An illustrated History of Russia

Edited by Georges and Rosamond Bernier

An illustrated History of Russia

by *Joel Carmichael*

Reynal & Company New York

Published in New York by Reynal & Company Inc. and in Toronto by Macmillan Company of Canada, Ltd
All rights reserved under International and Pan-American Copyright Conventions
Printed in Switzerland

Prologue: A Bird's Eye View

The most obvious thing about Russia may also be the most illuminating: her sheer size. One sixth of the land surface of the earth, and the equivalent of the entire North American continent, it is by far the largest country in the world.

Politically considered, modern Russia —the Soviet Union—is all the more striking because it began only some six centuries ago with the 500 square miles of the tiny principality of Moscow; a combination of territorial absorption and pervasive colonization has extended it from the Baltic Sea to the Pacific coast, from the Arctic Ocean to the Black and Caspian Seas, and all along the northern borders of Persia, Afganistan, India and China.

But in spite of its size and its wide variety of climatic zones, from the barren tundra of the extreme north to the lush orchard groves of the Crimea and Caucasus and the cotton plantations of Turkestan, a certain monotony, undisturbed by any abrupt elevations, gives an essential unity to the Eurasian plain that stretches from Hungary to China.

The Urals, which in schoolbooks still separate Europe from Asia, are altogether negligible—a chain of dwarf hills rising no more than 1,500 feet above sea level, with any number of easy passages. Passages so easy, in fact, that it has always been perfectly possible to go through them. There has never been any serious obstacle to movements back and forth across the great plain.

Extensive in space though Russia has been for so long, it is European Russia that must be looked to for an explanation of Russian history, and basic communications in European Russia have been ensured by a ramified waterway system. The lowlying watersheds of Central Russia are the sources of a number of great rivers like the Volga, the Dnieper, and the Western Dvina. Even in pre-Russian history the cluster of great waterways formed by the proximity of the outlets of the main rivers and their numerous tributaries were used by a variety of drifting peoples who settled and came into contact with other peoples both West and East. It was the waterways, also, that promoted the conquest of Siberia, since the Volga water system merges with the western Siberian system of the Ob.

This self-centred quality of Russian history is accentuated still further by the contrast between the relative insignificance of Russia's shoreline and her internal capaciousness. The Arctic Ocean and the White Sea are for all practical purposes useless; the Caspian Sea for all its size is quite landlocked. As for the Black Sea and the Baltic, they played no role in Russian history until the Eighteenth Century, when the cardinal traits of the nation-state were already formed.

The importance of the steppe in the formation of Russia has deflected atten-

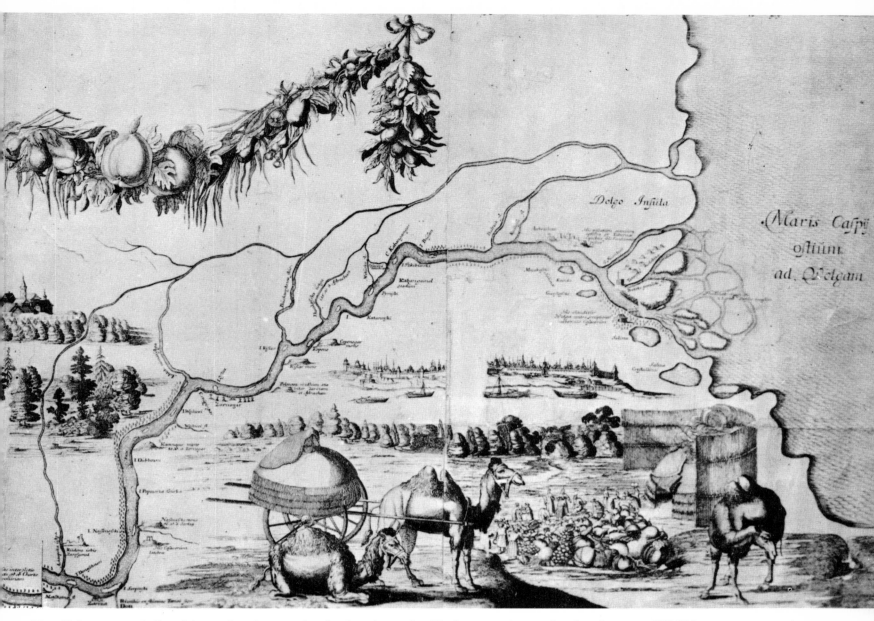

The Volga, *one of Russia's main river roads, flowing from the Ural mountains to the Caspian sea. XVIIth century engraving.*

tion from the preponderant role of the forest belt. Though the boundary line between the forests of the north and the steppes of the south is not definite, it was the forests that shaped the Russian people in its earliest days. Going much further south than it does now, the wooded zone started along a line passing as far south as Kiev, below present-day Moscow and Kazan. The timber zone then stretched out endlessly to the Pacific Ocean, paralleling the endlessness of the steppe to its south; after dipping slightly southward along the eastern slope of the Urals to the Saian Mountains, it resumed its eastward sweep. The steppe of European Russia merged imperceptibly with the steppe of Siberian Russia, flowing through the broad passage between the Urals and the Caspian Sea.

Most of us think of Russia today as primarily agricultural, because of its southern flatlands, but it was not until after

the middle of the Eighteenth Century that the forest belts receded into the background of Russian history proper, unlike the Asiatic invasions that influenced early Russian history so profoundly via this Ural-Caspian gateway. It was, indeed, just these timberlands of north and central Russia that served the Russians as shelter whenever the steppe disgorged its burden on them. The invaders generally moved with cattle and horses, often in entire caravans, and they found the forest zone an inhospitable medium.

The open steppe was an important factor of Russian history in a purely negative sense: not only was it the natural stamping ground for the mounted Asiatic nomads, but it also served for centuries as a refuge for all sorts of malcontents in flight from the oppressive regimes that have been a permanent feature of Russian life. It was the southern steppe, for in-

stance, that incubated the turbulent Cossack communities.

The creation of the Russian state was thus hampered by a two-pronged problem: on the one hand there was nothing to keep out periodic Asiatic invasions, while on the other there was no way of keeping its own people firmly tied down to the land. The free steppe constituted a chronic leak in the state, and until the rise of modern technology and its application to the control of populations it could not be stopped up.

The Russian hinterland in the northeast and center, marshy and forested, could only be permeated gradually by isolated individuals, while the broad streams of social life could only flow along rivers and roads, of which the steppe was the chief thoroughfare, and because of its far-flung unimpeded emptiness a source of disintegration both inside and out.

7

It is this emptiness that is the corollary of territorial space. The country was in fact too big to be occupied by a people till it grew numerous enough, and because of the constant incursions from without this was difficult.

But—more importantly—the spatial vacuum was the counterpart of a cultural vacuum. Civilization came to Russia, came with a heavy mortgage attached.

Civilization came with Christianity, oddly enough through the failure of Christianity elsewhere. The introduction of Christianity to Russia was a ricochet of the Muslim Arab conquests of the Seventh and Eighth Centuries. As the Muslims pushed toward the Caucasus they thrust back a Turkic-speaking ally of Byzantium, the Khazars, into the steppe of the Lower Volga and the Kuban, where they remained powerful enough to maintain themselves for a couple of centuries.

Some of the Bulgar tribes whom the Khazars had not absorbed emigrated north and west. One branch settled along the Middle Volga while another pushed on into the lower Danube. Here, after defeating the Byzantines, the Bulgars gradually came to dominate the whole of the eastern Balkan peninsula, adopting Slavic culture and language so thoroughly that they left nothing but their name to the modern Bulgarians.

The Khazars were rather versatile for nomads; not only did they become farmers and fishermen, but they developed a great merchant empire centered on the Volga, spread out laterally between the Far East and the Black Sea and vertically between the Muslim South and the primitive forest dwellers of the North.

Perhaps their chief distinction is their conversion to Judaism, the official religion of the rulers and a substantial part of the population: it was doubtless a way of fending off the Muslims on the one hand and the Byzantine Christians on the other. The Khazars were eventually undone by the Muslim advance, and the primitive Slavs they had been patronizing found themselves adrift.

It was by way of this pacific, trading empire that the first seeds of Christianity drifted into the land.

But while Christianity acted as a cultural channel, it was turned into a bottle-neck by the Byzantine form it took.

Byzantine Christianity had the paradoxical effect of depriving the Russians of a share in Greek civilization, for while Islam itself avidly sponged up classical Greek thought and passed it all on fruitfully to Latin Europe, and Byzantium itself dispatched scholars and manuscripts to Italy, there was no such migration of learning to Russia.

Through a quirk of circumstance Christianity was brought to her in her own language, not in Greek, so that the history of the Russian Church revolves around the poverty of Church Slavonic: Russian churchmen, to say nothing of their parishoners, had no need to learn Greek. Thus, with no Latin and no Greek the Russians were to find themselves cut off on the one hand from the civilized world at large, and on the other from their fellow Slavs who had become Roman Catholics.

What Russia received from Byzantium was what the court and the pious monks from Athos, Sinai, and the Oriental Churches could give her: a broad conception of sovereignty, in which the ruler's property was confounded with his authority; the canon law; an art that could only be religious, an ecclesiastical education —so meagre!—and the custom of secluding women, which lasted for centuries. The fact that Russian clerics learnt no Greek or Latin meant in effect that Russia missed Rome twice: the Roman Empire itself and the Roman Catholic Church, which inherited the values of classical civilization and the Judeo-Christian compound that emerged from it. For that matter she also missed the Renaissance, which owed so much to the rediscovery of Greek learning.

Byzantine Christianity in its Russian version was not a fountain of life, but a Chinese Wall, and because of the profoundly rooted tradition, inherited from Byzantium, of detestation of the Roman Catholic world, it was to insulate Russia against wider cultural influences for many centuries.

All this made the Russian Church profoundly and intimately national, but at the same time it condemned it to being a windowless chamber, the source of the backwardness endemic in Russian life down to our own generation.

A Russian churchman once said, rightly, that "the Russian Church knows no development". For just as Russian religion developed outside the Roman Catholic Church, so there was no occasion for a Reformation: Church and State were too densely interwoven. Nor was there the Counter-Reformation that, in reverse, reformed the Roman Catholic clergy and made them a potent factor in Western progress.

The closing of the seas to Russia proved culturally decisive. For having begun with the cultural tradition of Byzantium thinly filtered through Church Slavonic and reduced to a bagatelle in the process, Russia lost even that source in the Fifteenth Century, when the Ottoman Turks bypassed Russia via the South, entered the sphere of Islam in their turn, and wiped out Byzantium at the very moment Russia might have had most need of it. From the early Sixteenth Century on Russia was almost closed to Roman Catholics, and Byzantium had vanished. Both Latin and Greek civilization were unavailable, and Russia was cut loose in a sea of ignorance.

Thus Russia's physical isolation achieved its historic significance because of the spiritual isolation that accompanied it.

Ultimately, of course, the gap between Russia and the rest of Europe was bridged, but it took so long that by the time it happened there was a yawning chasm between the belated upper-class recipients of European culture and the masses of the people. The nation was flung into a profound imbalance that led to one explosion after another and has not, in fact, been righted to this day.

The Beginnings

Scythian saddle plaques, *wood, about Vth century B.C. Found in the barrow tomb excavations at Pasyryk in the Altai region (central Asia). The Scythians, of Iranian stock, were the first inhabitants of South Russia to appear in history. Both from the Hermitage Museum, Leningrad.*

Scythian gold work, *IVth-IIIrd c. B.C., the left section of a buckle, representing a horse attacked by a lion. From western Siberia. Herodotus wrote of the Scythians in the Vth century B.C. They were highly civilized and imported Greek luxury goods. From the Hermitage Museum, Leningrad.*

The mistiness of antiquity lasted much longer for Russia than for the rest of Europe. In fact nothing in any detail is known about the ancestors of the Russians until the Tenth and Eleventh Centuries. Even the Slavs as such are not mentioned until the Sixth Century A.D.; before that we must be content with archeological traces of the Scythians, mentioned in the Seventh Century B.C. as trading with some Greek colonists north of the Black Sea.

But the Scythians vanished before the Christian era, to be succeeded by the Sarmathians, who also remain a mere name for us; they were overcome in the Second and Third Centuries A.D. by the Teutonic Goths, after which events begin solidifying. The Goths spread throughout the eastern territories of the Roman Empire, to be finally halted, destroyed, and turned back by the first of the periodic Asiatic overflows, the Huns, who expelled them from the steppes north of the Black Sea and overran the Roman Empire in their turn.

The Huns were the first Asiatics to come within threatening distance of Europe as a whole: in the Fifth Century their leader, Attila, moved into what is today Hungary, and after him came the Avars, another obscure Turkic-speaking Asiatic tribe, who appeared in the southern steppes in the second half of the Sixth Century.

The Khazars, apparently a mixture of Turkic-speakers that included Huns and Bulgars, and their allies the Magyars—another intangible name for us—took control of the steppe north of the Black Sea by the middle of the Seventh Century; this is where they doubtless first came in contact with the great family of Slavic tribes, at this time still undifferentiated and all speaking much the same Indo-European language, the prototype of the various Slavic languages of today.

The Slavs are first mentioned by Latin and Greek writers as "Sclaveni, Sclavini, Sclavi"; they split up fairly early into the great divisions that have come down to us—the southern Slavs from the Balkans, the western Slavs, including the Czechs, Moravians, and Poles, and the eastern Slavs, later known as Russians. A dimness overhangs the movements of these vanished peoples, but it may be the collapse of the Hunnish Empire and the later invasion of the Avars that dislodged the Slavs from the Carpathian Mountains, and nudged the eastern Slavs into reaching the Dnieper some time during the Seventh Century and then infiltrating the Russian hinterland by river.

As they gradually drifted on, they occupied land formerly held by the Lithuanians, who by the Ninth Century were gradually pushed back to a stretch of land around the Baltic Sea, in the

basin of the Niemen River and the lower Western Dvina. The Slavs also seem to have pushed various Finnish tribes back into the North and the East; they were to come across them again later, as we shall see, when the Slavs in their turn, under the impulsion of still other ethnic drifts, began penetrating the northeastern forests.

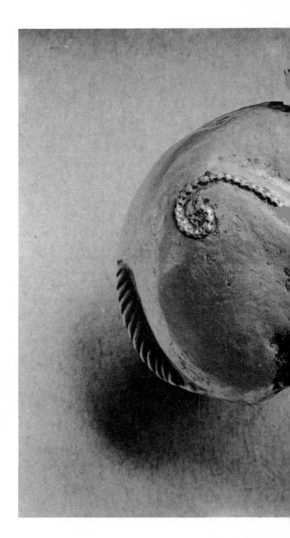

The Finns and the Lithuanians are two of the very few peoples the Slavs were culturally superior to; their first contact with the outside world, which was to give them the rudiments of civilization, came about because of the gradual investment by the Slavs, as they dislodged the Lithuanians and Finns in their sluggish migrations, of the great waterways that led from the Baltic to the Black and Caspian Seas.

The history of the eastern Slavs, and thus of the Russians, may be linked to this great international highway; primitive though the intervening country was, the highway led both to Byzantium and to Baghdad, and thus could serve as the spawning-ground for settlements that were essentially mercantile.

The primitive Slavs the Khazars conquered benefited a great deal by their subjugation. It brought them into contact with the international commerce of the new great mercantile centers, engendered by the meteoric rise of Islam, that were open to the various peoples in Russia. Slavic traders are reported by an Arab author as having gone as far as Baghdad.

The Slavs had the primitive products of the forest to sell: furs, honey, wax,

(it was finally extinguished in 1016); it had succumbed to a combination of the Slavs and another Turkic-speaking people, the Patsinaks, who were instrumental in expelling the Magyars eastward, a drift that had at least one important consequence: it cut off the southern Slavs from both the western and eastern Slavs. When two Slavic-

Finding their commerce endangered by the collapse of an established authority, the Slavic merchants were obliged to organize their own defence, and to do this effectively they now turned to another people that may be regarded as the catalyst in the crystalization of the Kievan federation, earliest Russian state.

Scythian gold work: *a crouching deer. Vth century B.C. National Museum, Budapest.*

and above all—people. They sold both their own people and any others they could enslave. The Slav stock-in-trade consisted of the natives, who handed over both the tribute levied on them and their own persons.

The earliest "cities" recorded for the ancestors of the Russians were military strongholds that owed their existence to the dual aspect of this primitive commerce; they were both storage points for goods and a rendez-vous for merchants. Thus these ancient centers —Kiev, Novgorod, Lyubech, Chernigov, Polotsk—were all established on the main trade routes, and gradually gave rise to a Russian state, or mock-state.

These politically disorganized traders found themselves in a difficult position on the collapse of the Khazar state during the Tenth and Eleventh Centuries

speaking Greek brothers from Saloniki, St. Cyril and St. Methodius, were invited to Moravia in the Ninth Century, the formal conversion of the Slavs to Orthodoxy was systematized, though some southern Slavs had been converted to Byzantine Orthodoxy before, soon after their settlement in the Balkan Peninsula. The two Greek brothers adapted Greek capital letters to a Bulgarian dialect from southern Macedonia, and since as late as the Eleventh Century the Slavonic languages as a whole were still undifferentiated enough for this so-called "Church Slavonic" to sound to each one of them like a standardized form of itself, this dialect ultimately became the language of the Russian Church and for many centuries the only literary medium available to speakers of Russian.

This was the Vikings. Businessmen and bandits simultaneously, a Swedish branch of the Vikings had long before established an important international trading center in the Isle of Gothland, and by the Eighth Century had come by way of the Caspian Sea and Persia to sell their slaves in the markets of Baghdad.

They had already made themselves felt elsewhere; they had rowed and sailed their small ships not only across the sea but up all the main rivers of Western Europe. In the Eighth Century they had raided Paris and London, and had, indeed, changed the history of France and England. Coming upon the Western Dvina and the Volga in the East, with all the commercial possibilities of a waterway that led from the Baltic, at their very doorstep, to the

Caspian Sea and thus made a market between Western Europe and the Muslim East, they began swarming over it.

Curiously enough it was the water route over the Western Dvina and the Volga, to Baghdad and the Middle East, that was discovered first, before the other and equally fruitful tradeway along the Neva, Volkhov and Dnieper,

became one of the principal stages in this encirclement of Europe.

Russian legend—i.e., the earliest chronicles—has it that the Vikings were actually invited by the ancestors of the Russians to "rule over them"; this must be an endearingly stylized account of something far more disordered, but whether or not the Vikings

The Russian word for Viking that has come down to us ("Varyag" = Varangians in most accounts) has always had a connotation of merchant, rather than warrior.

In any case the same Vikings who had produced such turmoil in Western Europe launched the Russians in their state-making. Buccaneers, adventurers, and above all merchants, founded the Russian state. They are personified in the figure of one Rurik.

According to the chronicle mentioned above, this Rurik established himself in Novgorod in 862. He is in all probability the same person as a Dane of the same name, who had ascended the Elbe and the Rhine with a band of Norsemen, obtained sections of Friesland in fief from Emperor Lothaire (a descendant of Charlemagne), and after betraying him was expelled by the Frisians to seek his fortune elsewhere.

The Vikings left scarcely anything in Russia beyond their names, including the word Russia itself, which the country has been known by for a millennium. The word comes from "Ros" or "Rhos"; whatever this might have meant, it seems to have referred first to the upper class, then to the people as a whole and their language, and finally to the country. It is an engaging illustration of the flux of human affairs that the biggest country in the world derives its name from some happy-go-lucky cutthroats and barterers from a tiny country known for little else. In any case the word "Russia" is a close parallel to other Viking operations commemorated by the Franks in the Lutetia region, the Normans in Normandy, and the Lombards in the Po Valley.

The Vikings were assimilated so quickly that they left no other mark. They melted into the Slav communities they were supposed to organize and carried on the traditional activities of the merchant princes, with the same twofold aim: to maintain commerce with the east and the south, and accordingly to defend the land and the waterways from the Turkish tribes. The continuous incursions of these tribes along the great steppe road and their constant harassing of the sedentary populations gave them a paramount role.

Though the first Russian organized state is traditionally supposed to have had Kiev as its base, there is nothing much worth saying about it. The available records, though of course indispensable as our sole source of information, are a theologically tinctured mixture of legend, fantasy and apology.

For that matter they were written down many generations after the events they are supposed to describe: the very term Russian state was not adopted

Prehistoric stone idol, *from the Dolmatovo and Akulinio excavations (near Podolsk). Historical Museum, Moscow.*

which later planted the Vikings before the gates of Constantinople itself.

This early intertwining of disparate elements is attested by the great hoards of Muslim coins found in Sweden and on the Isle of Gothland, which are much more numerous than the similar treasures troves of Byzantine coins.

Ultimately the Vikings found Byzantium more attractive, perhaps simply because it was nearer. From their point of view the Dnieper was superior to the Volga because it emptied into a real sea, and they established the great "Eastern route" by way of it: Kiev

were summoned by the Slavs or simply conquered them, and the legend was later built up out of self-regarding motives, they were employed by them along the middle Dnieper as mercenary soldiers and commission brokers. The Viking newcomers were supposed to conduct the boat trains from Kiev to the Dnieper Rapids, organize a portage from there, meanwhile protecting the merchandise against the Patsinaks, and then take the river again as far as the Black Sea, to land ultimately at the Byzantine quays where the goods and slaves were sold or bartered.

officially until the Fifteenth or Sixteenth Century. The extraordinary outburst of historiography as well as belles-lettres that was taking place in the Muslim East during the first few centuries of the beginnings of Russian self-consciousness gives us an arresting comparative example of Russian backwardness.

In any case, there is no doubt that there was a large number of Vikings in the Russian northwest from very early times on. The date assigned Rurik's settlement in Novgorod doubtless indicates that they were well established in the topmost stratum of the military-mercantile communities along the Russian waterways. These military-mercantile cities collectively made up the early Russian state.

The early Russian princes were not sovereigns in any national sense—they were simply adventurers in a vast, empty and at first foreign country; we perceive them too dimly to make a personal description of any interest. Perhaps the only one worth mentioning after Rurik, the forefather of the Russian aristocracy, is Vladimir Ist (978-1015), a pagan who was the first specifically Russian ruler to be converted to Christianity, which he imposed on the population by force. His choice of Greek Orthodox Christianity, which he is supposed to have made after weighing the claims of Judaism and Islam, was due to his love of strong drink, prohibited by Islam, and to the ornateness of the Byzantine Church services in Constantinople as reported to him by a visitor. Aside from his conviction that the Russian love of drinking made Christianity indispensable, his religious conversion did not interfere with his maintenance of a gigantic harem of at least 800 concubines.

Vladimir's conversion was really an echo of a Viking connection, since it had been during their trips to Constantinople that the Vikings had been impressed by the ritual and splendor of the Byzantine Church ritual at the Saint Sophia Cathedral. For that matter some compatriots of theirs serving in the Imperial bodyguard had already been converted; it was, indeed, in the interests of the Byzantine Empire to convert the outer barbarians as much as possible.

As indicated above, this conversion of Russian rulers by Byzantium was a decisive factor in Russian history, for whereas the Poles and Balts were converted by missionaries originating in Germany and Sweden, the Slav peoples of the Dnieper, like their fellow-Slavs in the Balkans, were converted by Greek monks. The Byzantine Empire exported, together with its wines and

Top and bottom: Silver figurines, VIth century A.D., from the Martynovka treasure, near Kiev. Historical Museum, Kiev.

13

brocades, the religion of the Eastern Church. It was to be typical of Russian history that the imposition of Christianity, as of so much else, was accomplished by fiat from above.

both then and later as a milch-cow. The more primitive form of tribute was naturally paid in kind, though it was also collected in the Arabic coins widely current in Russia during the Kievan

feuds that were to pulverize Russian life till the establishment of the Moscow autocracy centuries later.

Vladimir had held the title of Grand Duke of Kiev, which, since Kiev was

Stone bas-relief *from the south façade of the Opika monastery in Georgia: on the left the donor, David is at the right, on the throne. IXth century A.D. Tiflis Museum.*

It would be far-fetched to call Kievan Russia a genuine state. Not only were even its boundaries uncertain, but the Slavs themselves were still partly nomadic. What the cluster of rulers descended from the legendary Rurik did was simply to bring together under a loosely ramified and increasingly complicated, confused, and weakening family rule the variety of elements that populated the Russian plain. Their rule revolved around the combination of war and commerce that was the hallmark of the first few centuries of Russian history. The warfare carried on intermittently by the various Viking-Slav princelings was the source of the principal article of merchandise bartered and sold in the foreign markets—slaves, which is, of course, why the word for slave in most European languages is derived from the word Slav.

The sole administrative objective of the Kievan princelings was the collection of tribute: the country was treated

period: by this time the Muslim conquests had established a great network of markets throughout the Middle East and as far as Khorezm in Central Asia. The Kievan "state" was no more than a loosely articulated congeries of city-states, each one in its turn essentially amorphous.

A lasting accomplishment of Vladimir's was the setting up of his twelve sons as Governors: this linked each member of the ruling family to some specific, territorially defined headquarters and created a material basis for future dynastic claims by Rurik's descendants. But this apportioning of the land among Vladimir's sons naturally did not regulate affairs in a simple, incontestable way: it was itself a source of constant strife, chiefly because of the absence of any principle of succession, a confusion that exacerbated the amorphousness of the Kievan confederation. The moment Vladimir died his sons fell out, beginning the uninterrupted clan

the most important city in the region, was tantamount to acknowledging his senior authority in the Rurik clan, but the looseness of governmental relationships, as well as the sparsely settled state of the country and the continuous nomadic incursions along the ill-defined periphery of Kievan Russia, made the falling out between his sons inevitable: in fact Vladimir's son Yaroslav was the last Grand Duke of Kiev to exercise any direct control over the whole of the realm that in theory belonged to the Rurik clan and hence to its senior member.

Now, this whole question of the imprecision in the principle of succession had its roots in the primitive concept of state authority that Rurik's descendants—the "Rurikoviches"— developed as a guide to administration. During the early period of Kievan Russia the legal supremacy of the Grand Duke of Kiev was conceived of as an aspect of property law. Legality involved the recognition of paternal authority, plus the notion of the indivisibility of clan property. The whole area of Russia in the hands of the Rurikoviches was considered the joint property of the whole family, headed by the Grand Duke of Kiev.

The combination of these two notions of paternal authority and the indivisibility of property inevitably generated feuds between the Princes. When Yaroslav died he made an attempt to circumvent this baffling principle of succession by willing his eldest son more "authority", while simultaneously, however, partitioning the state. After his death his sons and their descendants considered the principalities and cities they ruled not as elements in an abstract entity known as Kievan Russia but as the actual property of themselves personally and of their own issue, to the exclusion of the other branches of the clan.

This notion of the primacy of actual property relationships simply signalized the profound change taking place in the adventurous character of the former roving Vikings: they were becoming squires and administrators.

Europe was so backward at the time that Yaroslav (1019-1054) was one of its greatest sovereigns. He believed in ramifying his family connections as much as possible; he married his sister to King Casimir I of Poland, whom he helped in the latter's own internal struggles, his daughter Elizabeth to King Harald Hardrada of Norway; his daughter Anastasia to King Andrew I of Hungary; his daughter Anne to Henry I of France, which makes him an ancestor of the reigning English house. His favorite son Vsevolod married the daughter of the Byzantine Emperor Constantine Monomachus.

The principle of seniority established by Yaroslav in an attempt to settle the succession in Kievan Russia, though it seemed clear at the time, led to even greater confusion.

He had wanted every death of a Prince to be succeeded by a movement of princes, each being promoted to a senior district. That is, the seniority of princes throughout the clan and the exact order of importance of the districts were correlated. Since the clan was very large and kept increasing at a great rate, what with early marriages, numerous wives, and the general high spirits of the Princes, both individuals and branches multiplied so rapidly that it soon became impossible to say whether a nephew in one line, for instance, was junior to the uncle in another or not.

Consequently, the fundamental notion of patrimony had to be reinterpreted, and it came to acquire the meaning settled on at a princely conclave convoked in Lyubech by Vladimir Monomakh, Vsevolod's son: it finally meant the right to succeed to one's own father's property, i.e., territory.

This modification in the original idea, though it merely acknowledged an existing state of affairs, eliminated even the pretence to unity that had been at least the theoretical goal of Kievan Russia: it was a source of copious feuds.

By the Twelfth Century the social composition of society was far more complicated than it had been before the Vikings. After they came the slaves naturally continued as before to be the dregs of society; though they were normally made up of prisoners of war, anyone at all could become one by birth, bankruptcy or voluntary agreement.

The princely clans constituted the apex of society, but they were essen-

Earliest Christian period: Bas-relief of an angel, *Xth century. Tiflis Museum.*

tially mobile and rootless. Each Prince had his retinue, which was the source of his power: there might well have been as many as 2,000 men in it. By the time the Princes came to number a hundred the drain on the countryside the clan lived off must have been very substantial. At first the princely retinue seems to have had a Scandinavian core: its duties were those of adjutants in the Prince's military, commercial, administrative and judicial activities. This retinue was quickly swallowed up by the native population, as well as by various other foreign elements that drifted in, such as Poles or Lithuanians. It was the Prince's retinue that was

Two early rulers: far left, Rurik, *the legendary Viking (about 862), and left,* Igor *(912-945). From the "Titulyarnik" manuscript of 1672 which listed the Tsars and the foreign sovereigns with whom the Tsars had diplomatic relations.*

the germ of the aristocracy or quasi-aristocracy that later developed; initially it was a military-mercantile aristocracy depending for its position on the Prince's favors, on the holding of high offices or on its wealth.

In the early days of the princely retinue the Prince was its source of revenue, but at the same time he found it indispensable for collecting his own revenue. Members of the retinue were sometimes paid off directly in money, but sometimes they were sent as satraps to the more remote parts of the country, where they were supposed to live by milking the population. This widespread practice was known, rather juicily, as "feeding": it lasted for centuries.

But the retinue was not tied to its Prince hand and foot: on the contrary, though it was customary for it to follow him about it was not a legal duty. The custom revolved essentially around either personal loyalty or egotistic interest, and was prevalent before society became stratified and developed a corresponding juridical structure.

As the original Viking bands settled down, the proto-aristocracy constituted by the princely retinue began splitting up in its turn, but though a group known as "boyars"—who were to play a role in Russian life for centuries—became the most influential group there was no clear-cut line of demarcation between them and the other free elements of society. What was to fix the aristocracy in one place as society developed was the ownership of land, which naturally became a criterion of position as society grew sedentary.

The boyars and other segments of the ruling groups were superimposed on the free townspeople—merchants and small artisans—and the free peasantry. It was possible even in the earliest days for a merchant to accumulate very considerable wealth, since it was after all the mercantile factor that was paramount in early society and was proportionally far better developed than crafts, farming and so on. The international markets based on the Muslim Caliphate and the Byzantine Empire were lush enough for traders even in the remote basin of the Dnieper to aggrandize themselves.

The real hallmark of the period was precisely this dependence of the economy not on agriculture but on the market: it was not the farming community that was politically influential during the Eleventh and Twelfth Centuries, but the cities, based on commerce. The merchants, consequently, were far too important to be helpless vis-à-vis their princes. The institution of the so-called "vyeche", or popular assembly, constituted one of the three foci of socio-legal authority in Kievan Russia, or the popular principle in contradistinction to the monarchical principle represented

by the princes and the aristocratic principle represented by the princely retinue and its offshoots.

The popular assembly spoke for the urban population, and though neither its composition nor jurisdiction was defined with any precision it was an effective element of government in primitive Russia.

This popular assembly was not supposed to be representative: it simply consisted of all the adult males in any given town; decisions had to be unanimous. In the absence of any formal way of resolving a dispute, if agreement couldn't be reached a free-for-all would break out and settle the question. In Novgorod, for instance, where because of the lengthy history of the city as an international trading center the popular assembly reached the zenith of its power, brawls, which became tremendously violent, would be settled as a rule on the bridge over the Volkhov River, with the losers being tossed into the freezing water.

The power of the aristocracy was greatest in Southwest Russia, in the principalities of Galicia and Volynia, where political life was dominated by the Boyar Council and the Prince was compelled to submit: he could only impose his own will on the boyars by actual combat.

The popular assembly was actually the closest approximation to democratic government in Russian history down to our own times. As the great commercial cities declined, the popular assembly declined with them; by the Thirteenth Century it was, except in Novgorod and Pskov, already extinct.

Kiev has come down to us as the symbol of early Russian statehood, but though it was the most magnificent Russian city of the period, as well as the seat of the head of the Church and the target of the incessant intrigues and feuds among the Princes, it had no real foundations. In an attempt to retroject the notion of unification as far back to the beginnings of national self-consciousness as possible, Russian piety has overemphasized the primacy of Kiev, which was never, after all, anything more than the largest center of an essentially informal federation of regional units, whose real demands were far stronger than the chimera of allegiance to a national capital.

During the Eleventh and Twelfth Centuries Russia was divided up into a number of substantial territorial subdivisions—Novgorod, Rostov, Suzdal, Pereyaslavl, Smolensk, Chernigov, Volynia, Galicia, Murom-Ryazan—that had grown up from the city-states deposited along the great waterways in the earliest historical times. None of the early Kievan Princes had ever managed to impose any unity on these principalities, and for that matter all

of them, with the exception of Kiev and Novgorod, acquired their own dynasties from the middle of the Eleventh Century on. But though a princely conference would occasionally take place, and there was a striking similarity in basic institutions and social conditions, perhaps even a general recognition of the need for unity, these Kievan principalities were for political reasons in a state of perpetual bickering and warfare. You might say that the nation had acquired its essential character in depth, while tempests kept agitating its surface.

In a comparison of Russia with Western Europe of the period, perhaps the most striking difference is just this rootlessness of the early rulers, that is, the absence of hierarchical social relations based on territorial attachments. While Western feudalism was a rigid pyramid, in which everyone from the King down occupied by birthright a fixed place, and a network of customs and contracts underlay the formation of classes and also welded these classes into a social organism called a state, the situation in Russia was quite different.

Kievan society was fluid. The hierarchical motionlessness of Western feudalism was based on a territorial theory: status depended on the connection between an individual and his *place*. The peasant was attached to his plot of land, the artisan to his guild, the bourgeois to his commune, the lord to his fief; each one of the classes formed a sort of building block, and all together made up the state.

The emptiness of Kievan Russia made this impossible. The country was too sparsely settled to be broken up into precise segments. With their economic life subject to the commerce of a great waterway the people were accustomed to moving back and forth, looking for opportunities to trade. Without natural frontiers the armed force had to be constantly prepared to move as quickly as possible to any point threatened. Consequently an individual was expected to perform the services required of him anywhere at all. In early Russia the criterion of status was function, not situation. This essentially horizontal character of society becomes even more evident when the roving, fluid Kievan society is overlaid centuries later by the

Miniature representing the invasion of ▶ Bulgaria by the Russians. *Above, Svyatoslav on a white horse. He was a warrior who fought against Byzantium, the earliest Kiev ruler to bear a Slavonic name. Below, the storming of Drostar in Silistria by the Russians in 969. Like the miniature on page 19, this comes from the "Manasses Chronicle", a XIVth century Bulgarian work, Vatican Library.*

ПЛѢНꙊРꙊСКЫ

НАЖꙂВЪДРꙊСТРЪ·

Above: Painted standard representing Vladimir the Saint, Tsar from 980-1015. Trading relations between Kiev and Byzantium led to the adoption of Greek Orthodoxy. Conversion began after a famous pilgrimage made to Constantinople by Olga, mother of the Kievan hero Svyatoslav. Christianity became the official religion when her grandson, Vladimir, later called "the Saint", came to the throne. According to the chronicles, Vladimir had led a wild youth and was "insatiable in debauch". Decided to marry Anne, sister of the two Byzantium emperors, he won her by defeating them in battle, and agreed to be converted to quiet their objections. Facing page: The Baptism of the Russians in 990. Miniature from the "Manasses Chronicle", a XIVth century Bulgarian work. Vatican Library.

evolving Moscow state, firmly rooted in land relationships.

In Kievan Russia, for instance, when the Prince changed residence, he took along his retinue, whose motives were nothing more than good wages or an occasion for trade or loot. The retinue at first had no links with the soil, since they were constantly on the move, nor with their lord, since they were perfectly free to leave him at will. They were functionaries more than vassals: they were not, that is, vassals of the lord of a fief that was always the same and who was in his turn the subordinate of a sovereign who remained the same. Kievan society had not yet been compartmentalized, nor was it to be for many centuries.

The emptiness of the country and its low cultural level were also reflected in its intellectual life. The chief source of culture in Kievan Russia was the Church, which was responsible for the introduction of letters and the arts. The hierarchy of the Church sprang up the moment the population of the big cities was either forced or cajoled into baptism, and in spite of the total illiteracy of the overwhelming mass of the people, clerical schools managed to mould preachers, primarily monks, with a smattering of knowledge.

For the first few centuries, to be sure, the conversion of Russia to Christianity was barely more than nominal: very often the higher clergy—to say nothing of the lower!—knew

nothing about Christian dogma at all. The primitive Slavs retained an essentially magical interest in their religion, which was facilitated by the utter unintelligibility of the Church Slavonic that was its medium. Linguistically, of course, it might have been considered a "standard" form of the local speech, but no one actually understood it, not even the scattering of educated people. It was perhaps just this obscure and unintelligible ritual of the Church, as well as the flowing robes and sacred vestments of the clergy, plus the threat of eternal damnation, that gave the Church its intellectual prestige.

But of course this general backwardness of the population did not prevent individual artists from achieving work of great distinction. There were many talented mosaists, painters of frescoes and ikons, and jewelers, who while adhering to their conception of the Byzantine tradition that inspired them gave their handiwork a national flavor, with considerable originality among the enamelists. It is true that though the Church introduced these activities it also quickly came to control them and standardize them into the lifelessness that later became their hallmark. But Russia's golden age of painting took place under the influence of Greek and Italian models, and it was only later that ecclesiastical conformity obliterated variety.

It must be recalled that the ikons, perhaps the primary form of artistic expression in Russia, were intended not as portraits but as semi-magical objects of veneration. Their very existence as objects of art was only made possible after the anti-iconoclastic party in Byzantium was defeated in the middle of the Ninth Century.

The type of architecture was indigenous; it can still be seen in the wooden churches of the northeast and the brick churches influenced by them, though Byzantium set a characteristic stamp on the architecture as well as on the painting and mosaics of Kievan Russia. Most of the churches built of wood have not survived, but there are some distinguished stone churches in Kiev and Chernigov; after the middle of the Twelfth Century the architecture of Suzdal and Novgorod began to strike an original note. Some of the finest examples of Old Russian art are to be found in these churches, which unaccountably show a great many foreign affinities, oddly enough, with the

Périgueux group of churches in southwest France. Masons imported from Germany, who plied their trade in Suzdal, are supposed to have been master craftsmen.

Much later, Russia acquired impressive architectural landscapes in the big cities that grew up, where though the building was done by Italians the results looked entirely at home on Russian soil. Sculpture, on the other hand, was practically non-existent, perhaps because the Church, though it allowed saints to be represented in the flat, forbade them to be done in the round.

As for literature, there was no question of this at all. Like Russian art in general it was an offshoot of a Greek transplant, but because the liturgical requirements of the Russian Church were satisfied by Church Slavonic, the cutting off of Russian literature from the Greek language made literature completely sterile: chronicles, lives of saints, etc. There was no acquaintance in Russia with any secular Greek literature, and the pre-Christian classical tradition was utterly unknown. Consequently, though Old Russian literature goes back to the middle of the Eleventh Century its interest is largely anthropological; the sole exception for the period, the *Saga of Igor's Host*, a prose-poem from about 1186 dealing with a campaign against the Qypchak Turks, is completely isolated: there is no continuity whatever between it and later Russian literature. It was in fact not even discovered until the end of the Eighteenth Century.

Thus, from its inception in the beginning or middle of the Eleventh Century to the end of the Seventeenth Century Russian literature was both

meagre and lifeless. Modern Russian literature has its origins in Russian life only after Western European influences of one sort or another began flowing into Russia in the modern period, beginning with the Seventeenth Century.

Thus, the general cultural isolation that afflicted Russia from its very beginnings was reflected with special intensity in the growth of her literature. Cut off from Latin Christendom and the West by her religious difference, and equally unable to benefit by Greek civilization because of the narrow channel it came to her in, Old Russia's aesthetic sense was expressed primarily in religious painting and church architecture.

Music seems to have been even more meagre: singing in unison was its chief manifestation, aside from the wealth of folk singing that must have existed and that evolved entirely outside the formulae of the Church, and so has come down to us very skimpily. Harmony did not develop until the Fifteenth and Sixteenth Centuries.

The Kievan period is generally thought to have ended in 1169, when Andrew Bogolyubsky, the son of Yuri Dolgoruki, Prince of Rostov and Suzdal, stormed Kiev and reduced it utterly. This was the first time a Russian Prince had given Kiev the treatment reserved as a rule for non-Russian cities: it was plundered and sacked, churches and monasteries were burned, the people slaughtered, expelled and enslaved. The sack of Kiev highlights the triumph of centrifugal forces in early Russia, which the competition of the Grand Dukes, unbridled by any constitutional regime, had precluded any attempt at unifying.

Actually, however, the primacy of Kiev was already declining just because it was dependent on its superb position along the great waterway from the Baltic to the Black Sea and on its commercial ties with Byzantium. Not only were new commercial links being forged between North Russia and Western Europe that bypassed Kiev altogether, but the Russian area as a whole was becoming increasingly vulnerable to Asiatic attacks. The Patsinaks had been succeeded by another Turkish people, the Qypchak Turks —the "Cumans"—who were both more numerous and better organized than their predecessors, and from the middle of the Eleventh Century on had been exerting more and more pressure on the Dnieper. The Cumans raided Russia annually, killing farmers, burning their barns and carting their wives and children off to slavery. They had made the great waterway "from the Varangians to the Greeks" unsafe in any case. Kiev was not only very close to the steppe, and the Kievan Princes were not only incapable of organizing any defence against the Cumans, but several of them married daughters of the Cuman Khans, who thus entered into the complex network of clan strife typical of early Russian history. The princely feuds were interminable; the Cumans were merely another element of discord.

From the beginning of the Eleventh Century on the sufferings of the Kievan Russians made them turn to an expedient that has been a leitmotif of Russian history: they took to their heels. The inhabitants of Kievan Russia began leaking out. There was no sudden exodus, but very gradually a migration began that cut into the population along the Dnieper. Both rich and poor began drifting, westward and northward, to elude at any rate the immediate prospect of being robbed, raped, slaughtered or enslaved.

It was the stream of migration along what was called the "straight road" from Kiev to the Volga—i.e., along a Dnieper tributary called the Desna— that ultimately led to the establishment of Moscow. It was another example of the characteristic phenomenon of Russian colonization via a river: this one, though it passed through dense thickets infested by robbers, was quite under-populated.

What the decline of Kiev meant concretely was that after the middle of the Twelfth Century the "Mother of Russian Cities" was no longer capable of even defending its inhabitants.

Politically speaking, the former principalities began drifting toward a re-

grouping that gave rise to different formations: the Moscow state in the northeast and the Lithuanian-White-Russian-Ukrainian state in the southwest, where the Russian territories were gradually absorbed by the Grand Duchy of Lithuania, which at the end

Svyatoslav II *(1073-1076), from a 1073 miniature taken from the "Izbornik" (manuscript) written upon the order of Svyatoslav by Deacon John.*

of the Fourteenth Century was to fuse with the Kingdom of Poland.

In short, the eastern Slav community concealed by the rubric of "Kievan Russia" was parcelled out in favor of all its immediate neighbors—Finns Lithuanians, Poles, and a number of Turkish peoples.

In the West the eastern Slavs were to develop ultimately into the White

Russians, within the frontiers of a Lithuanian-Polish state: in the South the Ukrainian grouping came into being as a partial reflection of the powerful influence of Lithuanian Poland, whereas the territory of what was to become Muscovy in the North served as the

spawning-ground for the Great Russians whose history we are concerned with.

To be sure, this division was not consummated until between the Fourteenth and Sixteenth Centuries. As Kiev subsided Galicia and Volynia grew in importance, only to find themselves outpaced by two different movements.

First the Mongols appeared: I shall speak of them in a moment.

◄ Council of Bishops. *"Svyatoslav codex", XIth century. Historical Museum, Moscow.*

Then, in the marshy forested region of the Niemen basin the Lithuanians, an ancient race still pagan, who had withstood the movement of proselytization launched by the German military monks, suddenly and surprisingly claimed the attention of history by embarking on a program of conquest under a number of able rulers. They extended their power to the Dnieper, turned Kiev into a Lithuanian city and subjected western Russia to Vilna, their capital. Greek Orthodox Christians found themselves in thrall to pagans in the West just as they were being politically effaced by Mongols in the East.

By the beginning of the Fifteenth Century, the Grand Duchy of Lithuania embraced a huge area, including the basin of the upper and the middle western Dvina, the Niemen, the southern Bug, the Dnieper and the upper Oka.

These Russian lands were to remain outside a Russian orbit for a long time; the harassed Russian Princes in the southwest were absorbed by the Lithuanian-Polish combination, chiefly because many of their economic interests were in the West, such as their trade with Germany, which used waterways under Lithuanian and Polish control, and also because the core of Russian society had been substantially disintegrated during the Thirteenth and Fourteenth Centuries by both internal dissension and the pressure of the Mongols. Also, both Lithuania and southwestern Russia had a common enemy in the form of the Teutonic monk-knights in the North.

Because of all this what was to become the Russian state only began to form when Muscovy emerged, during the Thirteenth and Fourteenth Centuries.

For those who like to focus historical patterns, Kiev's place was taken at first not by Moscow but by Vladimir, not far from Moscow, in the Principality of Rostov-Suzdal, which was taken by Andrew Bogolyubsky after he ravaged Kiev. Moscow, first mentioned in 1147, was wholly negligible in the Twelfth Century. Rostov and Suzdal were older than Vladimir, with relatively independent boyars and popular assemblies, while in Vladimir Andrew could do as he pleased.

The great migration that had drawn the Russians away from Kiev and the Dnieper Basin densened the population of northeastern Russia very considerably. The bulk of the migrants concentrated in the triangle formed by the upper Volga and the Oka, that is, the Principality of Rostov-Suzdal. It seems to have been the influx into the new area, which had formerly been inhabited by Finnish tribes, that changed the ethnic complexion of the region: part of the Great Russian people's ancestry is Finnish.

The forests, immune to the caravans and hordes of the nomads, gave the fleeing Russians a natural shelter, and since Russian peasants were pacific by nature and the Finns even more so, the Finns met by the Russian farmers in the forests of the northeast completely accepted them and intermingled with them. It was a typically frontier situation. The topography of northeast Russia militated against the creation of large villages, like those common in southern Russia; the country was covered by virgin timber and marshes that were difficult to cultivate.

As for the Princes, they too changed swiftly in response to the contrast between this environment and Kievan Russia. The new combination engendered a different social structure.

The northeast Princes were far more similar to the American pioneers who went West to carve their own estates out of the new lands: contemplating the land they had laid their hands on, they regarded it as personal property, theirs by virtue of their own toil and sweat, and disposable as they saw fit.

The boyars themselves began turning into a squirearchy, since the established tradition of princely rewards for services took the form of land-grants. This naturally broke the territory up into innumerable tiny principalities, and thus, by accentuating the fragmentation of the region, enabled the future Moscow dynasty to impose on the atomized principalities a degree of centralization that has remained the hallmark of Russian affairs ever since.

The atomization of northeast Russia, combined as it was with the principle of allocating land to the boyars in the service of any particular Prince, led to a clash of interests between Princes and boyars. The boyars were bound to be hostile to any change in their rulers, which simply meant that a new Prince, accompanied by new boyars, would be coming along to oust them. The selfish interests of the boyars tended to make them support their Prince's given dynastic ambitions insofar as these Princes were determined to maintain the local dynasty. But, as I have said above, since the Princes had inherited the tradition of looking on the principality they ruled as a piece of family real estate, and tended to divide it among their heirs, they would not only collide with the economic interests of the boyars, but the generally inevitable clan warfare that followed exacerbated the boyars, who by now had their roots in the soil. We shall see how the interplay of these factors led to the emergence of the Russian autocracy centuries later.

The boyar aristocracy was thus an element of stability; it was in its interest to establish order, which in contemporary conditions could naturally be accomplished only by the emergence of a strong house, in this case the Grand Duchy of Vladimir. To sum the period up politically, the main tendency was a growth in the strength of both Princes and boyars, with consequent collisions, while the popular assemblies declined rapidly. This process, so full of meaning for all subsequent Russian history, throughout which we see the chasm widening between the summits of society and the people, was consummated on the eve of the Mongol invasion.

Moreover, though the seniority of the Grand Duke of Vladimir was accepted, more or less theoretically, and the holders of the Vladimir office tended to act as though they were advancing the interests of the northeastern territory as a whole, this very process worked against the interests of the lesser principalities, with the upshot that the traditional concept of the Russian Princes as "brothers" became an almost empty fiction. Russia was pulverized by ferocious strife. The Princes detested each other, and were incapable of cooperating with the boyar aristocracy they depended on. Also, the decline of the popular assembly reflected the growing oppression of the rural population as well as the growth of the landed estates of the boyars and princes. Rural Russia had in fact been launched on the course that was to lead to bondage for most of her people.

But peace was about to be forced on the country for a time by the last of the Asiatic invaders, and the ablest —the Mongols.

The Mongols

With the advent of the Mongols, who became known to the Russians and thence to the world as Tatars, Russian history encounters a factor qualitatively different from any of the others that have affected it.

To give impartial consideration to the Mongols, who exacted tribute from the Russians for two hundred and forty years, we must change our perspective altogether: there is no point in looking at the Mongols through Russian eyes, the Russians must be seen through Mongol eyes. From the Mongol point

prehensible without the Mongol background. Fundamental decisions were made by the Great Khan of the Mongols, who held his residence in Mongolia or in China. This meant that the Russian vassals of the Khan of the Golden Horde—the Mongol unit encamped in Russia—were actually governed by the ruler of Peking. The structure and function of the Golden Horde itself and hence of Russia was established by the founder of the Mongol Empire, Chingis Khan, whose followers considered him enjoined by heaven to rule the world.

it was on the whole rather negligible, or on the contrary magnifying its negative effects and blaming the Mongols for Russian backwardness, their perhaps normal feeling of national identification cannot obscure the fact that Russian political and governmental life was moulded by Mongol politics for two centuries and more.

The Grand Dukes of Vladimir and Moscow, as well as all other Princes, were only rulers by the grace of the Khan, who was both the *de facto* and the *de jure* source of power throughout Russia. The Church, too, exercised its functions by virtue of Mongol authority, which from a religious point of view was quite benign, since the Mongols were wholly tolerant of religious differences, and though at first apparently Shamanists themselves had no objection to following Russian customary law. This, to be sure, did not eliminate discords, since Russian so-called immemorial tradition was a tissue of confusion, but at any rate it made for quiet.

The Mongols were utterly unknown in Europe and the Middle East before their sudden appearance in the Thirteenth Century. They were the last of the long line of invaders of the western steppe—the proto-Persians (Scythians and Sarmathians), and the Turkic-speaking Huns, Avars, Khazars, Patsinaks and Cumans. The interaction between Turks and Mongols was always intimate, and a substantial portion of the Mongol armies were Turks under Mongol officers: among the Russians the word Tatar, originally the name of one of the Mongolian tribes, came to encompass some of the Turks who settled in Russia later, such as the Kazan and Crimean Tatars.

To organize this confusion by giving it a name, modern Russian Orientalists sometimes use the word "Turco-Tatar" to take in these various related peoples.

In the part of the Golden Horde that occupied the lands west of the Volga the Turkish element actually consisted of Cumans, who as a people were simply absorbed once they had been defeated; there were also remnants of Khazars and Patsinaks.

Turkish elements predominated in the Golden Horde society to such an

Part of the Golden Gates of Kiev *dating from the reign of Yaroslav the Wise (1019-1054), during the period of Kievan supremacy. Yaroslav began uniting the scattered princely territories, built up his position through prolonged wars and dynastic marriages.*

of view the Russian adventure was simply an episode, and on the whole a minor episode, in a ramified campaign of conquest that included China and Central Asia; indeed, it failed in Russia not through Russian action but because the Mongol realm began to decompose from within.

Around 1300 the Mongol Empire extended from China to Poland, occupying the whole of Asia except India, Burma and Cambodia. When we consider that the Mongol people numbered possibly a million, while the peoples it controlled amounted to some 100,000,000, and that at its zenith it had fewer than 150,000 troops, it is obvious that under the leadership of this small group of nomads something special took place.

Russian history between the Thirteenth and Fifteenth Centuries is incom-

It was Chingis's "Great Yasa"—actually a constitution—that was the legal foundation of the whole Mongol empire, including Russia.

Conversely, Russia made a substantial contribution to the power both of the Golden Horde and of the Mongol empire it was part of. Russians drafted into the Mongol armies played an important role in the campaigns of the Khans of the Golden Horde as well as of the Great Khans themselves. During the 1330's there was a Russian division of Guards stationed in Peking that was an important pillar of the imperial regime in China. Russia was milked for craftsmen and artisans of all kinds, who worked in the Golden Horde and as far east as Mongolia.

In short, though Russian historians have generally had a biased view of Mongol influence, either pretending that

The mosaic-decorated interior of Saint ▶ Sophia, *of Kiev, one of the finest examples of Byzantine art in Russia, and of Kievan Russian civilization. The building of this church was started under Yaroslav the Wise in 1037. At the top of the curved apse, against a gold background, stands the isolated, colossal figure of the Virgin. Below, the Communion of the Apostles, with Christ shown twice, on the right and the left of the ciborium, each Christ offering bread and wine to six Apostles.*

—the Great Battue—that they held every year at the beginning of the winter, as a basic rite in the training of adult warriors.

During the Great Battue hunters would be deployed around a huge area comprising thousands of square miles. There was a center and a right and left wing, each with its special commander. After the columns had been deployed, the Great Khan himself, together with his concubines and his commissariat, set up camp in the center of the battue. The lines would then gradually converge—it took from one to three months—and drive the game into the presence of the Great Khan. Couriers kept the Khan informed of the progress, location, quantity etc. of the game. If any of the game slipped out through a badly manned section of the ring, the commanding officer would be personally liable to severe penalties.

After the game had been driven into a circle about ten miles in circumference, which would be marked off by lines of ropes, the ring was finally sealed. While huge numbers of panicky animals milled about inside, the Great Khan would go into the inner ring and begin the shooting, followed by Princes of the blood, army commanders and then ordinary soldiers, all slaughtering the animals in turn for a number of days.

Now, when the Mongols were about to launch a campaign, the Great Council —the *Kuriltai*—would convene as a staff headquarters. Operations and targets would be laid down, with the captains of all the major army units present to be given their orders. Special agents had already been sent to spy out the land to be attacked; as much information as possible about the people and the countryside was collected in advance. The marshalling grounds and take-off area for the army were designat-

Two panels (above, and on facing page) from the doors of Saint Sophia of Novgorod. The oldest monument of Novgorod, built between 1045-1052 by the son of Yaroslav the Wise (who built Saint Sophia of Kiev). The doors are of wood, covered with bronze plaques: simple repoussé work, German origin, XIIth century. Above, the Creation of Eve.

extent that the Mongols lost their language rather rapidly; even the ruling classes gradually began speaking Turkish. Documents of internal administration during the late Fourteenth and Fifteenth Centuries were actually kept in Chagatay Turkish.

The Mongols had an extraordinarily efficient striking force, based on the swift coordination of light and heavy cavalry, that was far superior to anything else at the time. It was not, to be sure, a total innovation, but the perfecting of the traditional steppe warfare based on horses. The horses, like their riders, had immense stamina.

The Mongol light cavalry was armed with bow and arrow; their heavy cavalry carried sabre, lance, a battle-axe or mace, and a lasso, with a helmet of leather (later of iron) and a leather cuirass or coat of mail.

But perhaps the most effective thing about the Mongol armies was their strategy: they were militarily successful by applying the principles of a hunt

Yuri Dolgoruki ("Longarm" 1154-1157) who cleared a space in the woods by a river bank to found what was to become Moscow. The "Titulyarnik" manuscript of 1672.

26

ed, and appropriate pasturing grounds reserved along the routes to be taken by the troops.

It was not a mere matter of military information: secret agents sent out long before the troops were to start marching carried on systematic propaganda and psychological warfare. The Mongol approach was to persuade the poor that the Mongols would be against the rich—which for that matter they actually were, i.e., the enemy rich—to persuade the merchants that the Mongol peace would make the routes safe for business, the religious minorities that the Mongols tolerated all religions. Everyone was promised safety if they surrendered, on the one hand, and frightful vengeance if they did not.

The Mongols' theory of war was political à outrance—their goal was the encirclement and physical extirpation of their opponents' armies.

This was where the Great Battue came in: the Mongols would first envelop a vast area as in the hunting battue, and then tighten the ring around it. The columns operated with astonishing coordination, communication between them being kept up by messenger couriers or smoke signals. If by some chance the enemy was too strong at first for the Mongols to burst through his lines they would pretend to retreat: as a rule the enemy would then break ranks and rush forward in hot pursuit, thinking they had been routed. The Mongols would then pivot about quickly on their agile little horses, reform their ring and this time finish things off.

Though at first the Mongols lacked siege machinery, after their first Turkestan campaign they developed an effective technique for taking strong fortified cities by storm. A wooden wall would be set up round the city some distance away, to stop supplies and cut off the besieged garrison from any contact with their kinsmen outside. Then captives picked up in prior campaigns, or natives drafted on the spot, would fill in the moat with anything available—stones, earth etc.; siege engines would be drawn up to bombard the city with rocks, containers of naphtha, and javelins, while battering rams would be turned against the gates.

Because the army was supposed to live off the conquered areas, and was only followed by a camel caravan with a minimum of supplies, the broad Mongol strategy was grounded on the assumption that the seizure of huge enemy territories was not only feasible, but lucrative, regardless of how small the Mongol armies were. As the Mongol army advanced through enemy territory it kept growing by levies on the native population. The peasants would be drafted to besiege fortresses and

drive carts, while urban craftsmen were drafted into the engineer corps, or to manufacture weapons and tools.

The Mongol army would often be stronger at the end of a campaign than at the beginning. When Chingis died the Mongol army proper numbered 129,000, probably its zenith: it made up for its size by the methods outlined above.

The Presentation in the Temple. *Bronze panel from the doors of Saint Sophia of Novgorod. Each door has thirteen panels. There were originally three doors, only two are left.*

All this of course sounds strikingly modern, both in the practice of living off the land in this planned way, and particularly in the principle of extreme mobility in warfare that became commonplace during the Second World War. Consequently, though military historians have traditionally disregarded Mongol strategy and tactics, interest in them has now revived precisely in the era of tanks and airplanes: the fast, far-flung Mongol columns of horsemen are startlingly reminiscent of the most effective techniques of the last war.

As far as we can see, the architect of the Mongol empire, Chingis Khan, seems to have made an arbitrary decision to conquer the world, though he was doubtless motivated by one of those intangible though pervasive geopolitical factors like the gradual desiccation of Central Asia etc. In any case, the initial stage in his program of world conquest—China—was quickly attained. Chingis's first China campaign, in 1211, ended with the surrender of Peking in 1215. His seizure of North China and Manchuria gave him not only a corps of army engineers, but a body of cultivated bureaucrats who

proved indispensable to the organization of the Mongol forces.

From the Mongols' point of view Russia was a quite unkown country lying vaguely to the west: when Chingis had conquered the ancient, cultivated state of Khorezm in Western Turkestan he gave one of his generals, Subudey, permission to reconnoitre "the western lands". Coming first upon the Cumans, allied by now to the Russian princes by marriage and other ties, Subudey routed both together at the celebrated battle of Kalka in 1222. The Mongols are reported to have celebrated their victory by a tremendous feast on a wooden floor, under which their Russian and Cuman captives were slowly crushed to death.

After destroying or enslaving the Cumans and Russians wholesale, and driving the remnants off to Galicia, the Balkans, Asia Minor and even Egypt, the Mongols vanished again, to the complete bewilderment of the Russians. Nothing was seen of them again for fourteen years, when a Mongol army headed by one of Chingis's grandsons, Batu, who had been appointed commander in-chief of one prong of the pan-Mongol drive westward, crossed the Volga; Subudey acted as chief-of-staff.

About 50,000 Mongols were the backbone of Batu's armies, which together with his Turks and various auxiliaries may have come to 120,000 or more; the territories to be governed and garrisoned by Batu were so vast that

Сотворися знамение в великом Нове городе Ш той иконы пр(е)стыя Б(огороди)цы иже на ильине улицы сице живущим новгородцем своею

области ико же ими Б(ог)ъ поручи кн(я)за держахъ себе посвоеа воли втоже врема двинане нехотахъ дани датiи нову городу

иидаша кн(я)зю андрею суздалскому новгородцыже послаша надвину данника исним Ш е ти концехъ посто мужеи послышакн(я)зь сiдас кiи посла воини
числомъ д i сотъ исретоша навели wзери иначаша битися ипоможе Б(ог)ъ новгородцемъ ипобиша мужеи ими побегоша итако кн(я)зь анреи разбiвы иначаша
копити воиство самъ же расволесд ипосла с(ы)на своего римана кн(я)дъ город

Приде кн(я)зь романъ суздалскии сомноже
ствомъ воинства квеликому нову
городу исоуставиша стрелы
послы новгородцки   послы суздалски

И молитвами пр(е)стыя Б(огороди)цы ипадины сослепоша ипопомъ
сами себе начаша росскати

his field army was probably never more than 50,000 in any given phase.

Batu's westward thrust was far more than a military advance: his troops were accompanied by whole caravans, including women and children. It was a migration more than an invasion.

The Mongols' preliminary raid in 1222-1223 had been aimed at southern Russia, but Subudey now thought it more prudent to reduce northeastern Russia first, perhaps because he thought that his success at Kalka fourteen years before had been facilitated by the inertia of the Grand Duke of Vladimir, the strongest of the Russian Princes. Since Subudey seems to have contemplated a far-ranging campaign all the way to Hungary he had to secure his northern flank.

In thinking of warfare in Russia our own point of view is nourished on literary recollections of "General Frost" etc., and the undoing of Napoleon and Hitler, but Subudey thought winter the best time for making war in northern Russia. Since the Mongols felt at home in the cold, what with their furs and general hardiness, and the Mongol horses were quite capable of foraging beneath the snow for leaves or stubble, the freezing over of the numerous rivers and lakes made their work much easier.

By 1240 Kiev was stormed and taken, after the Mongol envoys sent to demand its submission had been killed: there is an account of the city's being deafened by the rattle of wagons, the neighing of horses, and the bellowing of camels. The people of Kiev had built new wooden walls in the center of the town; when these were stormed there was the usual massacre, especially in the churches the townfolk had crowded into.

Six years after the destruction of Kiev a Minorite friar by the name of Plano Carpini, journeying eastward to visit the Mongols, described the city as having only 200 houses left, with nothing but skulls and bones round about the countryside. In Russia this was a common sight.

◄ *This ikon of the Novgorod School (2nd half of the XVth century), one of three panels, is the first representation of a scene from Russian history. It shows the battle between Novgorod and Suzdal, when Novgorod was besieged, in 1169. At the top, the town's most revered ikon is being carried for protection from its church into the fortified Kremlin. Negotiations between the adversaries broke down when the Suzdal forces shot arrows at the ikon. The Novgorod warriors avenged this blasphemy, with the miraculous help of warrior saints, by defeating the Suzdalians. Museum of Russian Art, Novgorod.*

The Mongols were anxious to get to Hungary, which was the farthest reach of the great Eurasian steppe and thus useful as a base for their cavalry in any Central European operations, just as it had been for Attila eight hundred years before. Also, the Magyars were excellent candidates by their origins for the Turco-Mongol alliance now in mid-ascent.

The Mongols seem to have been all set for a further advance into Central Europe until the spring of 1242, when Batu, who had reached Vienna and was camped in Klosterneuburg, heard that

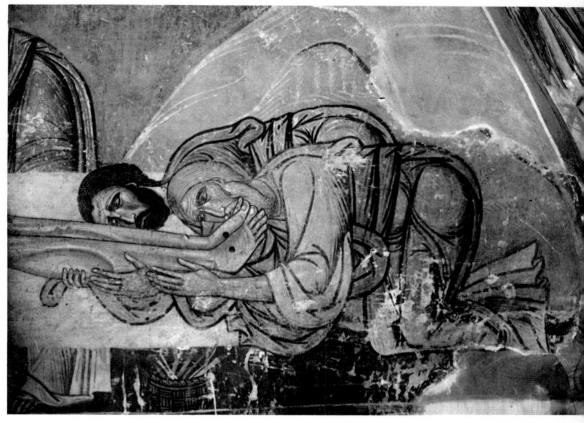

Apostles at the Feet of Christ, *fragment of a fresco of the Burial of Christ in the Cathedral of the Transfiguration of the Savior, Mirosh Monastery, Pskov. This painting, dating from the middle of the XIIth century, is characteristic of the earliest Russian frescos.*

his uncle Ugudey, the Great Khan since Chingis's death in 1226, had died, leaving the succession problematical.

Batu cancelled his offensive—by this time the Mongols were in Hungary and Croatia—and withdrew via northern Serbia and Bulgaria, to jockey for position in the new elections for the Great Khan, which as a descendant of Chingis he was eligible for. His campaign of 1237-1241 had brought immense areas under Mongol control; not only the south Russian steppe and the northern Russian forests, but also the lower Danube, Bulgaria and Moldavia were part of the Mongol empire for a century.

By 1242 the Mongol empire, centred in Karakorum, was consolidated. In one generation an entirely new and hitherto

unknown people had emerged with a claim to universal dominion. After having seized immense areas in Asia and Europe, the Mongols, as lords of the Eurasian steppe, were strategically capable of controlling both the northern half of Asia and the eastern half of Europe.

At least so it seemed. In the event, though the Mongols acquired some more territories, their conquest had now achieved what turned out to be its natural limits. From then on, it was to digest what it had swallowed, to settle down, and to begin decaying.

The cardinal event of Ugudey's reign was the establishment by his nephew Batu of the Qypchak Khanate in southern Russia, centred in the new city of Saray on the lower Volga. This became known as the Golden Horde, which for the first century of its existence was an *ulus*, or satrapy of the Mongol empire. The Golden Horde, in which the Mongol aristocracy was the topmost stratum, was ruled even after the Mongol empire disintegrated by the descendants of Chingis, who also ruled its successor-states.

Russia was only one of the departments of the Golden Horde's affairs: from the very beginning it governed an immensely complex variety of peoples in addition, more so even than the Mongol satrapies in China and Persia. Most of

One of the oldest examples of state regalia in the Kremlin's State Armory Museum, Moscow, is this fur-trimmed Monomachos Cap of State. *The top is in curving gold filigree against a flat gold ground, studded with cabuchon jewels and pearls. It is said to have belonged to Vladimir Monomakh, the Kievan leader who attempted to establish a centralized state, but Vladimir died over a hundred years before this cap was made.*

the Cumans were still pagans, as they had been when the Mongols first burst into the southeast Russian steppe, while the people of Khorezm and the Bulgars along the Volga were Muslims.

The Mongol dominion utterly liquidated Russian sovereignty. The Russian Princes were ordered to Saray in order to be licensed to rule; even after being confirmed in office by the Khan of the Golden Horde they often had to go all the way to Mongolia to get the ultimate sanction of the Great Khan himself.

Saray became a hotbed of princely intrigues aimed at the Mongols' favor; a considerable number of Russians were killed by their own people. The principal instrument of this bitter internecine struggle was the simplest—money. The license to govern a Grand Duchy or Principality was in effect auctioned off. Though the native Russian chronicles do their best to gloss over these facts, so distasteful to the national myth, enough traces remain to indicate that mutual denunciations to the Mongol rulers were a commonplace. The helplessness of the Russian Princes is

amply demonstrated by the nine voyages to Saray made by Ivan I of Moscow (1325-1341), and the five made by his son Simeon (1341-1353). The granting of the executive license, which took the form of a ceremony of enthronement, was carried out in the name of the Khan in the presence of his ambassador: it was a dramatic illustration of the peremptory reality of Mongol rule. All in all, between 1242 and 1430, some one hundred and thirty Russian Princes journeyed to the Khans and to the Great Khans, often for purely personal objectives.

The interests of the Golden Horde were simple: it wanted revenue and recruits, the basic requirements of the Mongol empire. The Russian Princes became tax collectors; by the Fourteenth Century they had replaced the Mongol officials who, supported by a police force, had originally been posted in charge of taxation all over the country.

The most effective way of getting a Khan's executive license for a desirable territory was to offer to increase its tax yield; this meant, of course, that the

Prince had to grind more out of it. Thus the constant intrigues at Saray all tended in the same direction, in a spiral, toward extracting as much as possible from the Russian subjects of the princely sub-vassals of the Khan. This naturally increased the friction between the Princes and the communities they governed; it even turned the Princes into active sponsors of Mongol interests.

The clashes between Princes did not take place merely around the Khan's court in Saray; the Mongols were invited to make punitive expeditions inside Russia again and again in order to help one of their favorites, i.e., a Prince who could offer more revenue. There are supposed to have been some 48 Mongol invasions of Russia between 1236 and 1462, some of which were merely punitive, and many of which came about at the invitation of the Russian Princes themselves. The Russian national hero, Alexander Nevsky, famous for having repulsed a Swedish army on the ice of the river Neva (whence his surname), who was canonized by the Russian Church, denounced his own brother Andrew to the Khan for having been remiss in his duty to the Golden Horde: it was in fact the Tatars (as I shall now call the Mongols) who installed Nevsky as Grand Duke of Vladimir in 1252, after ousting his brother.

Russians cooperated closely with the Tatars even in the earliest times: not only did the Russians take part in the military adventures of their conquerors, as I have indicated above, but the Tatars gave the Russian Princes great support in the struggle against their enemies on Russia's southern and western borders.

The symbiosis between Tatars and Russians was very dense. Tatar influence was not a mere matter of military domination; the Tatars had a great interest in commerce, which was promoted by the location of Saray on the lower Volga. This was the ancient trade route to the east, which enabled the Tatars to create a system of commercial exchange points between East and West. These commercial settlements stimulated exchange between merchants from many countries, and the Tatars themselves played a part in it, contributing horses, hides and leather goods.

The Russo-Tatar symbiosis was particularly intense in the summit of Russian society; Princes and boyars often married Tatar princesses. Oddly enough Tatar influence in Russian domestic affairs began to increase *after* the decline of the Golden Horde, which began about the middle of the Fourteenth Century and culminated in the collapse of the Tatar state a century later. After this collapse numerous detachments of Tatar princes and high functionaries poured into Russia, accompanied by throngs of servants and armed troops. As Moscow began to ascend it attracted them into its service, since it could offer them more than the crumbling Golden Horde.

This migration took on mass proportions after 1445, when Basil II of Moscow lost a battle to the Tatars and was taken prisoner. He seems to have bought himself off by a huge ransom and by undertaking a great many obligations delicately glossed over by the chronicler. He went back to Moscow together with a vast number of Tatar soldiers and grandees.

By the end of the Seventeenth Century the Moscow upper class is estimated to have been about 17 % Tatar or oriental. But the Tatar influence was far more than a question of blood lines: the state that evolved during the Sixteenth Century and lasted some four hundred years was an offshoot of the monolithic rule of the Tatars. The Tatars, once feared, then mingled with and imitated, were a model for the Tsarist autocracy. The Tatars had reduced the relatively independent squirearchy to subservience, first to the Grand Dukes of Moscow and later to the Tsars. The popular assembly, which had been declining rapidly in any case even before the Tatars' appearance, lost its most important function under the Golden Horde: the right it had once had to choose and oust its Princes. The Khans naturally took this over, and the popular assembly vanished, leaving the bulk of the people to subside still further under the twofold burden of domestic taxation and Tatar exactions.

There is an aspect of the Tatar expansion that is of general interest. The Tatar experiment in dominion, which in spite of its immense initial success finally failed, perhaps because with the technology of the time it was impossible to maintain a centralized empire spread

Combat between Russians and Tatars in 1238. *XVIth century miniature from the Historical Museum, Moscow. The Mongolian invasion, women and cattle included, swept across the Siberian steppe in 1237; their power was to last two and half centuries.*

so thin over such a vast territory, represents a curious parallel in embryo to the far more brilliant nomadic attempt to rule a sedentary civilization that was embodied in the Slave Household of the Ottoman Empire during the period of its efflorescence (roughly 1365-1565).

Nomads in general have all faced the same problem with respect to the

Prince Yaroslav Vsevolodovich presenting a model of a church to Christ. *Fresco in the Holy Savior church of Nereditsa near Novgorod (circa 1246). This church, once famous for its frescos, was totally destroyed during the Second World War.*

sedentary peoples they overrun. The problem is simply this: unless they give up nomadic ways and settle down themselves, intermingling with their subjects and sooner or later vanishing, what they must do is apply to men the methods that have been successful with their flocks and herds: they become shepherds of men. Nomads can only exist because of their horses, camels and dogs: what the Tatars did, though only partially, as we can see by the vastly greater system introduced by their Ottoman cousins, was to use the Russian Princes to ride herd. Eventually this failed because the fabric of Russian life was not, in fact, transformed or even changed substan-

The Hospitality of Abraham. *Armenian miniature, 1316.*

tially, so that when the Tatar empire began to crumble under its own internal tensions Russian society was still vigorous enough to take advantage of this enfeeblement of Tatar authority and resume its autonomous evolution.

The Ottoman Turks perfected a far more efficient device, which enabled their empire to survive into the modern era: not content with training their human auxiliaries they made a point of uprooting them in such a way as to cut them off from their origins entirely, thus making them far more malleable for the executive intentions of their masters. The Slave Household of the Ottoman Turks gave a career only to those born *outside* the Muslim Turkish fold, the children of infidels. Seized when young, these were then brought up in accordance with a program, organized in minute detail, that opened up to them the most influential posts in the empire

while keeping them subordinate as the Sultan's watch-dogs.

The social atomization of such slaves was evidently essential, since a new loyalty had to replace the old. This was why the children of the Ottoman Turkish Pashas were excluded from running the Ottoman Empire when it was at its height. The children of free Muslim feudal lords, full of race pride, with local and family connections, were obviously far from suited to run the empire on behalf of a centralized regime. In fact, when the ban was rescinded on the admission of free Muslims, in contrast with the children of Christians and pagans forcibly enslaved and converted to Islam while in a state of bondage, the Ottoman Turkish regime began decaying with great rapidity.

The charm of slavery, from an administrative and military point of view, lies in the purity of the executive

relationship between ruler and ruled: in effect the rulers commanded their slaves, Do our ruling for us!

The Ottoman Slave Household represented the perfection of what other Turks—the Tatars—tried in Russia; it was a superior application of the same principles of human herdsmanship tried out before the Tatars by the Avars and other nomads from Asia, as well as the Muslim Arabs in the initial phase of their expansion. The comparison is the more illuminating because in many ways the westward drive of the Ottoman Turks during the Fourteenth and Fifteenth Centuries was an after-effect of the Tatar overflow. The sinister impression made on Western Europe by the Tatar sack of Kiev in the Thirteenth Century was completely overshadowed by the Ottoman conquest of Constantinople in 1453, and though the Tatars threatened Vienna for a while they

32

soon went away, while the Ottoman menace to Vienna lasted until the late Seventeenth Century.

The slaughter wrought by the Tatar conquests amounted to several million dead, and few other periods before our own have seen so much killing, but the *Pax Mongolica*, by unifying most of Eurasia under a single regime and thus protecting the overland trade route from China to the Mediterranean, established a network of cultural exchanges between Europe, the Middle East and China.

The influence of the Tatars on Russian life, during the two hundred and forty years the Russians paid them tribute, was substantial. It must be remembered that of the many peoples the Tatars conquered the Russians were one of the few they could learn nothing from. Whereas they had borrowed many elements of civilization from others, notably the Chinese, Persians and Muslims, in Russia they found nothing at all to imitate. Saray was an industrial center with construction yards that ran on hydraulic power; the Tatars' palaces were very luxurious, and even had central heating; as indicated above their army engineering units had machines capable of reducing fortresses.

The Tatars have sometimes been held responsible for traits of cruelty characteristic of Russian life, especially in the treatment of criminals. It may have been under Tatar influence that Russians took with such enthusiasm to torture, flogging, mutilation and execution; in the Muscovy that slowly took shape beneath the shell of Tartar rule it was commonplace for criminals to have their noses, ears, hands or feet lopped off, to be impaled, quartered, racked on the wheel, and whipped to death: heretics and sorcerers were burnt alive; counterfeiters had melted lead poured down their throats; great ingenuity was unfolded in the interrogation of suspects.

Nevertheless the Russians thought the Tatars fascinating. Though one side of the Russian secular literature

Two miniatures from the XVIth century manuscript of the "Life of Saint Sergius" (Lenin Library, Moscow) showing repeated images of the saint in various activities. Above, with his brother Stephan, Saint Sergius builds a church out of wood. Below, he goes through the various stages of making bread at the Saint Sergius monastery named after him.

expressed a conventional feeling of hatred for the national oppressor, and the heroic folk-sagas recording the conflict with the previous enemy, the Cumans, were recast to fit the Tatars, a contrary fascination also rooted itself in literature and has, indeed, remained a permanent motif in Russian literature to this day. Tatar chivalry in warfare was much admired, as was what was thought to be the life of the steppe, with its free nomadic ways etc., which was to be very attractive to Russian writers during the Nineteenth Century.

In the Fifteenth Century the Tatar-Russian union in the upper classes was so intimate that the court of Basil II of Moscow actually spoke Turkish, which had meanwhile become the general language of the Golden Horde. Many

Russian noblemen in the Fifteenth, Sixteenth and Seventeenth Centuries even adopted Tatar surnames, perhaps the best known examples being the Velyaminovs, of Viking ancestry, who took the Turkish name of Aksakov: a descendant was to become a famous propagandist for the "Slavophile" viewpoint of the Nineteenth Century, while the philosopher Chaadayev, a zealous pro-Westerner, was a descendant of Chingis's son Chagatay. Many well-known Russian families are of Tatar descent—Yusupovs, Kutuzovs, Urusovs; the Tatars even produced a Russian Tsar—Boris Godunov.

Intimate association with the military adventures of the Khans naturally familiarized a great many Russians with the Tatar army system: it was natural for Tatar methods to be introduced into the Russian army. The Russians adopted the Tatar tactic of enveloping the enemy on both flanks, and also introduced Tatar armor and weapons. The articulation of the Russian army into five large units—center, right and left arms, vanguard, rearguard—was also modeled on the Tatar cavalry.

revival; there was a blossoming of religious painting both in frescoes and ikons. Though until the middle of the Fourteenth Century Russian painting remains obscure and Greek artists seem to have executed most of the better surviving ikons, neo-Byzantine influence streamed in during the second half of the Fourteenth Century and gave

a continuous native tradition. Rublyov's work is contemporary with Fra Angelico's, and is thought to resemble it. His most famous painting, distinguished by the serenity of the composition and the delicacy of the colors, is the ikon of the "Old Testament Trinity" in the great church of the Trinity Monastery.

The scarcity of the names of individual painters reflects the characteristically collective, impersonal spirit of the Russian Church. But as in so many of the other arts the origin of Old Russian painting was of course wholly Byzantine; this is surely the explanation of the curious contrast of Russian talent with its background of unrelieved barbarism. Russian art was not outdone by the finest Byzantine painting, though it had neither its emotional picturesqueness nor its realism. While conserving Byzantine grace and mobility, the stylization of Russian painting was wholly static —a counterpart of the liturgical formality of the Russian Church. The congealed adoration of rows of saints turned toward Christ expressed the motionless transcendence of the evolving Church-sponsored autocracy.

On the other hand, the devastation wrought by the Tatars was tremendous. Ancient centers of Russian civilization —Kiev, Chernigov, Pereyaslavl, Ryazan —were laid waste; the first three mentioned did not recover for centuries. Russian casualties were immense; also, the huge numbers of civilians of both sexes enslaved by the Tatars must have come to at least 10% of the population.

Perhaps even more importantly for Russian civilization, the cultural demands of the Tatars accentuated its intellectual impoverishment. The best jewellers and craftsmen, as well as artisans of various kinds such as smiths, armorers, saddlers, etc., were sent to work for the Great Khan or assigned to various Mongol hordes. This dispersion of Russia's best craftsmen for a time exhausted her reservoir of skills and interrupted the continuity of industrial traditions. When the enamel shops of Kiev were destroyed in 1240 and the artisans either killed or kidnapped, the Russian art of making cloisonné enamel, which had achieved such distinction in Kievan Russia, vanished altogether. It took a long time to recover from this; it was not until late in the Fourteenth Century that champlevé enamels were made in Moscow again. In the Sixteenth Century the making of cloisonné enamels by native craftsmen was resumed, but their handiwork was quite inferior to what had been produced in Kiev

Portrait of Grand Duke Dmitri Donskoy. *Fresco in the Archangel Cathedral of the Kremlin. Dmitri, one of the early rulers of Moscow (1363-1389), first dominated the neighboring princes, then beat the Tatars at the battle of Kulikovo near the Don, where he won the surname of Donskoy. Although this made him a national hero, the Golden Horde retaliated two years later, capturing Moscow. Dmitri had to give up his own son as hostage.*

The Tatars gave the Russian language a great many terms filtered through from Mongol and Turkish, or from Persian and Arabic through Turkish, not only for the vocabulary of trade and commerce, but for clothing, household objects, food and drink, fruit and vegetables, metals and gems etc. They also gave the Russians a census and a postal system.

The Tatar age stimulated a religious

birth to some remarkable painting, both in Moscow and Novgorod. Theophanes the Greek, who flourished between 1370 and 1410, played a stellar role in this artistic renaissance: he lived in Russia some thirty years before his death. Theophanes's influence was limited to his free brush-stroke technique, but his mastery was carried on by Andrew Rublyov, the only Russian painter whose name is embodied in

Dmitri Donskoy *subjugating the Tatars* ▶ *at the battle of Kulikovo, with a couple of helpful angels joining in the rout. From a XVIth century miniature recounting the life of St. Sergius. Lenin Library.*

Ivan Kalita, *"Moneybags", dispensing summary justice to the boyars. Ivan (1328-1341) was Grand Duke of Vladimir, Prince of Moscow, and chief revenue agent for the Tatar Khan, whence his nickname. "Life of Saint Sergius", XVIth century manuscript.*

centuries before. There was a halt in the making of filigree; when it was finally resumed it was visibly modified by the use of models from Central Asia. The niello technique also vanished with the Tatar invasion; it was not until the Sixteenth Century that it was taken up again. Glazed polychrome ceramics, as well as decorative tiles, also seem to have stopped being made until the Fifteenth Century. The art of masonry and fretwork, as well as construction crafts in general, was halted or impaired by the consequences of the Tatar invasion. The last masterpiece of stone-cutting was the reliefs in the Cathedral of St. George in Yuriev-Polsky in Suzdalia, finished just

before the Tatars struck. This depression lasted for a whole century in East Russia, and it was not until the middle of the Fourteenth Century, when Tatar control began weakening, that some branches of industry, especially metallurgy, began reviving.

The disappearance of urban crafts during the first century of Tatar control indirectly accentuated the growth of the manorial system. Since the absence of trained people to fill consumers' demands made the villagers and upper classes depend on themselves, the Princes, boyars and monasteries were obliged to sponsor crafts on their own estates. Ultimately, after the Princes and monasteries managed to redeem some cap-

tive craftsmen, while others came back from Tatar captivity, a large number of smiths, potters, carpenters and tailors

Cathedral of the Transfiguration, Novgorod, 1374. This characteristically Novgorod structure still has its original gabled roof; it is built around an apse and a single dome. Novgorod's unique position as a wealthy and independent mercantile city, added to a fortunate geographical position, allowed it to remain free of Tatar destruction. It also produced a class of wealthy merchant patrons; their trading contacts with foreigners opened the way to innovation. This group instigated Novgorod's intense building activity: during the XIIth century, sixty eight churches were raised. ▶

settled on princely and monastic estates: when the Grand Ducal manor became a major centre, as it did in Moscow, they continued to work for the local Prince or Grand Duke instead of for the market. This led to a marked growth of manorial industries during the Fourteenth to Sixteenth Centuries.

This process paralleled the growing importance of the large landed estates. It is true that the manor as a socio-political institution had been extending its role even before the Mongols, and that in the Twelfth Century both Princes and boyars owned great estates that were sources of copious revenue, but the cities were still the foci of political life; the Princes spent more time playing politics than attending to business.

But as the Tatars curtailed the political rights of all their subjects, the Princes were naturally reduced to the management of their estates; and as the cities declined the natural resources of the country—its forests, agriculture, etc.—became more important. Consequently the domains of the Grand Duke ultimately became the chief foundation of both his economic power and his administration. That is, his estates not only gave him an income, they became the axis of his material power. In this way patrimonial habits were to modify the very concept of princely power.

This happened to the boyars too: since the Princes, as former pretenders to sovereignty, were the ones most affected by the Tatar power, the boyars actually had greater relative influence on state affairs during the Tatar invasion than before. Until the Tatar invasion it had been only the Galician boyars who had successfully opposed the Princes, and who were actually responsible for drawing in first Lithuanian and then Polish rulers. In East Russia, on the other hand, as indicated above, the boyars became eager to sponsor the expansion of the Grand Duchy or principality they were counselors of, since this expansion benefited them both socially and individually. As the Tatar dominion waned, and it became clear that among the numerous petty Russian rulers it was the Moscow Princes who were in the forefront, this fact itself attracted more and more boyars to offer them their support. Thus the natural desire for self-aggrandizement on the part of the Prince merged in this early period with the spontaneous collaboration of the boyars.

Now, though Russian political life was not wiped out but merely distorted, the relationships between its constituent elements were completely upset: the paramount process in political life,

democratic institutions represented by the popular assembly, which had prospered variously throughout Russia, were wiped out. It was actually in the urban population of the surviving cities that

Saint Macarius, *detail of the head. Church of the Transfiguration, Novgorod. Fresco by the illustrious master Theophanes the Greek, who was working in Novgorod in 1378. Little is known of the artist; a contemporary letter mentions that he had been to Constantinople and that he was admired immensely as an outstanding craftsman. He painted in Moscow, but his frescos there were lost when the Kremlin churches were subsequently rebuilt. The church of the Transfiguration frescos and a few ikons are all that remain of his work. The subject of the painting above, Saint Macarius, was an ascetic who lived for thirty years in the Egyptian desert. He claimed that during all that time he never once ate, drank or slept as much as Nature required. His emaciated features indicate such trials.*

◄ Saint George, *late XIVth century ikon. Russian Museum, Leningrad. The patron saint of Russia often appears in frescos and ikons, with but little variation in the stylized treatment of the figure.*

as well as in economics, was the decline of the role of the cities.

Since most of the major cities of East Russia were actually destroyed during the Tatar invasion, the urban

the Tatars met with the only serious resistance during the first century of their rule. There was no basis for accomodation between the Tatars and the urban population: the townspeople,

An ikon, late XIVth century, representing Archangel Michael, *Novgorod school. Tretyakov Gallery, Moscow. The face and figure are treated in strongly linear style. The stern expression and vigorous manner suggest an Eastern influence.*

latter part of the Fourteenth Century, as the alliances between the Russian Princes and the Tatars began to break up, with the decomposition of the Tatar empire and the growing boldness of the Russian Princes, the consequent alienation of the Princes from the Tatars eliminated at least one cause of friction with the popular assembly, but even then the Princes and boyars remained suspicious of the unruliness inherent in the popular assembly, and even while appealing to the townsfolk for their cooperation against the Tatars they had no intention of allowing an actual popular assembly as an institution to take shape again. Thus, though the popular assembly kept springing up again at times of crisis, it never resumed its role as a permanent source of authority.

The Mongols had always been extremely tolerant—or indifferent— in religious matters; Chingis had admitted to his court every sort of religious persuasion—Buddhist monks, Nestorian and Franciscan Christians, Taoists, and Muslims. A grandson, Guyuk, wrote his "son" St. Louis that his aim was to protect all Christians regardless of denomination; another Great Khan, Mongka, said all religions were like the five fingers of a hand; according to Marco Polo, Kubilay, the ruler of China, kissed the Gospels presented to him by a Nestorian priest. In the West, however, though they remained broadminded, they gradually yielded to Islam; the most important cultural development within the Golden Horde during its efflorescence was the Muslim conversion that took place on a large scale in the reign of Uzbeg (1313-1341). Batu himself had been a skyworshipper and his son had accepted Christianity, and though his brother Berke became a Muslim it was not until Uzbeg's reign that Islam became the official religion of the Khan's court and was actually adopted by most of his Turco-Mongol subjects.

Since Mongols were actually a small minority of the Golden Horde, most of which consisted of Turks, the spread of Islam among both groups, already so closely intertwined, fused them still further; Muslim institutions gradually grew up alongside Mongol institutions.

Economically the Golden Horde itself was a symbiosis between nomadic and sedentary populations: the Tatars found pasturage for their cattle and horses in the steppes of southern Russia and the northern Caucasus, while the edges of the steppe were also used for crops.

It was the international trade underlying the Golden Horde that probably stimulated its conversion to Islam, because of the central role played in finance and trade by the Muslims of Central Asia and the Middle East; it was doubtless this conversion to Islam that in splitting the area ruled by the

especially the craftsmen, were constantly threatened by conscription; unlike the Princes and boyars, who swiftly both interacted and often intermingled with the Tatars, the city-dwellers were in a state of more or less continuous turbulence at each oppressive Tatar measure.

This naturally made the Tatars eager to stamp out the popular resistance rooted in the nature of city life. It led them to extend their dynastic or oligarchic combinations with the Russian Princes to the repression of urban opposition. The alliance was all the more organic because the Russian Princes were also inherently opposed to the unsettling tendencies of the popular

assembly. Both Tatars and Russian Princes, in fact, had a joint interest in combating the popular assembly, and thus, like so many other alliances concluded on the surface of Russian life against the stirrings beneath, for a long time they were welded together. The cooperation between Tatars and Princes forestalled the spread of urban rebellions during the second half of the Thirteenth Century and stamped out the isolated rebellions that flared up now and then.

The authority of the popular assembly thus dwindled sharply, and by the middle of the Fourteenth Century it no longer meant anything as an element of government. It is true that during the

Golden Horde into Muslim and Christian cultures postponed the unification of the Russian state.

Though the Golden Horde finally declined through a series of crises, splits and defeats, the dominion of Saray did not collapse completely until two new Tatar states sprang up over its ruins. The Kazan Turks, on the Volga, seceded in 1445, while the Crimean Turks set up a state of their own in Crimea with the support of the Poles. The Russian contribution to the shattering of the Golden Horde was minor; the Horde was in fact ultimately eliminated in 1502 by the Crimean Tatars.

The Golden Horde declined primarily because of something again outside the purview of Russian history—the rise of Timur (known to the West as Tamerlane) who was born in Transoxania in 1336.

Timur was one of the most devastating of Chingis's successors, though while a Mongol he was not a direct descendant, and he ruined the Golden Horde both economically and politically. During Timur's contest with the Khan of the Golden Horde, Tokhtamysh, all the great trading centres the power of the Golden Horde was rooted in were destroyed. Timur apparently intended not merely to defeat his rival in the field, but to reroute Western trade with China and India from the North Caspian and Black Sea regions to Persia and Syria, in this way starving out the Golden Horde and diverting its profits to himself. Timur, in fact did to the Golden Horde what Batu had done to the Russians: he destroyed the major cities, which were centers of crafts and industries as well as of trade, and thus eliminated their social elite. It was this victory of Timur's Central Asian empire,

and the consequent crumbling of the Golden Horde, that constituted a favorable medium for Russia's revival.

Generally speaking the Russians were incapable of coping with the Tatars

The Four Saints Ikon, *Pskov School, circa 1400. Tretyakov Gallery, Moscow. The heads of the famous saints, Paraskeva, Gregory the Theologian, John Chrysostom and Basil the Great, show a definite attempt at characterization. They are modelled so as to provide a three-dimensional effect, while the bodies are handled in a flat two-dimensional pattern.*

in a military way; they relied chiefly on inertia and guile. The celebrated victory won by Dmitri, Grand Duke of Moscow (1359-1389), over the Tatars at Kulikovo in 1380, which flabbergasted the Russians themselves, was not only the first but the only major setback imposed by them on the Golden Horde.

It is fashionable for historians, look-

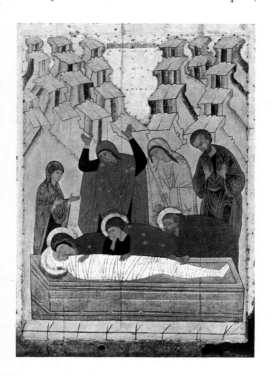

The burial of Christ, *Novgorod school, XVth century. The unknown artist of this ikon expresses sorrow beyond the usual stylized gestures. The Virgin bends over to kiss her son a final time; Mary Magdalen raises her arms like wings.*

ing for crucial turning-points in history and other aids to thought, to regard this battle as a pivotal event marking the definitive turning of the Asiatic tide from the heart of Europe, but in

fact the Russian victory inflicted no serious damage on the Tatar power; for a century afterwards the Russian Princes remained in thralldom, and probably never more so than during the first half of the Fifteenth Century. Even when the Tatar overlordship was definitely sloughed off in 1480, tribute to the Tatars was a matter of course: there is a curious testament left by Ivan the Terrible's father, who died in 1505, providing for a division of the tribute his heirs owed the Tatars, this time, to be sure, not the Golden Horde but the Crimean Tatars mentioned above, who formed one of its successor states.

The Rise of the Moscow State: Ivan the Terrible

Despite the heavy hand of the Tatars the inward development of Russian life went on, but it took forms of its own. I shall recapitulate some of the discussion on feudalism begun in connection with Kievan society, and indicate the development of the institutional pattern as Muscovy emerged.

In some ways Russian feudalism resembled that of Western Europe. The government principle was still only feebly centralized and the order was based on the existence of great estates and of a hierarchy among landlords, the landlords' enjoyment of delegated judicial and fiscal powers, and a contractual theory underlying the services to be performed by both boyars and tenants. But the principle paramount in Western Europe—the hereditariness of relationships and their objective, i.e. impersonal foundation—was generally absent.

Feudalism never crystallized as it did in Europe. Aside from the fact that the Russian Princes did not embody different dynastic claims like the great feudal houses in France and Germany, the people themselves had no regional characteristics. In a curious way the Russian nationality was formed long before the Russian nation-state. This was partly due to the above-mentioned social fluidity: in France a man would be far more a Burgundian than he was French, and a German much more a Bavarian than a German, while the two would have a basic allegiance, both spiritual and material, to an aristocratic house that in Russia was absent.

More importantly, as I have pointed out before, property was not symbolic of anything: a principality, in accordance with the ancient Viking attitude, was simply a piece of real estate. At bottom this is a profoundly anti-feudal notion. The wills left by Suzdalian and Muscovite Princes treated cities, villages, jewels and furs on exactly the same level. Russian feudalism is essentially different from Western European feudalism in the absolute revocability of contracts, and this was primarily because relations were not between things, but between people. Vassaldom in the West, for instance, was theoretically quite

◀ Andrew Rublyov *gilding an ikon on the façade of the Andronev monastery church near Moscow (late XIVth century). From the Life of Saint Sergius manuscript. Rublyov, who had assisted Theophanes, took his master's place as outstanding artist of the day. He died about 1427*

Old Testament Trinity, *by Andrew Rublyov, c. 1410-1420. Tretyakov Gallery, Moscow. This is one of the most famous ikons, still very beautiful in spite of its damaged condition. Here the artist interprets the theme of the Trinity symbolized by three angels. Painted for the Trinity and Saint Sergius Monastery near Moscow.* ▶

Cathedral of the Dormition, *in the Kremlin, Moscow, built between 1484-1489, on the site of an older church, by architects summoned from Pskov by Ivan the III. Future Tsars were to be married and christened here. Ivan, also known as Ivan the Great, married Sophie Paleologue, niece of the last Emperor of Byzantium. She had been brought up in Rome. Probably her influence decided Ivan to send to Italy for architects and craftsmen. Their work and their teaching resulted in the Italianate appearance of building during this reign.*

independent of the person of the vassal: a Baron of such and such a place was a vassal of the Count of such and such a place not because of any personal ties, of sympathy or material interest, but because the Baron's land was part of the Count's fief. The squires in Western Europe had their claims rooted in the land, which is why their titles contained the particle *de*. The Russian boyar custom of retaining family names is illuminating because it indicates the absence of a basic attachment to land. A Morozov or a Romanov might be a lord or a serf: the lineage of Russian nobles was purely genealogical and independent of the land.

This also meant the absence of a fixed hierarchy. There was no question

of "great vassals" as in France: Russia was divided up between the members of a theoretically single family who were all equal in terms of lineage and might go up or down in life in accordance with nothing but their luck. This also applied to the lords owning their land outright: whether they were descendants of the old princely retinues, or favorites of the moment, or people performing services for a Prince and rewarded by land, their material and spiritual status was a function of a contract they had concluded with him. As far as the Prince was concerned what they had was not a title of nobility but a function.

Consequently there was not even a clear line between plebeians and

nobility. The basest villein could be elevated by receiving a charter of immunity from a Prince, just like a boyar or the head of a convent.

In Russia, in a word, the whole complex of relations revolving around the notions of privilege, status, immunity, etc., was based on an economic and not a political concept. Thus all functionaries of the state, however exalted, were mere employees who could be sacked at will.

In a way, of course, this system was democratic, in the sense that status did not depend on a concept of the person, but on a relationship between functions. Boyars were not obliged to "acknowledge" a more powerful boyar: their domain was not attached to a domain that was larger, but directly to the person of a prince; thus there was no question in Russia of that vertical ladder of status that distinguished the Middle Ages in the West. The Russian functional, democratic, plebeian system might be called a horizontal checkerboard, in which the criterion of status remained what it had been in Kievan Russia—function, not situation.

Perhaps the contrast is best illustrated in the absence among the Russians of any concept of honor: chivalry was an alien idea. The success of the Roman Catholic Church in moralizing combat by creating the dual concept of the knight "without fear and without reproach" had no counterpart in the Russian Church, which was indifferent to the organization of society. Everything in Western Europe to do with honor, whether of the class, family, or individual—chivalric orders, duals, tournaments, heraldry, etc.—was completely missing in Russia.

When boyars and Princes spoke of "honor", what they meant was a rank they claimed in a genealogical hierarchy: it involved no duties. The extraordinary unscrupulousness of the society was unbridled even by lip service to any ideal: neither lying, perjury nor assassination was regarded as something beneath a Prince's dignity. Deceit was not only commonplace, but admired; treachery with the aim of securing a brother's or cousin's death was entirely acceptable. The customs of Russia in this as in other things seem an echo of a more ancient past, of France, for instance, under the Merovingians and Carolingians, before the rise of a moral ethos humanized manners.

It seems clear that in a regime where vassaldom was a link between individuals regardless of land, where aris-

tocratic hierarchy was inherently indefinite, where there was no genuine nobility, no chivalry, no knighthood and no concept of honor, there is no point referring to feudalism. It would be better to say that Russia missed the Middle Ages just as she missed the influence of Rome and the Renaissance. If the Middle Ages are taken to span the end of Roman civilization and the beginning of the Renaissance, then Russia, unacquainted with both one and the other, simply remained unarticulated throughout this period, and moreover, was completely submerged in the religious conception of both individual and social life until the reign of Peter the Great, and even for generations afterwards, if the masses of the people are thought of.

It must be recalled that Russian backwardness, so often referred to here, is not a mere epithet, but a structural concept: Dante's composition of the *Divine Comedy* some one hundred and fifty years before the unification of Russia by Moscow is a useful coefficient of relativity, as is the fact that five centuries after her conversion to Christianity Russia remained almost a hundred per cent illiterate, and at bottom profoundly pagan.

This general background of course affected everything: even below the level of state politics, for instance, there was no genuine concept of hierarchy. Of the three social groups dependent on the Prince—the boyars, the Prince's administrative personnel, i.e., the "courtiers", and the taxpayers, or "blacks", who cultivated his land—relationships were governed by contract; the slaves, who were outside all this, were possessions, and were in any case as we have seen a minor factor in the growth of Muscovy. The purpose of the Prince's governmental apparatus was not the

maintenance of society, but the aggrandizement of his treasury.

The dependent Princes, i.e., those invested by the so-called patrimonial Princes with appanages, had the same sort of court on a smaller scale. They too had their "courtiers", functionaries

Interior of the Cathedral of the Annunciation, *Moscow, showing a blend of Italian Renaissance and Russian themes.*

and domestics, either free or slave. A large part of their land would be rented to tenant farmers, and in the Russia of the time would form a universe to itself, separated from others by vast forests or impassable marshes. Whenever it rained or the snows melted the roads would dissolve into a vast sea of mush: when communications were made easier by the big winter freeze they would be more vulnerable to attacks by marauders, usually Tatars.

The point about such Princes is that they were essentially landowners and not gentlemen. Their point of view was highly materialistic. If things went badly on a Prince's land and he found himself ruined, there was nothing in his habit of mind that would prevent his hiring himself out to some luckier landowner, as a farmer or even a voluntary slave.

Foreign trade had long since vanished with the retirement of the Russians into the nooks and crannies of the vast timbered northeast; there was no merchant class to carry on the role it had played in Kievan Russia. Muscovy slumped into the squirarchal, peasant life that was to be its hallmark for centuries. There was a sort of middle

Belvedere *built between 1485-1508 on the Kremlin walls by Italian architects, in the style of the Castello Sforzesco in Milan.*

class, made up of the Prince's functionaries, who took up taxes and collected the tributes for the Tatars, and scribes who coped with the administrative red tape that was the forerunner of the bureaucratic jungle of a later day. Every individual was enmeshed in a network of liabilities: everything had to be paid for—crossing a bridge, hunting

taxation altogether. These privileges were all defined in some detail in actual letters patent issued by the Prince to a landowner; the lands held in outright possession under such conditions were known as patrimonial or hereditary estates.

The patrimonial domain was distinct from another source of land ownership

patrimonial and service estates became altogether blurred and all landlords were subject to government service.

The upper class was growing far more stratified. The boyars, who owned land they exploited with servile or semi-servile labor, depended for their economic independence on the size of their estates, though their independence as individuals still benefited by the custom inherited from the ancient retinues of the Viking Princes and their successors, according to which they were under no obligation to serve their Prince simply because they lived or held land within his political sphere. This privilege was always paid lip service to in agreements between boyars and Princes; since this was the only guarantee of the landed aristocracy's independence it was highly cherished. Boyars never showed the slightest hesitation in changing sides at their convenience, nor was there ever any legal impediment to this. The Princes were in no position to challenge this privilege, since they were often weak and found the boyars indispensable; for that matter the custom often worked in their favor. To be sure, if a Prince lost his own boyars a *de facto* question of retaliation would arise regardless of theoretical rights. Boyars who left their Prince would find that their traditional immunity would simply be laughed at; they found themselves ruined by having their estates taxed beyond endurance, pillaged or confiscated outright. With the consolidation of princely authority in the rise of the Moscow dynasty the ancient right that had been breached more and more frequently was simply forgotten, and by the second half of the Fifteenth Century it was a dead letter, though never abolished by any edict. By the Sixteenth Century, when all landlords found themselves burdened by compulsory service, the independence of the former landed aristocracy had vanished: as the Moscow state consolidated itself it turned the former aristocrats into its servants.

This gradual imposition on the population of the duty of service was even more important in the case of the farmers, who had formerly been free and were now gradually slipping into a network of obligations to the owner of the land they worked as well as to the state. Though the process in its early phases is obscure, it seems that

Cathedral of the Dormition *in Moscow, where the Tsars were crowned, built between 1475-1479 by one of the architects, Fioraventi, brought to the Russian court from Italy by Ivan the III's wife. Fioraventi avoided his native style and bellowed Vladimir models.*

beavers, tolls for the marketplace, being tried, acquitted or condemned. The most trivial transactions of daily life were grist for the Prince.

In Muscovy, with production negligible and commerce sharply reduced, land relations formed the matrix of society. The concepts underlying them were to evolve rapidly and exercise a profound effect on politics.

At the very beginning of Russian society the original source of the ownership of land had doubtless been the fact of occupation or purchase. Land acquired in this way was simply the absolute property of the owner, who had no obligations to the authorities but that of paying taxes. A landowner might be granted all sorts of exemptions and privileges by the Prince controlling his land, such as the right to act as judge over those living on it. He might also be designated tax collector for the Prince; also, the estate, for one reason or another, might be exempt from

—service-tenure—that became widespread during the Thirteenth and Fourteenth Centuries, when the problem afflicting the country as a whole was still the scarcity of manpower. Land was very abundant, but without development it meant nothing; the problem of the local Princes was manpower for the exploitation of the land. Their revenues would be magnified immensely if waste or fallow lands were converted into agricultural settlements, which they might secure by granting individuals and monasteries estates, and they did so.

But they did not always do so unconditionally; they would make the land-grant, unlike the patrimonial estates, dependent on the performance of various duties, primarily military service. Though its actual point of origin is obscure, service-tenure in land became very common, especially during the second half of the Fifteenth Century, and was the general rule in the Sixteenth, when the line of demarcation between

Ο ΑΓΙΟC   ΓΕωΡΓΙΟC

the formerly independent farmers eventually became tenants on land owned variously by Princes, boyars or the Church. In some cases big landlords, both secular and ecclesiastical, would simply seize land belonging to weaker neighbors, but more generally the privileges the Princes could bestow on estates both of boyars and of the Church, especially in taxation, were a great inducement for the farmer to exchange his nominal independence for the protection of a powerful lord. This inducement grew during the Tatar occupation; and since both before and after this landlords had a vital interest in manpower, the farmer himself might well come to think it better to have a protector interposed between himself and the voracious treasury official.

In any case, by the Fourteenth Century tenant farming seems to have been far more common than independent small farming. Slavery had meanwhile become a negligible factor, especially since prisoners of war, its chief source, had vanished with the pacification of the national territory.

Relations both between tenants and landlords and between Princes and boyars evolved in the same direction. At first the tenant could theoretically leave his landlord and work for whomever he pleased, whenever his contract had expired, while contrariwise the landlord could also dismiss his tenants. But the tenant's right to go wherever he wished to soon began being encroached on. The Prince had a fundamental interest in keeping his tax-paying population within his reach, and the farmer's freedom of movement began to be hampered, initially through agreements made by the Grand Dukes of Moscow with other Princes mutually binding themselves not to accept free peasants leaving each other's domains.

Such restrictions did not touch the actual freedom of the tenant, but increased the difficulty of finding a new landlord by limiting the freedom of the landlords themselves in this respect. But this was actually only the first step; a further restriction, applied by the middle of the Fifteenth Century, made it impossible for the tenant to leave whenever he chose to during the year, which had formerly been his right, and restricted him to the fortnight preceding and following St. George's Day (26 November). This restriction was the beginning of a general trend.

But quite apart from these administrative restrictions, what ultimately bound the tenant to his landlord was the burden of indebtedness he incurred for purely economic reasons. Since farmers, then as always, needed help to carry on from one season to another, they were bound to turn for it to their landlords, both secular and ecclesiastical; the loans they got paid heavy interest, and though at first the existence of a debt outstanding between tenant and landlord did not in and for itself stop a farmer from leaving it came to much the same thing, since a debt could be enforced. As the debtor could never repay the loan in any case, he was compelled to work for his creditor until the debt was paid. In practise this was tantamount to bondage for life; even by the Thirteenth Century indebtedness had become a substantial force for the enslavement in fact of people who were free in law.

It was against this complex background that the Moscow dynasty emerged, a powerful centralizing and state-making factor that in the space of a few generations began playing a positive role abroad as well as at home. The components of the new Moscow state were not themselves new—if only to judge by their churches Rostov, Suzdal and Vladimir had a substantial history behind them—but in the event the collapse of Kiev turned out to have marked the end of an epoch, and the rise of Moscow the beginning.

Moscow, as I have indicated above, was to achieve the unification of the diverse Russian-speaking territories, and ultimately of the vast country in existence today, precisely because of their fragmentation through centrifugal tendencies in Russian life that antedated even the Tatar invasion. By reaction the Tatars gave Russia an attitude of collective identity, on the one hand, and on the other magnified the relative position of specific rulers by the pressure of their demands.

Moscow was the focus of three groups of water-routes: the western group to North Europe via the Baltic, the Volga-Middle East route it acquired in 1552-1556, and the northeastern routes to Siberia, where the precious furs came from that have always produced so much foreign revenue for Russia. The first two routes, which were a basic transit route from North Europe to Persia, connected Moscow with the world market, and Moscow became firmly embedded in the rapidly developing commercial revolution then sweeping Europe as a whole, especially after the English discovered the White Sea route to Russia in 1553.

In addition, Moscow was one of the natural goals for immigrants fleeing northeastward from the chaos of southwest Russia, and thus benefited by an increase in population as well as by the growing commerce based on this far-flung river-complex.

Politically speaking, the emergence of Moscow was conditioned by its relationship to the Tatars, who may, indeed, be regarded as having given this emergence its initial stimulus. A good example of the interaction between Russian domestic and foreign policy is the career of Alexander Nevsky, whom I have mentioned above as a shrewd manœuvrer between Tatars and Russians. Nevsky, though in some sense representing the collective interests of northeastern Russia on the Western frontier, *vis-à-vis* Swedes and Germans, was in domestic affairs a mere tool of the Khan. After winning his surname in his victory over the Swedes on the Neva River in 1240, he beat the German knights in 1242 after their entry into Pskov, and the Lithuanians three years later with a motley army from all over the country. All the while he took his orders in domestic affairs from the Tatars. This position of Alexander's as Grand Duke of Vladimir by grace of a Khan illustrated the subtle dynamics in the evolution of Russian national interests.

Nevsky's son Daniel was the first ruler who was definitely Prince of Moscow as such: before him there had been no pre-eminence of any Russian prince at all. The history of Vladimir during the last quarter of the Thirteenth and the beginning of the Fourteenth Century had been chaotic; the feuds between Princes with equal claims, making coalitions and freely using Tatar troops, precluded the emergence of a paramount Prince. Moscow suddenly emerged from parochialism at the beginning of the Fourteenth Century, about a hundred and fifty years after its first mention in 1147.

The expansion of the Moscow ruling house may have been stimulated psychologically, so to speak, by the ineligibility of the Moscow rulers, as a younger branch of the Rurik line, for the Grand Dukedom of Vladimir. When Ivan I (Ivan "Moneybags"), Nevsky's grandson, the first to launch the territorial aggrandizement of Moscow, was licensed by the Tatar Khan, he was repaid for his subservience by being appointed Grand Duke of Vladimir as well as Prince of Moscow. This helped ensure the primacy of the Moscow line over various other princelings.

The fact that Ivan I was the chief revenue agent increased his prestige among the Russian princes, on the one hand, and on the other gave him an effective instrument for the exercise of pressure.

Since none of the Russian Princes had any better claims to "legitimacy" this was at least a negative factor in the growth of the Moscow dynasty. Dmitri's substantial, though ephemeral victory over the Tatars at Kulikovo also enabled the Moscow ruler to present himself as the spearhead of an eventual emancipation from the burden of Tatar rule.

◄ Saint George and the Dragon. *Georgian enamel, XVth century. Tiflis Museum.*

Ivan Moneybags, who died in 1341, began a custom among the Moscow Grand Dukes of leaving a constantly increasing share of the family patrimony to the son who actually inherited the title, enabling him constantly to increase his material primacy among the Princes

controlled by the Princes. This control included the right of testamentary disposition: thus, though theoretically independent, or semi-independent, they could be bequeathed at will by the Grand Duke; and this combination of circumstances was the lever used by

tunities, especially in the form of land-grants, which might very well be scattered throughout several principalities. The landed aristocracy had the most to lose from the bloodshed and sacrifices attendant on feuds between Princes. Not only was their land subject

Ambassadors sent by Ivan the Terrible *(1533-1584)* to the Emperor of Germany in 1576. In the center, boyars carrying furs and precious gifts for the Emperor. XVIth century engraving. Ivan sought contacts with the West, and proposed an alliance to Queen Elizabeth.

of Muscovy, which around this time, like the other Grand Duchies in Russia, consisted of a group of tiny and theoretically independent principalities that were actually a form of appanage

Basil III, *father of Ivan the Terrible (1505-1533). Engraving from an album entitled "Portraits and Lives of Illustrious Men" by André Thevet, Paris, 1584.*

the Moscow Grand Duke to eliminate the very appanage order that gave him these advantages.

Moscow focussed all the forces hostile to the permanent dismemberment of the country: its chief rival at the time, Tver, was preoccupied by complex political and economic relations in the West, while Moscow's own interests were simultaneously more comprehensive and because of its central position more "national": in the West they took in Novgorod, Tver, Lithuania, the Baltic countries, in the south and east the Golden Horde, and as a permanent accompaniment to all this the currents of colonization and commerce along the Volga.

It is impossible to discern any actual *movement* for Russian union: perhaps the most important single factor amidst the endless internecine clashes that enabled Moscow to emerge as the unifying element in Russian history was the concurrent sponsorship of unification by the boyars and the Church, each group for its own reasons.

The boyars, to be sure, were unconscious of any altruistic goals: the aggrandizement of the Grand Duke they served naturally offered them lucrative oppor-

to confiscation, but they were the first to be slaughtered by their Prince's enemies.

As a great land-owner the Church shared these material preoccupations of the landed aristocracy; at the same time it had the further goal, as the heir of the Byzantine claims to universality, of having one Russian metropolitan as the sole head of the Church. This naturally made it a strong supporter of union as against princely strife.

Ivan Moneybags's name refers to his supposed methods of acquiring territory, but this may be a misunderstanding, since the growth of the Muscovite State did not arise out of the acquisition of land so much as out of the accumulation of political authority by the Moscow Grand Dukes. Ivan Moneybags actually increased his power not merely by thrift, as the historical legend has it, but by his skill in acting as a Tatar agent—docile toward the Tatars, ruthless toward the Russians.

Russian unification may be summed up as the consequence of two interwoven processes: the unification of the Principality of Moscow under its "senior" Princes, their fusion with the Grand Dukes of Vladimir, and the establishment as a result of the "Grand Duchy of Moscow, of Vladimir, and all Russia" the forerunner of the Muscovite Tsardom.

The extension of Muscovite authority to other Russian territories took place with the full sanction of the Tatars:

from their point of view it was just another and more efficient way of running their herds. But the process, while promoted by the Tatars for their own reasons, had to overcome the conflict between two principles I have mentioned before: the contradiction between the idea of "patrimonial" succession, or the right of a descendant to share in his father's principality, conceived in accordance with traditional Russian law as a piece of real estate, and the other principle, just as accepted, that called for unification under the rule of a "senior" Prince. Russian unification had to overcome serious obstacles.

Basil II may be said to have laid the foundations of the Muscovite autocracy. The first genuinely energetic, strong-willed and rapacious ruler in his line, he managed to concentrate in his own hands all the fragments of political

Two engravings from an album by Desprez, published in Paris in 1567, entitled "Anthology of the diversity of the costumes now worn in all the countries of Europe, Asia, Africa and the savage Islands, all done from real models". The Moscow woman is described as having skates, and the man as being wrapped in a mantle and caring most "to make war and acquire the goods of this earth".

power scattered among the hodge-podge of Russian principalities. Leaning even more heavily than his forerunners on a hired Tatar force he became famous even in this blood-drenched country for cruelty in dealing with his enemies, both former and potential.

But while an effective man of action he was faithful to a sort of muzziness characteristic of early Russian political thought: he failed to recognize or formulate any change of principle in what he was doing. Without discarding the outmoded dogma of the patriarchal family and while retaining the same traditional formulae in his testament as other Princes, he paved the way for a new source of authority by disregarding the former distinction between the Grand Duchy of Vladimir and the portion of the "senior Moscow Prince". Thus, the Grand Duchy he bequeathed his eldest son as his "patrimony" left the way clear by virtue of its geographical re-definition for the aggrandizement of the territory comprised in the new "patrimony" and the eventual investing of the growing region with an evolving concept of autocracy. In effect this fused Vladimir and Moscow both territorially and constitutionnally; it may be said that the Muscovite State had now been born.

When Basil II died, he controlled some 15,000 square miles: the reigns of his son and grandson added at least 40,000 square miles. The Tatar rule, already declining toward the end of Basil II's reign, as indicated above, was officially terminated in 1480, while the Golden Horde was liquidated in 1502 by the Crimean Tatars.

La Mosquovide.

La Mosquovide ainsi comme i'ay leu,
Se vest ainsi, & d'vne bonne grace.
Ayant en teste vn gros chapeau velu,
Portant patins qui sont ferréz à glace.

Both Muscovy and America were discovered by Western Europe at about the same time, as it gradually became evident with the growth of Muscovy that Europe did not end, as had been thought, on the northeastern frontier of Lithuania and Poland.

The growth in the importance of Muscovy led to a momentous development in the history of the Russian Church. When Moscow became a sovereign state in 1480, in the wake of the Golden Horde's dissolution, it grew up into a situation in which it found itself the only independent Greek Orthodox community. Byzantium had been conquered and suppressed by the Ottoman Turks in 1453, only five years after Russia herself had acquired the right to elect and consecrate her own metropolitans, as a by-product of the Council between Roman Catholic and Greek Orthodox dignitaries that had met in Ferrara and Florence in 1438 to bridge over the Great Schism.

The Russian Church no longer could look to Byzantium on the one hand and the Tatars on the other to protect it against the growing power of the Grand Dukes. Weak, primitive, and utterly unlettered, the Church not only tacitly submitted to the primacy of the Grand Ducal power, but actively promoted the expansion of Muscovy by expanding a theory of allegiance that made of Moscow a "Third Rome".

This theory was engagingly simple: since the first Rome had fallen because it had betrayed true (i. e., Greek Orthodox) Christianity, and Constantinople, the second Rome, had been taken by the infidel for the same reason,

Le Mosquovide.

Le Mosquovide auec sa grand' mante,
Dessus la mer gelee fait la guerre,
Et le desir qui plus fort le tourmente,
C'est d'acquerir des biens dessus la terre.

Moscow was the natural heir of these two other backsliding Romes and would, moreover, continue forever. This piece of narcissism was actually an adaptation of earlier theories commonly held in other Slavic and Balkan countries, especially Bulgaria, but it lacked the element of a definite material link between Constantinople and Moscow.

ciated with the name of Joseph Sanin, the founder of the Volokolam Monastery and a contemporary of Ivan III. His theological fanaticism was put to the service of Muscovite absolutism; it was summed up in his remark that though the Tsar did resemble other human beings physically, "in his power he was similar to God in Heaven".

substantially toward the end of the Fifteenth Century, enjoying the protection of both the Russian Princes and the Khans. When the Moscow government under Ivan III needed land-grants for his retainers, etc., the tradition was broken; Ivan III confiscated a great many Church lands when he incorporated Novgorod into the Moscow state.

Thus on this one point Sanin and his followers were at odds with the Muscovite regime, and since the Judaizers advocated secularization for their own reasons, the Moscow government handled them with unusual leniency.

The Judaizers were especially annoying to the Church because they were much better theologians. Though the name Judaizer itself may be an epithet, it is also possible that it originated with three actual Jews who had come to Novgorod in the Fifteenth Century: their teachings seem to have some connection, also, with the small sect of the *Strigolniki*, which had appeared even earlier in Novgorod and Pskov and repudiated the ecclesiastical hierarchy, its sacraments, and prayers for the dead. The leaders of this sect had all been executed, but their followers survived to form a germinating nucleus for other currents of dissent.

The simple-mindedness of the orthodox Church theologians was to give the Judaizers a first-rate polemical victory: 1492 was officially considered the 7,000th year from creation, and for some reason it was thought certain that the Second Coming of Christ and the Last Judgement were now scheduled. These forecasts were naturally supported by an endless array of incontrovertible proofs drawn from scriptures, especially Revelation and the Apocrypha. Actually the Judaizers had exactly the same theory, but their chronology was different: since they used the Jewish calendar they were sure that the world still had another 1,747 years to go before it arrived at 7,000.

Consequently, when the Last Judgement missed its cue the Judaizers derived a great polemical advantage over their adversaries by claiming that if the official Church had misfired on a matter of such primordial importance as the end of the world, it might be wrong on other things as well. This argument was so persuasive that after 1492 the Judaizing movement forged ahead for a time.

Another dissenting movement, which was to keep producing ripples and cross-currents in Russian life for generations, was that of the so-called Volga hermits, whose leader was one of the few outstanding personalities of the

Bas relief from the Royal Seat of Ivan IV the Terrible *(1547-1584). The elaborately carved Royal Seat, topped by barbaric pinnacles, is kept in the Uspensky cathedral of the Kremlin.*

Logic required some factual support to enable Ivan III and Basil III to assume the mantle of Byzantium.

Ivan III had married Sophie Paleologue, the niece of the last Byzantine emperor, who had been killed by the Turks when they took Constantinople; this was now supplemented by a brilliant lyrical invention that made the Moscow house not only the direct descendant of a so-called Pruss, supposed to be a brother of Caesar Augustus, but also traced the transmission of Christianity in the first place not to Byzantium but directly back to one Andrew, a brother of the Apostle Peter.

With these additions the old theory was enough to give the Moscow Grand Dukes the most splendid genealogy imaginable, and to make them leaders in their own right of Greek Orthodoxy. This theoretical cornerstone of the growing Muscovite absolutism was reinforced by some further apologetic philosophy that buttressed the alliance between the Church and State by laying it down that blind, obedient faith was the only road to salvation and proscribing the use of reason altogether. The slightest show of independent thought was heresy and blasphemy *per se*: the only acceptable arguments were scriptural quotations. This school is asso-

The fanatical Sanin school started some counter-reactions. A sect of dissenters called the "Judaizers" had been discovered about 1470 in Novgorod, just about the time it was carrying on its final and losing battle against absorption by the Muscovite state. These Judaizers seem to have denied the Holy Trinity, claimed that the Messiah had not yet come, that Christ was only a man, and consequently that Christianity could not be the true religion. Of course these views imply not a heresy but a secession from Christianity altogether. The Judaizers also denounced monasticism, repudiated the need for church and church services, denounced the ecclesiastical hierarchy for simony, and went so far as to claim that reason was paramount, not faith.

This attitude naturally irritated the Church authorities, since by denouncing monasticism and prayers for the dead the Judaizers were undermining the foundations of the Church's wealth.

Now, this dissenting sect was looked upon with a kindly eye, oddly enough, by Ivan III for its advocacy of the one thing that the official church was reluctant to concede the Moscow state it otherwise supported with such zeal. This was the secularization of the vast Church estates, which had grown very

Ikon of Saint John the Evangelist *at* ▶ *Patmos. Dionysius school. Early XVIth century. Tretyakov Gallery, Moscow.*

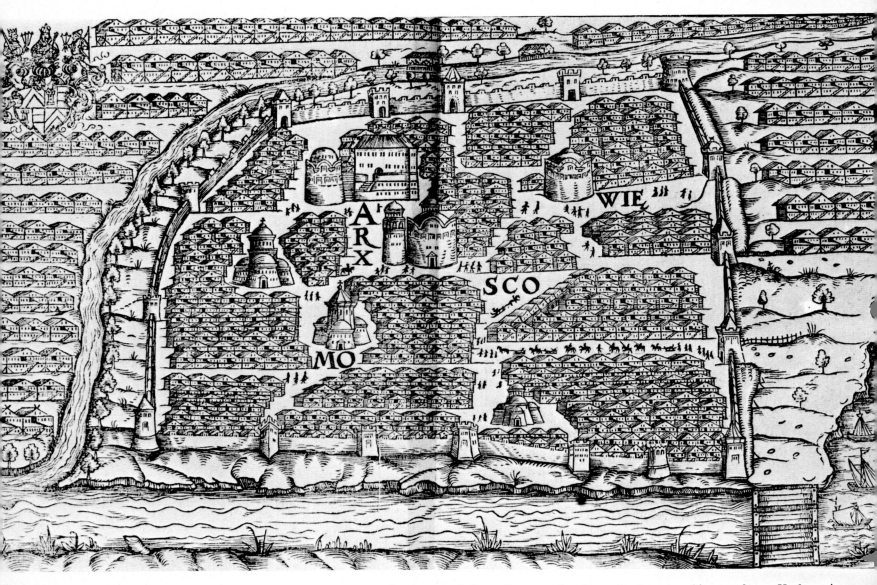

Moscow *at the time of Ivan the Terrible (1549), engraving by one of the earliest travel writers, the Austrian Siegmund von Herberstein, in his "Voyage in Muscovy". Herberstein was sent twice as ambassador to the Grand Duke of Moscow: first by the Emperor Maximilian in 1517, then by Charles V in 1526. His accounts remained classics, drawn upon by other writers for several centuries.*

Fifteenth Century—Nil Sorsky (1433-1508). This movement was also strongly in favor of secularizing church lands, and consequently also fell foul of the official Churchmen. On the religious side Sorsky was a mystic, persuaded that inner conviction and not external observance was the core of Christianity; he also thought this inner conviction could be arrived at by a diligent, though critical study of the scriptures. Sorsky was a monastic reformer: he had spent some time at Mount Athos, and when he came back to Russia after extensive travels in the eastern Christian communities he tried to reform monastic life by founding a hermitage east of the Volga, on the very rim of the Russian sphere. This accentuated the drift into the woods on the part of individual seekers after salvation; hermitages were scattered everywhere throughout the woods of northeastern Russia.

When the Sorskyites, who believed that the Church must never use violence but must confine itself to moral suasion and prayer, were attacked by the official hierarchy, they were, oddly enough, backed by a group of boyars, who for their own reasons favored the Church's independence so that there might be some check on the Grand Dukes. They also wanted the monastic estates secularized in order to stop the state from encroaching any further on their own privileges.

But the Church won out, over the hesitations of both Ivan III and Basil III, at the price of becoming utterly subservient to the state power in all questions. It is illuminating to read the kernel of Joseph of Volokolam's argument concerning relations between Church and State:

"If the monasteries are deprived of the villages they own, how would it be possible for an honorable and noble man to take orders? And if there are no honorable monks, where shall we find candidates for the metropolitanate, the archbishopric, the bishopric and other honorable offices? And if there are no honorable and noble monks, then faith itself will be undermined".

The net effect was that both the Church and the landed aristocracy, which had jointly sponsored the rise of absolutism, found themselves completely undone and engulfed by the jaws of the beast they had unleashed. The ancient privilege of the landed aristocracy—the acceptance of service on its own terms and under its own chosen Princes—was outmoded the moment Ivan III and Basil III acquired a monopoly of political authority. By the end of Basil's reign any boyar malcontents could actually no longer find any independent Princes to serve. The only alternative was leaving the Russian sphere and entering the service of a foreign state outright, such as Lithuania and Poland, but the new rulers of Muscovy found what was now explicitly called treason a convenient pretext for confiscating the culprits' estates.

The allocation of service-land had been widely applied by Ivan III and

Basil III. It was this that had countervailed the second source of the landed aristocracy's authority—its right to the absolute ownership of its own estates. The expenses involved in the expansion of Muscovy could only be met by the lavish distribution of land under service tenure: the former juridical distinction between hereditary estates, and those held on service tenure simply vanished. This was actually part of the disappearance of the ancient right of the boyars to opt for any Prince at will while retaining title to their estates wherever located. Thus, just as failure in allegiance to Moscow ultimately brought about the confiscation of the offenders, estates, so the corollary was equally valid: the holder of an estate in Muscovy was bound to serve the Grand Duke, its ruler.

This too was never actually formulated as a principle: it simply evolved pragmatically during the Fifteenth and Sixteenth Centuries. It affected minor Princes and boyars in basically the same way: just as the traditional privileges of princes who had previously been sovereign on their own territories were gradually curtailed as the Moscow Grand Dukes extended their control, so the old practice of defining the privileges of monastic and secular landlords in letters patent issued by the sovereign came to be the source *in law* of the actual ownership of the land itself, as the once unambiguous distinction between hereditary and service estates was blurred.

In this way the custom gradually developed of allowing a given estate to be enjoyed only on condition that the crown was served. Though introduced haphazardly and pragmatically, the change-over from tenure derived from purchase to tenure derived from service ultimately revolutionized the basis of the relations between the sovereign and the upper classes. In spite of the failure to formulate it juridically the change

was unmistakable: the new principle underlying the regime was shown in the mass deportations of landlords to remote parts of the country, where they received land in service tenure, while their own estates were allocated to others on the same principle.

Nor was the aristocracy capable of defending itself: despite the general discontent there was no solidarity of any kind. In the Fifteenth and Sixteenth Centuries the Moscow aristocracy was a mere hodge-podge that included all sorts of newcomers, adventurers, dispossessed Princes and princelets, and boyars: the diversity in the origins of the aristocracy produced a scramble for cushy jobs handed out by the court. This primordial process of socio-political manœuvring was congealed in a special institution called by the Russian equivalent of something like "placement". This involved the fixation of the aristocratic families in a hierarchical order, based primarily on their genealogical standing in terms of the previous government offices they had held. Special books had to be kept in special government departments to handle this confused system, which was arrived at in an attempt to counteract the flood of nondescripts thronging into Moscow. Unlike the feudal system in Europe the placement system did not establish hereditary rights, but simply tried to lay down a hereditary relationship between various families in terms of offices historically held by them in government service. Thus it was the relative position of the office-holder that mattered rather than the office itself.

The system was so cumbersome that it was a permanent source of dissension among the boyar families and achieved nothing beyond curbing the efficiency of the official hierarchy. It lasted until the end of the Seventeenth Century only because in order to get anything done at all various pockets were created in the higher military offices that were

exempt from what has been called the placement arithmetics.

The boyars spent an immense amount of time and energy in litigation designed to protect their positions in the place-

Ivan the Terrible; *Italian engraving.*

ment system. They even fought each other physically to defend what was thought of as their "honor". The ethos of the time made death itself preferable to serving in the army or sitting at the Grand Duke's table "below" someone whose ancestors lacked a record that was sufficiently distinguished.

The concentration of power in the Muscovite autocracy, on such a great and novel scale, changed life in Moscow and at court. The new status of the crown had to be made manifest by the embellishment of the city, and both Ivan III and Basil III exerted themselves to do this. Italian architects were imported for the building of cathedrals and churches: the palaces of the Grand Dukes were built of stone, instead of the wood that had been used in the much less pretentious houses they had been living in: the Kremlin was given a ring of stone walls and towers. The court developed an elaborate ceremonial, possibly under the influence of Sophie Paleologue. Ivan III, who often used the title of "Sovereign of all Russia by the Grace of God", was occasionally also referred to as "Tsar and Autocrat" though the Russian connotation of this

Far left: Departure of the Tsarina Anastasia, ill *(she is shown lying in a carriage); Anastasia was the Tsar's first wife, he is thought to have had seven. Left:* The fleet of Ivan the Terrible leaving to attack the Tatar stronghold of Kazan. *Russian manuscript, XVIIth cent.*

was simply that he was independent of the Tatars. The unification of the realm was symbolized by the adoption of the two-headed eagle of Byzantium.

The development of a strong centralized monarchy in Russia was not at all peculiar to her: Ivan III (1462-1505) was contemporary with the English Wars of the Roses and the rise of the Tudor dynasty, while strong monarchies were pushing forward in other countries in Europe.

But the growth of the Muscovite autocracy far outstripped the parallel development of monarchy elsewhere in Europe. In 1517, when an envoy from the Holy Roman Empire, the Austrian Baron Siegmund von Herberstein, visited Moscow, he felt as though he were entering an entirely different political atmosphere, and that Basil III had completely outdone any other monarch in power over his subjects.

The Muscovite Tsardom of the Sixteenth and Seventeenth Centuries was in fact based on a different concept of society and state. Whereas Kievan society may be called with all due qualification a free or semi-free society, the Muscovite Tsardom was based on the principle that all classes from top to bottom except, curiously, the slaves themselves, were yoked to the state.

Basil II had laid the foundations of the autocracy, and Ivan III and Basil III had set it up. Though the emancipation of northeastern Russia from the Tatars was the result of a combined national effort involving the Moscow Grand Dukes, the Church, gentry and commoners, the new monarchy that now anchored itself in Russian society was based on principles that would have seemed alien to the Kievan Russians:

the subordination to the state of society *in toto*. The profundity of this process is indicated by the fact that the regimentation of the social classes that had begun under the Tatars grew progressively afterwards, and in fact reached its peak about 1650, two whole centuries after the Tatar rule had dissolved.

This is far from paradoxical: the new monarchy grew up under the aegis of both unceasing warfare on its borders and the suppression of elements contending for power at home.

In the southeast and south there was still a Tatar threat; in the west there was a constant struggle for power going on between Moscow and Lithuania (after 1569 between Moscow and Poland), whereas in the northwest the absorption of Novgorod by Moscow meant that Moscow was now thrust into the forefront of a struggle to contain the Teutonic Knights and the Swedes around the Gulf of Finland. The defiance of the Golden Horde by Moscow did not mean peace, since even after the collapse of the Golden Horde there were several Tatar successor-states, which continued making almost annual raids on the southern and eastern provinces of Muscovy, pillaging systematically and capturing thousands of people.

The Tatars remained an exceptionally difficult problem, since in the absence of any natural boundaries on the broad highway of the steppe the Moscow government had to keep the whole border under constant guard. The Moscow regime, reversing the historic process, had set up a vassal Tatar state of its own, the Kasimov Khanate, about 1450, and while the Kasimov Tatars and the Cossacks hired by the Moscow

regime as irregulars were very useful, regular army troops were needed as well. The Tatars kept piercing the complex and expensive systems of fortified defense lines the Muscovites set up and pouring into the country beyond.

Thus Moscow had to control the steppe lands, either by conquest or

Russian horseman *at the time of Ivan the Terrible, from the diplomat-historian Herberstein's "Voyage in Muscovy", 1549.*

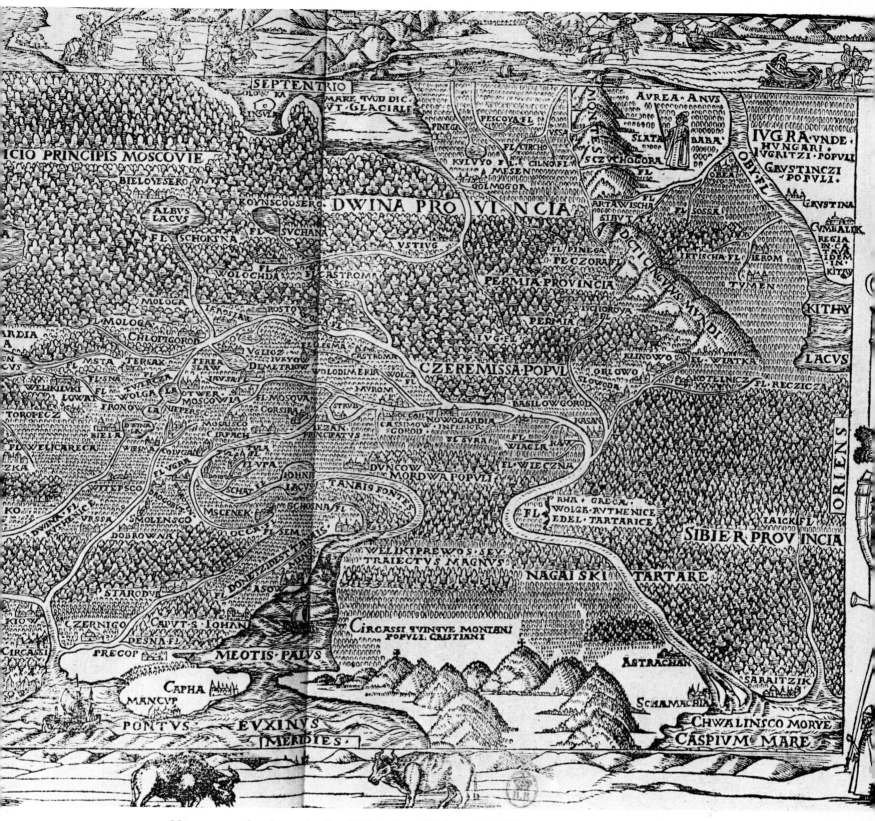

Muscovy *under Ivan the Terrible's reign. Herberstein's "Voyage in Muscovy", 1549.*

diplomacy, a problem that was duplicated by its harassment in the West, where the struggle, though not so relentless as against the Tatars, cost just as much money, since whenever a genuine crisis developed stronger and more methodically equipped armies had to be put into the field. Armaments made taxation heavier, which in its turn called for increasing centralization to tighten the government screw.

The whole process was a many-linked vicious circle. The struggle against the west called for recruits, which was what the grants of land held in service-tenure were supposed to supply; the provision of recruits meant a crisis in manpower to till the soil, with the further consequence that the peasants had to be tied down to the land they had originally been free to leave on the expiration of their contract with the landowner.

In this complex fashion the regimentation of the social classes that had begun under the Tatars, in response to the Tatar principle of centralized administration, was developed still further by the Muscovite regime. A chain reaction was started that lasted for centuries; it was signalized by the spiralling interaction of autocracy and serfdom. Social chaos was the other side of the autocratic coin: it was doubtless because Russian

society was so backward and chaotically organized that it was possible for the Moscow autocracy to suppress rival elements of authority and establish its own monopoly.

And it was during the reign of Ivan the Terrible, the longest in Russian history (1533-1584), that this autocratic complex was streamlined and formulated. He was the first to rule Russia as a wholly autocratic Tsar in theory as well as in practise. Three years old at the death of his father, Basil III, he grew up in a period when the savagery of the princely and boyar cliques and clans kept lapsing into the violence that had been largely repressed under the thumb of Basil III, but kept breaking out under the regency of Ivan's mother. Deportations, confiscations of estates, tortures, assassinations, and executions were commonplace.

Ivan's nickname seems well deserved, though in Russian it properly denotes menace and has been translated into English as "Dread". He became known for an extreme kind of sadism while still a boy, and grew up with a combination of intense piety of the Russian type—obsessive devotion to the external observances of the Church and utter indifference to the inner meaning of the religion, to say nothing of its ethics—and extravagant sexual license.

He had himself crowned "Tsar of all the Russias" at the age of seventeen, and thus made official a title that had been used only casually during the preceding century. The word "Tsar" had meant nothing characteristic beforehand: it was also used to refer to the Khan of the Golden Horde.

The new title set an official stamp on the uncontested paramountcy of the Moscow regime; its resonant comprehensiveness reflected Ivan's view of his role. A highly talented though erratic writer, and unquestionably the only articulate Russian ruler except possibly Catherine the Great, he was the first Russian ruler who openly established monarchical absolutism as a political philosophy. In contrast to his predecessors, who with all their ruthlessness had been mere land-grabbers, Ivan articulated a rough but comprehensive theory: he regarded himself as the actual vicar of God on earth, and consequently a completely unhampered ruler both in theory and in practise.

◄ The cathedral of Saint Basil *on Red Square, Moscow, built by Ivan the Terrible to commemorate his victories over the Tatars between 1554 and 1560. The Russian architects used traditional forms of wood construction and added eight cupolas, all different, and a central pyramid. The exuberant variety of the exterior is made even more exotic by multi-colored decoration of tiles and paint.*

Since his legitimacy was based on heredity, he not only emphasized descent from Rurik but took over the theory I have mentioned above of the Third Rome; in negotiations with foreign powers Ivan and his envoys made great play of his descent from Augustus Caesar's brother Pruss.

Ivan seems to have been a paranoiac: his mistrustfulness led to his killing off almost anyone who came into contact with him. Executions by him were commonplace on all levels of society, generally accompanied by the most ingeniously contrived tortures. After 1560 especially, when Ivan decided he had been a mere tool of his counselors during his early days, he made a wholesale slaughter of members of his family, church dignitaries, Princes, boyars and commoners.

He was devoted to the Church. Though during an expedition he undertook against Novgorod in 1570 to punish it for remissness churches were desecrated, pillaged and burnt, while priests were flogged, tortured and executed in public, it would be rare for him to miss mass; he spent a great deal of his time composing monastic rules, or contriving complicated ceremonies for the consecration of the Metropolitan. This did not stop him from treating his actual Metropolitans with the utmost ferocity. An archbishop of Novgorod is said to have been sewn into a bear's skin and thrown to the dogs.

Ivan's prey generally met their deaths in churches, quite often during the actual mass. In the midst of the most extravagant blood-baths he kept lists of the people he had murdered, and distributed money to monasteries to pay for their eternal repose. Some 4,000 names of those he killed were actually listed; the true number is thought to have been much larger. Obsessed by terror of plots and political catastrophe in general—doubtless quite rightly—he wrote Queen Elizabeth in 1569 asking for asylum should he be ejected from Russia and offering to make the arrangement reciprocal. She declined.

The general tendency of Ivan's rule may be summed up as the elevation of state authority so that it became supreme institutionally as well as practically. To some extent this involved the apparent magnification of local authorities, since Ivan curtailed the highhandedness of some of the provincial governors still battening off the local populations under them, but socially speaking his contribution to the centralization of state authority took the form of destroying the power of the landed aristocracy, whom his wrath, generally quite indiscriminate in its choice of target, eventually fixed on and blighted.

The isolation and annihilation of the landed gentry was begun by Ivan's suddenly and unexpectedly leaving Moscow, in what seems to have been a naive but successful piece of guile. In December 1564 he simply left, with his family and a huge retinue carrying treasure,

The interior of Saint Basil *is low, dark and painted like the inside of wood churches.*

jewels, and household goods; at first the caravan seemed to be heading into the unknown, but it stopped a short distance from Moscow at Alexandrovskaya Sloboda, which remained a sort of second capital throughout his reign. A month later he sent two messages back to Moscow: one was a bitter denunciation of the landed gentry and clergy as being all of them traitors and thieves. The second was addressed to the merchants, artisans and commoners, who were cleared of any responsibility for the others' misdeeds. The whole manœuvre, doubtless intended to sound like an abdication, was obviously a trick to facilitate his setting up a new regime: he was invited back to Moscow by a delegation that «persuaded» him to reconsider.

Of course he came back on his own terms, celebrating his return by the slaughter of some leading boyars. The most significant change he instituted was the so-called *oprichnina*, a curious old word meaning an entailed domain, generally the portion of a sovereign Prince's widow. He split up his entire realm into the *oprichnina* and the remainder, which was to be run by the normal administration. The *oprichnina* was to be Ivan's personal realm, whose cardinal function and duty was the wiping out of "treason" in the other half of the realm.

The *oprichnina* was autocracy institutionalized. It was an omnipotent security police that raised the Tsar's personal authority far beyond any other institution in the country. The members of the *oprichnina* were dressed in black and rode black horses, carrying a dog's head and a broom attached to their saddles. The symbolism was potent.

It was the *oprichnina* that finally pulverized the political power of the landed gentry. The *oprichnina* had a spatial location: provinces, cities and even a number of streets in Moscow were cleared of their gentry and landowners, who were deported to other parts of their country while their estates were distributed among the officials of the *oprichnina*. The provinces handed over to the *oprichnina* eventually took in almost half the whole country; the distribution was calculated so as to dislodge the former princely families, whose estates were granted to newcomers whose title to the land derived from Ivan's caprice and nothing else.

Though the *oprichnina* and the rest of the country were theoretically to remain separate, the *oprichnina* gradually took over the chief trade routes and markets; ultimately it dominated the country completely. Thus, in addition to destroying the aristocracy's political influence and changing its composition, it brought about a transfer of land on a huge scale.

The very fact that the personnel of the *oprichnina* included some of the oldest names in the country, such as Trubetskoy and Shuisky, indicates that it was a novelty *institutionally*. The *oprichnina* officers were not, of course, immune from Ivan's sadism either; he put some of them to death in a particularly gruesome manner.

The imaginative ferocity of the tortures that became so commonplace under Ivan blurred the institutional significance of the *oprichnina*: observers both in Russia and abroad were so struck by the incredible ritualism and fantasy in the activities of Ivan and the *oprichnina* that the long-range effects were only gradually perceived. The new capital, for instance, was transformed into a sort of semi-monastic fortress run by rules Ivan wrote himself; he and his favorites of the moment would dress like monks and divide their time between lengthy church services and extravagant orgies, punctuated by long sojourns in the torture-chamber.

Aside from these long-range sociological innovations Ivan's reign was marked by the decisive beginnings of the protracted eastward expansion of the Russian state. Strife between the Tatar states of Kazan and Astrakhan on the Volga enabled Ivan to conquer and annex them both, Kazan in 1552 and Astrakhan in 1556. This eastward movement led to the absorption of Western Siberia, which was actually carried on by purely private initiative, as a result of the trading operations of the Stroganov family, which had been assigned large estates near the Urals with permission to extract metals and salt and to extend its domain beyond the mountains. The Stroganovs had a private army, formed of Cossacks and the various Lithuanian and Muscovite fugitives who roamed the southern Russian steppe in haphazard bands. One of these Cossacks, Yermak, who was actually under sentence of death for rebellion, led a few freebooters, about 150, into Siberia in September 1581: by 1582 he had a hold on two great Siberian rivers, the Irtysh and the Obi. In return for a full pardon and a few presents he presented his conquests to the Moscow crown. This marked the beginning of the long Russian advance to the Pacific Ocean, which was reached by 1643, mainly through a process of permeation, with very few armed conflicts and scarcely any government help at all.

The annexation of Kazan and Astrakhan did not end the Tatar danger, since the southern border was still subject to invasion at will by the Crimean Tatars, impregnably ensconced in the Crimea. These Crimean Tatars were not interested in territorial acquisition but in booty, primarily in the form of prisoners of war. They flooded the slave markets of Europe, Africa and Asia with people dragged from Muscovy, Lithuania, and Poland. Their raids were endless: in 1571 they laid siege to Moscow; they burnt its suburbs and carried off some 150,000 captives. The next year they followed this up by sending in an army of 120,000 to invade Russia, this time being stopped before reaching Moscow.

Moscow in fact remained in a state of permanent tension because of the Tatars, with an element of danger added by their willingness to ally themselves with Russia's enemies in the west.

Under Ivan it was only in the east that Russia began expanding; she never broke through to the Baltic Sea, and though this was made up for to some extent through the unexpected discovery by some Englishmen of a new maritime route to Western Europe in 1553, it involved crossing the White Sea, which was much inferior to a warm-water route. It had the odd by-product of anchoring British tradesmen in Russian life for a long time to come: the leader of the expedition, Richard Chancellor, was treated very well by Ivan, who developed a great fancy for the English and gave the Muscovy Company of London very valuable monopolistic privileges. Characteristically, this did not stop him from arresting all the English merchants and confiscating their goods after his failure to secure an English alliance. He expressed his irritation in a letter to Queen Elizabeth, calling her the rough equivalent of "common slut".

Ivan himself was one of the few literate people in his kingdom. Officials in charge of vital administrative positions were quite incapable of signing their names, and the country, by and large, was utterly illiterate.

Ivan's main achievement was the creation of a complete vacuum around the Moscow autocracy, consummating the process of suppressing all other sources of power and many old institutions in favor of the unification of the realm that had already been set in motion by Ivan the Great and Basil III. Ivan, however, by elevating the executive power above the mêlée did not devise an instrument for quieting the turmoil; on the contrary, he ruled out any but an explosive solution.

By the end of Ivan the Terrible's reign the whole country had been churned up: the fabric of society had been rent asunder. The older aristocracy found itself expelled from its ancestral lands, deprived of most of its political influence, and dragooned into the service of the state. Many individual aristocrats had been tortured to death and executed. Landowners generally, both boyars and the descendants of former ruling Princes, were staring ruin in the face because of the dearth of manpower on their estates. In addition, the military expenditures involved in Ivan's ruinous wars constituted an intolerable burden for everyone.

Nor was there any compensation to be looked for in the new parvenu class, the rapidly increasing "service people" —those with land-grants subject to military service. In the Sixteenth Century this was a very motley group drawn from every social element, including slaves. The size of the land-grant might be a mere parcel of land with only one peasant household on it; it might even be farmed by the service-noble. The diversification of elements in the parvenu nobility precluded any solidarity.

Even more basically, the dearth of manpower, especially in the central and western areas, led to a tremendous competition among the landlords for available hands. The country, never densely inhabited in any case, was now actually depopulated because of the general state of disorder, the military defeats caused by Ivan's abortive attempts to break through to the Baltic,

The Dormition Cathedral (1585) in the ▶ Trinity-Sergius Monastery at Zagorsk, sixty miles north of Moscow. It is one of several ecclesiastical buildings copied from Moscow's Cathedral of the Dormition with its five domes. Inside are Boris Godunov's tomb and many XVIIth century frescos.

and especially the repeated Tatar raids, in particular the actual invasions of 1571 and 1572 mentioned above. Also, the combination of the expansion eastward and the spread of service-tenure, with its creation of a new class of agricultural overseers in the shape of the motley beneficiaries of the land-grants, emptied out the country not only eastward, but also toward the free life of the Cossacks in the Southern steppe. As in Kievan Russia huge numbers of people simply began drifting away.

The regime had a twofold reason to halt this migratory movement: not only was it deprived by the flight of the population of potential taxpayers, but the very foundations of the military class it depended on were corroded. It was essential to find a way out of the cul-de-sac inherent in the worthlessness of a service-holding without manpower; the measures that were developed to solve this problem were, as we shall see, the source of the gradual imposition of bondage on the bulk of the population that became known as serfdom.

The competition for manpower was particularly burdensome for the smaller service-nobles, since the greater lords, both secular and ecclesiastical, could secure tax exemptions from the state that enabled them in their turn to promise their tenants lower taxation. Such tax exemptions were given most often to the big landlords, especially the Church. In the long run, of course, these promises did the tenant no good, since the additional burdens would more than counterbalance the slight, though immediate tax saving: but it goes without saying that few tenants were in a position to think of the long run.

Now, a tenant could leave the land he worked if he settled his debt to his landlord, and since he was scarcely ever able to find the money he needed he would have to turn to a prospective landlord. This increased the advantage of the wealthy landlords even more; on top of all this the devastation likely to befall a service-holding with no tenants made it easy for a big landlord, particularly a monastery, to take it over. Consequently, the service-nobles were in dire straits; there was a tremendous clamor for relief that was never given.

On the other hand, while the smaller landlords were squeezed by the bigger, the landed class as a whole was bound to benefit by the peasants' indebtedness. Consequently, it was to their interest, supported by the state, to halt the flight of the tenants.

An illuminating instance of the severity of the tenants' plight is a provision in the Code of 1550 that if the tenant sold himself into slavery he cancelled the usual restrictions on giving up tenancy.

Thus, since an indebted tenant could only be bought off as a rule by some other landlord and there was keen competition for manpower, whenever the time came for tenants to be transferred—during the fortnight before and after St. George's Day—the violent outbursts accompanying this would reach their height. Petty landowners would often take up arms to resist the big landlords' recruiting agents, sack the houses of tenants who wanted to leave them, and actually shackle the tenants themselves.

It was these two roots—the combination of the fiscal regime of the Moscow state and the burden of peasant indebtedness—that gradually gave rise to serfdom, which evolved in a spasmodic and piecemeal, but relentless fashion, and was consummated in the middle of the Seventeenth Century. During Ivan the Terrible's reign the combination of circumstances referred to above accelerated the process of tenant enslavement.

This process was eased only slightly by the opening up of the lands to the east: the newly acquired territories were soon distributed as service-land in their turn, and so the fugitives from the steady march of serfdom kept finding the same system catching up with them. The other refuge, the southern steppe that separated Muscovy from the Crimean Tatars, also attracted many. In the Sixteenth Century the entire area north of the Black Sea was teeming with fugitives from Muscovy, Poland and Lithuania. A Turkish word, Cossack, was applied to them; they had a loose semi-military organization under a leader they elected and lived by banditry and mercenary soldiering.

There was a development parallel to this in the cities, which in the Sixteenth Century were often no more than military centers producing nothing. Indeed, Russian city life in general was very slow in developing. Throughout Russia's history, especially her early history, her cities have generally been trading-posts or military establishments; production was the last thing to develop. Since the government was primarily interested in collecting taxes it tried to centralize commercial activities in a restricted number of localities, and thus hindered the development of commerce. The richer merchants would be appointed revenue agents by the state; there was no direct payment for their services, and they had to depend on being exempted from taxes and the jurisdiction of ordinary courts. Thus they had to be rich in order to ensure their carrying out their duties. When such privileges were granted the other burghers naturally had to make up for the gap in the tax yield, and in the social stratification promoted by this process the underprivileged burghers found themselves struggling for existence. Their situation was made still more difficult by the thronging into the cities of military officials who, since they weren't supposed to be in trade, were exempt from the burghers' taxes, though in fact they took advantage of their immunity to compete with the burghers on more favorable terms. Big landlords, especially the monasteries, would start competitive businesses run by their tenants or slaves on their estates, next to the trading centers.

Because of all this the cities also began expiring slowly; the urban population began drifting away, and the government was compelled to nail down the urban burghers to their shops and trades just as it had tried to do with the peasants in the countryside.

The Moscow regime thus found itself caught in a situation that was inherently contradictory: in order to be able to benefit fiscally from the labor of the population it had to tie it down, and when it tied it down the exacerbated conditions led to even greater distress. The state's reaction to the immense turbulence it was itself responsible for throughout the country constituted a process of ruthless straitjacketing that wiped out all vestiges of freedom.

The Russian people is the only people in recorded history that has been completely enslaved by itself. Slaves have generally been people uprooted by brute force and transported elsewhere, as a rule in the wake of wars. But Russian history so worked out that almost the whole of the population was enslaved by its own leaders.

The ruthless concentration of authority in the Moscow state, consummated during the reign of Ivan the Terrible, plus the disastrous evolution of socio-economic conditions throughout the rapidly growing country, soon led to an extraordinary upheaval, which though prepared for over many decades was launched by a dynastic crisis.

In 1581, Ivan, in a fit of rage, had killed his son and heir with a metal-tipped staff he used to carry: the young man had apparently been trying to shield his pregnant wife against his father's brutality. Ivan naturally spent a good deal of time repenting, but when he died in 1584—characteristically after taking monastic vows on his death-bed—the only heir was his feebleminded other son, Theodore, who died in 1598. His death extinguished the Muscovite dynasty and led directly to the "Time of Troubles".

Peter the Great

The fifteen years that followed the death of Ivan's feebleminded son were a period of constant and ungovernable turbulence. Since the Tsar himself was feebleminded, wholly concentrated on the ringing of churchbells, his brother-in-law, Boris Godunov, who had been

Tsar Theodore Ivanovich *(1584-1598), son of Ivan the Terrible, was a religious eccentric who spent his time prostrating himself before ikons and ringing bells.*

a favorite of Ivan the Terrible's, took advantage of his sister's influence over the sickly Tsar and made himself the *de facto* ruler of the country: he was temporary victor in the dense swarm of palace intrigues and internecine boyar conflicts that had broken out upon the death of Ivan the Terrible. These intrigues, far too complex for even a brief summing up, were rooted in the bitterness between the ancient nobility —Shuiskys, Vorotynskys, Golitsyns, Kurakins, etc.—and the less distinguished families that may be referred to as the nobility based on court influence, such as the Romanovs and Godunovs.

Godunov established himself so thoroughly that on Tsar Theodore's death without issue he easily arranged to have himself elected Tsar by a so-called Territorial Assembly, but the election did no more than inflame the old intrigues all over again. Godunov, formerly considered charming and amiable, soon lost his appeal; the upper classes found themselves once again in much the same situation as under Ivan the Terrible,

Throne of Boris Godunov, *covered with pure gold, studded with ruby and turquoise cabochons. Iranian work, late XVIth or beginning XVIIth centuries. Armoury Museum of the Kremlin, Moscow.*

with deportations, confiscations, and executions an everyday event.

All this was climaxed by a great famine that lasted from 1601-1603; both merchants and landlords became profiteers, and confiscations were accompanied by the release of slaves, who were forbidden to find another master, while many slaves were merely turned out to forage for themselves. Banditry grew rife, and the flood of peasants already drifting away from the encroachments of serfdom was increased by a torrent of famished and dislocated people.

The general disaffection crystallized in the form of a Pretender to the throne —the first of many—who with the assistance of the Polish government led the movement against Godunov. The "False Dmitri" claimed to be a son of Ivan the Terrible who was supposed to have died in 1591 under enigmatic circumstances: his actual identity seems irremediably obscure. In any case in 1603 the False Dmitri took up headquarters with an adventurous Polish nobleman called Mniszek. Though he had numerous Polish connections, actually marrying his host's daughter Marina, Dmitri's emergence was a reflection of the disaffection among the boyar groups, doubtless primarily the Romanovs, who ultimately benefited by his enterprise. The whole Romanov clan had been accused by Godunov of having used witchcraft in an attempt to usurp Godunov's crown, and the head of the

family, Theodore Romanov, father of the future Tsar Michael, had been forced to become a monk, under the name of Philaret, in a distant monastery where he was kept imprisoned.

Dmitri's army was made up of some 3,500 to 4,000 men; an altogether random assortment of Polish knights, soldiers of fortune, runaway Russian peasants, etc. Polish complicity had enabled him to organize this group on Polish terrain, but its rapid successes were due to the feebleness of the Moscow regime. The unruly Cossacks and discontented small landowners of the southern regions went over to him in a body, as did many of the petty nobles and burghers; the Russians in fact engulfed the small Polish core of his army. When Godunov died unexpectedly in 1605 the Pretender made a triumphal entry into Moscow.

But this anti-Godunov coalition fell apart at once: the Pretender's backing was contradictory in composition. The boyars hoped for a restoration of their ancient privileges; petty nobles wanted bigger land-grants, more money and

Boris Godunov. *XVIth century miniature. This wily Tatar regent made himself Tsar in 1598. Surrounded by plots, driven by dark suspicions, he established an early version of the police state based on a network of informers. He was a favorite figure for Russian writers. Pushkin and Mussorgsky immortalized him in an opera.* ▶

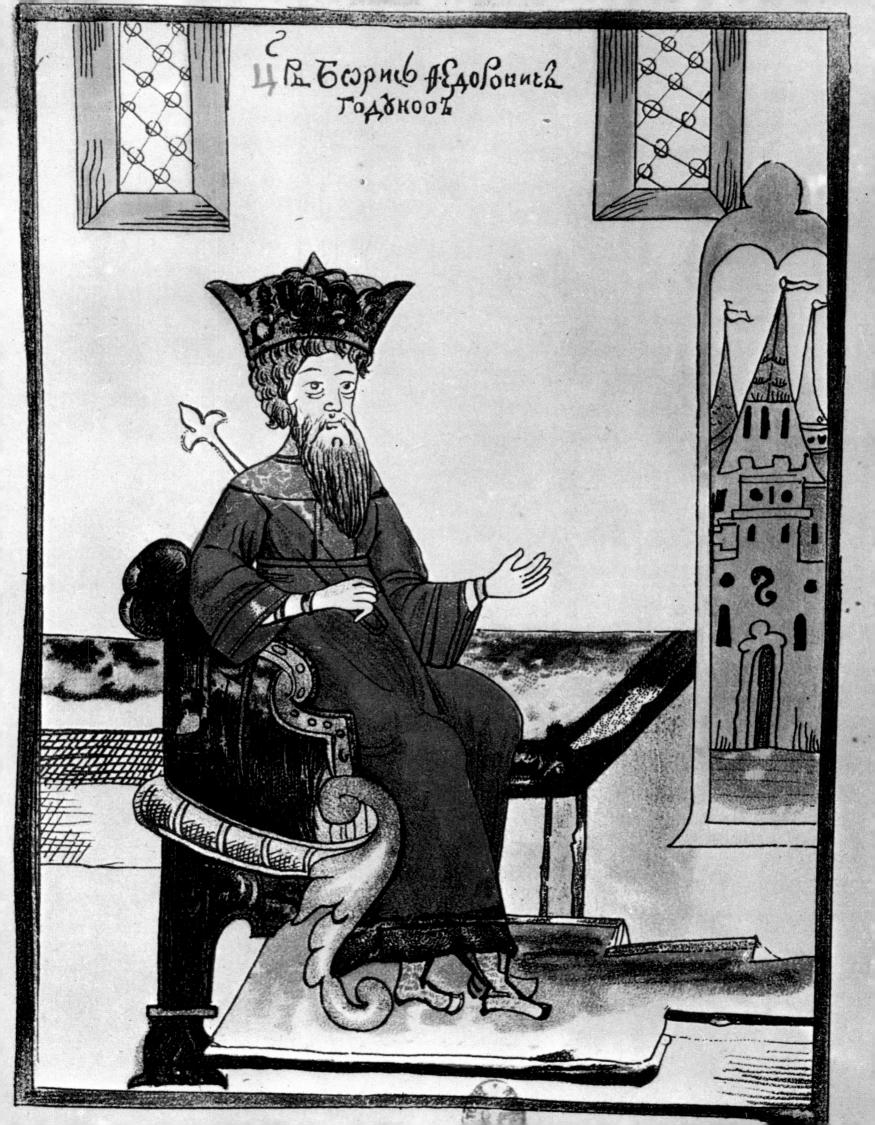

Ц Р҃Ь Борисъ Ѳедоровичъ
Годуновъ

Inside the engraving the following labels appear: *per flauus.* · SCHMOLEN SKA. · *Des Herm Wrasenski* · *leger vnd Bat torej* · *Ludwig weger mit seinen kosathe*

A. Wachthurn.
B. Kloster.
C. Die vorstatt so die Moscobiten selbs angesteckt vnd verlassen haben.
D. Einzug 1000 soldaten so der statt zurhilff sind geschickt worden.
E. ein truckener graben.

Siege of Smolensk *by the Poles in 1611. German engraving.*

a tighter grip on the peasants working their estates; the peasants, especially the Cossacks, were longing vaguely for land and freedom; the foreign mercenaries clamored for their pay; Jesuits and Polish clericals were intriguing for a reunion of the two churches under the Vatican.

These conflicting currents undid the Pretender, who was murdered by May of 1606, as they did the next Tsar, Basil Shuisky, who was merely appointed by the aristocracy without even a pretence of formality. A scion of the senior branch of the house of Rurik with no reservations about absolutism, he represented, socially speaking, the people who had appointed him, which immediately made him the target of the radically inclined Cossack masses and small landowners.

For the first time in Russian history a movement of disaffection was launched that injected a social element into essentially dynastic conflicts. A runaway slave, Ivan Bolotnikov, rallied the fugitive peasants and slaves who made up the main body of the Cossacks, and under the guise of restoring Dmitri proclaimed a program of actual social revolution: this included the slaughter of the upper classes, the incitement of the poor against the rich and peasants and slaves against their masters, and promises to the exploited of the land, wealth and women of their oppressors.

This movement, which oddly enough fought together with a detachment of some of the petty service nobility, came within sight of Moscow by October, 1606; here, as it turned out, the very extremism of Bolotnikov's movement enabled Tsar Boris Shuisky to rally around himself the proprietary and conservative groups appalled by the potentialities of Bolotnikov's program. Bolotnikov quickly lost his own allies among the nobility, and his movement was suppressed by the most savage means: the rebel provinces, about a third of the country, were flung open to plunder, and thousands of prisoners were executed, a great many by slow drowning, a peculiarly cruel form of torture.

Pretenders kept springing up like mushrooms in 1607-1608. A score of rebels took the name of "Tsarevich": imaginations were strained to provide the flimsiest of connections with the Moscow dynasty. The most effective of these Pretenders became famous as the Tushino Bandit, from the location of his headquarters, set up in the spring of 1608 in Tushino, a few miles from Moscow. Even less is known about this second False Dmitri, as he was also known, than about the first. In his case there was not even a pretence of belief in his dynastic claims, though to be sure the names taken by all the impostors were merely a pretext for attacking the official regime.

Shuisky appealed to foreign governments for help, as well as to the Russian cities whose support he could depend on, but perhaps the chief reason for the failure of the Tushino Bandit's rebellion was its invasion of the northern provinces, which were not so disaffected as the southern and had continued to enjoy a slight degree of self-government that was disregarded entirely by the Polish mercenaries, Russian gentry and Cossacks in the Bandit's entourage. Even the northern peasants resented their savagery, and by 1610 the siege of Moscow had fallen apart.

For two years Tushino played the role of a second capital because of the radical instability of Shuisky's regime as well as of the Bandit's. There was an unusual number of boyars, churchmen, nobles, functionaries, merchants and commoners who kept switching back and forth between Tushino and Moscow hoping for the best. As the price of their slippery support they traded the grants and promotions they managed to secure from Shuisky for still greater benefits from the Bandit and the other way round. It was the desperation of both camps and the country's exhaustion that made this situation possible: one of the chief notables in the Bandit's camp, for instance, was Philaret Romanov, who while presumably a prisoner was revered by the insurgents as their patriarch.

When things looked black for the Bandit, Philaret Romanov and the Tushino aristocracy turned to Poland, and signed an agreement in February 1610 that made the Polish King's son Tsar of Muscovy, while ensuring the inviolability of the existing Russian state and the Orthodox Church.

Shuisky finally had to abdicate, and Polish troops occupied Moscow and the Kremlin, whereupon Sigismund, the King of Poland, made an attempt to get the throne for himself, not his son. But this infuriated everyone; in addition it aroused the anti-Catholic mood of the masses, and for that matter irritated the Swedes, who had joined the Polish-led anti-Shuisky coalition, while at the same time becoming rivals of the Poles on the Baltic coast. The Swedes actually started a False Dmitri of their own.

From the Russian point of view the Protestant Swedes in Novgorod, the

The "False Dmitri". *Tsarevitch Dmitri was put to death, presumably on Boris Godunov's orders. Later a rumor spread, growing to epic proportions, that he had not really died, and a "false Dmitri" appeared as Pretender. The new Dmitri won massive support, including the King of Poland's. With his armies he marched on Moscow. After Boris's sudden death the "False Dmitri" was enthroned and ruled for a year (1605-1606) before being assassinated. English XVIIth cent. engraving by Compton Holland.*

Catholic Poles in Moscow, and the huge bands of brigands roaming about the country were a sign of utter political devastation, which was finally ended by a popular uprising. This was launched, curiously enough, by a wealthy butcher, Kuzma Minin, who together with a Prince Pozharsky defeated the Poles. Russia was confronted by the urgent need of settling once and for all on a Tsar who would be genuinely accepted.

A Territorial Assembly began forming in Moscow in January 1613; though there is hardly any information about it this may be the first representative

Skopin-Shuisky, *head of the Russian troops in the struggle against the second "False Dmitri" during the prolonged period of civil wars known as the "Time of Troubles". Anon. painting. XVIIth cent.*

group ever to have convened in Moscow. The numerous candidates for the throne included many foreigners, among them some Habsburgs, but eventually Michael Romanov, a totally unknown boy of sixteen, was elected in February and proclaimed Tsar.

Favored partly by his family status, since the Romanovs were related to the house of Rurik and had been immersed in Moscow court affairs for a few hundred years, he was chosen as a compromise between conservative and radical elements; he was also a nephew of Ivan the Terrible's son Theodore. Both factors made him attractive to the legitimists. From a different angle, since his father Philaret had been made Metropolitan of Rostov by the first False Dmitri and Patriarch by the Second, the Romanovs were ensured the backing of the Cossacks.

But perhaps what promoted Michael s candidacy most was his insignificance, taken by his backers to mean pliability. He was so little known that the delegation sent by the Assembly to offer him the crown had no idea where he was.

In spite of all the social turmoil that had been going on for fifteen years the new Tsar ascended the throne with no limitation whatsoever on his power: he was invested with all the traditional absolutism of the autocracy developed by Ivan the Terrible and his forebears.

For that matter the country had not changed in the slightest degree during the preceding period of anarchy: it was just the same, simply more exhausted. It had had a social upheaval expressed in various ways and under various leaders, but with a quite unmistakable element of revolutionary unrest; dynasties had changed kaleidoscopically, foreign powers had invaded the country, there had been the usual devastation, impoverishment and slaughter typical of civil wars, but nothing had changed in the state structure. Indeed, though it was undoubtedly the revolutionary nature of the Time of Troubles, both comprehensive and profound, that accounts for the extravagant churning up of the whole country, the strangest

◀ Tsar Michael Romanov *(1613-1645). The Time of Troubles came to an end with the Poles pushed out of Moscow and the boyars electing young Michael Romanov Tsar—the first of this dynasty to occupy the throne. The new ruler was grandnephew of Ivan the Terrible. Anonymous Russian painting, XVIIth cent.*

Scenes from the marriage of Michael ▶ Romanov. *Actually the Tsar was married twice. His first wife only lived a year. With his second, Eudoxia, he had a son, Alexis, who was sixteen years old at the time of his father's death. Alexis became Tsar and, later, father of Peter the Great.*

thing about it is the total subsidence of the whole movement. The masses of peasants and slaves were simply given back to their masters; the institution of serfdom itself emerged from the chaos rejuvenated and stronger than ever, the foundation of the Muscovite state.

Nor did the number of parvenus represent a change in structure: on the contrary, the Time of Troubles, which had accelerated the political decomposition of the old boyar and princely families, simply replaced them with

Medallion representing Tsar Alexis Mikhailovich *and his second wife. From the Bibliothèque Nationale, Paris.*

a different group of service-nobles who owed their wealth and power to the Tsar's favor. This merely rounded off a process begun with the unification of the realm under Ivan the Terrible's immediate forebears and consummated by his own institution of the *oprichnina*.

The formation of this new social group, distinct from the old families, had been well advanced during the Sixteenth Century; the Time of Troubles made the process irrevocable. For that matter the parvenus who had rocketed to the surface wanted to make themselves respectable as quickly as possible; they had no interest at all in overhauling society. As for the Church, throughout the storm and stress of the civil war neither its vast estates nor its old privileges were touched.

In a way the primordial chaos of the Time of Troubles is another illustration of Russia's political inarticulateness: none of the currents of unrest was capable of creating a new idea, or even a new slogan to symbolize its dissidence. The peasants followed only leaders who claimed the authority of the Tsarist tradition; the royal principle was indispensable as the theoretical justification of any movement, however lawless in essence. It was the contradictory combination of royalist legalism, organiza-

tional incapacity, and the leaders' short-sightedness that was responsible for the inherent sterility of all the dissident movements; they inevitably slumped back into the old forms.

When Michael ascended the throne, the first of a line that was to last three hundred years, the country was actually ruined. Foreign travelers reported that to stop for the night in abandoned villages they had to sleep on their sledges, since the stench of rotting corpses still filled the huts. The collapse of the country was almost total: villages and towns were abandoned wholesale, fields were rapidly becoming woods again; the commercial communities had deteriorated completely.

The classic answer to this desperate situation remained flight. The mass desertion of taxpayers naturally undermined the treasury while drying up the manpower reserves needed for the army as well as for the fields; it also increased the tax burden of those remaining. The only solution that occurred to the Moscow regime was one of stricter regimentation. A police-state gradually formed that was the institutional expression of absolutist theory.

During the Sixteenth Century the growth of serfdom was accentuated by some other factors: the practice formerly permitted of serving a lord personally without losing one's personal liberty —distinct from tenancy, since it had nothing to do with the use of land— was drastically restricted: the celebrated Code of Laws *(Ulozhenie)* of 1649 laid it down that anyone who served a lord for even three months renounced his status as a freeman. It also became usual during the second quarter of the Seventeenth Century for a tenant to give his landlord a written promise to live on the land assigned him until his death: this amounted to a renunciation of his former right to give up his tenancy, which meant that the tenant's dependence on his landlord, formerly based on his indebtedness, now assumed the character of a contract.

This was a reflection of the government's need to pin down its taxpayers, since peasants still paid taxes and did so even after they became serfs.

But the peasants could still run away, and the government constricted them still further, in the Code of 1649, by abolishing any limit on the time run-

Map of Moscow made in 1647 to illustrate the "Voyage in Muscovy" by Olearius. This illustration comes from a volume entitled "Agreeable Gallery of the World" published at Leyden in the XVIIth cent. Olearius, the Saxon (Adam Oelschläger), had been sent to Russia by Holstein merchants who wanted to negotiate with the Tsar for the right to cross his country in order to trade with Persia and India.

MOSCOU,
Capitale de la Moscovie
Suivant Olearius.

Kremelin.

Porte du Sauveur.

Château Kremelin, dans la Ville de Moscou, avec la celebration de la Fête de Pâques Fl...

aways could be searched for. This enabled squires to recover runaway peasants whenever they found them; it riveted the tenant to his landlord even more strongly than before, since what had been a contractual relation now became an hereditary one backed by law.

The situation, though altogether incoherent in its juridical formulation, ultimately boiled down to forging a link between the servile population and the person of the landlord; the tendency developed for bondsmen no longer to be attached to the land itself, but to be bound over to the landlord as *individuals*. The Code of 1649 and other legislation never defined the personal services the landlord was entitled to, nor did it define the property rights of the bondsmen.

In fact, from the middle of the Seventeenth Century on what had once been a clear-cut line of division between former peasant tenants and slaves tended to vanish, despite the survival of some technicalities that were not wiped out until a decree of January 1723 laid a poll-tax on the whole servile population.

For generations the energies of the service-nobility were exhausted in cantankerous disputes about fugitive serfs. The nobles were so preoccupied by the problem of keeping the serfs tied down that they were quite unable to curb the powers of the autocracy; indeed, since they derived their privileges only from the whim of the sovereign they had no desire to. Relations between master and man were dominated by a hunt for runaway serfs, in which churchmen and monasteries vied with secular landlords in ferocity and imaginativeness.

This was naturally echoed by the peasants themselves: landlords were assassinated right and left and manor houses burnt. By the Sixties the cauldron boiled over once again in the revolt, still celebrated in folk-songs today, of Stenka Razin, who started a campaign in the summer of 1670 against Moscow. Once again this was not aimed at the Tsar, but at the boyars and landlords. Despite his initial successes, with peasants rushing to slaughter their masters and joining him *en masse*, which gave him control of the Volga river from its mouth to Simbirsk, he was defeated, after exterminating landlords wholesale, and executed in 1671.

His movement had been typically spontaneous and shapelessly ferocious.

Palm Sunday in Moscow, with the walled Kremlin in the background. From the "Agreeable Gallery of the World", XVIIth century. The boyars wear their traditional long gowns and beards; Peter the Great was to prohibit both in his efforts to westernize his court and his people.

Its persistence as a motif in the folk imagination doubtless reflects the permanence of conditions underlying Razin's career: the legend has it that he miraculously escaped death, eluded his executioners and turned up again a century later during the reign of Catherine the Great. The paradox of his career was characteristic of Russian

Oil portrait of the Patriarch Nikon, painted about 1660. Nikon led a movement in 1652 to reform the liturgies and the service books of the Russian Orthodox church. His slight changes were passionately contested by traditionalists; he ended in deportation in a distant monastery.

society: while even the most extremist elements of society vehemently proclaimed their devotion to the crown, the Tsar himself was in constant terror of his own people.

The Time of Troubles had given vent to so many different kinds of social pressure that in the Seventeenth Century the unity of the Russian Church itself was destroyed, in a way that was far more radical than the relative pinpricks of the Judaizing and rationalist heresies of two centuries before. The piety of the people had been deeply impressed by the afflictions and plagues Russia was enduring: wholesale impoverishment, devastations of war, treacheries of boyars and Princes, bogus Tsars, and heretics ruling in the very heart of Russia. The Russian Church was feeble in every way: politically because of its total subjection to the state power, morally, in its indifference to the secular order amidst its own material self-aggrandizement, and dogmatically, in the utter inability of the Church authorities to contrive anything that could be passed off as moral or mystic content for

View of the town of Tver. *Engraving by Nicholas Witsen, from the "Agreeable Gallery of the World", XVIIth century.*

the rigidly maintained superstructure of rites and dogmas. Michael's son Alexis, the second Romanov Tsar, was so pious he often stood in church for five or six hours on end; at the great festivals he would prostrate himself fifteen hundred times: his library contained six note-books of religious music, copied in his own hand. His chief counsellor was Basil "Barefoot", an "innocent", i.e., one of the psychopathic Godfearers the country has always been full of.

The repercussions of the Reformation had penetrated as far as Moscow, to some extent via the influence of Kiev, which finally re-entered the Russian orbit as a result of a peace treaty made by Muscovy with Poland and Turkey in the aftermath of a war that had gone on intermittently from 1672-1681.

The Ukrainians brought along some Western culture; there was an influx of outright foreigners into Muscovy. Catholics, Lutherans, Calvinists and all sorts of heterodox elements seemed to be corroding the one true faith of the Russian Church. At Narva Swedes were attacking Orthodoxy in works printed in Russian; foreign Protestants had a temple in Moscow; Poles had planted some Roman Catholic germs during the Time of Troubles itself. Some boyars had stopped wearing their long robes, and were even cutting their beards to the scandal of the right-thinking. Tobacco had even penetrated the customs of the people, in spite of the punishment smokers were subject to—the slashing away of their nostrils.

The Patriarch Nikon, who was venerated by the pious Tsar Alexis, undertook a reform of the Church. This was actually no reform at all but simply a return to certain ancient usages of the parent Byzantine Church that involved minute changes in the phrasing of certain texts retranslated from the Greek, a slightly altered spelling of Jesus's name, the use of three instead of two fingers in making the sign of the cross, saying Hallelujah three times instead of twice during church services, and having religious processions walk in the direction of the sun instead of against it.

The contrast between the triviality of these "reforms" and the incredible violence they were opposed with indicates the degree to which Russian society as a whole was insulated against any humanizing influences. The virulent concentration on such bagatelles, quite unconnected with any dogmatic changes, illustrates the purely magical value of the rites and formulae of the Russian Church: interminable controversies raged around these details, and while of course

Nikon's enterprise sprang out of a broader cultural context the curious narrowmindedness of the Russian clergy made them regard any deviation whatever from established custom, regardless of questions of content, as heresy and blasphemy.

The underlying reasoning was that the credit of the Byzantine Church had been gravely impaired by its having accepted the notion of union with the hated Vatican at the Council of Florence; despite its later repudiation of this its debased status under Muslim rule in Turkey was taken to be a sign of divine wrath, reflected in its inability to have kept up the purity of the ancient faith.

Nikon himself was completely fanatical, and eventually brought about a breach with Tsar Alexis himself, despite the latter's veneration, by proclaiming the primacy of the ecclesiastical power over the secular, and by repudiating the limitations in the Code of 1649 on the Church's traditional privileges in jurisdiction and landownership. Nikon's high-handedness had created enemies everywhere; in the upshot the dispute about details broadened into an actual schism. The dissenters rejected Nikon's trivial alterations as heresy and called themselves the "Old Believers;" they were anathematized by 1677.

This heresy of the Old Believers was coped with by the government, which backed the so-called reform despite Nikon's falling out with the Tsar, in the same way as Christianity had been introduced into Russia—by fire and sword. In 1681 Avvakum, the most famous of the dissenters, a talented, fanatical priest and the only gifted writer of the period, was burned at the stake. His party considered the changes in the spelling and the number of fingers

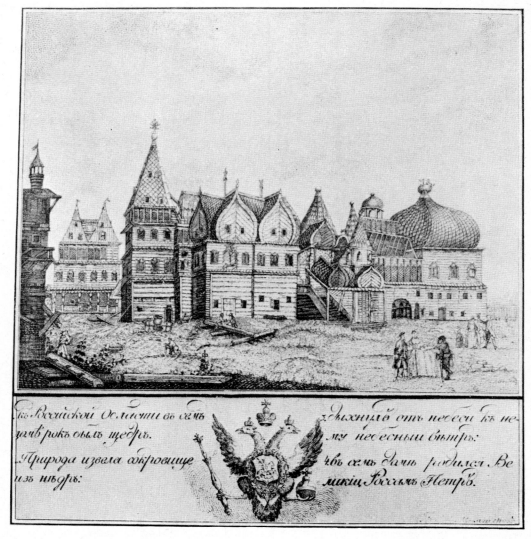

Engraving by Hilferdine, 1768, of the timber palace of Kolomenskoye *near Moscow, demolished by Catherine the Great who had a wooden model made. It was used as a country residence by the Tsars from Ivan Kalita ("Moneybags") to Peter the Great. An assembly of buildings, decorated with all the carving virtuosity of local workmen, it has been called "a gigantic dictionary of all the architectural terms invented by the Russian carpenters". Wood was used extensively in Russia; whole towns, in fact Moscow itself, were built of it.*

used in making the sign of the cross cardinal criteria of Christianity itself, while the masses of the peasantry, the burghers, and many of the nobility were desperate at the prospect of being deprived by the state of the priceless hope of eternal salvation.

Avvakum and his disciples actually thought Nikon's spelling changes heralded the advent of the Anti-Christ; the ardor of the movement expressed itself in an epidemic of mass suicide by burning. The dissenters considered this martyr's death preferable to being burned forever in the eternal flames. As a matter of fact, they thought the end of the

The ecclesiastical Kremlin of Rostov, *built on the order of the Metropolitan Jonas Sysoevich (1652-1691) when this city was at the peak of its prosperity. Though dating from over a century later than the Moscow Kremlin, its thick walls and many towers reflect the archaic style.*

Interior of the Dormition cathedral *within the Kremlin walls, in Moscow (see page 46).*

(see page 46)

world was on them once again in any case: it was supposed to take place in 1666 or 1669; when it failed to turn up new calculations were made, fixing the date at 1698. Between 1672 and 1691, when the movement slacked off, 20,000 people burned themselves to death, sometimes as many as 2,500 at a time, especially after a ukaze of 1684 threatened heretics with burning at the stake. Groups of people would lock themselves into huts filled with hay, tar or something similar and burn themselves to death.

The dissenting movement, nourished by political and social factors, proved indestructible. Its stronghold was in the remote and almost unapproachable timbered wilderness of the north and northeast, spreading to Siberia along the Volga, to the regions of the Don and Dnieper, and finding a good deal of Cossack support, which gave this religious controversy a definite revolutionary tinge. The Church lost some of its most pious followers, since the loyalty of the official flock was a reflection only of fear, and found itself still more dependent on the state, the police and the army.

The intellectual level on which these profound internal stresses of Russian society expressed themselves is of course appalling. The movement of the Old Believers might hyperbolically be called a counter-reformation, if Nikon's reforms could legitimately be compared with the Reformation. When the Protestants in the West shook loose of the Roman Catholic Church, they turned upside down the whole universe of thought and usage; the struggle was waged in the name of definite and peremptory principles. Protestantism also induced a counter-reaction within the Catholic Church itself, actually reinvigorating it. But for all its blind violence the Russian dispute produced nothing but dissident sects mouldering in a dogmatic and intellectual penury that could only resist the official Church because that was more penurious still.

No new prospects were opened up either by the official churchmen or by the Old Believers. The intellectual isolation of Russia is demonstrated most dramatically by this mindless schism: Muscovy had not been touched by a single movement of the European Middle Ages. In the epoch of Louis XIV it had the look of Eleventh Century France. In a Europe utterly transformed, and with religious civilization succeeded by a secular civilization and a subsistence economy by the money economy that gave rise to modern capitalism, Muscovy was an anachronism.

It remained practically untouched at a time when Europe had been set in ferment intellectually by the Reformation, the Renaissance, the invention of printing, and the discovery of America.

Both Nikonians and Old Believers had the same rigid attitude: while the latter rejected any changes at all, however trivial, the Nikonians themselves simply believed in going back to the Greek source of the religion. Both parties were incapable of intellectualizing their positions by devising any new dogmatic ideas; thus both clung to the dead letter of unintelligible doctrine.

The Church in Russia lacked the strength to stamp out heresy, as the Inquisition had succeeded in doing in Spain and Italy. The fervor of the dissidents kept generating new sects, and once this process of breaking away from the mother Church was launched with no intellectual inspiration to guide the wanderers, there was nothing to act as a curb on fantasy. There had actually been a fission at the very beginning between the "moderates" who accepted priests ordained before Nikon, and the extremists who preferred to live with no sacrament at all rather than be tainted by Nikonianism. The latter came to be known as the "priestless"; they spread chiefly in the northern wilderness, where the custom, rooted in necessity, had already been prevalent of dispensing with priests: settlers had to baptize their children themselves and confess to each other.

The knotty question of whether marriage was possible without an official blessing was given a special answer by the sect of the "White Doves"; they thought the simplest way out of the dilemma was to castrate themselves. The flagellants, on the other hand, would dress in long white blouses and whip themselves while chanting hymns; when they had reached a climax of ecstasy

they would have a collective orgy. Other sects were quieter, such as the "Milk-Drinkers," and the "Spirit-Wrestlers," or Dukhobors, who eventually moved to their present location in Canada.

Church of St. Elias, *built at Yaroslav by wealthy merchants (1647-1650), typical of local construction by its ample proportions and three apses surmounted by five cupolas.*

But despite the absence of intellectual content in all this sectarian atomization, the schism was the first time Russian peasants and burghers were infected by

an emotion tinged with social protest, and an emotion they were actually willing to sacrifice their lives for. In this sense the schism, infused by a substantial element of non-egotistic mutinousness, takes its place by the side of the persistent rebellions of the peasant masses after Bolotnikov.

It may not be far-fetched to think that this deep-rooted, anti-intellectual spirit of sectarianism has remained a persistent trait of Russian life to this day; it reached its apotheosis in the endlessly casuistical political discussion during the Nineteenth and Twentieth Centuries in precisely the most "intellectual" of the sectarian groups—the revolutionaries.

For centuries Russia was an arresting combination of dreariness, coarseness, and brutality. Debauchery, drunkenness and illiteracy were universal. The so-called courtiers around the sovereign were not courtiers in any European sense: there was nothing social about life at the court. Upper-class women, including the Tsarina, were secluded in a Byzantine type of harem: they never went out unless hermetically veiled; they looked on at palace ceremonies from behind a gallery grillwork. The Kremlin looked like a convent, night-

Drawing illustrating "Iter in Moscoviam" by Mayerberg, 1667, showing Tsar Alexis Mikhailovich (Peter the Great's father) giving audience on April 24, 1662.

A Cossack, *XVIIth century engraving. The accompanying caption say the Cossacks "make all their neighbors fear them, they spare no one, they apply iron and fire to everything, their manner is so fierce as to surprise, so that even their glance is horrible".*

the Sixteenth Century, when the Papal Legate Possevinus spent some time in Moscow, only one member of the Boyar Duma knew any Latin, and though a few knew Polish they were nearly all clergymen: a great many of the boyars could not read or write at all.

Business preoccupied the Muscovite gentry. Possevinus was astounded at seeing Russian envoys, supposed to be negotiating peace with Poland, set up shop on the side in order to sell some goods they had brought from Moscow. The Tsar himself set the example: he was the country's chief businessman, monopolizing the sale of vodka and furs, as well as the sale abroad of caviar and codliver oil. He actually rented out from his personal wardrobe festive garments for marriage.

The extraordinarily low standard of culture obliterated any serious differentiation between the classes: the boyar, merchant and peasant, and even the priest, were all equally boorish. There was a vacuum between the aristocracy and the plebeians, with no genuine middle class on either side: the bourgeoisie was not marked off either by education or by social function, and both aristocrats and plebeians had the same manners.

Moral standards were equally primitive. In the arranged marriages a trick was commonly played on the bridegroom by switching a less attractive daughter in on him at the last moment. Homosexuality was very widespread, and a favorite topic of comedy: few pains were taken to conceal it.

Though there was a trickle of learning in spite of all this, and printing gradually increased the amount of reading material for the few who could read, there was scarcely any progress. Mathematics, for instance, made none at all. Arabic numerals were not used generally until the Eighteenth Century: because

club and shop simultaneously: services were frequent and long, the drinking on feast-days was tremendous, and Russian noblemen spent most of their time discussing sales of hemp, furs and tar.

Ignorance was profound: secular reading was out of the question, nor was any foreign language known. Even in the highest clergy those who knew Greek were rare exceptions. At a Territorial Assembly in 1648, 141 of the 292 delegates were quite illiterate; and the Assembly was supposed to be of the "best people in the Russian land". When the Patriarch Philaret, father of Michael, the first Romanov Tsar, wanted to learn Latin he had to ask an Englishman who happened to be passing through Moscow

to write down a few words for him in Russian characters.

Nobody actually learned to read or write at all except the Tsar himself, future priests, and children of the wealthiest boyars. It was not until 1696 that Latin was made part of the curriculum at the Ecclesiastical Academy newly opened in Moscow: at the end of

Stenka Razin, *the legendary leader of the ruthless Cossacks who embarked on one of the first large scale rebellions. His uprising started in 1670 with a campaign of piracy, developed into sweeping social conflicts. He was finally caught, tortured at length and quartered alive. Bib. Nat. Paris.*

The massacres of Stenka Razin at Astrakan. *The Cossack leader, gathering adherents as he pillaged, ravaged the Persian coast of the Caspian sea with his flotilla. His successes drew more followers. At the head of a large force he attacked towns along the banks of the Volga, then seized Astrakan in 1670. Later, Stenka Razin was defeated by Prince Bariatinsky and fled towards the Don. The engraving from "The Voyage of Jehan Struys in Muscovy, in India and other foreign countries" (Amsterdam, 1681), shows Razin's men killing off the population of Astrakan within the walled city, while others flee, arms raised in horror.*

of the Slavonic characters still current hardly anyone could go beyond addition and subtraction. The only textbook used in the Seventeenth Century was an adaptation of one more than a hundred years old. Euclid, who had been rediscovered by Western Europe during the Twelfth Century, was not given the Russians until 1719. Algebra and trigonometry were not available in Russia until 1730, when the first textbooks were published. Copernicus, Kepler, Galileo and Newton might never have existed. Ideas concerning medicine and natural history were still taken from the scholastic handbooks of the Thirteenth and Fourteenth Centuries.

Though the schism gave impetus, paradoxically, to the advancement of theological studies, because of the Church's excommunication of the Old Believers, who damned Western science and thus made the Church in its turn relatively more indulgent toward learning, obscurantism remained global. No one was allowed to have a teacher of any foreign language, including Greek and Latin, without the permission of the so-called Slavonic-Greek-Latin Academy. Only the graduates of this Academy were allowed to own foreign language books, or to discuss religious questions even in private. Foreign scholars could only come to Russia with this Academy's permission, and had to be supervised. Anyone expressing any doubt whatever concerning Greek orthodoxy was liable to Siberian exile: the stake was the punishment for conversion to any other faith, or any slighting remarks about Orthodoxy, ikons or holy relics.

But this apparently opaque wall of parochial self-centredness in fact had too many chinks and crevices to keep Old Russia watertight. By the end of the Seventeenth Century, in spite of everything, a thin layer of foreign culture had formed that linked Russia with Western thought; however alien, it was a germinating-bed for new ideas. Physi-

Bogdan Khmelnitsky led a bloody Cossack Tatar uprising of serfs against their Polish gentry masters in the Ukraine (1648). Amidst dreadful atrocities against the Poles and the Jews, Khmelnitsky's forces decimated two Polish armies. The Cossack negotiated with the Polish King and actually ruled a year himself. He died in 1657.

cal contact with Europeans had of course long since been established. Ever since the end of the Fifteenth Century foreigners had been trickling into Moscow looking for gain: Chancellor

liberally minded upper-class individuals on its slovenliness. A signal was needed for a change of pace and direction—a serious effort to realize the slogan, put forward by the Soviet Union more than

other sons and six daughters; the resulting situation was so confused, when Alexis's first son died in 1682 after a brief reign, that intrigues between the two clans flared up again.

Winter coach of a XVIIth century Tsarina, by Erich Palmquist, a contemporary Swedish artist and engineer, 1674.

had counted three hundred of them at Ivan the Terrible's court. Popular xenophobia had kept them confined in a sort of ghetto called the German Suburb, which after a lengthy interruption during the Time of Troubles was restored in 1652, to survive well into the Eighteenth Century.

Even the first Romanovs, historically speaking all nonentities, had had to use foreigners to develop Russia's much needed natural resources. It was plain to the few thoughtful members of the upper class that something had to be done to reform Russia, if only technically. In the seventy years between the first Romanov's accession and the death of Peter the Great's father the Muscovite autocracy had been at war for about thirty, sometimes fighting on several fronts at once. It had focussed the attention of both the rebellious masses and

two hundred years later, of "catching up with and passing" the West.

This signal was given by Peter the Great; by the time he appeared Russia had fallen so far behind that his attempts to change her took the form of a strenuous effort to recast the whole of society.

Despite the opposition he was to encounter it must be recalled, however, that he was backed by the bulk of the service-nobility and a small but active minority of the mercantile community: the conventional picture of him as a titan fighting against terrible odds on behalf of civilization, or conversely of a tyrant obliged to overcome universal recalcitrance, is highly misleading.

Peter was born in 1672, the fourteenth child of the pious Tsar Alexis by his second wife, a member of the Naryshkin clan. Alexis's first wife had been a Miloslavsky, by whom he had three

In the Russia of his time Peter might have come from another planet, or even from Nineteenth Century America: he had an altogether secular, democratic view of life. Physically huge, with fabulous energy and stamina—amazing in a Romanov—he grew up completely outside of and indifferent to the traditional life of Muscovy. He was completely self-made; he never learned any

The church of Saint John the Baptist ▶ *is part of the Rostov ecclesiastical Kremlin (see page 77), built in 1683.*

Pages 84-85

Reval *in Esthonia, annexed by Peter the Great during his Baltic wars. Today part of the USSR. One of a series of XVIIth century engravings of Russian cities.*

REUALIA i

fol. 10

LIUONIA.

A die ThumbPfort   F S Nicolaj Pfarrkirch   M s Olaj Pfarrki
B der Lange Harmen   G Rahthausz   N die Kleinestrant
C dasz Schlosz   H die Karie Pforte   O die grosse strant
D die Kick in de kack   I Kirche zum Heil.G P das Wacht Blo
E der Thumb vnd die   K Kloster Kirch vnd   hüsz vnd Hase
    Thumbkirch   Gymnasium   Q dasz Eiland
    L die Lehmpforte   Wülff

grammar or spelling, and had scarcely any formal education.

He soon found himself enthralled by the purely material achievements of European civilization, in the form of the scraps of technical information he picked up hanging about the motley assortment of expatriates in the German

ambitious and beautiful Menshikov, who had started life as a street-peddlar, was one of the most powerful figures in the state until Peter's death and after.

Peter's inner circle was bound together by liquor and debauchery. Their orgies were distinguished by a complicated and imaginative ceremonial devis-

himself was characteristic: in the procession celebrating his first signal military success, the capture of Azov on the Black Sea, he marched in the ranks dressed as a naval captain.

There are voluminous records in Peter's own hand describing the structure and activities of this Assembly. People had to take part in public celebrations in which a stellar role was assigned the Assembly, or else they would be liable to severe punishment. Parades and masquerades that lasted for days on end had to be attended by the royal family and court and state functionaries, as well as by diplomats, all playing peculiar musical instruments and all in costume. Peter would be present dressed as a Dutch seaman, pounding away at his favorite instrument, the drums. These enforced celebrations were to become more and more common.

He had a weakness for arranging pseudo-weddings that he would contrive fantastic and obscene rituals for. When one of the two heads of the Assembly, Zotov, a septuagenarian drunkard, formerly Peter's tutor, who had been given the mock title of Pope or Patriarch of the Assembly, was "married," the preparations for the mock-ceremony kept everyone at court and in the government busy for months; Peter himself supervised every detail. In the thick of his war with Sweden he never neglected his ribald, silly correspondence with drunken friends.

Historians have naturally devoted a good deal of effort to extracting some point from this curious rigmarole. It is a futile enterprise: the Assembly was exactly what it sounds like.

Peter was very free-and-easy in his manner, with a peculiar sense of humor. On noticing his friends' disgust during a visit to an anatomical laboratory in Holland, he made them tear a corpse to shreds with their bare teeth; once, on overhearing a maid-in-waiting complain of a wasted youth, he gave her a lesson at first hand, in front of the whole court, in the sexual experience she had been missing.

Gouache by Lossenko of the equestrian statue of Peter the Great *designed by the French artist Falconet for the Senate of St. Petersburg. Lossenko painted his gouache in 1770, probably as a compliment to Falconet; the statue was not in place at that time, it was not inaugurated until 1782, after Falconet had left Russia. The Neva quays are on the right, the Senate and the Synod at the back, as they looked before being rebuilt in 1830.*

Suburb. He made his first contact with Western civilization, in fact, through a friendship with a Dutch seaman; throughout his life he retained the dress, speech, and bearing of his first Western tutor.

Western Europe, as represented in the German Suburb, which he became familiar with before he was twenty, dominated his mind as long as he lived.

As a boy he had lived most of his life in a small village, where he collected a large group of young men of the lowest social origins to drill with. Beginning when he was only eleven years old, though exceptionally big and well developed, he turned them into the nucleus of a military force. His taste for low companionship continued throughout his life; one of the "stableboys," a childhood friend he seems to have been in love with, the illiterate, unscrupulous,

ed by Peter; unlike other erratic and fleeting interests this remained a constant preoccupation of his.

When he was eighteen he organized his disreputable associates into a sort of satirical organization called "The Most Drunken Assembly of Fools and Jesters", sworn to the worship of Venus and Bacchus, with an elaborate ceremonial parodying both the Roman Catholic and the Greek Orthodox Churches. In this drunken hierarchy Peter was a mere deacon. This ostentatious humbling of

1703 medallion of Peter the Great's son Alexis, born in 1690. There was constant strife between father and son. Alexis was forced to renounce his rights to the throne. He sought asylum at the Viennese court, was tricked into returning to Russia, was charged with treason and put to death.

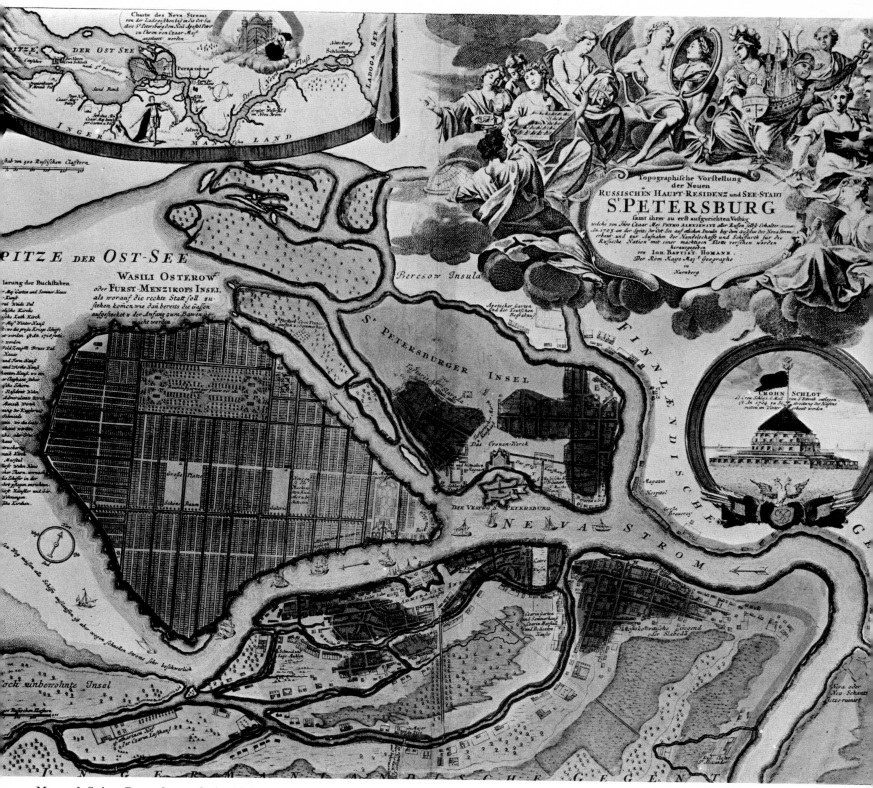

Map of Saint Petersburg *dating from 1717-1725, by Johann Baptist Homann, Nuremberg. Peter the Great decided to build his own capital on the northern stretches of marshland captured from Sweden at the mouth of the Neva. Construction started in 1703 under his personal supervision. Hundreds of thousands of workmen died as Peter's "window on the west" was reclaimed from the dank and foul swamps.*

At the age of twenty-four he decided to see Western Europe for himself, and after imposing himself on the attention of European governments by defeating the Turks in an impromptu campaign, he set out on his own idea of a Grand Tour. He had already shown his interest in foreign countries by resuming the practice of Boris Godunov of sending young Russians abroad for study, but he was the first Russian sovereign to

leave his country on a peaceful mission since the legendary Princess Olga's trip to Constantinople in the Tenth Century.

At the European courts he visited he struck everyone as most peculiar: his behavior was bizarre, his anger volcanic, his person sloppy, his manners non-existent, his attitude toward knives and forks hostile.

Of course he had a certain air: the Duke of Saint-Simon, who saw him in

1717, when Peter was forty-five years old, portrays him vividly:

"He was a very big man, well built and fairly thin, with a rather round face. He had a large forehead, fine eyebrows, and a moderately small nose fleshy at the tip. His lips were rather thick; his complexion ruddy and brown. He had large, fine black eyes, well marked, lively and piercing. His look, when he was aware of it, was majestic

breeches, stockings; no gloves and no cuffs, the star of his order on his coat with the loop below; his coat often completely unbuttoned, his hat on a table and never on his head, even out-of-doors. This simplicity, however plain his coach or attendants, made him unmistakable for the majestic air that was native to him.

"The amount of food and drink he consumed at two regular meals is inconceivable, disregarding the quantities of beer, lemonade and other drinks he swallowed between meals. His whole retinue drank even more: a bottle or two of beer, as much and sometimes more of wine, followed by liqueur wines, and, at the end of the meal, blended whiskies, a pint and sometimes a quart: this was more or less the usual fare at every meal."

On his first trip, to be sure, Peter had no intention of spending too much time at stuffy court functions: he wanted to learn ship-building, navigation and warfare. His visit to Holland was enough to start a legend, still alive, about the "royal carpenter of Zaandam", though he stayed there no more than a few days. He traveled round looking at factories, shipyards, museums, hospitals: he studied architecture, engineering, book-printing, anatomy, drawing, and for that matter dentistry.

Then, having heard that the English knew more than the Dutch about building ships, he did much the same thing in England, where he also spent a great deal of time carousing. He left a house lent him as though a tornado had struck it.

Peter had upset enough people in Russia for a dissident movement to spring up. Shortly before he left for

Coat of arms of Russia and the Russian provinces at the time of Peter the Great. Korb "Diarium Itineris in Moscoviam".

and charming; when not, it was stern and fierce, with a tic that, though not recurring often, convulsed his eyes and his whole face: it was terrifying. It lasted only a moment, giving him a distraught and frightful look, then vanished at once. His whole bearing attested intellect, thoughtfulness, and majesty, and was not without a certain grace. He wore only a linen collar, a round wig, brown and seemingly unpowdered, which fell short of his shoulders, a brown jacket, a tunic with gold buttons, a waistcoat,

Peter tried to make his new capital look as much like western cities as possible. Among the foreign architects recruited for this purpose was a Frenchman, Jean Baptiste Alexandre Le Blond (1679-1719) who organized an Office of Construction and built the palace of Peterhof, the Tsar's country residence on the Gulf. From a drawing by N. Michetti now in the Hermitage Museum, Leningrad.

Peter had visited Versailles and probably wanted something equivalent. Peterhof was designed in the classic manner with straight wings, formal gardens, terraces and cascades. Later Empress Elizabeth's Italian architect, Rastrelli, enlarged and altered the plan.

Western Europe, in March 1697, a conspiracy against him was discovered: it involved the so-called "Archers" (*Streltsy*) and the Cossacks, and was aimed at reinstating Peter's older half-sister Sophie, who had been regent in Peter's boyhood.

These *Streltsy* were a peculiar semi-military formation of Seventeenth Century Muscovy: though organized as regiments in reserved areas in Moscow they actually plied a variety of trades, and were highly accessible to political currents. Many of them sympathized strongly with the Old Believers, and as an armed and mutinous group were a constant menace to the government; they had been used before by Sophie and the Miloslavskys, who made them all sorts of promises. The *Streltsy* had installed her in power with great bloodshed

slaughtering a number of young Peter's relatives, including his uncles, in full view of Peter and his mother, and then erupting throughout the city, killing anyone in their bad books.

After Peter's unexpected return to Moscow he started a reign of terror unheard of since Ivan the Terrible. He personally kept fourteen torture chambers busy twenty-four hours a day, and in an attempt to involve Sophie and his other half-sisters in the plot he personally, together with his intimates and henchmen, tortured more than 1,700 people. But in spite of great imaginativeness he failed to get enough evidence. The tortures were followed by mass executions, hundreds of people being killed. Peter led his friends in the head-lopping. The corpses were left to rot in public for five months. One

hundred and ninety-seven were hanged in the convent where Sophie was imprisoned, three in front of her window, their dead hands clinging to letters allegedly written her by the *Streltsy*.

Peter then left Moscow for a few days; when he came back in January 1699 the slaughter was resumed with equal savagery, preceded by a riotous celebration of the Most Drunken Assembly, including a particularly obscene masquerade, to consecrate a new and luxurious mansion Peter had had built for one of his oldest friends, the Swiss Lefort. After paying their respects to Venus and Bacchus, the merrymakers surged back to the torture chambers, execution blocks and gallows.

By the end of February, more than 1,000 mutilated bodies had been taken away. The *Streltsy* were shattered.

This extravaganza of ferocity was accompanied, typically enough, by Peter's first spectacular attempt to start Westernizing Russia, or at least the shaving customs of the upper classes. The day after his return Peter showed himself in Western dress in public, and took a pair of shears to the flowing beards of the court dignitaries. This was bound

warfare: he was obliged to use the antiquated Russian army, and when he found himself confronted by better organized states in the west he was led, haphazardly and planlessly, into an assault on the whole social structure. Out of the thirty-five years of his reign, only the last was free of war: the rest of the time Russia was at peace for

"Hungarian" dress, and all men and women, except the clergy and peasants, to wear "German, Saxon or French" clothes on pain of "cruel punishments". By 1705 most of the upper classes had yielded, though for some time the aristocracy preferred its traditional high bonnets and long robes with flowing sleeves.

The cat buried by mice, XVIIIth century Russian caricature of Peter the Great, represented here as a fat cat. Political satire appeared for the first time in the XVIIIth century. This famous popular print, instigated by the Old Believers who saw Peter as the Antichrist himself, was a thinly disguised jibe at his funeral (1725), with the eight horses pulling the hearse transformed into eight mice.

to inflame sentiment: a beard was of the utmost importance to pious Muscovites; the Russian Church taught that it was indispensable to the "image of God" man was made in, and its loss therefore meant that people were no better than cats and dogs, which in its turn led to eternal damnation.

Peter's effort to transform Russia sprang out of his preoccupation with

◄ Peter *and his rowdy courtiers went on a tour of Europe to learn and to carouse. In England he had his portrait painted by G. Kneller, a German artist established there, and gave the picture to William III as a farewell present when he left in 1698. Kensington Palace, London.*

only thirteen months. These wars were not imposed on him in any way: they were launched arbitrarily, with no clear view of their aims.

His most demonstrative attempt at catching up with the West had to do with changing the way Russians looked: his cutting the beards of the court functionaries in 1698, after coming back from Western Europe, turned out to be not merely one of the pranks the young Tsar was famous for, but the beginning of a systematic regime of savagely enforced modernization in the dress and appearance of the boyars, the nobility, and for that matter the entire city population. Decrees in 1700 and 1701 ordered all these classes to adopt

A special tax was laid on beards, graduated according to the social status of their owners. The peasants' beards were tax-free, as long as they were kept in their villages, but every time a beard came into a city or left its owner was charged a copeck.

Peter also forced the Russians to start mingling socially like Western Europeans, or at any rate like the patrons of a Dutch tavern. A decree of 1718 gave precise instructions for informal parties to be held in private houses, attended not only by officers and noblemen, but by merchants and artisans. Women were forced to attend: this broke up the tradition of Byzantine seclusion they had still been subject to at the beginning of the century.

Peter launched an immense series of cultural reforms, beginning with the reform of the calendar, which had reckoned time since the beginning of the world and started the year on September 1st. This calendar, an object of veneration, especially to the Old Believers, was

teach young Muscovities the trade. In 1702-3 they played fifteen tragedies and comedies, mostly translations of current German plays about mythological and celebrated personages. Molière was also played, but the defectiveness of the Russian translation made his *Précieuses*

much because of the translators' incompetence as because the Russians of the period were nonplussed by the basic situations of the German and French plays: their bafflement was reflected in the lack of any language to express them.

Peter made a tremendous effort to launch higher education, at least his own version of it, formed largely by his obsession with navigation and related studies, but he kept colliding with the currently irremediable absence of textbooks and properly trained teachers, and the equally marked absence of pupils. School discipline was grotesquely harsh even for the period, and most parents were reluctant to allow their children to get an education. The student quota, laid down by fiat, was difficult to fill; the schools were deserted by the students *en masse*.

The entire conception of an educational program was lopsided: at a time when the country had no schools worth mentioning, either elementary or secondary, Peter, apparently inspired by Leibniz, arranged to launch a Russian Academy of Science; seventeen professors were imported from Germany, but since no Russians were qualified to take the courses some eight students had to be scraped up in Germany too, and as this number was not enough to listen to the seventeen professors' lectures, they were obliged to attend each other's. The oddity is that in spite of everything the scholarly ability of the

The foreign quarter in XVIIth century Moscow *from Mayerberg's "Iter in Moscoviam", 1661. Baron von Mayerberg was Emperor Leopold of Austria's ambassador to Russia. He wrote trenchantly unflattering descriptions of the inhabitants' table manners and manners in general. In his day the city was divided into separate quarters: for the Tsar, for commerce—with separate streets for each different trade—and for foreigners.*

changed in 1699 to the Julian calendar. The first Russian newspaper appeared in 1703, and in 1708 the alphabet was simplified, but the fact that the ancient Slavonic alphabet was retained for the Church accentuated the alienation between the Church and other educated groups that was to leave its stamp on later intellectual development.

Peter thought geometry the key to all knowledge, and since his interests in general had a narrowly "practical" tinge there was a steady output of dictionaries and translations of textbooks in arithmetic, geometry, fortification, etc. No literature was published to speak of. The light side of life was coped with in a book on etiquette translated from German; since the Russians had been commanded to behave according to Peter's view of polite society the book was very popular.

Peter hired a troupe of German actors to come to Russia, both to act and to

Ridicules as well as most of the other plays utterly incomprehensible, not so

The summer palace of Oranienbaum near Saint Petersburg, built for Peter the Great's powerful favorite Menshikov. A German architect, Theodor Schwertfeger, designed the central building with semicircular galleries attached to pavilions on each wing. Terraces sloping down to a canal linked the palace to the gulf. Peter's Italian architect Antonio Rinaldi later added some pleasure pavilions and a fancy "Sliding Hill". (See page 144.)

The police were given the most diversified duties: they were not only supposed to make everyone work at an honorable trade, but to "prohibit excessive domestic expenditures," "bring satisfaction of all human needs," and "educate the young in... moral purity and train them in honorable sciences". These statements, from statutes enacted in 1721, conclude by proclaiming the police the "very soul of citizenship." The Church itself was subordinated even more than before to Peter's police notions. A civil body, the Holy Synod, was substituted for the Patriarchate; it was organized in just the same way as other administrative units of the government, except that the members were clericals; the following year the Holy Synod came under the rule of a Chief Procurator, who was invariably a layman. This office grew steadily in importance; the Chief Procurator was finally made a Minister of the crown. The office lasted until the revolution of 1917: it nullified any political influence the Church might have had.

Peter, while making a point of attending church services, was personally

first fellows was quite respectable; the capital benefited after Peter's death by this novel note of intellectual life.

Peter's alienation from the parochialism of his native milieu constituted a chasm that could only be bridged by will-power; his social ideal, institutionally expressed, was the police-state.

irreverent; this indifference of his to religion made for some slight tolerance, and though all forms of dissent were still persecuted—he resumed the hounding of the Old Believers—the driving force behind the persecution was now not so much a fanatical desire to stamp out heresy as a campaign against a

political opposition. This was part of Peter's secularization of life in general: during his reign and after Swedes and Turks were no longer to be hated as heretics or infidels, but simply as national enemies. He thus consummated the end of the Church's role as a symbol of

Portrait of Catherine, *second wife of Peter the Great, as a young woman. She was a Baltic servant girl who had been his friend Menshikov's mistress. After bearing the Tsar four illegitimate children they were married, to the scandal of the court. Catherine made a most devoted wife.*

national unity, which in any case, to be sure, had been shattered by the schism.

The combination of Peter's wars and the military-administrative reforms they necessitated had the most far-reaching effects on the social structure, especially the organization of the nobility. The growing bureaucratization of the government and its heightened meddling in all social life made the burden on the nobility much heavier. The aristocrats were

supposed to give the army its officers and the civil service its functionaries; since the government was taking on an immense variety of novel industrial and construction activities it had to have large numbers of superintendents to run the masses of drafted workmen. Peter made it impossible for the nobles to go on stewing quietly on their estates; they were obliged to fit themselves into the evolving bureaucratic machine as best they could.

Peter did not abolish the privileges of the aristocracy, but simply formalized the old Russian concept of state service. The originally clear distinction between patrimonial estates, owned outright by the noble, and estates subject to service had been confounded for some time: Peter wiped it out altogether. A decree of 1721 made every army officer regardless of origin a hereditary noble; the concept was developed and ramified in a decree of the following year that established the celebrated Table of Ranks, which included an attribution of personal lifetime nobility, a notion curiously at variance with any Western European idea. The upshot was that you were no longer an officer because you were noble, but noble because you were an officer. All landowners became nobles with the same obligations to the state; the distinction between the great and the petty nobility vanished.

The Table of Ranks drew a clear line, for the first time, between civilian and military service. All officers in each of these two branches were put into a hierarchical order of fourteen classes, each of which had to be passed through, beginning from the bottom. The Table of Ranks extended the privilege of hereditary ennoblement to civil servants who had attained a certain rank.

In this way government service was formally acknowledged to be the source of nobility in all its forms. The terms of the basic decrees establishing the Table

of Ranks sound like an attempt at democratization, but it did not have that effect at all: the facts of life—status, connections, wealth, etc.—still made opportunity accessible chiefly to those already on the summits of society. What it did do, however, was emasculate the notion of an hereditary aristocracy even more than before, by making the bureaucratic function of an individual the source of his status: a bureaucracy dependent on a sovereign's favor is ob-

Allegorical XVIIIth century engraving, *with Saint Petersburg in the background, glorifying the Russian fleet. During over twenty years of the Great Northern War, Peter captured the Baltic coast from Viborg to Riga with his personally created navy.*

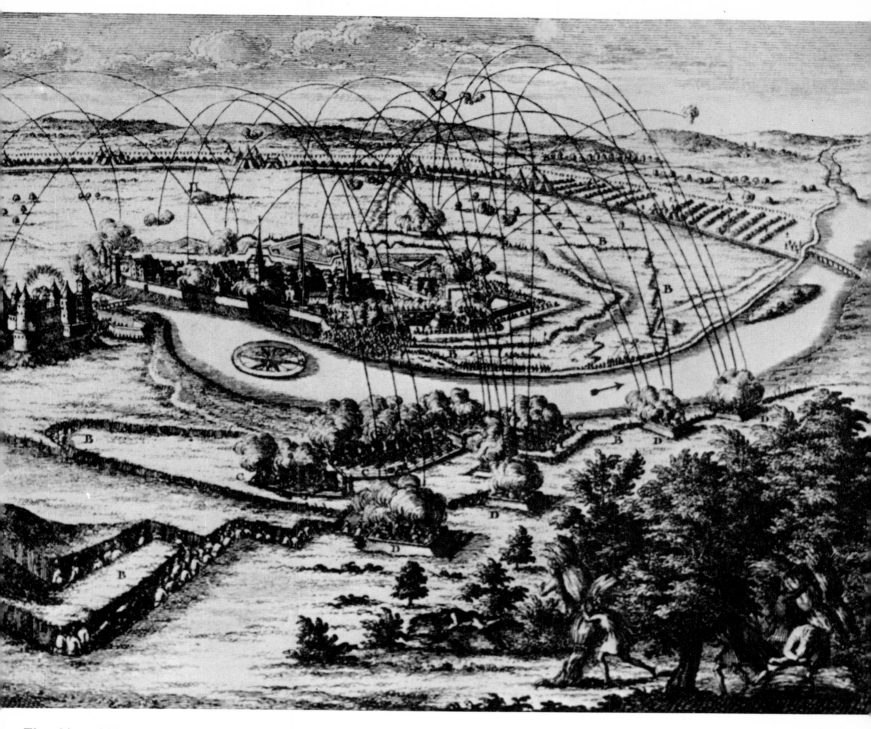

The taking of Narva by Moscovite forces in August 1704. Peter's first attack against the Swedish fortress on the Gulf of Finland (1700) was ill-prepared and disastrous. The 28-year-old Tsar's large army was routed by the forces of Sweden's 18-year-old king Charles XII. Four years later Peter organized the victory against his adversary. Contemporary French engraving.

viously more pliable than an aristocracy with autonomous pretensions.

The Table of Ranks was one of Peter's most durable reforms: it gave a sharp outline to the bureaucratic state that had begun developing in Muscovy even before him, and created a bureaucratic tradition that was to survive the revolution of 1917. Peter replaced the easy-going sloppiness of patriarchal Muscovy by a ramified system of protocol and etiquette, ranks, titles, emblems of obsequiousness, and above all of uniforms. These became compulsory for anyone even remotely connected with the state:

they were worn by civil servants as well as army officers, and later on by students, including secondary school students of both sexes. On its upper levels the country became a sort of gigantic barrack-house. The pervasive regimentation was relaxed to some extent during the liberalization of the upper classes in the Nineteenth Century, but it never entirely disappeared.

The regimentation of the landlords was naturally passed on to their serfs: the poll-tax not only added to the burden of the already servile population, but extended serfdom to groups that

formerly had been relatively free. Discontent seethed constantly, with mass desertions to the southern steppe and northeastern wilderness, and rebellions, all of them drowned in blood, flaring up at one point after another, especially along the Volga and to the south.

Peasant discontent was heightened by grotesque, though well-founded rumors about Peter's personal life as well as that of his entourage. From reports in the files of the security police, which had become all-powerful, a nightmarish picture emerges, especially after the Old Believers began being persecuted again.

The universal denunciations naturally led to the medieval torture chambers, which were in constant operation, and from the records it seems that a very large number of people caught up in the police network thought Peter the living in the world for his deeds; but he has the right and power to govern his realm and his lands as a Christian sovereign, according to his will". A Church statute of 1721 said the same thing in a form that was to be retained with slight

Of course it had nothing to do, as it were functionally, with his "democratic" feelings: his second wife, Catherine, was a Latvian peasant. She had first been a servant-girl at a Protestant pastor's, then a mistress of a Swedish dragoon: imprisoned by the Russians at the sack of Marienburg in 1702, she soared aloft in an amazing career. She passed through a great many hands before becoming the mistress of Peter's boyhood friend Menshikov, who passed her on to Peter in 1703, whereupon she was converted to Greek Orthodoxy. Though plain, quite illiterate and completely vulgar in manner, she had a very lively mind; she and Peter were entirely devoted to each other. She actually followed him to war, slept outdoors with him, and ate the soldiers' food. She was the only one who could soothe his epileptic crises. He had four bastards by her before marrying her in 1711: Muscovite public opinion, of a pre-medieval strictness in such matters, nevertheless had to swallow the peasant Empress. It is entertaining to recall that Louis XIV required years of persistent effort to secure the legitimization of his bastards by Mme de Montespan, who was, after all, the daughter of a Duke.

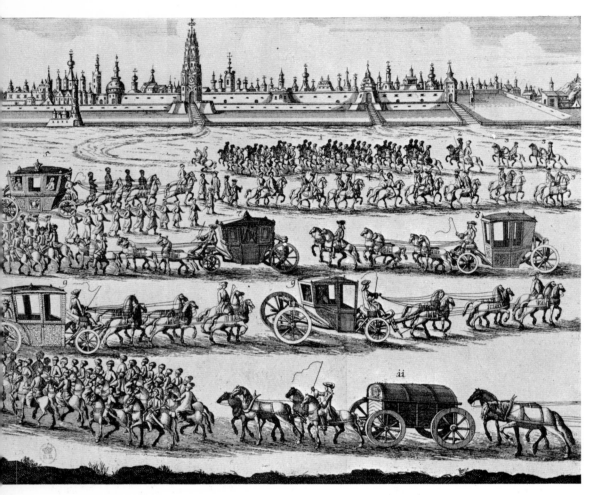

The ambassadorial mission extraordinary *sent by Leopold I, Emperor of Germany, to Peter the Great in 1698. At the top, left, Peter in his carriage has come to meet the ambassadors. From Korb's "Diarium Itineris in Moscoviam", Vienna 1700.*

incarnation of the Apocalyptic Beast, an opinion shared by many beside the Old Believers.

Peter did a great deal to lay the foundations of the mass espionage and security police methods that have never since left Russia.

Peter did have enough intellectual consistency to concretize the autocratic principle already expressed theoretically by Ivan the Terrible. He proclaimed himself Emperor for the first time in 1711, and in 1716 the army regulations he had drawn up gave this notion legislative form. This was the formula he used: "his Majesty is an absolute monarch who is not responsible to anyone

modifications until 1917: "The power of monarchs is autocratic; conscientious obedience to it is ordained by God Himself." This formula summed up Peter's "theory" as well as practise.

Since Peter's basic motive had been the assimilation of Western technology in order to wage war, his indefatigable energies were flung into the substitution of "factories" for the tawdry workshops of the Russian natural economy. The objective was dual: the army had to be equipped and the country enriched simultaneously. Peter attempted to organize the production of saltpeter, silk, wine, etc. He imported foreign engineers and foremen, as well as machines and technical handbooks. He tried to create an entire industrial structure by fiat from above, both by offering premiums to private initiative and by flogging delinquents and recalcitrants. The factories were all built at the treasury's expense, and leased out to individuals with varying degrees of competence. It was the first effort at the creation of a state-economy. But it remained

Far right: A Russian medal commemorating the victory at Narva *in 1704. Right: Russian medal celebrating the taking of Schlüsselburg fortress in 1702. Both from the Bib. Nat. Dept. of Medals, Paris.*

inherently unviable: as Peter once exclaimed in despair, "There are no people!" There was not enough experience or education in the country for such an enterprise, and though government-grown Russian industry finally became capable of supplying uniforms to the army—at an extravagant cost— it was never able to withstand the flood of foreign imports.

The founding of St. Petersburg may have been his most successful, and surely his most dramatic and expensive enterprise, in human as well as material terms. The new capital was situated at the farthermost reach of the empire simply for Peter to be near his beloved navy. The terrain he chose was so watery—at the point when the Neva, the shortest and widest river in Europe, pours into the Gulf of Karelia in four arms—that the mud had to be fortified by means of buoys and piles: the workers died by the thousands in the freezing marshlands. St. Petersburg, which was to become one of the finest cities in Europe, was at first built out of wood. Great palaces along concrete quays were to grow up later. The new capital, which Peter referred to as his paradise, was a sepulchre for hundreds of thousands of people and a bottomless well for an inestimable loss of wealth.

The whole problem of Peter's reign, which unflagging controversy has raged round ever since, was created by the curiously haphazard, practical limitations of his mind hacking away at his milieu. In the brief span he devoted to the problem it was doubtless inherently insoluble.

For despite his fabulous energy Peter's mind was essentially elementary. Altogether "practical", he had no grasp of general ideas. Though he has gone down in history as the great Reformer (or rather Transformer) he never had any real plan. He was merely obsessed by a desire to catch up with the West technologically, and it was in his determination to combine this general obsession with his other obsession for

Campaign against the Turks *in 1710, showing the Tsar's camp retrenched at Pruth. Agents of Charles XII of Sweden and the French incited the Turks to fight against Peter the Great. Peter was almost taken prisoner; he was forced to give back the Azov fortress wrested from the Turks a few years before. Anonymous French engraving.*

warmaking that he had to initiate an immense variety of changes in government, taxation, etc., to carry on his wars. Though he was quick and inquisitive, his ignorance was fatal. Since his

obsession was always with a practical goal and he was incapable of formulating general principles, his method was inevitably one of trial and error, nearly always error: his practical policies generally cancelled each other out.

Medal commemorating Peter the Great's victory at Poltava *against the Swedish army, in 1709. Wounded before the battle, Charles XII led his forces from a stretcher, he was able to escape to Turkey. This medal represents the Russian cavalry. Paris, Bib. Nat. Department of Medals.*

Pages 98-99

Peter the Great's victory at Hangou *on the Baltic in 1714 over the Swedes was the first great naval success in Russian history. Engraving by Maurice Baquoy.*

Both the imposition of industrialization from on top and the growth of the bureaucratic apparatus as a means of organizing society may be looked on as the inevitable response to the nology, not vice-versa, and that traditional Russian institutions eluded the superficial control of his administrative improvisations, he ran head-on into an almost solid wall of resistance.

Despite the conventional eulogies addressed to Peter even by Russians who disliked his methods, the fact is that the population of the country was more than decimated by Peter's ruinous

The battle of Poltava, *where the Russians beat the Swedish army in 1709 (see page 97). Painted and drawn by Martin the Younger. Engraving by Nicolas de l'Armessin, made for Emperor Peter the Great.*

gigantic gap between Russia and Europe that had been allowed to develop as the material counterpart of her spiritual isolation. Just as Russia disregarded the cultivation of Latin Europe for seven hundred years, while deriving a thin trickle of culture from Byzantium, so now, when Peter, like a newborn child, determined to cultivate his country, he turned to Germany and Holland for technique. But since it was only technique he was looking for he never could clarify to himself what it was that made technique possible: he thought he could convert sleepy paternalistic Russians into energetic businessmen and engineers by changing their clothes and thrusting into their hands a series of technical handbooks, largely unintelligible.

Peter was a mixture of energy, practicality, and intellectual limitation; it made his reforms both artificial and fragmentary. By failing to perceive both that civilization underlies tech-

His reforms were fragmentary in any case; they touched only a minute class, with no effect on the people as a whole. Not only did the Russian masses remain inert and lethargic as before, since in their vast numbers they could only be conceived of by Peter as targets of the knout, but since Peter did succeed in forcing Russia into the Procrustean bed of Western culture he did so at the cost of alienating the upper classes from the masses far more completely than anywhere else. The comfortable national identity of ignorance, squalor and coarseness, based on an identity of customs and beliefs, yielded to a society divided by a broader chasm than before.

The landed nobility had to extract even more from their serfs in order to live up to Peter's demands; the more streamlined bureaucracy became tamer than ever. Together they constituted the summit of society. Underneath them lay the people, groaning.

wars. Hosts of Russian soldiers, badly dressed, badly armed, and badly trained, died on countless battlefields. Many thousands of conscripted workmen died of hunger, cold and disease in Peter's vast enterprises, including the construction of a canal, the waterway system, Petersburg itself, etc. It is enough to recall that during Peter's reign Russia's population, in spite of a proverbial fecundity, decreased by 20 %. Russia was devastated, as she had been during the Time of Troubles and was to be so often again.

Peter the Great *made a second European tour in 1717, this time he came to the French court where he was received by the boy King Louis XV. This drawing by J. Desmarets, 1718, records the meeting, at which Peter later scandalized onlookers by picking up the little King in his arms.* ▶

Le Czar Pierre le grand, *venant de hollande, arriva à Paris
le 7. mai. Il descendit au louvre, d'où le maréchal de Tessé le conduisit à
l'hôtel de L'Esdiguières. Le lendemain il fut visité par le Régent. Le 10.
par le Roi lui même. Le Czar le vint prendre à la descente de son carosse.
et le reconduisit au même endroit. Le 11. il vint voir le Roi au Palais des
Thuileries, qui le reçût avec les mêmes honneurs. Il partit de Paris le 21. Juin
pour aller à Spa. Pendant son séjour, il visita tout, soit dans Paris, soit dans les
environs, tant maisons roiales, académies, manufactures, laboratoires, &c. et il fut reçû
partout et traité avec magnificence.*

Catherine the Great

During the thirty-seven years between Peter the Great and Catherine the Great the throne was occupied by a grotesque assembly: it was kicked back and forth seven times, between ignorant sluts, feebleminded German princes, and children, each representing the power of the guards regiments founded by Peter, which remained a decisive factor throughout this period.

Having tortured his heir Alexis to death, with the only remaining heir a grandson he wanted to eliminate, Peter had formally decreed the Emperor's right to appoint his successor. Thus he projected the autocrat's own power beyond the very principle of monarchy, and after a life spent magnifying the autocracy left Russia without a ruler, since he died too soon to nominate one.

The feverish instability of the regime may be traced to these two acts of Peter's: his arbitrary negation of the monarchical principle and the immense importance he bestowed on the guards regiments. These factors came into play against the background of the dynastic alliances Peter had zealously entered into with a number of German princely houses.

With no stable principle of authority, and with a variety of contending elements of power, policy in St. Petersburg increasingly became a foot-ball of competing cliques, especially since the country had acquired international consequence. The political horizon was no longer confined to parochial disputes with Turkey, Poland and Sweden; Russia was now a factor in Western Europe as well.

What may be called the regimental principle in the Russian state was launched in a very natural way. Peter's social upheaval, which struck at the very heart of the old-line aristocracy, had inevitably produced a cleavage between the parvenu clique that had prospered under his wing and the victims of his various persecutions. These people, who were longing to restore tradition, were fortified by the general revulsion of feeling at Peter's extravagant personal behavior and especially at the murder of his son Alexis, and considered Peter's grandson a legitimate successor ready to sweep away the plebeian adventurers who under Peter had been battening off the state.

These adventurers, equally naturally, were vitally interested in the immobility of the status quo. None of Peter's favorites, especially his peasant Empress, Menshikov, and Theophanes Prokopovich, his tame Metropolitan and professional eulogizer, could expect anything from a change of regime but death or at the very least imprisonment, exile or confiscation of property.

It must have been obvious that the guards would have the final word in deciding who was to ascend the throne, and during Peter's last illness they were sounded out to see whether they would help keep Catherine on the throne. In any case Catherine, who had accompanied Peter on so many campaigns, was personally popular with the army, both officers and men, and troops thought to favor her were rushed to the capital. Their approval of Catherine was stimulated by the simple device of giving them their pay, by now almost a year and a half in arrears, and promising them rewards in future with understandable generosity.

This facile procedure established a mould for the palace revolutions that characterized the Eighteenth Century. During the forty years after Peter the Great's death the throne was claimed by many: his grandson Peter, his two

Coronation of Empress Anne *(1730), from an album printed in Moscow the same year. After Peter the Great's death (1725) the crown passed in rapid succession to his widow, his grandson, then to his niece Anne, widowed Duchess of Courland.*

Fireworks given August 12, 1741 for the ▶ anniversary of Ivan VI. *Although the celebration looked impressive, Ivan, infant grand-nephew of Anne, only ruled a year, with Anne's lover Biron as Regent.*

Engraving of St. Petersburg *(1733) showing the Academy of Sciences on the left, naval cadets training in the center of the Neva river, and on the right, the Admiralty Quarter and the façade of the Winter Palace, which now houses the Hermitage Museum. The name of Peter's capital was changed to Petrograd during the First World War and is now Leningrad.*

daughters by Catherine, Anne and Elizabeth, born out of wedlock, and his three nieces, Catherine, Anne and Praskovie (the last of whom played no political role). The success of one or another depended on the decision of a clique of fortuitously organized higher officials enforced by the guards regiments.

The justification given of making Catherine Empress of Russia in her own right, which took place even before Peter's actual death, was that she had been "crowned" a year before by Peter himself; the curious thing is that this extraordinary innovation failed to create any serious disturbance. Some stick-in-the-muds, to be sure, at first felt there was something wrong about taking an oath of allegiance to a woman who on top of being a Latvian peasant to begin with had been the mistress of so many people and borne Peter so many bastards, but these traditionalists were soon shown the light by the security police.

Since Catherine did not even pretend to rule but simply devoted herself to debauchery of one kind or another, Menshikov, who had been instrumental in putting her on the throne, remained the chief power in the land. He managed to consolidate his power still further even after Catherine's death in May 1727 by marrying off his daughter to Peter's young grandson, and on the death of Catherine Menshikov's prospective son-in-law, Peter II, was hailed as Emperor, at the age of eleven.

But Menshikov's career, seemingly at its peak, failed to live up to its prospects: the arrogance of the "overbearing Goliath", as he was called, had multiplied his enemies beyond control. He had alienated the young Emperor and even lost his hold over the guards in whose ranks he had started out himself. Only three months later, after a short illness, he was banished with his whole family; he died a couple of years later.

For a short time the fall of Menshikov cleared the way for a restoration of

Moscow as capital and a return to the traditional life Peter the Great had upset. Young Peter was crowned there in January 1728, and that summer some major departments of the government were shifted to the old capital; many observers thought that everything symbolized by St. Petersburg was done for.

But Peter II's career was very brief, though full of fun. Very tall and sexually precocious, like his grandfather, he spent most of his time with some young friends; life was one long round of parties, hunting, and love-making. His festive career was ended by small-pox: he died in January 1730, leaving Russia without a ruler for the third time in five years and the male Romanov line a thing of the past.

The dynastic situation remained as amorphous as ever: after considering the various candidates the Supreme Privy Council, plus a number of other highly placed personages, arbitrarily selected Anne, Duchess of Courland, Ivan V's second daughter, apparently

because she was considered a model of submissiveness. The throne was offered her on the basis of certain "Conditions" that substantially curtailed her power as sovereign. These Conditions were intended to ensure the influence of the great Dolgoruki clan, and were thus construed at the time as an attempt to replace the monarchy with an oligarchy. But the resistance to the novel scheme of curbed autocracy among the noblemen who were even more against the oligarchy than against the autocracy, and their confusion as to any alternative to these two types of government, facilitated the restoration of an autocracy proper.

The guards and noblemen outside the inner circle of the would-be oligarchy insisted on the restoration of absolutism, and Anne literally tore up the restrictive Conditions in front of a large group of army officers and notables. Thus, what might have been an experiment in a monarchy based on an aristocratic oligarchy came to an end

XVIIIth cent. popular engraving *of a combat between a Cossack and a Prussian.*

less than a fortnight after Anne's entrance into Moscow in February 1730.

Anne was thirty-seven at the time. She had been married at the age of seventeen to the Duke of Courland, but was widowed only a few weeks after the marriage; she had been obliged to spend nineteen years in the eccentric

position of a Duchess without a Duchy. A bigoted ignoramus and highly sensual, she was dependent on the niggardly subsidies of the Russian court, whose agent was in charge of the affairs of the Duchy. All this time she had been writing humble illiterate notes to her imperial relatives and to the favorites in

Medal *commemorating the oaths exchanged between the Preobrazhensky Guards and Elizabeth, youngest daughter of Peter the Great, in 1741. Elizabeth was brought to the throne after conspiracies between the French ambassador and dissatisfied elements at court led to a palace revolution that banished the infant Tsar and his mother and got rid of the hated German officials. Medals Department, Bibliothèque Nationale, Paris.*

began to ail toward the end of her reign the regime found itself once again confronted by a dynastic muddle.

This was given a stop-gap solution by the birth of an heir to Anne's niece, Princess Anne of Mecklenburg, or Anna Leopoldovna, the only descendant of the senior Romanov branch. Biron had attempted to anchor himself more firmly in the ruling circle by marrying his son off to the young Princess, but he was unable to withstand the opposition of his rivals and the unwillingness of the bride herself, who chose to marry a German Prince, Anthony Ulric of Brunswick-Bevern-Luneburg, whom she

power, and when she finally found herself on the throne, after this lengthy and generally hopeless-looking exile, she quickly made up for lost time.

She had been involved in a liaison with Ernst Johann Biron (Bühren), a minor functionary of German ancestry, who was supposed to be dropped on her return to Russia; like the other Conditions, however, this was also disregarded. Biron became the real ruler of Russia during her reign, which is actually known in Russian history as the *Bironovshchina*—the rule of Biron.

The moment Anne became Empress she flung aside the docile impersonation she had been forced to carry on for so long, and plunged into an unflagging series of splendid palace and Church festivities. She had inherited Peter the Great's predilection for peculiar people: she filled the imperial residences not only with animals, especially those that could perform amusing tricks, but with all sorts of giants, midgets, cripples, beggars and clowns: she kept a large corps of women on hand who did nothing but entertain her by telling stories. Anne also had Peter the Great's liking for practical jokes and satirical rites: she celebrated a "marriage" between two princes—a Golitsyn and a Volkonsky—and once made this Goli-

tsyn the bridegroom of a famously repulsive Kalmyk woman, in a grotesque ceremony performed in a palace made of ice.

In accordance with Anne's often proclaimed motto of ruling in the "spirit of Peter the Great", she moved the court and government back to St. Petersburg the year after her accession, putting an end to the short-lived experiment of reviving Moscow as the capital of the realm.

As part of a campaign to crush the great clans that had attempted to curb the autocracy in their own interests —Dolgorukis, Golitsyns, *et al.*—Anne intensified the police reign of terror. Once again the torture chambers began churning out their full quota of people, often on the mere suspicion of disapproval of Anne's regime; thousands were sent to Siberia, often to vanish completely.

Anne remained childless, and as she

The coronation of Empress Elizabeth *in 1742, from an album published in St. Petersburg in 1744. Peter's daughter was young, handsome, and pleasure loving. Her fondness for France substituted French for German at court and introduced French fashions and intellectual currents.*

had no liking for either. This match produced a boy in August 1740, and when Anne died a few months later she appointed the infant her heir: the best Biron managed out of this was his appointment as Regent until the baby, called Ivan VI, reached the age of seventeen. This negotiation was so private that this time no one at all, not even the guards, was consulted.

But in the uncurbed flux of interests around the Russian throne the arrangement lasted only thirteen months. Biron had incurred great hostility, and more especially had failed to secure the support of the guards; he was

arrested only a few weeks later, being deported to Siberia with his family. He was to languish in exile for more than twenty years.

He had been replaced as Regent by Ivan VI's mother, Princess Anne of Mecklenburg, possibly the most muddle-headed ruler even of the confused interregnum that followed Peter the Great's death. She spent days at a time closeted in her bedroom seeing no one but her lady-in-waiting and her lover Count Lynar, whom she was planning, curiously enough, to join in marriage: she was passionately attached to her lady-in-waiting. Throughout Princess

Anne's regency the contention for the helm of Russia between various German cliques and individuals was incessant; it was brought to an end only by a palace revolution at the end of 1741 that resulted in the arrest of the Brunswick family, the deposition of the infant Ivan VI, and the accession to the throne of Peter the Great's daughter Elizabeth.

Elizabeth was thirty years old: she was to reign for twenty years, until her death in 1762. Peter the Great, hoping to fit her for a major role at the court of Versailles, had taught her German, French and dancing: otherwise she was uneducated.

Contemporaries considered her personal beauty and charm irresistible. Gay and amorous, she concentrated exclusively on carnal amusements with a disconcerting lack of inhibition. The Spanish Ambassador, the Duke de

Portrait of Empress Elizabeth, *crayon, by Moreau the younger, 1758. Bibliothèque Nationale, Paris. The Empress had many lovers and many clothes; at her death her cupboard contained 15,000 dresses.*

Liria, said she "shamelessly indulged in practices that would have made even the least modest person blush". It was, indeed, her amorous nature and taste for low company, inherited from her parents in the form of a weakness for handsome guardsmen, that was to give her the throne. Lightminded and irresponsible, she seems to have frequented the guards' barracks for simple pleasure rather than in pursuit of any elaborate political objectives, but her charming accessibility nevertheless created a faithful following for her among the guardsmen, who were used to regarding the throne as their private preserve. This following was taken advantage of by those who were against the Brunswick family and the German connection generally. St. Petersburg, now deeply involved in European affairs, was simply another arena for power politics, and it suited France and Sweden to choose Elizabeth and her guardsmen as a means of getting rid of politicians whom they could easily claim to be alien to Russia's interests without harping unnecessarily on their own.

Elizabeth's rule brought life in St. Petersburg much nearer to the European model the elite were longing for so ardently. The festivities were far more conventional: the relays of masquerades, spectacles, and hunts were no longer marred by the grotesqueries of Empress Anne's reign; the cripples and clowns had vanished, while Elizabeth's beloved guardsmen did much to elevate the standard of looks around the court if not its urbanity.

Elizabeth's agreeable frivolousness was merely reinforced by her imperial status. The wobbly Russian treasury was completely outdistanced by her quest for amusement. Though she thought it politic to recommend thriftiness in dress to everyone else, when she died she left behind 15,000 dresses, as well as many items needed for the masculine attire she was very attached to. She liked traveling, and on her frequent trips to Moscow and other cities, as well as to monasteries, she was escorted not only by the court but by various government agencies. The huge governmental caravan required thousands of horses and carts for all

the officials, including their servants, furniture, and household utensils. The imperial residences even in Moscow were unprepared for the massive descents of the sovereign's entourage and government.

Caprice was elevated to a state principle during Elizabeth's reign: the "merry Tsarina" was generally inaccessible to anyone but her private chancery, which was not even acknowledged as a state institution. Russian statesmen and foreign diplomats alike were reduced to lurking about in the hope of catching the Empress in an off-moment and making her sign indispensable state

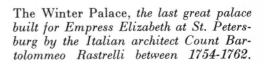

The Winter Palace, *the last great palace built for Empress Elizabeth at St. Petersburg by the Italian architect Count Bartolommeo Rastrelli between 1754-1762.*

The Summer Palace, *built by Rastrelli for Empress Elizabeth between 1741-1744, on the site where Peter had erected a cottage for his Queen. The new palace became one of St. Petersburg's most magnificent constructions in the Russian rococo style. Rastrelli not only designed the large government buildings for Elizabeth, he supervised all architectural activity in Russia and formed many pupils.*

papers, which otherwise might lie about for months and often be shelved altogether.

Even more than at other times the reign of Elizabeth was distinguished, as has been observed, not by "the authority of state institutions" but by the "power of persons".

In addition the German element in society, so influential ever since the acquisition of the Baltic lands, was given permanent roots through Elizabeth's importation of her nephew, the Duke of Holstein-Gottorp, to St. Petersburg after her accession. On his conversion to Greek Orthodoxy he took the name of Grand Duke Peter, and in November 1742 was proclaimed heir.

His marriage to a German Princess, the future Catherine the Great, was to put a German stamp on the Russian monarchy that remained fundamental until the extinction of Tsarism.

But with all the changes of regime during the period of turmoil that followed the death of Peter the Great, with all the personal corruption of the rotating backstage favorites, with all the capriciousness of the policies that emerged through the complex filtering-chamber of the ramified alliances with German houses, there was, nevertheless, a certain unity of development. Serfdom progressed steadily; not only did it become more comprehensive, but it also became a hallmark of class privilege.

A number of laws passed between 1730 and 1759 limited the right of anyone but a member of the nobility to own serfs; concomitantly the peasantry grew progressively more desperate. Impoverished and decimated by the cost of Peter the Great's imperial expansion and the exorbitant exactions of its owners, it did what it always did: it ran away and revolted. The monarchs who succeeded Peter the Great, especially his daughter Elizabeth, found themselves coping with one peasant rebellion after another. These uprisings were especially frequent and savage on the monasteries' estates and in the industrial enterprises worked by serfs. It was a common occurrence for great bands of armed peasants, numbering sometimes several thousand, to wage regular pitched battles with the punitive expeditions sent against them. The private soldiers, who were subject to a life term of service, often joined them, only to be overcome ultimately by still other government troops. Every uprising was crushed; its leaders were all killed on the wheel, or the gallows,

solidly anchored in its privileges, the personal security of any individual nobleman was much the same as that of his serfs. The greatest personalities in the country were subject to the most abrupt changes of fortune.

Thus, while the official policy was savage repression of the peasantry plus the conciliation of the nobility as a class,

come down in history as a depraved and drunken moron (chiefly because of Catherine's tireless literary energies), but his chief political shortcoming seems to have been that he was one of the few Russian monarchs in the Eighteenth Century to mount the throne legally, and hence had no effective support at all. Catherine herself was quite unknown outside the court; she was wholly a usurper and could at most have claimed to hold the throne as regent for her son, Paul. But after Peter III was murdered, apparently with Catherine's at least tacit approval, she clung tenaciously to the throne nevertheless.

Paul's claim to the throne was incontestable, and since its only obstacle was Catherine's will-power, there was a profound estrangement between the two: when Paul visited Vienna in 1781 it was considered prudent to cancel a performance of *Hamlet*, and a license to put it on in St. Petersburg was cancelled when the authorities found out what the play was about: by titillating the curiosity of the reading public this decision greatly stimulated Russian interest in Shakespeare.

Catherine II has gone down as one of the most glamorous monarchs in history: this is largely due to her extraordinary talent for press agentry and the immense zeal she devoted to it. Her position enabled her, also, to hire the services of still more talented press agents like Voltaire. One of her cardinal objectives was to be on friendly terms with Voltaire, Diderot and d'Alembert, not only because of snobbery, but because she saw very clearly how useful such indefatigable writers and opinion-moulders could be in singing her praises. She was, as Frederick II said about her, "very proud, very ambitious, and very vain."

Voltaire, unusually available, became a completely pliant instrument. He praised her at all times and endorsed everything she did, lauding the first partition of Poland as a victory of "tolerance" over "fanaticism," etc. Much the same was done by his colleagues and the growing band of their Russian followers. By acquiring the public support of internationally known French writers and thinkers, Catherine secured her own position at home.

The moment Catherine took power—nine days later, to be precise—she invited Diderot to shift to Russia the publication of the *Encyclopédie*, suspended in France; a few years later she bought his library, allowing him to keep the books and draw a pension of

Russian popular engraving of an officer. XVIIIth century.

or at the whipping post, or deported to the Siberian wilderness.

The harshness of peasant life had its counterpart in the general insecurity arising from the arbitrariness underlying the government. The rulers themselves, placed on the throne by capricious combinations of palace officials and guardsmen, never knew what was going to happen next. This arbitrariness applied to the nobility as well. Though as a class it was more and more

there was at the same time a pervasive disaffection that showed itself in palace conspiracies, the evasion by the nobility of its obligations, mass desertion, and peasant revolts.

A palace revolution put Catherine the Great, born Princess of Anhalt-Zerbst, on the throne for thirty-four years; she ascended it over her murdered husband Peter III, with the support of the Preobrazhensky Regiment. Peter III has a peculiarly bad reputation, having

The rococo church of St Andrew, in Kiev, built for Empress Elizabeth's favorite, Razumovsky, by Bartolommeo Rastrelli between 1747-1767. It combines western style columns with Russian cupolas. ▶

1,000 *livres* as Her Majesty's Librarian. This openhanded policy paid off richly: at bottom such acts are the underpinnings of Catherine's reputation for enlightenment. After Diderot's visit to Russia in 1773 he gave Catherine *carte*

copiously with Frederick II, Joseph II, Prince de Ligne, Falconet and a great many others. Mme Geoffrin, who had a famous salon in Paris, and Frau Bielke, her counterpart in Hamburg, were particularly effective propagandists.

preferred turkey to chicken." Some months later she assured him that Russia had always benefited from wars; the Turkish war then going on was just the same: "There are no shortages of any kind; people spend their time in singing thanksgiving masses, dancing, and rejoicing." Voltaire may have believed these droll comments on the Russian scene, or merely pretended to: even those who thought them nonsense were flattered at being in the confidence of such a powerful sovereign. This kind of personal propaganda was fairly effective in securing the proper attitude on the part of Catherine's correspondents.

Favoritism had always had a lush growth at the Russian court, but Catherine made it a semi-official institution. Her ten chief favorites, in succession, were given apartments next to hers and treated magnificently: titles, lucrative estates, vast fortunes were the index of her affections. An oddity of hers was an absence of any vindictiveness toward her lovers for straying; she never persecuted the ones she sacked. Among her lovers Orlov, Potyomkin and Zubov were powerful influences on government policy, both domestic and foreign.

Potyomkin actually outlived his lovership: he influenced Catherine until his death. He was mysteriously skilful in influencing the choice of his successors; they were nearly all his tools. For years he was practically an all-powerful counselor of Catherine's: he was one of the inspirers of her ambitious project for the expulsion of the Turks from Europe.

In spite of her frivolous early education, Catherine had become a voracious reader during the seclusion forced on her under the reign of her aunt-in-law, the Empress Elizabeth. She was also a tireless, thoroughly mediocre writer of tragedies, comedies, polemical works, musical comedy librettos, treaties on pedagogy, allegorical tales, and historical writings, as well as memoirs, which have become celebrated. Her collected works, apart from her vast correspondence and her "Instruction"—a philosophical draft constitution for Russia—fill a dozen bulky volumes. Though her Russian was good enough for speaking it was scarcely a literary medium: her ideas about grammar and spelling were vague. In a very common Russian word of only three letters she made four mistakes in spelling. As for what she wrote in French, it was all thoroughly processed and corrected in the most modern manner before being released.

Alexis Razumovsky, *favorite of Empress Elizabeth. His good looks and fine voice attracted her attention to him when Razumovsky was singing in the imperial chapel choir. The Empress had several children by him made him a field-marshal. Indolent and good-natured, the favorite had little personal ambition and preferred to further the career of his younger brother Cyril. The Razumovskys were given 120,000 serfs by the Empress.*

blanche in the way of moral support: he praised her as combining "the soul of Brutus and with the charm of Cleopatra." Intellectuals are a cheap and fruitful investment.

Besides Voltaire, Diderot and d'Alembert, Catherine corresponded

Catherine showed an engaging effrontery in what she wrote Voltaire about Russian conditions: in 1769 she told him that since taxes were very low "there was not a single peasant in Russia who could not eat chicken whenever he pleased, though he had recently

The great staircase at Peterhof, *the* ▶ *palace built by the sea thirty miles from his capital for Peter the Great by Le Blond. Elizabeth had the palace considerably enlarged by Rastrelli. While it was damaged severely in the last war, Rastrelli's rococo staircase still exists.*

Rastrelli completed the plan to convert Peterhof *for Empress Elizabeth into a large palace in 1747. Five years later he had doubled the length of the façade, added a storey and the square pavilions at each end. The clipped geometrical garden is in the French style.*

Under Catherine Russian life—social, economic, and political—remained much the same. The gulf between her superficial aping of French liberalism and the facts of Russian life was unbridgeable. The above-mentioned "Instruction", for instance—one more in a long series of abortive governmental attempts to cope with the chaos, corruption and wastefulness of Russian society—was not a specific program for legislation, but a mere plagiarism of Montesquieu's and Beccaria's philosophical generalities. Catherine's throne was too shaky, aside from the shallow confusion of her ideas, for her to undertake surmounting the massive obstacles in the way of any genuine reform, to say nothing of her grandiose projects for the remapping of Europe and Asia, which were equally abortive.

Under Catherine Russia added some 200,000 square miles to her area, and established herself firmly on the shores of the Baltic and the Black Seas. Her population had increased substantially, partly through these territorial acquisitions, from 19,000,000 in 1762 to

36,000,000 in 1796, the year of her death. This expansion cost a good deal both in lives and in wealth, and led to the assimilation of some peoples, such as the Tatars and Poles, who remained constant sources of disaffection, especially the Poles, who throughout the Nineteenth Century and into the Twentieth were a permanent target of bloody repressions.

Russian annexations seem particularly pointless if we recall that the Empire as a whole was scarcely exploited at all, as for that matter it is not even today. Catherine had Louis XIV's view that "to aggrandize oneself is the worthiest and most agreeable occupation of a sovereign." The actual driving force of most of the warfare carried on during Catherine's reign was nothing more than a powerful imagination, abetted by the equal flights of fancy of her various lovers.

As a matter of fact, not only did Russia's wars during the second half of the Eighteenth Century hold up her economic development, but by extending her rule to the Polish provinces,

which were never reconciled to Muscovite control and in fact combatted it stubbornly until Poland was restored to the map one hundred and fifty years later, they set up a source of disaffection very close to home. It is true that Catherine extended the boundaries of the Empire more than any other Russian sovereign since Ivan the Terrible, but this merely heightened the contrast between the area of Russia and her degree of underdevelopment, a leitmotif for centuries.

There is a celebrated anecdote about Potyomkin's building some cheery bungalows, surrounded by merry peasants dressed in their Sunday best, in order to regale Catherine and some foreign diplomats who were sailing down the Dnieper to witness the conquest of the Turks. The territory was still uninhabited, and since Potyomkin wanted to show the visitors a going concern both the scenery and the extras were transported upstream at night and the spectacle duplicated. The story actually seems to be apocryphal, but its meaning is splendidly apt: all Russia was a vast

Potyomkin village. It was like a brilliantly illuminated comic-opera stage, with elegantly costumed lords and ladies strolling back and forth exchanging duets and witticisms in French while the mangling-machines were grinding away backstage.

In fact, just because Catherine was such a voluminous correspondent and gave free expression to the loftiest ideas she could lay her hands on, the contrast between what she said and what she did is all the more striking. She is best known for the acquisition of the littoral of the Black Sea and of new outlets on the Baltic, but she failed to undo the Ottoman Empire, which had been her declared aim, not to mention her really extravagant schemes. She is reported to have said: "If I could live for two hundred years the whole of Europe would be brought under Russian rule." Also: "I shall not die before I have ejected the Turks from Europe, broken the insolence of China, and established trade relations with India."

Though the autocracy she believed in so firmly was kept unchanged, her attempts at administrative reform im-

Left: Count Bartolommeo Rastrelli, *(1700-1777) Italian-born favorite architect and decorator of Empress Elizabeth. He built, prodigiously, palaces and public buildings all over Russia. Trained in France, his work shows the influence of central European rococo and also of purely Russian sources: the fortified church architecture of Moscow. Far left:* Michael *Lomonosov. Poet, grammarian, scientist, one of the pioneers of Russian literature. Of humble origins, a hard drinker, he had heated disputes with the German members of the Academy of Sciences.*

Russian Baptism *by the French artist Jean-Baptiste Le Prince, who travelled in Russia from 1758 to 1763. He not only stayed and worked in St. Petersburg, where he painted some ceilings for the Winter Palace, but went through Finland and Livonia to Moscow and as far as Siberia. When he presented this picture at the Paris Salon of 1765 it had the greatest success; the exotic subject matter and such details as the silver baptismal fount were particularly appreciated.*

paired the efficiency of the central government, while her attempt to multiply expensive local agencies of self-

◄ Peter III *goes down in history not in his own right but as having been Catherine the Great's husband. He was Empress Elizabeth's nephew, weak in mind and in body. His stay on the throne was brief (1761-1762): hated by the court, despised by his wife, he was deposed and done away with by Catherine's supporters.*

government failed to bring about any self-government, or even to curb the corruption of government officials. The much-publicized Legislative Commission she had written her "Instruction" for failed to produce even a draft of the exemplary code she had wanted.

Even in the sphere of abstract thought, the moment Catherine's freely professed ideas were put to the acid test of the French Revolution she reacted like a perfectly conventional European ruler of the period and recoiled in horror, repu-

diating the superficial liberalism of her whole life. The French Republic was boycotted, and even individual French nationals who refused to take an oath to monarchism were expelled from Russia while, on the contrary, the most reactionary French aristocrats were received with open arms. After the French Revolution French education, which remained fashionable, took the form of education by "Monsieur l'Abbé," in spite of the risk of the children's being seduced by Roman Catholic propaganda.

119

Catherine II the Great (1762-1796) as a young woman. This most Russian of monarchs was born wholly German: Princesse Sophia Augusta of Anhalt-Zerbst. At 17 she married her cousin Grand Duke Peter, later Peter III. His short, inept reign was ended by a palace revolution instigated by Catherine and the Guards. Engraving by J. Stenglin. 1745.

It is true that in areas of public activity where there was no danger Catherine actually did try to apply some of her liberal principles as well as talk about them. She let up to some extent on the persecution of dissenters, though the question of eliminating their legal disabilities was never raised. As for the Jews, who had always been subject to a great variety of legal disabilities in addition to outright oppression on the part of the populace as well as the government, they now found their position legalized, with some negligible exceptions; they were allowed to settle in what became known as the Jewish Pale, though even there they were more heavily taxed than others. With modifications this remained characteristic of Russia until 1917.

The fact was that the shakiness of Catherine's throne counteracted the dragooning of the nobility into state service that previous sovereigns, particularly Peter the Great, had tried to accomplish. The dynastic upheaval following Peter's death had given the landed gentry a hold on the sovereign, who though in theory was absolutely autocratic had in practice arrived at a *modus vivendi* with the landed aristocrats that made them relatively more powerful than the boyars of old Muscovy. Since in this agricultural country the land was held by the nobility it was *ipso facto* a vital economic force, and since it provided the officers the military strength of the regime was organizationally dependent on it. Because of this, as well as because of the vacuum surrounding the sovereign, especially Catherine, it was now necessary to bribe the landed nobility with lavish concessions in the exploitation of the manpower that was the source of its wealth.

In fact, the second half of the Eighteenth Century put the landed nobility in a better position than ever. Catherine's consort had freed them from the obligation of service in 1762, and Catherine sustained this concession. Until 1785, when a new Charter of the Nobility was published, the nobles did not have to enroll in government service; they simply resumed life on their country estates, this time not as idlers, however, but as a group with privileges that included the direction of rural affairs. The Charter was very wordy and somewhat incoherent: it simply extended the privileges

of the nobility and set up a framework for its corporate existence. The Charter protected the noble against deprivation of his "honor", life, property and title (except for "personal" and non-hereditary titles) without a trial by his peers. Nobles could leave government service whenever they wanted to, travel abroad as much as they liked, and serve friendly foreign states. They were exempt from corporal punishment and the poll-tax, and could own estates with people and houses in cities, trade in the produce of their estates, and own industries.

The notion of service that had underlain the social structure of Russia was altered by the lightening of the nobility's obligations to the state. The theory, so to speak, of serfdom, or in any case its historical dynamics, had been rooted in its having enabled the nobility to serve the state by forcing the serfs to carry on the nation's economic activities. But with the concessions made by both Catherine II and her consort Peter III, as formulated in the 1785 Charter of the Nobility, a social group was now created for the first time that had many privileges but no direct personal duties to the state. This was a continuation and amplification of the characteristically Russian conception of the aristocracy as a class with privileges but no duties. It was essentially a profiteering institution, in contrast with the Western view of aristocracy as involving an ideal of service to something beyond individual gain.

At the same time this basically materialist view of the aristocracy was given a functional component by rooting the source of nobility in service understood bureaucratically: individuals would acquire a coveted title by serving the government as individual functionaries, while the influence of the nobility as a class would be secured not by anything it did within the realm of its class privileges as such, but because it was the ultimate reservoir of bureaucratic manpower.

Catherine was said to have had twenty lovers. They were given monthly stipends and rich possessions, and a number of them had considerable influence over state affairs. From top to bottom: Gregory Potyomkin, handsome Guards officer whose dash and courage helped promote him to Prince, Prime Minister and Field Marshal. Portrait by Lampi. Stanislas Poniatowski was first made Polish ambassador to St. Petersburg, then Catherine had him elected King of Poland; he was the last Polish king. Serge Saltikov, another royal favorite. Prince Platon Zubov, the Empress's last passion. Catherine was in her sixties when she became infatuated with the twenty-two-year-old Zubov. He advised her recklessly and envenomed her troubled relationship with her son.

Thus the emancipation of the nobility from its previous dependence on the state made the primacy of the bureaucratic machine more unambiguous; indeed, it reinforced the vast and ramified bureaucracy that governed the country till the 1917 revolution, and for that matter survived even the revolution and left its imprint on the Soviet Union.

Catherine was not merely the tool of the nobility's shortsightedness: not all landowners were blind to the dangers

conversation of a tiny circle around the Empress, and were quite irrelevant to the social legislation of "the age of enlightenment."

Serfdom, though not formulated in specific legislation, had been established by the end of the Eighteenth Century; Catherine's legislation, piecemeal though it was, consolidated it completely. Noble landowners had gradually acquired the power, not unambiguously given them by law, to dispose of their serfs as they

cial authority over them except for murder and theft. The rights of possessing land and of litigation, already taken away from the serf by two of Catherine's predecessors, were now supplemented by Catherine's denying him even the right to lay a complaint against his owner.

Announcements like the following were common in contemporary newspapers: "For sale: Two domestic servants, one a leatherstitcher, who can also repair shoes. Thirty years of age, married: his wife is laundress and can tend cattle; twenty-five years old. The other is a musician and singer, seventeen years of age, plays the bassoon, with a bass voice. Also for sale at same place: a Hungarian horse, three years old, very tall, English-bred, not yet ridden."

The price of serfs varied considerably: a girl might be sold for ten rubles and a cook for 2,500. There was nothing to prevent a landowner from running actual torture chambers: there was one in Orel who had thirty professional torturers and assistants. Others actually had full-fledged penal codes applied on their estates. The cruelty that was common throughout Russia assumed psychopathic forms in individual cases. A noblewoman, Darya Saltykov, was accused of having tortured to death some seventy-five of her serfs: it amused her to pass a red-hot iron over her servant-girls' breasts. This caused such a scandal that she was deprived of her title and imprisoned for life in the prison cell of a convent, where she incidentally had a child by one of the guards. But this case, which for that matter was unsuccessfully brought before a court twenty-one times before it was finally settled six years later (1768), was quite exceptional. The law actually said nothing about the punishment of landlords who killed their serfs: there are only twenty cases, nine of them women, known throughout Catherine's reign: there were only six sentences of forced labor and two deportations to Siberia. The others were simply imprisoned in convents or monasteries for terms varying between one week and a year.

The only recourse the serfs had was to petition the crown, but this often boomeranged: while Catherine was making a trip along the Volga in the spring of 1767 she was approached by some delegations of serfs asking for her help against their masters. This produced a decree of the same year forbidding any complaint *at all* by a serf against his master: a breach of this made a serf

Catherine's armies waged lengthy and successful war against the Turks at the beginning of her reign. This engraving by D. Chodowiecki commemorates the victory of General Golitsyn *near Choczim (Bessarabia) on Sept. 18, 1769. The General points out the decimated armies to the subdued Turks on the right. The war continued until 1774.*

inherent in the plight of the peasants. On various occasions even highly conservative noblemen recommended alleviations of serfdom without even suggesting abolition, while the records of the abortive Legislative Commission of 1767-68 show some support for a more liberal policy on the peasant question even among the rank-and-file of the nobility. Catherine was obdurate, and in her defence of what she conceived to be the interests of the class she owed her throne to invariably took the most narrow-minded and reactionary conception of those interests, consistently disregarding all counsels of common sense as well as of humanity. By the end of her reign serfdom was more solidly rooted in Russian life and more grinding than ever before. Voltaire's and Montesquieu's theories were confined to the elegant

chose. They could transport them at will, sell them with land or without, mortgage them, settle debts with them, etc. The sale of serfs often led to the break-up of families, and this had been condemned in principle as far back as 1721 by Peter the Great; but one of Catherine's decrees half a century later did no more than stipulate that the transaction must not take place at a public auction, presumably not to shock Catherine's French friends. This treatment of serfs as chattels was to continue until the emancipation of 1861: it was, of course, slavery.

A rich landowner might have a vast number of what were called household serfs, consisting of hundreds of men and women, from stableboys to cooks, tailors, artists, actors, musicians, and astronomers. The master had complete judi-

Prince Gregory Orlov *was Catherine's* ▶ *lover while she was still Grand Duchess, one of five brothers who conspired to do away with Peter and enthrone Catherine. Painted by the Italian artist S. Torelli.*

A popular Russian amusement at public parks and fairs were the Sliding Hills: *fun-lovers climbed up wooden steps and whizzed down a steep incline covered with ice (in summer they went down in little carts). These artificial slopes had particular appeal to northern Russians who lived in a mountain-less country. Foreign artists were always intrigued by the local pastime. This scene on the frozen Neva river is by the French engraver Damane-Demartrais (1763-1827).*

Gold medal *representing horsemanship games at the court of Catherine the Great in 1766. Medals Dept., Bib. Nat., Paris.*

liable to flogging and penal servitude for life.

Serfs were the index of wealth: a nobleman's status was calculated in terms of the number of "registered" serfs in his possession, i.e., the number of male serfs allocated him by the preceding census.

A few figures are in order. The following do not include the Ukraine, and may not be precise, but they are illuminating. In the second half of the Eighteenth Century 59% of the landowners owned fewer than 21 male serfs each; 25% from 21 to 100; and 16% over 100. By 1834, however, 80% of the male serfs belonged to the big landowners with over 100, and so on. The concentration was actually much greater: in 1834 the 3% of the landowners who owned over *500* each together owned 45% of all the serfs, while only 870 magnates (about 1% of the landowners) owned some 2,038,000 male serfs, or 30% of the total.

At the beginning of Catherine's reign about 45% of her people were serfs.

Serfdom was not only for life but was hereditary; it could only be brought to an end by army enrollment, Siberian deportation, or emancipation voluntarily granted by the owner. The first two remedies were dependent on the owner, the superintendent of the estate, or the village council, and were probably worse than serfdom itself: the other was very rare.

One of the anomalies of the period was the serfs' economic position: their right to private property was subject to all sorts of restrictions. Movable property, though not immune to expropriation by their masters, could be enjoyed by serfs as long as they owed nothing to their masters or to the state, and though they were forbidden to own real estate outright, there were many serfs who had *de facto* possession of town houses, populated estates, and even industrial enterprises registered in their owners' names. Serfs belonging to a great landowner, Count Sheremetiev, in fact founded and owned many cotton mills technically belonging to him: some serfs even accumulated large fortunes, and could do as they pleased with them if they got their owners' formal agreement.

But these were of course exceptional instances: by and large there was no escape from the network of rules and customs that imprisoned most of the serfs, and when serfdom was formally introduced in the Ukraine and southeastern Russia there was no longer any refuge from bondage.

It is this plain and simple fact that made Catherine's copy of Montesquieu's ideas in her Instruction a mere quip: she was in fact repaying the landed nobility for their support by giving them free rein with their human cattle. The minor measures she passed mitigating grosser abuses, such as forbidding the enslavement of peasants once emancipated, or liberating some peasants upon the promotion of a village to a city, were more or less cancelled out by the wholesale distribution of vast troops of peasants to her favorites and generals. She was robbing Peter to pay Paul. In fact the Russian peasantry was at the very nadir of its long and miserable existence during the reign of the Philosophers' friend.

In reaction the classical flight of the peasants continued without let-up: constant attempts to curb it, by both threats and cajolement, met with little success. Poland was one of the favorite refuges of runaway serfs until it was wiped out as a sovereign state: Catherine's foreign policy, which led to the partition of Poland and extended serfdom to the Ukraine and southeastern Russia, was welcomed with pleasure by

serf-owners. Her regime could not remedy the oppression, but it could at least stop up the escape hatches.

Mass flight and desertion kept the vicious circle in full heart: the owners were vitally concerned by the problem,

Fonvizin *(1715-1792) playwright, who wrote comedies satirizing the provincial nobility and its efforts to imitate French manners. In spite of the censorhip imposed on the press at the end of Catherine's reign—when her "liberal" ideas dissolved in shock at the French Revolution— literature began to flower. Young aristocrats thought it fashionable to write poetry.*

since not only did it cut into the revenues represented by the serfs' labor, but it increased the burdens of those remaining, by making them bear the taxes and furnish the contingents of recruits that the runaways would have had to meet. This naturally increased discontent, which incited the serfs to further flight or rebellion, etc.

The growing mood of rebellion, ex-

Pugachov *the shrewd, illiterate Cossack who led a serf revolt under Catherine II. Passing himself off as Peter III having escaped assassination, he rallied the peasants to massacre property owners and to march on the capital. His movement became a real social revolution. He captured Kazan and defeated generals sent against him. Finally betrayed by bribery, he was sent to Moscow in a metal cage and decapitated on Red Square in Moscow in 1775. Underneath this anonymous engraving is written in Russian: "If you have never seen a great enemy of the country, then look upon Emilian Pugachov in person".*

acerbated by the tightening of serfdom at the very moment, and in consequence of the relative emancipation of the nobility, culminated in the Peasant War of 1773-74, led by one more obscure, illiterate and adventurous Cossack—Pugachov.

Alexander Radischchev *(1749 - 1802) nobleman of liberal ideas, author of a passionate protest against the horrors of serfdom and the condition of the peasants entitled "Journey from St. Petersburg to Moscow". Catherine first sentenced him to death, then altered the punishment to exile for life to Siberia. Later Catherine's son, Paul I, had him brought back.*

This revolt, begun by Pugachov with an initial following of only eighty men, mushroomed so rapidly that like the upheaval of the Time of Troubles it actually endangered the throne.

The widely publicized Legislative Commission for which Catherine had written her equally publicized Instruction had fortified long-standing rumors about an emancipation of the serfs; when this optimistic mood was dashed by repressive measures such as the abovementioned decree of August 1767 forbidding the serfs to complain against their masters, and the Commission itself was dissolved, an ugly mood struck root throughout the country. This, combined with the damaged prestige of the throne itself as a result of the constant series of palace revolutions since the reign of Peter the Great, accentuated by the murders of both Catherine's husband, Peter III in 1762 and another claimant, Ivan VI, in 1764, generated the usual flock of imposters claiming to be one miraculously escaped Tsar or another. There were at least half a dozen pretenders in the

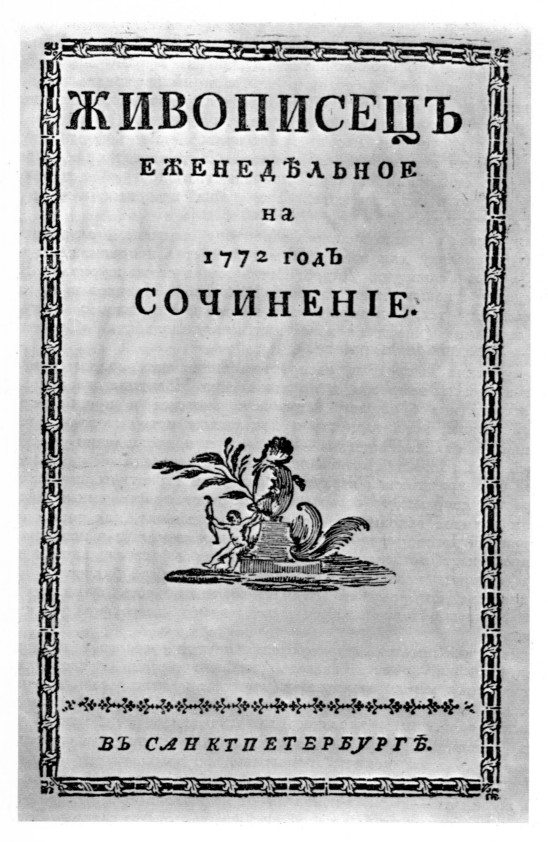

ЖИВОПИСЕЦЪ

ЕЖЕНЕДѢЛЬНОЕ

на

1772 ГОДЪ

СОЧИНЕНІЕ.

ВЪ САНКТПЕТЕРБУРГѢ.

Title page of a satirical journal Zhivopisets *(The Painter) edited and published by Nicholas Novikov. At one time, while still influenced by advanced French thinkers, the Empress herself contributed to Novikov's publications. After her attitude stiffened, Novikov's publishing house was closed; he was confined to Schlüsselburg fortress for his Freemasonry ideals.*

it was also vague and contradictory. He promised an end to the landowners' regime, the restoration of the Old Faith, a prohibition on the shaving of beards, old-fashioned dress, and happiness for everyone. He said he would not rule the country himself, but would simply depose Catherine as a usurper and install his son the Grand Duke Paul on the throne. His entourage was a clumsy burlesque of the Petersburg court.

Once again a peasant revolt was presenting itself in the shape of a demand for the restoration of the rightful Tsar.

In practice Pugachov unleashed a reign of terror. Though the noble landowners were the natural targets of his revolutionary program, the Cossacks and peasants did not do very well either. The same situation faced the population that was later to turn Russia into a shambles during the civil war that followed the Bolshevik seizure of power in 1917: if the people rejected Pugachov they were flogged to death or hanged, if they yielded the punitive troops the government sent to put him down would behave in the same way.

Pugachov was helped by the enthusiasm of the nomadic Turkic-speaking tribes like the Bashkirs, Kirghizes, Tatars and others, the forced laborers in the mines and workshops of the Urals, and the runaway serfs the provinces of Orienburg and Kazan were teeming with. On the negative side, he was also favored by the feebleness of the local authorities, the shortage of reliable troops and the incompetence of the central government. He occasionally assembled as many as twenty and even thirty thousand troops, or rather large groups of guerrillas incapable of any sustained elan. Whenever these casual stragglers encountered even a semblance of organized action from government troops they melted away again: the regime was still capable of coping with an essentially anarchic uprising. By 1775 he was executed in Moscow: his head was flaunted on a pole, and sections of his dismembered body were broken on the wheel in public and then burnt. The authorities had been so alarmed by the success of the movement, and especially by the obvious fact that it was due not to any positive qualities but simply to a pervasive state of discontent, that the Holy Synod actually anathematized Pugachov's followers: both his house and the whole of his native village were levelled to the ground; the village was

Russian costumes *from an album published in St. Petersburg in 1774, called "Russia presented, or complete collection of the attire of all the nations found in the Russian empire". Above, from left to right: women from the extreme north of Russia and from Finland. Below: Yakut woman and Tatar woman from Kazan.* ►

decade after Catherine's seizure of power.

Pugachov's uprising was the most effective. After an extraordinary saga of adventure—commonplace for a Russian frontiersman of the time—he escaped from a jail in Kazan in 1773 and passed

himself off as Peter III, a name he had been using intermittently for some months.

Pugachov's program was immensely effective among the dissident element of the population, whose name was legion;

transported to the opposite bank of the Don River and given a different name. The government's retaliation was as ferocious as the movement itself had been.

In a sense the Pugachov revolt enabled the bureaucratic arm of the absolutist regime to justify itself: the nobility saw itself defended—incompetently but in the long run effectively—against a common enemy. The course embarked on by Catherine in the wake of her predecessors was bound to lead to the yoking of the peasant countryside to the economic needs of the nobility. Before the industrial revolution and the development of both a middle class and an industrial working-class, the peasants by themselves proved incapable of summoning up the technical capacities needed for an assault on the existing order.

In spite of everything, however, Catherine's regime, by flinging open the gates of at least upper-class Russia to the fructifying influences of French civilization, was another crucial stage in Russian history. This time Russia, after having been harnessed to Dutch and German technology, was thrust into the schoolrooms of France; French influence, which had been very much in vogue even under Peter's daughter Elizabeth, now had the field to itself.

Catherine's reign marked the beginning of the French tutelage of Russian society that lasted down to 1917. The French language and a smattering of French literature became an emblem of social status and the precondition of a successful career. French tutors and private schools run by foreigners became astonishingly fashionable, so much so that any number of French barbers, coachmen from Marseilles, and often downright criminals would guide budding Russian nobles in the arts of civilization.

All this took place, of course, in the summits of society. Since Catherine was far too taken up with expensive foreign wars and the repression of peasant uprisings to cope with the universal absence of popular education, there were practically no schools at all. The upper classes had not yet swallowed their aversion to schools sponsored by the government; the few schools in existence could scarcely find the quota of pupils laid down for them. Throughout the whole of Catherine's reign only one M.D. was conferred by the University of Moscow.

The influx of influences of all kinds into Russia was matched by the exodus of noblemen abroad: their right to travel, granted by Peter III and confirmed by Catherine, for the first time gave them a chance to see Western Europe for themselves. There was a stampede to Paris, which while offering the conventional nobleman an opportunity to ruin himself in gambling-dens, bro-

thels, cafés, restaurants and dress-shops, also opened the eyes of many others to Western European ways of life. It was the beginning of a ferment that was to churn up the Russian educated classes during the next few generations.

Under the influence of Western European models and inspirers, artistic life began changing at an increasing pace. St. Petersburg had grown with tremendous speed, much more rapidly than any other Eighteenth Century city. What had been an icy quagmire in 1703 was to become a celebrated metropolis a century later. Since Peter the Great had been determined to make St. Petersburg an arresting symbol of Russia's new orientation—a "window to the West"—and thus a complete contrast to the ancient capital, it was the chief focus of the innovations initiated by him and carried on by his successors. The Europeanization of the new capital symbolized the growing cleavage between Russia's elite and the rest of the population that was the outcome of Peter's determination to overhaul Russia.

About 1713 Peter the Great had begun employing great numbers of European artists, architects, and engineers, more or less indiscriminately: a Frenchman, Le Blond, and a Swiss Italian, Tressini, were the only men of real distinction he found. His urgency set them all to work helter-skelter, often side by side on buildings standing next to each other. It was common for a building to be designed by an Italian or Frenchman, started by a German or Dutchman, and finished off by still another architect.

A certain unity was given by the domination of the baroque then in international vogue, but of course each architect interpreted the general style in terms of his own inclinations.

In Peter's time, accordingly, the city was a curious mixture of German, French, Dutch and Italian baroque that had not yet been fused into a Russian harmony.

The first thirty-five years of the city's existence were marked by a certain planless groping; the final establishment of its centre on the land side instead of on the islands during the 1730s ended an era of purely utilitarian

At the top of this town plan is the mention in French and in Russian: "New map of the city and the fortress of St. Petersburg. An exact copy of the original that is in the Police Archives by C.M. Roth, 1776". Under Catherine, new public buildings and palaces continued to be erected. New foreign architects, and some Russians, continued to enlarge the city. The rococo character of architecture under the previous Empress gave way to a classicism influenced by the French spirit.

ЧАСТЬ ФИН-СКАГО ЗА-

ЛИВА

PARTIE DU

GOLFE DE FINLANDE

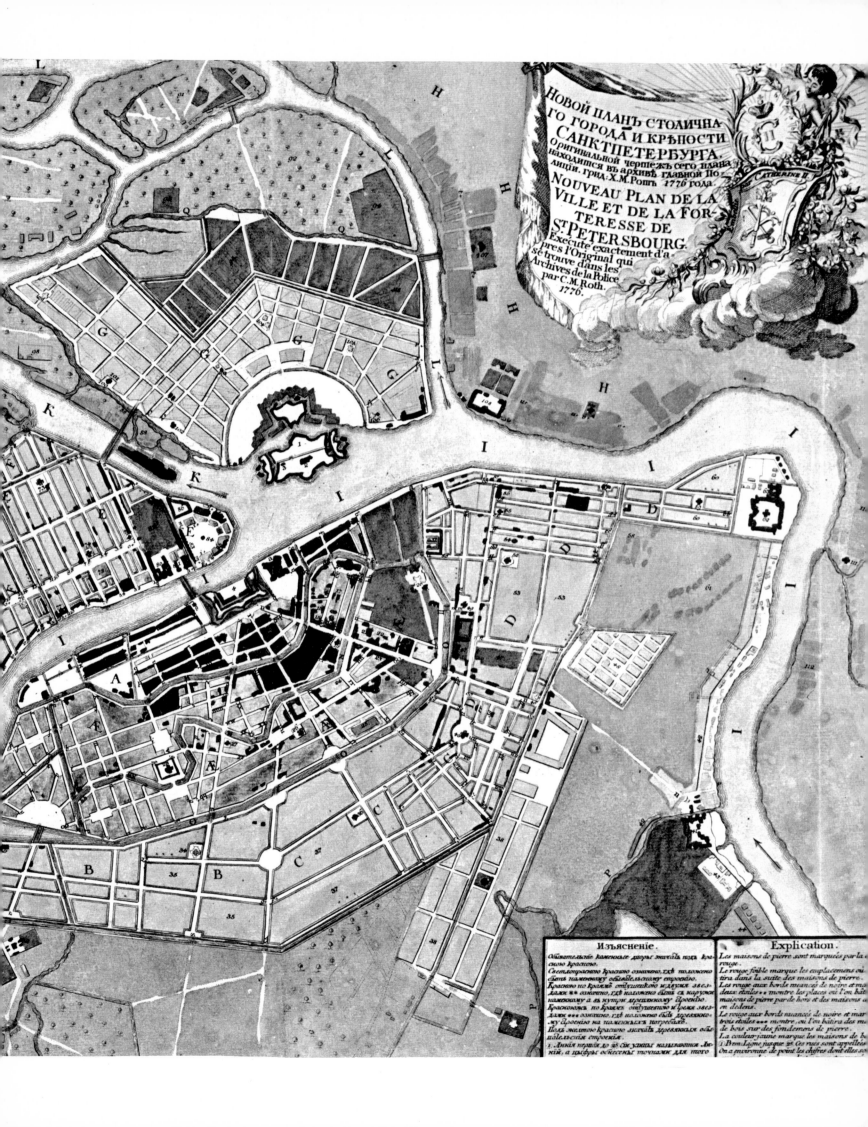

НОВОЙ ПЛАНЪ СТОЛИЧНА-
ГО ГОРОДА И КРѢПОСТИ
САНКТПЕТЕРБУРГА.
Оригинальной чертежъ сего плана
находится въ архивѣ главной По
лиціи. Грид: Х. М. Рошъ 1776 года.

NOUVEAU PLAN DE LA
VILLE ET DE LA FOR-
TERESSE DE
St. PETERSBOURG.
Exécuté exactement d'a
près l'Original qui
se trouve dans les
Archives de la Police
par C. M. Roth.
1776.

CATHERINE II

Tsarskoye Selo palace and the park; *engraving by Damane-Demartrais. The Great Palace had been built for Elizabeth by Rastrelli, who added long wings onto the original small palace that already existed there. At that time Rastrelli had laid out formal gardens in the French geometrical style inspired by Versailles. Later Catherine, sharing her century's romantic leanings, altered this. She wrote to Voltaire "I now passionately love the English style of garden, the curving lines, the gentle slopes, the ponds in the shape of lakes"...*

construction, signalized by the Empress Anne's building of the Winter Palace.

Elizabeth's unrestrained love of amusement laid its imprint on what may be considered the second phase in the integration of Petersburg. The city added the attributes of an imperial residence to its commercial, maritime, and military establishments.

Under Catherine the Great the capital was given its definitive character as a centre of government, transcending its use as a port, military outpost, or imperial seat. The centre was devoted to government offices and ministries, and new palaces were erected primarily in the suburbs.

In spite of the disparate sources of the new architecture a fusion was finally effected between the foreign architects and their Russian environment that established a characteristically Russian monumental style, partly because of the increasing familiarity of

Russians with foreign countries, and even more because of the gradual melting together of specific national traditions into a more or less unitary international style, promoted by the growing influence of the European academies and of the numerous architectural publications, all of which tended toward a unification of theory and practice.

Perhaps the primary unifying factor was the revival of an interest in antiquity, which proved a magnet for the most widely differing political and social tendencies. The excavations of Herculaneum and Pompeii, accompanied by the assumption of the superiority of classical art that became fashionable, established a concert of opinion unknown since the Middle Ages. A supranational point of view came to be accepted as a matter of course; the similarities between contemporary public buildings in Russia, England and

America are striking. Since symbols are inherently plastic, American republicanism, English aristocratic romanticism and Russian absolutism could derive equal inspiration from the admiration of the rediscovered beauties of the classical world.

Though the "merry Tsarina" Elizabeth's tastes were quite different from Catherine the Great's, she left her far more to build on than is generally recognized. Elizabeth's favorite architect, Count Bartolommeo Rastrelli (1700-1771), was the son of an Italian sculptor (the title was papal) who had come to Russia in 1715 with Le Blond. During the formative years of St. Petersburg he showed such talent that he was sent abroad to study, once to Paris, where he worked under Robert de Cotte, and the second time on a lengthy visit to Saxony, Bohemia, Austria, and Italy. Empress Anne had been the first to recognize his gifts : in 1752 she commissioned him to rebuild the Winter Palace designed by Tressini and another Italian architect, Niccoló Michetti.

But it was under Elizabeth that Rastrelli established his authority. He not only designed the major government buildings for twenty years, but acted as general supervisor of all architectural construction in the country. Since the younger generation gradually came under his sway his talents became embedded in the mid-century Russian style.

Both in the magnificent Summer Palace (torn down at the end of the century) and in the Anichkov Palace (extensively rebuilt) as well as in a variety of other palaces, churches and town houses for the nobility, Rastrelli demonstrated eclecticism at its best; while not wholly derivative, nor on the other completely untraditional, his work combined the best elements of a variety of styles in something that somehow looked Russian. In his churches especially he went beyond Peter the Great's tastes to a recollection of the older Orthodox style; in his Cathedral of St. Andrew in Kiev and the Smolny Convent in Petersburg—ultimately to become the seat of the Soviet of Workers' Deputies—he achieved an extraordinary combination of spontaneity and sensitivity of balance. These buildings are considered to be rococo in the broadest sense: they manifest a highly personal attitude toward the baroque, infused with a wordly lightheartedness.

The Catherine Palace in Tsarskoye Selo and the Winter Palace in St. Petersburg, which Rastrelli reconstructed, were the chief imperial palaces; they were the last great works he undertook for Elizabeth, and they gave formal expression to the symbolism embodied in the residences of the autocracy.

Rastrelli's achievement may be summed up as the creation of a Russian baroque that was both consistent and distinguished by its scale, its use of colors, and its protean lushness of contrivance. It had a peculiarly theatrical quality that made it a bridge between the life of spectacle, exemplified in Elizabeth's passion for masquerade balls, and the grandeur of official institutions.

During the last fifteen years of her reign, Catherine the Great had a Scottish architect with Jacobite convictions, Charles Cameron (c. 1740-1812/20), do considerable work at Tsarskoye Selo. He had lived in Rome, and brought with him a love of antiquity and a feeling for Palladian style. He built intimate but sumptuous apartments for the Empress out of such exotic materials as malachite, agate, colored marbles, moulded glass and Wedgwood medallions. Above, sketch for Cameron's Gallery *attached to the palace, with open and closed galleries supported by pillars. On the left of the Gallery, the* Agate Pavilion.

Below, Cameron's Agate Pavilion: *a diminutive gem in the Greco-Roman manner with pillared façade and a central rotunda, and set-in stuccoed medallions. It was connected to the Gallery by a sloping ramp so the ageing Empress would not be tired by stairs. The inside, still intact has a main marble room, smaller rooms with domed ceilings, and agate columns, encrustations of lapis lazuli, porphyry, mother-of-pearl and malachite.*

Catherine's accession put an abrupt end to Rastrelli's influence: perhaps partly because of her contempt for Elizabeth, Catherine did her best during the 1760s to obliterate in one way or another the rococo inherited from her aunt.

a distinction between public life and private. In ancient Muscovy this would have been unthinkable, and it was quite alien to the interests of Peter the Great and Elizabeth, but since Catherine was, after all, thoroughly European, it was natural for her to carry on a

Rinaldi, an Italian, and Bazhenov, a Russian. These three may be taken as a transition between the baroque and the later classical influence generally associated with Catherine; each was responsible for at least one major building that while baroque in design or

The green dining room at Tsarskoye Selo, *by Charles Cameron, an early example of his work for Catherine the Great. Cameron used moulded neo-classic plaster reliefs of figures, pilasters and garlands.*

Full of ideas, her own and others', and set on making Russia fittingly European in order to deserve the admiration of her foreign friends, Catherine introduced a novel point of view that stimulated a branching out of the revival of classical architecture in two different directions. For the first time in Russian history a sovereign made

◄ Catherine the Great *towards the end of her life, in the park of Tsarskoye Selo near St. Petersburg. The original palace had been built by Peter the Great for his wife. Her daughter Empress Elizabeth had it enlarged by Rastrelli, who planned the extended façade and the gardens with its pavilions. Catherine had the park filled with obelisks and monuments commemorating everything from victories to her favorite dogs. Engraving by Borovikovski.*

private life while establishing the external symbols of an imperial apparatus.

Thus two types of buildings came into vogue during her reign: public buildings of unprecedented scope, and dwellings for private, though of course regal use. An intermediate category might be considered to be those buildings erected for her lovers or buildings she inspired the wealthier nobility to undertake. As Empress, Catherine was powerful enough to indulge a desire for privacy, while the greater nobility, who owned vast estates and troops of serfs, had to be content with indulging an addiction to conspicuous magnificence.

After turning away abruptly from Elizabeth's fancies, Catherine spent the first two decades of her reign in stimulating innovation through the work of three architects: Velten, a German,

elevation marked a definite shift toward the classical in detail.

Catherine also made use of a talented Frenchman, Vallin de la Mothe, who was summoned to Russia in 1759 and made a professor in the newly established Academy of Fine Arts in Moscow. Catherine, who must have been impressed by the Academy, commissioned De la Mothe to build the first Hermitage as a private residence for her to retire to from the wind-swept splendors of the Winter Palace. De la Mothe made a skilful graft of a characteristic annex of his own onto Rastrelli's ornate structure. He also gave St. Petersburg its Markets (Gostinny Dvor) on the Nevsky Prospect.

It is in the third and last phase of Catherine's patronage of architecture that the character of St. Petersburg, and thus of so much of Eighteenth Century Russian architecture, was consummated: classicism, in the version of a fusion of ancient Roman architecture and the revival of Palladio, the Six-

Cameron, a Scottish Jacobite, came to Russia at Catherine's invitation in 1779: he stayed on as her favorite architect until her death in 1796. There is some mystery about his antecedents in general

His style was modelled on Roman patterns as popularized by the Adams referred to above. It combined classical forms with comfort, and made flexible use of scale to provide for both intimacy

The Alexander Palace at Tsarskoye Selo *was built by Catherine the Great in 1795 for her favorite grandson, the future Alexander I. It was designed by the great Italian architect Giacomo Quarenghi (1744-1817) who built extensively in and around St. Petersburg during the last decades of Catherine's reign. The low structure of columns, the unadorned façade and the sober grandeur of proportion are typical of this architect's style. Quarenghi had left Italy early after studying Greek temples and Palladio's work, and spent the rest of his life in Russia. Below: Drawings by Quarenghi for the Alexander Palace. The palace was a favorite residence of the last Tsar, Nicholas II, who left from here for deportation and death in Siberia. From Quarenghi: "Fabriche e Disegni illustrate", Milan, 1820.*

teenth Century master, carried the day.

This classical efflorescence under Catherine, who had a weakness for the mere activity of building as well as for ancient Rome, was executed by another trio of gifted architects: the Scotsman Cameron, the Italian Quarenghi, and the Russian Starov.

Starov's most distinguished work was perhaps his design for the Tauride Palace Catherine gave her lover Potyomkin; it was remodelled again and again, and ultimately became the seat of government during the 1917 revolution. Its splendid colonnade became a favorite object of imitation in numerous palaces and private houses. Indeed, it infected all Russia: the aristocratic islets scattered throughout the countryside began sprouting manors based on Starov's imitation of patrician Roman architecture. They somehow blended intimately with the birch-copses and rolling hills of the Russian woodlands and plains.

and the circumstances of his arrival in Russia in particular. He was known for his admiration of classical art and of Palladio, as well as for his interest in eastern Europe. He may have had a fancy for Russia because of the likelihood of his being regarded in England as a rival of the famous Adam brothers; also, on the continent his being a Jacobite would not be a disadvantage.

Cameron's talent, formed by a study of Palladio, had been refined by the French architect Charles-Louis Clérisseau, another foreigner Catherine liked.

and austere dignity as required. It also displayed a novel opulence in accordance with Catherine's taste for luxurious materials, in contrast with the old St. Petersburg custom of using brick and plaster. Cameron was particularly fond of the exotic; he specialized in intricate ornamentation and a subtle use of color, in contrast with the strong primary colors characteristic of Tsarskoye Selo under Elizabeth.

By carrying on the tradition of the Adam brothers Cameron was important as a link in the preparation of the style that came to fruition under Catherine's grandson Alexander I. More immediately, his influence is visible in the "Pantheon" of the Tauride Palace. His talent was characteristically express-

elements that made Catherine continually refer to his work as "charming". His first commission, the English Palace, which was to remain typical, mingled a classical quality, a Palladian design,

Rembrandt, and many others. The Hermitage collection had been based on the acquisition of a small number of valuable collections, notably those of Baron de Thiers, Sir Robert Walpole,

ed in Tsarskoye Selo and Pavlovsk, indissolubly associated with him, and also in the provinces, in Baturin, etc.

Giacomo Quarenghi arrived in Russia only about a year after Cameron. He was perhaps the most distinguished

and Russian dimensions in a characteristic manner.

Quarenghi's talent extended beyond the buildings he designed: he was used as an adviser to such an extent that he influenced the last twenty years of the

and Count Heinrich Brühl, but it was soon substantially increased. By the end of the century St. Petersburg had become one of the major art centres in Europe.

Catherine dutifully devoted herself to music too, in spite of her being prac-

architect of Catherine's reign as well as one of the most prominent architects of the later Eighteenth Century. Catherine, apparently displeased—rather unaccountably—with most of her architects except Cameron, had asked a friend, Grimm, to send her "two good architects, Italian by nationality and skilled at their trade". The two were Trombara and Quarenghi.

Quarenghi remained classical without ever becoming merely archeological, and majestic while retaining human dimensions. It was this deft combination of

Eighteenth Century more than any other architect in Russia, though during the confusion of Catherine's son Paul's reign he was reduced to designing barracks and riding-halls.

Catherine's lavish spending on public buildings, private palaces and churches, emulated by her favorites and the wealthier nobles, established the huge art collections Russia was to become famous for. De la Mothe's Hermitage sheltered a vast collection of cameos, statues, drawings and paintings by Raphael, Murillo, Poussin, Van Dyck,

Pages 136-137

Russian bath, *from an album published in Paris in 1812-1813 by two French writers, Count Charles de Rechberg and G.B. Depping, called "The peoples of Russia, or description of the customs, habits, costumes of the diverse nations of the Russian empire, accompanied by colored figures". The illustrations were engraved and hand-colored after drawings by Karnajef, Men and women are shown enjoying a steam bath, beating themselves with sticks and cooling off with vats of cold water.*

tically tone-deaf; she seemed to like the opera, Paisiello, who conducted his own works at the Hermitage, the theatre, and the lighter forms of music. But no native Russian composer worth mentioning appeared until the Nineteenth Century.

Socially speaking Russian society, that is, the tiny upper-class elite accessible to European influences, was flooded by secular music from the West, both instrumental and vocal. It became fashionable to use music for entertainment of all kinds, banquets, balls, performances, etc. The court was imitated by wealthy squires who organized orchestras and choirs among their serfs. The Italian Opera came to Petersburg in 1835, and gave rise to a few only moderately successful attempts to write operas in the Italian manner.

In the continuing blight that afflicted Russian literature throughout the Seventeenth Century, leaving scarcely any names worth reminding the unpedantic of, there were nevertheless two figures whose influence was disproportionate; they may be thought of as the precursors of the intelligentsia that was to play such an important role in Russian life.

Alexander Radishchev (1749-1802), who had come under the influence of French philosophy at the University of Leipzig before becoming a deceptively demure civil servant in Russia, wrote a bitter and effective castigation of serfdom in *A Journey from St. Petersburg to Moscow*, modeled on Lawrence Sterne's *Sentimental Journey*. It attacked both bureaucratic incompetence and even more importantly the very principle of monarchical absolutism. Slipping past the censorship in 1790, it was shown to Catherine, who was consumed by rage: Radishchev was sentenced to death, but finally exiled to Eastern Siberia for ten years. His book scarcely deserves any literary attention; it is altogether rhetorical and despite its fury is perhaps no more than an exercise on a set theme: but the factual background and its free and extravagant expression of the stimulus of the French Revolution, which was to have such a sweeping effect on Russian intellectual life, were to make the later intelligentsia consider Radishchev one of its first martyrs and spokesmen.

He was released by Catherine's son Paul in 1797, rehabilitated by Alexander I in 1801 and taken back into the Civil Service. But he seems to have become a melancholic in exile; he committed suicide the following year.

Nicholas Novikov (1744-1818) became the leader of Russian Freemasonry, which had been introduced into Russia about 1730 and had considerable success among the upper classes; it was to remain an influence of varying importance for generations. Novikov became a figure in publishing, which because of Catherine's mistrust of Freemasonry and his acquisition of a huge following undid him: he was sentenced in 1792 to fifteen years in the Schlüsselburg Fortress, only to be pardoned like Radishchev by Emperor Paul, when already broken in health and spirit.

These are only two examples of the infiltration of new ideas that marked the life of the Russian upper classes during the second half of the Eighteenth Century. These ideas, though confined to the tiny social elite, generated an intense fermentation. But just because the upper classes adopted French language, thought, and various exotic theories, the gulf between them and their totally ignorant serfs was made even wider. The divergence grew progressively with the succeeding generations as education, while encompassing more and more people in the upper strata, failed to penetrate any further. It was to have a decisive effect on the intelligentsia that developed during the Nineteenth Century, and on the character of the 1917 revolution.

The Modernization of Tsarism

The Great Theatre *(Bolshoi) of Saint Petersburg, lithograph by Gabriel Lory from an album published in 1799 in Russia under Paul I. The theatre was built by a French architect, Thomas de Thomon (1754-1813), in the French "Greek revival" style. It closely resembles the Odéon Théâtre in Paris. It was destroyed by fire in 1813.*

For a generation following Catherine's death nothing changed much in Russian society, though during the reign of her grandson, Alexander I, Russia broadened the scope of her influence from mere territorial expansion in Eastern Europe and Asia and began to exercise an important, indeed in many ways decisive influence on all continental questions, both during and after the immense agitation of the Napoleonic wars. Nevertheless things had been changing behind the smooth and lustrous façade of the Empire. An awareness of the shortcomings of absolutism began to affect even the sovereigns.

In a preamble he wrote for a plan of constitutional reform in the beginning of the Nineteenth Century, Speransky, one of Russia's few imaginative statesmen, wrote that there were only two classes in Russia: "the slaves of the autocrat and the slaves of the landowners. The former are free merely by comparison with the latter; in actual fact there are no free men in Russia except beggars and philosophers. The relationship between these two classes

of slaves destroys the energy of the Russian people."

This thought had been expressed before, but it was now put into words by one of the Tsar's ministers. Speransky was ultimately undone by the clarity of his insight into the thorny tangle of Russia's problems, but the cleavage between illusion and fact was at last becoming unmistakable even to the topmost stratum of officialdom.

Yet externally all would have seemed well. Though Alexander came to the throne in a way that had become rather banal, that is, through his father's murder—which he seems to have connived at—there was no question of his own legitimacy. Full of the French philosophy and enlightenment that had made Catherine's intelligent conversation such an ornament of her salons, he had imbibed the most grandiose ideas wholesale from a Swiss tutor, La Harpe.

His father, Paul I (1796-1801) after waiting with growing bitterness in the antechambers of the power wielded by his mother Catherine, ascended the

throne at the age of 43, to rule a mere five years until his personality, German-trained rigidity, and above all the drillmaster's discipline he wished to apply to the nobility as well as to the people at large, left him dangling in a vacuum, exposed to the rancor incurred by his narrow view of the nobility's privileges.

Paul I had no intention of undertaking anything like a radical solution of the peasant question, though he seems to have thought of alleviating the peasants' burdens, but he had reverted to the eccentric view that the aristocracy was supposed to serve as well as be served. Without repealing the 1785 Charter of the Nobility, he reinstated service, especially military service, for every nobleman, and moreover laid a tax on their estates. Even more annoyingly, and symptomatic of his drillmaster's attitude, he regarded any nobleman convicted of a crime as having forfeited his noble title, thus laying himself open to the corporal punishment the nobility was theoretically immune to. Under his reign the loss of a noble title, rare under Catherine, became much more common; once again the nobility was bound to feel a certain insecurity in its relations with the sovereign. By adopting the same disciplinarian attitude toward the officers' corps, and a genuinely paternal attitude toward private soldiers, as well as insisting on the fulfillment of all forms of discipline, including court etiquette, Paul gradually made himself so unpopular that his assassination created no ripple of resentment in any responsible group. Like his father before him, he had been guided too exclusively by an abstract view of his absolutist power, disregarding the practical consideration that even abstract views must be sustained by some vested interest.

In fact, regardless of his theories, which revolved around the institution of a rule of law, Paul's political regime became more and more arbitrary. His hatred of republican France, one of the few tastes he shared with his deceased mother, made him heighten the oppressiveness of his regime after he declared war on France. Foreign books, newspapers, and even music were forbidden; foreign travel was prohibited; the censorship became even more severe, and was extended even to private correspondence; functionaries were often sacked, and sometimes deported and degraded as well. This social program, so to speak, was further accentuated by Paul's numerous personal eccentricities, and in 1801, when he was murdered in his bedchamber through a plot undoubtedly launched by three of his intimates, with Alexander's consent, there was not the slightest opposition, but in fact a great deal of rejoicing. It was the last palace revolution in Russian history.

Born in 1777, Alexander I was brought up away from his parents, under Catherine's direct supervision. One of his most characteristic traits, an ambiguously sphinx-like charm of manner, was due doubtless to his early training: his formal schooling was ended when he was only seventeen, and his Swiss teacher, La Harpe, was a fervent revolutionary in the fashion of his time, full of French radical ideas yet willing to trim his sail to the wind of autocracy when it suited him. Alexander was brought up in two entirely conflicting atmospheres, the

rhetorical liberalism of Catherine's court on the one hand, and his father's Prussian entourage in Gatchina, where he was often allowed to visit toward the end of Catherine's reign. In any event Alexander, doubtless by having learned at an early age to navigate skilfully between two conflicting winds, exemplified throughout his life the two attitudes taught him as a youth: liberalism in rhetoric and devotion in fact to the barrack-room regimentation identified with his father. It may have been the need he felt to plaster over the basic difference in these points of view that led to his charm of manner, which was successful with almost everyone and which in combination with his personal appearance—he was tall, fair, handsome, and limped a little, from a horseback fall while young—lent him a peculiar aura of attractiveness.

Alexander's character, indeed, embodied the same contrast as his grandmother Catherine's: extravagant lipservice to the ideals of the French education they had been nurtured on, and in practical affairs an iron hand. It is this basic contrast that may underly Alexander I's reputation as the "Sphinx" and the "enigmatic Tsar".

Pages 142-143

View of the solemn celebration at Saint Petersburg *given by Alexander I on May 12, 1803 to commemorate the foundation of this city by Peter the Great a century before. This color engraving by the Swiss artist Gabriel Lory, published in 1804, shows the crowd flowing from the Senate Square and past the equestrian monument erected to Peter by Catherine the Great.*

Paul I, *Tsar from 1796 to 1801, portrait by Argunov. Catherine's son, whom she had systematically kept away from affairs of state, ruled only four years. Unbalanced and erratic, with a passion for military procedures, he antagonized the nobility and increased the already rigid censorhip. His son Alexander was a party to the plot to dethrone him; the conspirators strangled Paul with an officer's scarf.*

Vue de la fête solemnelle à St. Petersbourg donnée

jour de l'Anniversaire du siecle de la fondation de cette ville à l'honneur de son fondateur Pierre I.er sur l

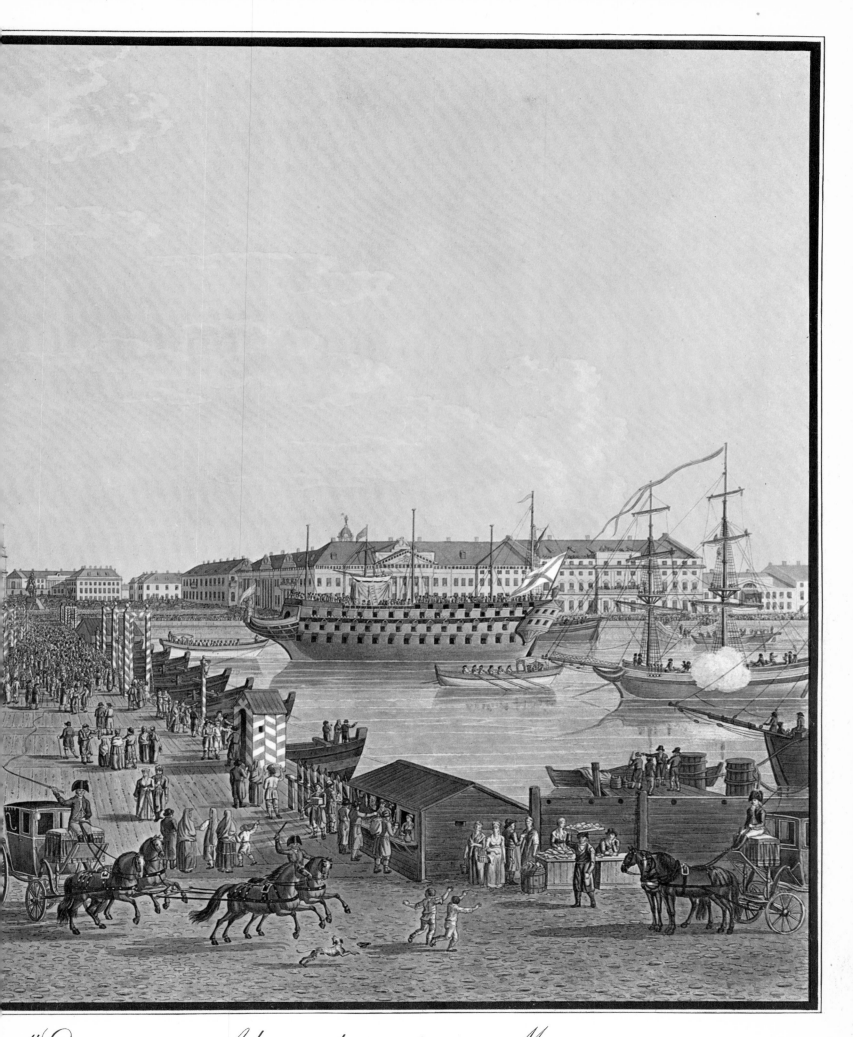

l'Empereur Alexandre I. le 12. Mai 1803.

du Senat vis-à-vis du monument érigé à ce Souverain par l'Impératrice Catherine II.

It is significant that the most powerful personality associated with Alexander I was Arakcheyev (1769-1834) whose name is a synonym in Russian for administrative ruthlessness. Arakcheyev's ascendency coincided with that of the liberal Speransky, a coincidence that must be taken as a tribute to Alexander's simultaneously adroit and strong-willed manœuvring, since both Speransky and Arakcheyev were disliked by court and bureaucratic circles. For that matter, despite great personal differences, the universally charming Alexander and the universally loathed Arakcheyev had a great deal in common: they were both obsessed by the sort of orderliness and external symmetry achieved by close-order regimental drilling, an obsession that underlay a common religiosity.

Alexander's mysticism may have been responsible for a growing detachment from practical affairs that began around 1812. It was made up of many elements focussed on the study of the Bible, which in its turn of course was interpreted in terms of Alexander's highly capricious mixture of personal whims that combined Swedenborg, the Quakers, the Freemasons, Russian dissenters, individual visionaries, etc.

Despite Alexander's public manner of supple charm, there can be no doubt of his firm, though capricious willpower. In foreign policy, for instance, the alliance he contracted with Bonaparte in 1807, and the Russian leadership in the anti-Napoleonic coalition of 1813-1815, which was crowned by Waterloo and the Russian entry into Paris, and especially his Holy Alliance itself, were actually pushed through against domestic opposition.

Since the condition of the peasants remained unchanged throughout Alexander's reign, the mutinousness endemic in Russian life kept breaking out: when

Alexander I, *Tsar from 1801-1825, brought up by his grandmother Catherine the Great and a Swiss tutor, La Harpe, was gentle, charming and unstable. Vague liberal impulses marked the first years of his reign, but the last decade saw a return to reaction and bigotry. Engraving by Theodore Wright of a portrait by G. Dawe.*

The French Ambassador at St. Petersburg, Count de La Ferronays, summed it up in 1820: "He talks of the rights of man, of those of peoples, and of the duties of a monarch as the disciple of a philosopher can and should talk, but at the same time he enforces his most arbitrary wishes with a greater despotism and ruthlessness than Peter the Great."

Speransky's rapid rise may be explained by his ability to grasp the general principles involved in Alexander's essentially declamatory view of affairs, while his even more abrupt

decline was due to exactly the same thing. The moment Speransky approached the nub of the conclusions liberal principles inevitably led to in the Russia of his time, the very exactitude in their realization inevitably dispelled the mysterious enchantment of gushing verbiage and left Alexander confronted by chill reality.

Elizabeth, *Princess of Baden, wife of Alexander I. Their children died in infancy. The couple lived apart much of the time. Engraving of a portrait by Monier.*

Moscow in flames after the entry of Napoleon's forces September 11, 1812, *as "drawn on the spot" by an English artist, John Vedramini. The French Emperor entered the Kremlin September 14 and remained for a month, and quartered his horses in the Dormition Cathedral. The city had been abandoned by most of the inhabitants and was aflame. It has been said that the Russians set it on fire themselves to stir native patriotism; in any case the arson was probably more accidental than due to the French.*

Napoleon invaded Russia in 1812 rumors sprang up as usual about the imminent liberation of the serfs, a minority of them believing that Napoleon would free them, while most thought the Tsar would reward them for fighting off the invaders. Despite Napoleon's generally liberal influence throughout Central Europe he seems never even to have considered improving his military position by emancipating the serfs: like Hitler more than a century later he relied on exclusively military factors.

Alexander's death created a slight mystery, well in keeping with his enigmatic character: a legend sprang up to the effect that he had not died at Taganrog on the Black Sea in 1825, but had vanished and taken up the guise of a holy monk, Theodore Kuzmich, dying at last in Siberia in 1864. Though this seems to be no more than a legend there are so many convincing details about it that many knowledgeable people have believed it, including Tolstoy, who wrote an affecting story about it that was published posthumously.

It was during Alexander I's reign that Russia for the first time achieved a position of international primacy, as a result of her decisive role in the undoing of Napoleon. Throughout the Napoleonic epoch and its aftermath, which was dominated by the unraveling of Napoleon's empire, Russia, despite her sustained and savage defeats, occupied a focal position by virtue of the shifting imbalances of the remainder of the continent. Alexander's public gifts played a great role and gave him the nickname of the Blessed. During his reign extensive new territories fell to the Russian crown: Finland, Bessarabia, and extensive territories in Poland and the Caucasus were added to the vast, relatively uninhabited empire; both Finland and Poland created additional centres of disaffection.

The War of 1812, which has received so much publicity from nationally-minded Russian historians as well as, more strikingly, from the immense popularity of Tolstoy's *War and Peace*, was far less important than generally thought: Napoleon's invasion lasted only six months, and it took the Grand Army a mere seven weeks to get out of the country. Indeed, the whole invasion was both preceded and followed by far more ruinous Russian invasions of a score of countries.

The Allies enter Paris, March 31, 1814. *After Napoleon was defeated, the leaders of the Coalition (Alexander of Russia, Francis of Austria, Frederick William of Prussia) and their troops entered the French capital. This German engraving shows them riding by the Porte St. Martin, causing considerable emotion among the on-lookers.*

As for the Holy Alliance, which Alexander's name is associated with, though he seems to have had sincerely idealistic or mystical ambitions for it, it never achieved the status of the "universal union" Alexander had dreamed of for it. Its influence, to some extent because of Metternich's skill in playing on Alexander's illusions, remained negative, a bulwark against revolutionary movements in Germany, Italy or Spain.

By and large the imbalance of Russian society remained the same. The cities continued growing, but very slowly. Though domestic trade increased somewhat, the small and socially declassed

bourgeoisie still had no say in public affairs. Despite his growing harshness Alexander had not continued with his assassinated father's attempt to discipline the nobility as well as the rest of the country, but though still in possession of its privileges the nobility was becoming increasingly restive. Its more alert or cosmopolitan members were chafing more and more at the very principle of autocracy. The alliance between the crown and its mainstay was beginning to crack.

There were still no elementary schools at all when Alexander's reign began, practically no state-sponsored secondary schools except military academies, and

only three universities. An attempt was made to overhaul this skimpy educational system in 1803, but it collided with the same difficulties as all such previous attempts throughout the Eighteenth Century: the absence of funds, the profound mistrust of state-sponsored schools, and the dearth of teachers. The 1803 plan had pathetic results: in 1824 only some 4,465 pupils attended lower schools throughout the vast St. Petersburg region, and enrollment in secondary schools had risen from 5,600 in 1809 to 7,700 in 1825. There were only 820 students attending Moscow University in 1824, almost half the total number of students in Russia.

This was of course in sharp contrast with the private schools of the nobility, which emphasized such "useful" accomplishments as French and dancing: in 1824 there were over 2,000 students attending these private schools in the St. Petersburg region, as against the 450 in the state-sponsored secondary school and the fifty-one in the University of St. Petersburg.

The utter disproportion between the ideas of the "enlightened" summit of society and the material institutions of Russia, an imbalance that characterized Alexander's reign as much as Catherine's, remained a source of growing tension that was to be pregnant with consequence. Western liberal and revolutionary ideas had played a great role in the drawing-room talk under Catherine, but toward the second decade of the Nineteenth Century they finally began to acquire flesh and blood. While the bulk of the nobility—that is, those settled on and living off their own estates—were inherently conservative for fear of disturbing the serfdom that was the source of their wealth, the young officers who had been floating about Western and Central Europe during the Napoleonic upheaval had been brought into close contact both with the turbulent intellectual currents released by the French revolution, and with the moral and material superiority of the Western masses in contrast with the Russian.

The simple fact that European peasants, however heavy their burdens, were freemen who were not subject to corporal punishment, was an arresting example of the abyss that separated Russia from the West even in a period of general turmoil and breakdown. The contrast between the backwardness of the Russian masses and the military prowess of the Russian armies had a stimulating effect,

and when these young officers got back to Russia aflame with enthusiasm for the new ideas they had encountered their renewed contact with the obscurantist regime of Arakcheyev and Alexander kindled the sparks of a political opposition.

European influence had a dual effect. The tiny minority influenced by liberal ideas was disappointed by the course of events after the settlement of the Napoleonic turmoil: the growth of the security police, the harshness of the censorship, the promotion of military colonies—a peculiarly silly idea, both oppressive and futile, that was one of Alexander's quirks—as well as the general ascendancy of religiosity, both mystical and orthodox, in the Tsar's entourage, all gave the ardent liberal aristocrats a feeling of suffocation. In addition, the actual evolution of Alexander's Holy Alliance into an agency for the suppression of the liberty and national independence he had so often praised, was inherently unpopular: Russian liberals found it both pointless and reprehensible for Russian troops to intervene in Spain and Italy. Contrariwise, the more radical of the liberal aristocrats were immensely stimulated by the upheavals that had become commonplace in Southern Europe, to say nothing of Central and South America.

The aristocratic opposition to the existing order coagulated in secret societies, a natural consequence of the concealment of strongly felt ideas. It was expressed solely by the most aristocratic segment of society, under the leadership of some of the greatest names in Russia. These secret societies, themselves the reflection of the great European current of thought aimed at "reaction" with parallels in the Italian *Carbonari*, the French *charbonnerie*, and the German *Tugendbund*, had a quite

specific political character: some of the aristocrats involved even accepted the assassination of the Tsar as a means to their goal. They were in sharp contrast with the somewhat dreamily humani-

Alexis Arakcheyev *(1769-1834) brutal disciplinarian, advisor first to Paul I (he succeeded Speransky) then Alexander I. All-powerful between 1810-1825, he dictated interior affairs under Paul, then supervised the hated "military colonies" under Alexander. These forced peasants to maintain the regular army and be trained themselves. Brutal punishments abounded; the subsequent uprisings were mercilessly punished. Portrait by Dawe.*

tarian Masonic Lodges that had returned to Russia under Alexander I, after a long period of suppression under Catherine the Great and Paul I.

The aristocratic mutineers had any number of reasons for their disaffection:

Pages 148-149

Military parade before the Imperial Palace *in St. Petersburg, 1815. Anon. engraving.*

◄ *Leaders of the* Decembrist conspiracy. *The Decembrist revolt, the first entirely altruistic uprising in Russian history, exploded in December 1825, as Nicholas I took over the throne. Its aristocratic protagonists had vastly differing opinions and were completely disorganized; a fiasco insued. A leader of the conspiracy was a brilliant staff officer, Paul Pestel (first on left), whose opinions—not just reforms but revolution was essential, a temporary dictatorship should precede a reorganization of society—somewhat resembled Lenin's.*

the corruption of the court, the deplorable condition of the armed forces, to which as officers they were particularly

Alexander Pushkin (1799-1837), Russia's greatest poet. He was the author of "Eugene Onegin", made into an opera by Tchaikovsky, and "Boris Godunov", set to music by Mussorgsky. His liberal friends and affiliations got him into trouble on several occasions. Twice he was banished. Suspected of being involved in the Decembrist uprisings, Nicholas personally censored every line he wrote. Pushkin had colored blood. His grandfather, an Abyssinian prince, was taken as a hostage by the Turks, then sent to Peter the Great's court as a black page. The poet's matrimonial life was stormy and led to a duel in which he was killed.

sensitive, the abysmally low salaries of government officials and the resulting corruption, the savage conditions in the packed prisons, the economic stagnation, and the staggering burden of taxation, which oppressed all strata of the population, including the nobility. Above all the condition of the peasantry particularly oppressed liberal Russians, who saw in the reformation of serfdom not merely the fulfilment of abstract considerations of compassion but the furthering of their self-interest.

The general malaise was doubtless heightened by the widespread impression made by Alexander's personal brand of liberalism. There was an inherent tendency toward action even in the vague theoretical liberalism of Eighteenth Century Russia, and Alexander's personal liking for constitutional government, and his detestation of serfdom, were taken seriously in aristocratic and military circles. For that matter something had actually been done about it: constitutions had really been given Finland and Poland, and there was perennial hope for a constitutional reform in Russia too.

In December 1825 all these factors culminated in an insurrection, the first one in Russian history that was engendered by an attitude based on principle, in contrast with the play of selfish interests. It was halted instantly.

Only a handful of people were involved in the preparations, but they were in a state of hopeless disagreement on all practical points, and for that matter were split from the very outset into wings with basically different perspec-

tives. The great aristocrats and Guards officers from Petersburg, while agreeing that representative government and the emancipation of the serfs would be good things, were entirely in favor of property rights; they actually leaned towards a constitutional monarchy, while the lesser nobles, who served in line regiments, were far more radical. Paul Pestel, for instance, a founder of the so-called Union of Salvation, was a republican: he envisaged a centralized egalitarian and democratic republic that would exclude all privileges arising out of status or wealth. He was also a Great Russian expansionist: he wanted to expell the Jews from Russia wholesale and conquer various territories still inhabited by Mongols. Prince Trubetskoy, on the other hand, thought that the dynasty could be retained by forcing it to grant a few reforms.

It was the inherent irreconcilability between these differing aims that doubtless explains the extraordinary slovenliness in the preparations for the insurrection, which in the event was a complete fiasco.

Alexander's unexpected death in November 1825 forced the conspirators to advance the date that in spite of all internal friction had been settled on. His death and some uncertainty about the succession because of the ambiguous position of his brother Constantine, who was heir-apparent, were a great opportunity for the conspirators, but all they could demonstrate was their unripeness. Trubetskoy's primary anxiety was to forestall any popular intervention; he believed that the insurrection had to be

The Virgin of Kazan Cathedral, Saint Petersburg, *an 1812 impression of city life. The new cathedral had been built (1801-1811) by Emperor Paul in honor of a miraculous ikon. Originally Quarenghi made the plans, but Paul decided it must be an entirely Russian affair and accepted Count Stroganov's suggestion to give the work to Andrei N. Voronikhin. Voronikhin had been a serf on the Stroganov estate; his masters recognized his talents, attended to his education and sent him on a tour to Europe. The design for the cathedral shows the influence of Saint Peter's in Rome and of Bernini in its handling of the colonnade.*

kept strictly within the bounds of an action by the armed forces under the closest possible control of their officers. What he actually wanted was an orderly upheaval. But the membership of the secret societies involved was minute,

◄ *The erection of the* Alexander Column *in the Winter Palace Square, Saint Petersburg, 1829. This monument, the largest granite monolith in the world, was to outshine the memorial monuments of Paris and Rome. Its transportation from the Lake Ladoga stone quarries and its erection on the Square were triumphs of engineering, but the results were more impressive for size than beauty. The column was designed by a French draughtsman, R. de Montferrand, who also raised the giant bell in the Moscow Kremlin.*

and more importantly consisted of almost nothing but junior officers. It was obvious that their effect on the rank-and-file, unaware of the broader implications of the insurrection, would be less effective than the authority of their superiors. There was no question of any solidarity, to use a modern term, between the junior officers and the soldiery.

The fiasco was grotesque: Trubetskoy simply vanished from the Senate square, where the actual seizure of power was to take place, and Prince Eugene Obolensky, who took charge, had no idea what orders to give. Everyone stood around doing nothing at all, while government troops under the personal command of Nicholas, who had succeeded his brother Alexander, thronged into the square and the adjacent streets. The insurgents,

though listless and unled, refused to surrender, and since their resistance was encouraged by a great many civilians who mingled with them and occasionally attacked the government troops with stones and logs, Nicholas decided on firmer action to forestall any transformation of the army mutiny into a popular rebellion. A few field guns were brought up; after the third volley the insurgents were routed. By the time darkness set in the Senate square was cleared except for seventy or eighty corpses, including some civilians.

Nicholas also supervised the commission of enquiry, demonstrating a love for interrogation that was one of his traits. Most of the insurgent leaders hurried to surrender, and with the exception of Pestel and a few others made a most embarrassing display of extra-

vagant remorse. In pouring out their hearts they freely implicated quite innocent people; of the almost six hundred people interrogated one hundred and twenty-one were finally tried, in such a way that some of them did not realize their hearing had been before an actual court. Five of them were sentenced to death, including Pestel, while more than a hundred were deported to prison in Siberia.

The Decembrist revolt was futile because on the one hand the people were utterly uninvolved, with nothing between the peasantry and the aristocracy-bureaucracy to provide the pseudo-revolt with any social support, while on the other hand it could not have been successful in the manner of the traditional palace revolutions because its makers were indifferent to such considerations.

They tried to ideologize and socialize a mutiny precisely in an ambiance that simply had no place for it. They were blinded by a form of sentimental confusion about what they "represented": fundamentally they represented only themselves, but since their education had projected them beyond the sphere of vulgar egotistic or cliquish ambitions, and provided them with an arsenal of 'ideas', they failed to see through these ideas to the brute fact that socially they were merely in a void. They were in effect championing a nation that had never heard of them, or could have.

Their sincere desire to restrain the autocracy foundered on their reluctance to give up their own social primacy, which was dependent on the service of the peasantry they were consequently afraid to risk arousing. Thus, however brilliant the individuals among these aristocratic officers, their isolated position was doubtless responsible for their most characteristic collective trait: indecisiveness.

On the other hand, of course, it is only too easy to produce such *post facto* generalizations: in fact, if the insurgents had not been so slack, and had been more practical in concrete preparations, the December enterprise might have produced an altogether different result. Aside from Nicholas's personal unpopularity, the sympathies of a whole section of the population were obviously with the movement. This is doubtless one of those cases in which an inherently practicable scheme was wrecked by its executors.

But despite the lackadaisical, inept and to some extent cowardly character of the Decembrist enterprise, it became a symbol for future generations of dissident Russians. It is true that the

◀ Empress Alexandra Feodorovna, *daughter of Frederick William the III of Prussia, wife of Nicholas I. Lithograph by Maurin of a painting by Christina Robertson.*

crushing of the insurrection itself for a time pulverized Russian liberal thought; since with rare exceptions the Decembrists had no desire to uproot the existing order, they had no motive in sustaining a revolutionary attitude the regime now intransigeantly opposed. Most of the former liberals melted back into their milieu: some members of the secret

Nicholas I with his wife and son in a boat. *Nicholas (ruled from 1825-1855), a military martinet, introduced Tsarism in the Prussian manner. His reign started amidst the violence of the Decembrist conspiracy, which sought to put his elder brother Constantine on the throne. Under Nicholas the police state took over. Fittingly, this disciplinarian always wore a military uniform, even when on a pleasure outing with his family.*

societies who had escaped Siberia covered themselves with distinction in the service of Nicholas; the exceptions whose personal convictions made such surrender impossible eased themselves into what was to become the "underground."

The fact is that while the secret societies were eliminated as a result of the Decembrist failure, the conditions that had spawned them continued; this kept alive the ideals they had professed. These ideals were a negative reflection of the various imbalances in Russia, and their survival was ensured by the failure of the regime to right them.

Perhaps one of the chief effects of the Decembrist mutiny was its reinforcement of the repressive party in court

circles. The dilemma facing authority in a situation of disaffection may be said to be universal: it is bound to turn either toward mollification and compromise, or toward repression.

Nicholas, who had a drillmaster's mind trained on Prussian discipline like his predecessors, was profoundly moved by the abortive mutiny. It remained a constant preoccupation of his, all the more so because it had involved the Guards, the flower of the Army he regarded as the bulwark of the autocracy. He showed a keen interest in the Decembrists he had exiled to Siberia; even more, he was far from blind to the cause of their rebelliousness. Indeed, Nicholas was quite aware throughout his life of the necessity of some kind of reform, even though nothing was ever attempted during his reign. His attitude toward the master institution, serfdom, which was doubtless the source of the suppurating wound in Russian society, sums up the contradictoriness and paralysis inherent in this dilemma: "There is no doubt that in its present form serfdom is a flagrant

Emperor Nicholas I and the Empress reviewing cavalry troops. *Nicholas wanted to imprint a military aspect on every possible branch of his domain. He himself invented uniforms to be worn by everyone from bureaucrats to students. Engraving by the French artist Auguste Raffet for a famous book by Count Demidov "Travels in Southern Russia and the Crimea".*

evil everyone is aware of, yet to attempt to remedy it now would be, of course, an evil still more disastrous," he said at a State Council meeting in March 1842.

It was doubtless the awareness of the deep-rootedness of serfdom, as well as of its inherent perniciousness, that in fact paralyzed Nicholas's will-power and intelligence, and throughout his reign gave Russia a look of frozen immobility —an immobility that as events were soon to show was highly deceptive.

The twenty-year reign of Nicholas I saw absolutism at its apogee. He had received a rather good education, at any rate in languages, though like Alexander's it ended at 17, but he showed no interest in such things as political economy, government, etc.—subjects he sneered at as "abstractions." His chief interest was warfare, particularly military engineering. Nicholas gave the classical principle of Russian autocracy a slight twist of his own by emphasizing dynastic

and religious elements, the supreme virtue of duty and discipline, and national tradition. His view of the state was essentially that of a smoothly running regiment, based on a detailed hierarchy, rigid specification of duties, and the unquestionable authority of the head. This splendidly lucid outlook was summed up by his Minister of Education, Uvarov, in a formula that was to become famous: "Orthodoxy, autocracy, and nationality," though there is reason to believe the slightly ambiguous final word of the formula was actually a euphemism substituted out of tact for the more downright—and accurate—word "serfdom."

"Nationality" meant nothing definite at all: it was generally used so as to convey the notion of "official patriotism", etc., which is how Uvarov's slogan is generally referred to in Russian literature. Uvarov's obsequious inflation of Russia's past and present was parti-

cularly engaging because he himself had never read a Russian book in his life, and was at home only in French and German.

The application of this slogan to education implied the preservation of the existing order via the elimination of subversive, i. e., liberal influences. The goal of the authorities was to discourage students from studying anything beyond their social station and to concentrate in the government's hands complete control of all intellectual life, but they were inevitably disappointed. In fact Nicholas's regime somehow coincided with one of the greatest bursts of literacy as well as intellectual activity: not only were some of the greatest Russian literary masterpieces produced, but the seeds of almost the whole of the subsequent cultural development were contained in the outburst of creativity that took place in the intellectual vanguard, constricted though it was.

Nicholas had close ties to the Hohenzollerns: he had married King Frederick William III's daughter, sister of the future King Frederick William IV, at the age of 23 and had seven children by her. He admired his father-in-law enormously, especially since Prussian monarchism seemed ideal to him. It was during his reign that Russia, which had always aped one European country or another, definitely turned her face toward Germany. In Peter the Great's time advanced Russians chiefly admired technique and the economic life as exemplified by Holland, Germany and Sweden; France had been the magnet for the elegant thinkers of the Eighteenth Century, and England had a short period of tutorship after 1815, when the utilitarians, the Byronic movement, and the economists were looked up to. During Nicholas's reign once again Germany became on the one hand a lodestone for the official classes, because of her absolutism and bureaucratic organization, while at the other pole the intellectuals looked to her for philosophy and rounded *Weltanschauungen.*

There was a wholesale absorption of German stock into the upper classes and the ruling dynasty itself. Germans had first become prominent in Russia because of Peter's personal taste for ability and accuracy, and in mass terms through his Baltic acquisitions, which had a broad upper segment of German landowners and townspeople. The ruling dynasty itself was completely submerged in German blood as a result of the union of Catherine the Great, a German princess, with Peter III, the son of Peter the Great's daughter Anne and of the Duke of Holstein-Gottorp. It is curious to reflect that every Russian sovereign since Catherine the Great married a German, so that even if her son Paul was not Peter III's son but was, as is likely, the son of a lover of hers called Saltykov, the amount of Russian blood to be attributed to any Romanov after Catherine is infinitesimal. If Paul was Peter III's son, the blood of Nicholas II, the last Romanov sovereign, was only one-128th-part Russian.

Thus German influence had an altogether sweeping effect on both Russian officialdom and the Russian intelligentsia. Because of the force of ideas it was of course to be much more far-reaching in the intellectual sphere and ultimately, through the influence of Marxism and kindred philosophies, of cardinal consequence in Russian history.

Nicholas's political rigidity, his fear of popular discontent and of the principle of national self-determination that was making such headway in Europe during the Nineteenth Century, and his natural concern with the interests of the landed aristocracy, made reform at home impossible. It also spurred him on to an aggressive and universally irritating policy abroad. Thus, while his theoretically paternalistic regime was in fact a ramified police state, his foreign policy, though relatively successful at first, laying the foundations for the conquest of the Caucasus and making some Asiatic acquisitions while definitely enfeebling Turkey, ultimately led to the Russian catastrophe in the Crimean War of 1853-56. A major factor in the confusions that led up to this war was another reflection of Nicholas's dynastic obsessions and his lack of any conception of either abstract law or the conduct of states: he believed in the settlement of all questions by direct negotiations between heads of states. This produced a

Grand Duke Constantine, elder brother of Nicholas I. The Decembrists had wanted to put Constantine on the throne after Alexander's death. No one knew for a while which of the two brothers had been named by Alexander as his successor. After considerable confusion, sharpened by the disclosure of the projected Decembrist rising, constantine renounced his rights.

curious sort of personal diplomacy that in the Crimean calamity ended up by impairing the prestige of the regime and

Nicholas I *as seen by Auguste Raffet in an illustration for Demidov's "Travels in Southern Russia and the Crimea". The Emperor was vain and always careful about his appearance. Raffet travelled through Russia and Turkey with Count Demidov and made very exact drawings and paintings of events, people and places.*

pulverizing the myth of Russian military power.

Despite the bitterness between the throne and the landed aristocracy that had exploded in the December revolt, they were bound to each other by common interests. Nicholas I liked re-

One of the earliest war photographs ever made. Here, during the Crimean campaign *(1854), the 71st regiment of Highlanders. The sergeant on the right is a colored man.*

ferring to the aristocracy as the "mainstay of the throne", and sometimes even described himself as "the first nobleman". For their part, the bulk of the noble landowners, blinded by a narrow view of their own class interests and desperately anxious about losing their privileges—i.e., the right to exploit servile labor—were in fact solidly behind the throne and what it stood for in the way of stability.

Nicholas evidently had grave doubts about the viability of serfdom, as indicated above, but there was nothing he could make up his mind to do about it. It is true that he abandoned his policy of non-intervention between landowners and serfs in the case of the Polish provinces he annexed after crushing a Polish insurrection that took place in 1830-31, and undertook some measures designed to weaken the Polish landowners relative to their Russian serfs, but this was merely part of a general policy of russification. It had nothing to do with emancipation and amounted to a mere definition of mutual rights and duties.

The famous English nurse Florence Nightingale *(1820-1910) in a hospital at Scutari during the Crimean war. Her organization for nursing the wounded in this campaign grew into the Red Cross. Contemporary drawing by W. Simpson.*

A way out of the impasse created by serfdom would have been an improvement in farming technique, but only a small minority of the more open-minded nobles took to this. Except for some sugar refineries, most attempts to rationalize farms took place against too general a background of backwardness; they were almost uniformly fiascoes. The basic difficulty was pervasive: rationalization could only be done with capital investments, but since the only capital most of the landowners had was their serfs, any attempt to modernize technique collided with the unwillingness and ineptitude of the uneducated and traditionally-minded servile population. This interacted with the fluctuating international prices for produce and the limited capacity of the market, both foreign and domestic, which made the profitability of even a major capital investment dubious. It was this combination of circumstances that forced some of the more progressive landowners into a blanket condemnation of serfdom in and for itself as the source of evil.

But most landowners were reluctant to take such a leap into the unknown: the alternative to emancipation and technical progress that they inclined toward was squeezing the screws still further on their serfs. There was a tendency on the part of many landowners, especially where the land was rich, to extend the areas farmed by themselves directly, so that increasing numbers of serfs were forced both to pay an annual tribute and to perform services for their owners.

The fact is that both peasants and landowners were being squeezed. The position of the aristocracy was only powerful from an external point of view: though some 102,870 nobles owned about a third of the territory of Russia in 1859, the great majority of the landowners were rather impoverished. Of the above total, for instance, more than three-quarters was made up of estates of less than 100 male serfs, while those of over 500 male serfs made up only 3.6%. The landowners were heavily mortgaged; their debts kept running up, and it was quite common for them to be foreclosed. It was obviously just those proprietors who had the least capital who needed it most, and it was they who were in the worst straits.

The uneven pace of development that now began to be more and more marked in Russia was also, oddly enough, responsible at the same time for an increase in workers' wages. Industrialization, though still primitive, was progressing rapidly; the relative shortage of labor due to serfdom and the prevalence of cottage industry, which before the emancipation of the serfs could compete successfully with big industrial plants—before the widespread use of machinery simple manufacturing processes could be done just as well by craftsmen as by big enterprises—gave the workers a favorable position. The number of manufacturing workers actually more than doubled during Nicholas I's reign, from 210,000 in 1825 to 483,000 in 1855. In 1860 they numbered some 565,000. It seems likely that servile labor was actually being forced out by paid labor between 1825-1860. The situation was different in the development of mining and metallurgy, most of which enterprises were located in remote provinces. By 1860 the number of workers in mining

Cap Kerson (Chersonèse)

Landing por of the french army

A colored wash drawing by the French artist Constantin Guys (1805-1892) made during the Crimean war of a landing of the French army. Guys was sent as artist-reporter to cover the war for the English periodical "The Illustrated London News". This extremely gifted draughtsman had an adventurous character: he had previously joined Byron in Greece, then travelled in Europe and in Turkey where he made drawings of Constantinople and oriental costumes. Musée des Arts Décoratifs, Paris.

and metallurgy was about 245,000, of which hired as distinct from servile labor amounted to 30%.

By 1860 the total number of industrial workers, accordingly, came to about 800,000, or a little more than 1% of the population, with servile labor accounting for about a third of the total. This was four times as many as there had been at the beginning of the century.

Mechanization began to become a substantial factor toward the end of the 1840's, and first made itself felt in textiles, where the technical process was particularly adaptable to machinery.

As for education, it remained something for a small elite, in spite of the fact that Russian scholarship was finally launched: in the first part of his reign Nicholas had sent some gifted Russian students abroad to be trained as scholars. This created a core of professors who were personally often very distinguished, and capable of arousing the zeal of their abler students. But the actual number of students remained small: after an increase from 1,700 in 1825 to 4,600 in 1848, it declined to 3,600 in 1854, when Petersburg had only 379 and Moscow 1,061. Nicholas I, who remained hypersensitive to all signs of popular disaffection and upheaval, was reinforced in this attitude by the French revolution of 1848 and its European repercussions. In March 1848 officers of the Ministry of Education, including teachers, were forbidden to leave the country: the number of independent students was severely limited. Teaching of the constitutional law of European states, and even of philosophy, was stopped, while logic and psychology were put in the hands of theological professors to make sure they fitted in with Orthodox views.

The standards of instruction in lower schools were exceptionally debased, to say nothing of the infinitesimal number of pupils involved. Literacy among the peasants was practically unknown: a peasant child could only learn something from informal classes where quite unqualified teachers, often retired soldiers with only glimmerings of literacy themselves, would teach the rudiments of reading and writing.

Jews were under special restrictions; their number in Russian schools was very small. Out of 15,000 students enrolled in 58 high schools in 1853 only 155 were Jews, who were the target of Nicholas's special dislike. He wanted to have them completely assimilated after the elimination of their "religious fanaticism and racial exclusiveness". His anti-Jewish policy was part of an intensified persecution of all forms of Russian dissenters as well; their religious particularism was taken as a pretext to persecute them for purely political reasons. But the policy of russification failed in the case of the Jews as well as the Old Believers. What happened was that the draconian regime applied to the Jews—including compulsory army service of 25 years, prohibi-

157

tion against employing Gentiles, the dissolution of the Jewish autonomous communities, and the compulsory wearing of Jewish traditional dress—was often evaded, furnishing the police and other government officials with a splendid occasion to thrive on the intensified misery.

Foreign policy during Nicholas's reign revolved around a question that was considered to have become cardinal for Russia: the survival of the Ottoman Empire. The Russian attitude toward this question, as expressed by Nicholas with a combination of insolence and ambiguousness that exasperated the British and French, ultimately led to the Crimean War. Historians are of course fond of demonstrating the inevitability of past events; here, however, it seems likely that it was the incalculable element of personal capriciousness that led to this preposterous and futile war.

Generally speaking Nicholas seemed to believe that the maintenance of the *status quo* in Turkey was to Russia's interest, but at the same time he made no secret of his view that the collapse of the "sick man" of Europe was inevitable. Since not many people agreed with him about this, his making pacific statements while preparing to bury the Ottoman corpse was considered mere hypocrisy. Further, as a legitimist he was indifferent or hostile to the claims of the Greeks and the Balkan Slavs —he regarded them as disloyal subjects of their legitimate ruler—but at the same time he kept encroaching on the Ottoman power in Moldavia and Wallachia. This was naturally taken as another sign of deceitfulness.

Also, Nicholas's irrepressible loathing

for France made it difficult for him to secure the working-agreement he desired with the British, which was complicated still further by his congenital inability to grasp the dynamics of the British constitution, and hence of the powers of the Queen and her ministers. Of course these limitations of Nicholas's found a counterpart in Napoleon's desire for showy military triumphs, and especially in the obsessive hatred of Russia shown by Palmerston and Canning, the British Ambassador at Constantinople.

For Nicholas the Crimean War was a crushing blow: not only did it mark the checkmate of the international diplomacy he had specialized in, but the army he had been so proud of was defeated.

The Crimean defeat had, as usual, an advantage: just because Russia was so humiliated and the autocracy's shortcomings were suddenly and dramatically displayed, even conservatives were forced to face the necessity of a serious reform. A reformist mood came to a head after Nicholas's death in 1885 and the accession to the throne of his eldest son Alexander.

It is difficult to perceive the personal element in most of Alexander's behavior; like his uncle Alexander I he remains immune to psychological analysis. His practice of keeping people of irreconcilably opposed views simultaneously in office alone makes him elusive. Also, a curious streak of well-publicized sentimentality, perhaps acquired as a boy from his chief tutor Zhukovsky, an emotional humanitarian, blurs the outline of his character: during the war with Turkey in 1877-1878 he proposed

attending the wounded in person as a male nurse.

Actually, however, he was just as conservative as his father; he remained true to the autocratic traditions he had inherited by maintaining a very harsh police regime, and exiling thousands of people without trial of any kind. The traditional division of his reign into a liberal part ending with the era of Great Reforms in 1866, when the first attempt at assassinating him was made, and the reaction afterwards, is wishful thinking: haphazardly mingled "reactionary" and "liberal" elements characterized his whole reign.

General Bosquet, *Commander of the French Division of the Crimean war. He witnessed the Charge of the Light Brigade and became famous for his remark "It is splendid, but it is not war". This early war photograph shows him explaining the action, on the spot where it took place.*

The signing of the Treaty of Paris, in 1856, which ended the Crimean war. Russia had to renounce the right to have her fleet in the Black Sea and other advantages. Standing, left, is Count Walewski who presided the conference representing France. The Russian envoy, Count Orlov, is standing, right. After the first signature an electric message was sent to Napoleon III informing him, and the Emperor signaled back he would be happy to meet all the plenipotentiaries afterwards. From the English "Illustrated Family Paper" of the same year.

Alexander II is known as the "Tsar-Emancipator", the inspirer of the "Era of Great Reforms". His reign spans a general, though of course far from systematic overhauling of Russian society, in addition to a number of far-reaching changes in public life. One of the most notable of these was a sweeping reform of the judiciary in 1864, which finally, though hesitantly and imperfectly, introduced the accepted principles of Western European jurisprudence—equality of individuals before the law, the impartiality and accessibility of courts, trial by jury, public proceedings, immunity of judges to removal except for misconduct in office, etc. These new measures gradually eliminated or softened many of the abuses that had given Russian courts a well-deserved reputation for corruption and inequity, though against the background of Russian society as a whole the effects of the judicial reform were superficial.

But of course the most far-reaching reform was the abolition of serfdom. After generations of social and individual malaise this basic Russian institution was finally sloughed off.

But it was done half-heartedly. The procedure was cumbersome and the results defective. The upshot was a regime of elusive complexity socially, administratively and economically. While giving the peasants something, it did not give them enough to satisfy them; it left profound grievances, and in the event, indeed, satisfied no one.

Alexander's decision to emancipate the serfs was not a reflection of a general attitude: on the whole he seems to have admired his father's version of the police-state. His change of heart was doubtless due to the revelation of Russia's ineptitude in the Crimean War, as well as to another conviction, widespread at the time, that emancipation was the only way to forestall a major peasant upheaval.

It was first hinted at in a royal manifesto of March, 1856 announcing the end of the Crimean War. In order to enable the public to swallow the depressing terms of the Treaty of Paris it alluded significantly to all the benefits peace was supposed to bring Russia, but since the wording of the manifesto was so indefinite it was taken to be merely another sop to piety. Even after emancipation was decided on by

159

Alexander, the government proceeded with as much caution as possible, to avoid frightening the landowners. Alexander had tried to persuade the aristocratic landowners to collaborate in preparing the reform but since they naturally dragged their feet the reform

were not obliged to surrender too much land. Contrariwise, of course, in the less fertile and more industrialized central and northern provinces, where the landlords were often absentees and lived principally off the annual cash tribute paid by their serfs, they were

tocracy keep a tight hold on the peasant population through police and judicial powers: it was natural for them to wish to retain at least their position in the social hierarchy.

The provincial committees finished their work by the end of 1859; the statutes agreed on were finally enacted in February 1861 and the end of serfdom was solemnly proclaimed, typically enough by a well-known enemy of emancipation, the Metropolitan Philaret. The statutes were originally published in a big volume of 360 pages, which had to be amended over and over again. The vagueness and discrepancies in the official text were due to a conflict of opinion in the government agencies supposed to formulate the emancipation legislation, their inadequate legal training, and the pressure they had been working under.

The enactments of February 1861 gave personal freedom to 47 million peasants, of whom the 21 million belonging to the country squires were for all practical purposes slaves; the 20 million who had been crown dependents had been in somewhat better circumstances, while the approximately 6,000,000 others were artisans, factory industrial workers, or the household personnel of the squires.

But the problem remained that personal liberty was not accompanied by an outright ownership of individual property. The entire discussion of emancipation had, after all, revolved around a complex question: should the serfs be freed with or without land? Also, how could the serf-owners be indemnified for the loss of their human proper-

A caricature by the French artist Gustave Doré (1833-1883) showing wealthy Russians with the national passion for cards. They not only gamble away their estates but also their peasants, considered to be chattels.

had to be prepared, typically enough, by the bureaucratic agencies—in the absence of any effective public opinion a traditional resource of Russian governments.

The landowners were called upon in 1857 to set up provincial committees to recommend practical steps. Since the landed aristocracy was at heart against the emancipation, they did this as slowly as they could; they saw that serfdom was doomed, but they were determined to hold out for as high a ransom as possible for the liberation of their serfs. The great variety in their recommendations had nothing to do with degrees of conservatism, but was rooted in the actual diversity of economic conditions throughout Russia. The chief factors that weighed with the serf-owners were the quality of the soil, the type of estate management, and the density of the population. In the celebrated "black soil" belt, where it was the land itself that made the estate valuable, the serf-owners were prepared not to be reimbursed for liberating their serfs as long as they

quite willing to be openhanded with their land as long as they were compensated by high indemnities. The provincial committees were at one in recommending that the landed aris-

Two muzhiks in the province of Moscow photographed in 1878, with the kind of agricultural implements available at the time to the peasantry. Only large estates had more up-to-date technical equipment.

Peasants drinking tea in the province of Moscow, 1878. Idealistic young intellectuals, often aristocratic, tried to appeal directly to the "people" to revolt. Looking at this photograph one can understand why their mission was a failure: the crusaders lacked any experience in common with their audience and were unable to communicate their message.

ty? In the event a complex regime of "more or less" had been instituted.

The reform was to take place in three stages, in the first of which, after the substitution of government agencies to perform the administrative functions formerly exercized by the noble land-owners, the serfs were to be freed of their personal dependence on their masters. They were free to marry, own property, engage in commerce and litigate. This was considered a temporary regime —though no time limit was laid down for it—after which land was supposed to be allotted to former serfs by a cumbersome system of "redemption" payments. The government handled the redemption debt, intended to make the serfs small farmers, by capitalizing at 6 % the yearly charges the peasant allottments were assessed at, and advancing to the landowners interest-

bearing securities amounting to 75 % to 80 % of the total idemnification due them, the peasants usually providing the remainder. The government was supposed to be repaid by the peasants for the advances to the former owners: at first they were given 49 years to do this in, and the annual installments were supposed to come to the equivalent of the advance on each allotment, plus interest. Only after this obligation was settled could the serf regard himself as emancipated, with a clear title to his allotment.

The hitch was that the redemption payments were assessed far in excess of the value of the allotments: the plan simply broke down. Arrears kept accumulating over and over; ultimately all redemption payments had to be cancelled, in the wake of the revolutionary upheaval of 1905.

The procedural complications of the reform were overshadowed by even more basic questions: How big was the allotment to be? How much had to be paid for it? What was the legal status of the emancipated serfs?

The 1861 reformers agreed that the former serfs should be given their homesteads and an "adequate" allotment of farming land. "Adequacy" is of course a slippery concept, and the expedient was adopted that allotments worked by the serfs before the reform should be considered adequate. This was quite dubious, of course, since under serfdom the peasants had had to spend at least half their time laboring for their masters. An attempt was made to compensate for the known disparity in the size of the pre-reform holdings; the whole of Russia was split up into zones with maximum and minimum norms

for each zone's allotments. The maximum varied from a little more than 32 acres to about 7 ½ acres: the minimum was one-third of the maximum. However, in most places the landowners were entitled to hold one-third (in some places one-half) of their arable land regardless of what this might do to the size of the allotment.

The cumbersomeness of the arrangements could not conceal the fact that in a great many cases, even though the maximum norms were from 100 % to 300 % bigger than the allotments actually proposed, they were still substantially less than what the peasants had been holding before the reform.

The government repeatedly declared that there could be no question of the landowners' being indemnified for the loss of their service labor, as distinct from the loss of their land, but this principle was constantly being infringed on. It is obvious that many landowners would have been seriously embarrassed if they were to receive no indemnification for their serfs, especially in the less fertile regions of the country, where the value of an estate lay in labor and not land.

The reform acts of 1861 set up an elaborately graded schedule of charges that in effect gave the landowners the ransom it was too distasteful to discuss openly. In Great Russia, for instance, the charges were levied in inverse proportion to the size of the allotment: the smaller the allotment, the bigger the charge. This is actually, of course, the converse of the principle of the modern income-tax; its explanation is that the heavier charge on the smaller holdings was a way of indemnifying the former serfowner for the loss of his serfs. Because of the system of capitalization embodied in the 1861 statutes, as indicated above, the redemption payments were often more than the rental value of the allotments.

But perhaps the chief irritation in the new regime from the peasants' point of view was that the land allocated the peasants was not handed over to the peasants individually, but to the so-called Mir, or village commune,

◄ *The cathedral of Saint Isaac of Dalmatia in what is now Leningrad is the fourth building of that name to be raised on the same spot. Peter the Great built the first ones in wood, then brick. Catherine the Great had Rinaldi replace these by a marble church with five cupolas. Alexander ordered a completely new cathedral to suit his taste for the monumental. Ricard de Montferrand (see page 151) won the competition for the commission, submitting drawings in the Chinese, Indian, Gothic and Byzantine style. His classical project with central dome was chosen. The cathedral was consecrated in 1858.*

which the peasants were compelled to belong to. Since the commune was basically in the hands of government functionaries, the emancipated serfs, though euphemistically described in the emancipation statutes of 1861 as "free village dwellers," were actually under the control of the commune. In this way, despite the ending of the

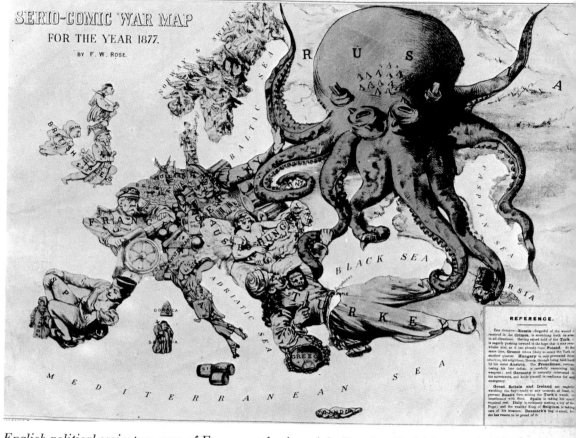

English political caricature map of Europe *at the time of the* Russian-Turkish war of 1877. *Russia is shown as a great octopus ready to dismember prostrate Turkey, with the British Isles on their way to the rescue. Russia almost reached Constantinople, goal of her immemorial dreams, but was checked by the presence of the British fleet in the Sea of Marmora.*

peasants' personal dependence on their former masters, the village commune nevertheless exercized a quasi-dictatorial power over them. Thus the property relations in a family, for instance the rights of inheritance, were not under a regime of law, but depended on the working out of old unwritten local customs.

The sponsorship of the village commune was based primarily on the theory, supported by both bureaucrats and sentimental theoreticians, that Russian peasants were instinctively cooperative, and would remain immune to the charms of materialistic Western Socialism by clinging firmly to the land while mollified by having their "own" institution to guide them. Thus they would not float into the cities to swell the new and dangerously uprooted working-class.

The peasants also remained subject

to corporal punishment (abolished for other members of society in 1863); they paid a poll-tax, gave recruits to the army, and had a number of other duties the "privileged" classes were exempt from. Some of these restrictions were, to be sure, removed soon enough: liability to recruitment in 1874, the poll-tax in 1885, corporal punishment in 1904, while between 1906 and 1911 an attempt was made to loosen the network of communal organization in rural Russia as a whole.

The peasants' reaction to the emancipation was one of bitter disappointment. The emancipation procedure was so complicated that it baffled professional historians and economists for decades; the peasants themselves, of course, were totally at a loss to undestand it, but their common sense told them the plain fact that the "land and freedom" they had been longing for had somehow eluded them. The extension of the redemption process over forty-nine years, for instance, was met with widespread mockery. A legend usual in Russia sprang up that the emancipation of 1861 was somehow not the "real" emancipation but that the well-meaning Tsar had once again been thwarted by the wily landowners and bureaucrats—in short that the peasants had been tricked once again.

The execution of the reform encountered a great deal of resistance, both active and passive; peasant revolts sprang up intermittently in many places.

Broadly speaking, what the reform had failed to do was to free the peasant either materially or juridically and, most important of all, to provide him with an economically viable situation.

It was not the mere size of the allotments that irritated the peasants. Actually they had been given the use of quite a lot of land: more than 300 million acres were transferred to the peasants between 1861 and 1870 in European Russia (not counting Poland, Finland and the Caucasus); the peasant allotments amounted to 31 % of the country in 1877, private owners holding almost a quarter and the state and various public bodies the rest. Much of the vast state domain consisted of forests and land unfit for cultivation; the Church held only some 5.67 million acres.

It was accordingly not so much a question of the absolute size of the land as the inability of the allotments to provide for a family, with the prevailing agricultural methods, or to give it enough work.

The difficulty of alleviating the plight of the peasants even after the reform was once again rooted in the general backwardness of the country, accentuated by the deadening influence of the village commune and the obtuseness of the government.

There was neither the capital nor the knowledge required for the introduction of a rational agriculture: intensive cultivation was prevented by the absence of technical knowledge, by a lack of capital and credit, and by the communal organization, which subdivided the fields assigned peasant households into thin strips mixed in together so that it was necessary to rotate the crops in a uniform way. This meant that one-third of the plough-land lay fallow every year. This was common until well into the Twentieth Century. There was no increase in crop yields: the grain-plantings scarcely increased, and failed even to keep pace with the growth of the rural population, a large portion of which, moreover, remained idle, since freedom of movement was still inhibited by restrictions of one kind or another. Poverty, the tutelage of the commune—i.e., the government —as well as the natural conservatism of the illiterate peasant community, in effect prolonged the existence of serfdom. The peasants were forced to lease land to make ends meet, and since they never could manage this they continued to be crushed by indebtedness.

In short, though the element of legal constraint involved in the juridical status of serfdom had disappeared, it had been replaced by economic necessity, and from this economic point of view the relations between landowners and their former serfs were in some ways not changed at all by the 1861 reforms.

Thus the peasants remained impoverished, with few prospects of betterment. A word often used for the general situation was "rural overpopulation", or conversely, "shortage of land". The oddity of this in a vast and relatively uninhabited country like Russia is of course just another way of referring to the contrast between the number of people and the inadequate means of subsistence available, but in the minds of the peasants the feeling that it was the land that was somehow in short supply became a fixed idea. The masses came to look on the seizure of the lands held by the state and the nobility as the only way out of their impasse, as the only cure for the "shortage of land", and of course as a primordial act of justice that should long since have been accomplished. This basic economic fact, combined with the bitterness caused by the execution of the 1861 reform, led to a tenacious belief in the inevitability of a "second emancipation". It was a decisive factor in the 1917 revolution.

Parallels with the American emancipation of the slaves in 1860 have often been noted; they are, indeed, obvious enough. An entertaining sidelight on social psychology is afforded by the recollection that both American Negroes and Russian serfs were uniformly thought of by their owners—before emancipation!—as childlike, musical, simple-hearted, etc. (also, of course, lazy and shiftless). But the American Negro community could never escape from its ghetto, nor was it large enough to kick the lid off the cauldron it was simmering in, while the Russian peasantry, on the other hand, as part of a homogeneous society, was to prove capable of providing a powerful lever for change throughout the country.

An ironic thing about the emancipation was that it failed to benefit the nobility either. Proportionately the big estates suffered most from the general absence of technical knowledge, lack of capital, and the lackadaisical inefficiency that characterized the rural nobility. The nobility itself was mortgaged up to the hilt, and even though it received very substantial sums for the land transferred to former serfs—nearly 600,000,000 rubles the first decade after emancipation—almost half had to be handed over to the treasury at once, to settle mortgage loans, while only a small part of the remainder was invested in the land again. At the same time, of course, the nobles went on borrowing in order to live as they had been accustomed to. The employment of hired labor that could use machinery and livestock furnished by the owners —the transition to capitalism—was very difficult. Since most of the nobles could not or would not spend the necessary money to run their estates on a capitalist basis, they continued working the land under pre-reform conditions; they would rent the land to the peasants, who would use their own horses and machines as they had under serfdom. The average yield per acre on the nobility's estates remained much lower than almost anywhere else in Europe.

The recurrent famines at home were in contrast with the rapid increase in Russian grain exports, which the building of railways promoted substantially. This was made possible not by any greater yields but, on the contrary, by extending the cultivated land still further. Here too the nobles were inefficient: most of the profits were appropriated by middlemen.

Thus the nobility was badly squeezed: in European Russia it lost more than half its land between 1862 and 1911, chiefly to merchants, burghers, and well-to-do peasants. A graphic description of this process, from the point of view of the nobility, is given in personal terms by Tolstoy, in *Anna Karenina*.

In fact, the reign of Alexander II marked the end of noble Russia.

Gradually constricted by the newly evolving class of merchants, burghers, financiers and industrialists brought into existence by the new expansion of foreign trade, the construction of railways and ports, and the establishment of new mines and factories, the nobility slowly began declining both economically and politically. It came to have little to depend on but the personal benevolence of the sovereign. The Russian nobility was finally eclipsed; aristocratic Russia had in fact become an external sheath under which, little by little, new social forces took shape.

This process was promoted by some of Alexander II's administrative reforms. The abolition of serfdom made it impossible for the squirarchy to play a cardinal role in administration and judicial life: the local institutions set up in the provinces by Catherine the Great had to yield to the 1861 reform. The village commune, which inherited the proprietary functions of the squires on the land cultivated by the peasants, also assumed their supervision of the rural population.

Principles of local self-government were extended to the administration of

Grand Duke Nicholas after the victory at San Stefano during the Russian-Turkish war, 1878. Although the goal of Constantinople and the Straits seemed in sight, subsequent pressure from Britain and Austria forced Russia to abandon some of her gains. ▶

the provinces and districts Russia was divided into: the economic and administrative interests of both were assigned to an assembly composed of all classes of the population with a president who was, however, invariably a Marshal of the Nobility. The whole complex of these institutions was called a Rural Council (*zemstvo*); it administered everything concerning schools, hospitals, sanitation, outbreaks of animal disease, etc.

These Rural Councils were probably Alexander II's most effective innovation: they created a channel for the most idealistic feelings, which inflamed not only the evolving intelligentsia, as we shall see, but even those provincial nobles who prided themselves on their advanced liberal opinions. The feeling that it was high time things were accomplished, which had marked the accession of Alexander II to the throne, engaged the most energetic elements in thinking Russia in the labor of overhauling the countryside. Liberal squires often became diligent, benign tutors of their former serfs, furnishing them with doctors, nurses, and veterinaries; they taught them new methods of cultivation that they themselves had only learned with difficulty, and that their own class often found no use for.

Defective though the emancipation was, it nevertheless levelled to a large extent the dam that had been keeping the Nineteenth Century out of rural Russia. This newfound enthusiasm of the liberal and "conscience-stricken" nobility, to be sure, waned gradually as the country, once caught up in the millstream of Russia's Industrial Revolution, began to develop new turbulences, and as the intelligentsia, with more sharply defined and less exclusively humanitarian ideals, began to encompass the newly emerging conscious elements of the peasantry and working-class.

For an industrial proletariat was gradually forming. Lenin, restricting the term "factory" to enterprises employing at least 16 workers, calculated that Russia had about 2,500 to 3,000 factories in 1866, 4,500 in 1879, 6,000 in 1890, and 9,000 in 1903. The gradual introduction of the industrial revolution to Russia was accompanied by abuses usual in every country: long hours, disagreeable working conditions, low wages, and the exploitation of women and children. In Russia, of course, such conditions were not noticeably different from the general situation, though they were sometimes worse. The working-day was twelve hours as a rule, occasionally going as high as eighteen. Women and children as well as men commonly worked at night; workers were often crowded into dirty barracks, sleeping on the floor or on tiers of bare bunks.

Many cottage industries were gradually shut down by the gradual growth of cheap mass-produced articles, which, while increasing the flow of cheap manpower into the factories gradually being built, exacerbated the conditions still further: the development of industry, while rapid enough to squeeze people out of cottage trades, was not rapid enough to absorb them all. This depressed wages and living conditions still further, and it was not until the great industrial boom toward the end of the Nineteenth Century that real wages resumed an upward rise, after a substantial depression (20%-30%) between the 1860s and the 1890s.

One of the factors that enabled the newly forming class of Russian workers to endure the low wages was the very fact of its newness: most of them were peasants still tied to their native villages, with an interest in the farm homesteads still being maintained by their families. Thus they did not have to maintain a family near where they worked; before they could abandon the land completely, they would have had to receive higher wages.

But this, of course, was only a transitional phenomenon. It was just this emergence of an industrial working-class, which paralleled the appearance of the familiar modern complex of entrepreneur, financial and banking groups, that is surely the most significant phenomenon of the era that followed the emancipation.

Perhaps the cardinal factor in Russian economic progress was the great increase in railway construction mentioned above, again a result of the Crimean War, which had demonstrated the need of good communications for modern armies. In 1860, curiously enough, railways had been commonly denounced as a pernicious luxury: in 1855 Russia had had less than 660 miles of railways, with another 330 added by 1860, when they began to boom. Twenty-five years later the mileage came to 21,780, a substantial increase even for Russia's vastness, and even though it left her with proportionately less railway mileage than any major country in Europe.

Russia was reacting in her own way to the intensification of life everywhere that marked the second half of the Nineteenth Century. Population was skyrocketing, commodity consumption and production were shooting up, transport was revolutionized in consequence; the whole process was solidly embedded in the new techniques. Both economically and socially the Russia of Alexander II reflected this general expansion of the capitalist world. Of course the lack of "culture" referred to so often was a factor that impeded the assimilation of the new technique of production and organization, and Russian life retained many old-fashioned elements jumbled together with the novelties of the era. Russian capitalism developed slowly; the change was slow enough for dynamic lopsidedness to become firmly embedded in Russian life, with consequences we are still living through today.

Externally speaking Russia had made substantial achievements by the end of Alexander II's reign: her foothold on the Pacific Ocean was consolidated; vast areas in Central Asia as well as the Near East were added to the realm; she had thrown off the restrictions of the Treaty of Paris, the seal of her defeat in the Crimean War, made Turkey powerless, and started a ferment among the Balkan Slavs. To be sure this was no grandiose march of history, but a rather casual jumble of events; ambitious bureaucrats and generals kept encumbering a country already far too large for its population, extremely backward technically and culturally, with wastelands in Asia, and squandered men and money in pointless adventures in the Balkans. The 1877-1878 war with Turkey, for instance, was wholly futile from any economic point of view. Russia had never had the slightest business interest in the impoverished Balkans, even more backward and peasant-bound than herself. It resulted in a diplomatic defeat after a military victory, chiefly because the British had been antagonized by feverish and futile Russian manœuvrings in Central Asia; since the British overestimated Russian abilities they were nervous about India.

It is true that the Turkish war of 1877-1878 has been mythologized very successfully in Russian and Balkan tradition: by injecting into international affairs a novel element of what may be called ethnic sponsorship, the so-called "War of Liberation", as it is referred to by Russians, has had an enduring influence.

The Intelligentsia

We have seen what an extraordinary identity of outlook and behavior prevailed throughout Russia until well after the upheaval launched by Peter the Great. Afterwards Russian society changed rapidly, though in its own way. European influences poured into Russia with the Eighteenth Century, but they were channelized into the nobility, which found itself elevated into a totally different world. This sharply focussed and exclusive cultural impact split Russian society into basically two classes—the aristocrats and the plebeians, separated by a chasm that did not even begin to be spanned until the end of the Eighteenth Century.

They lived in different universes. Cities outside Moscow and St. Petersburg were no more than big villages. The merchants, with their beards and long cloaks, could scarcely be distinguished from the peasants. Even after becoming rich they did not abandon their old-fashioned manners; they did not become a bourgeoisie until almost into the Twentieth Century, when industrialization began remoulding society at an ever increasing pace. The countryside itself reflected this contrast between the overwhelming sea of peasant humanity and the isolated islets of European manners. Monotonous fields and forests were studded by villages made up of squalid huts; at one end of the village would be found a splendid park, a huge mansion, probably with columns, and elegant people with works of art, libraries and French tutors.

A step away were the peasants, utterly unlike the aristocracy in looks, clothes, manners, and for that matter in language. Pious, respectful, sunk in folklore and a life of toil, both exhilarating and exhausting, the peasants remained untouched by the Western currents that had turned their masters into a different race.

It is true that as early as the reign of Catherine II the growth of the public services had given rise to a group that was intermediate between the nobility and the plebeians—the functionaries, but they remained essentially peripheral, a sort of ragtag-and-bobtail with neither real estate, money, nor influence; there could be no question of their replacing the bourgeoisie Russia was not to develop till much later. This early, diffuse, bureaucratic milieu—described so depressingly by Gogol and Dostoyevsky—never influenced Russian history.

The uneven evolution of Russia,

◄ Alexander Herzen *(1812-1870) pioneer revolutionary agitator, novelist and journalist: founder of the newspaper "The Bell". Later the Populist movement grew out of his faith in the Russian peasantry as depository of Socialism. Photograph by the famous French photographer Nadar.*

her failure to develop her economic resources and the consequent delay in the formation of a modern spectrum of social categories, created a vacuum. As education developed, however slowly, and the liberal professions increased in numbers, this vacuum became the medium for a class known by the odd name of "intelligentsia", a word long since incorporated into the international vocabulary.

The intelligentsia was never actually a social class, in the sense of a fragment of society distinguished by characteristic roots, livelihoods, or manners. It was actually made up of all sorts of people from all sorts of groups: academic people, students and lawyers were generally members of the intelligentsia; a great squire or a high functionary might or might not be, while a peasant would not, though his son, if he could become a teacher, might be. A good criterion might be its "world-outlook", an outlook that was rooted essentially in the notion that life was important, that ideas were important, and that the world should and doubtless could be changed.

This is, of course, a fundamentally religious view, and it may be that the intelligentsia grew up from the deep roots of Russian mysticism. The secularization of Russian society effected by Peter the Great and even more by Catherine II had touched only the summit: when education began trickling out of the preserves of the aristocracy into the lives of commoners who, after 1857, began invading the universities, though in pathetically restricted numbers, the mystical element inherent in the people shot up to the surface at once and rapidly coagulated in a new and essentially messianic outlook. It engulfed the most influential stratum of Russian society, and in following the logic of its own development it created by the latter half of the Nineteenth Century one of the most dedicated forces in history—the Russian revolutionary movement, which ultimately destroyed the Tsarist regime and poured its own apocalyptic spirit abroad upon the world.

But the distillation of the Russian revolutionary movement happened gradually: the intelligentsia had to mature before it could give birth.

The Decembrist uprising of 1825 had been repressed with great vigor, but a ferment began to work that was to affect the newcomers to the universities. In the University of Moscow we can see its germ: the government, instead of finding a philosophy to justify autocracy, naively shut down the chair of philosophy on the theory that a study of it could lead to no good. This parochial Tsarist error had fateful consequences: the professor of physics undertook to quench the thirst of the student body for new ideas, and physics became

Above, Dostoyevsky *(1822-1881) and top,* Petrashevsky. *Petrashevsky, a Foreign Affairs official, gathered together a "subversive" group of officers, students, artists and tradesmen to discuss social conditions. Among them was the young Dostoyevsky. The group was denounced and arrested. Nicholas I led the questioning and was doubtless responsible for the gruesome idea of condemning the five leaders to death and only informing them on the gallows that the sentence had been commuted to exile in Siberia. Later, in "The Idiot" and "Memories of the House of the Dead", Dostoyevsky wrote of his feelings in prison. The early drawing of Dostoyevsky was made two years before these events (1847).*

Pages 170-171.

View of St. Petersburg showing the Exchange designed by Thomas de Thomon at the beginning of the XIXth century and the Marble Palace built by Antonio Rinaldi. Engraving by Damame-Demartrais.

exceptionally popular. People began bubbling with ideas; informal groups leaped into being that spent their time discussing all sorts of scientific, philosophical, social and political questions, united only by a general and often quite personal disaffection and by what Herzen called a "profound feeling of alienation from official Russia". This element of alienation was to be the imprint of the intelligentsia throughout its existence.

The informal discussion groups, though small, had a disproportionate influence: they included almost everyone of any distinction at all outside official circles. There was of course no program or organization; these passionate debaters flitted freely about from one bough to another. In retrospect, however, a general design emerges against the background of the clamor.

The influence of the French age of enlightenment, with its detached rationalism and empiricism, was still powerful, but it was gradually caught up with and overcome by German ideas. The tormented, uprooted Russian Hamlets who, floating about in a social no-man's land, with neither family, wealth nor position, passionately longed to *believe* as well as to *know*, were revenging themselves on the elegant salon-learning of the Frenchified aristocracy. The scepticism, atheism and liberalism of aristocratic salons since Catherine II gave way to a yearning for faith and a desire to change the world.

The rationalism of the French Encyclopedists was too cerebral; the romantic Germany that had aroused the imagination of Victor Hugo, Michelet, and Edgar Quinet among the French, made a similar and far more profound appeal to the early Russian intellectuals.

◀ *Fedotov: The Aristocrat's breakfast. 1849. This canvas, by a painter known for his scenes of everyday life in the prosperous classes, gives a good idea of what their surroundings looked like towards the end of Nicholas I's reign. The young man in informal morning attire would know French—the indispensable language for moving in polite society—play the piano, recite poetry, and dance gracefully. That would probably be the limit of his education, although as a member of the nobility or as the son of an official the university would be open to him. Nicholas had made study abroad practically impossible, and had limited the subjects to be taught at home. Cut off from the stimulation of foreign contacts, hedged in by the régime's intellectual restrictions in Russia, the young aristocrat no doubt spent much of his time losing more at gambling than he could afford. Ladies considering him as a son-in-law would inquire in French "How many souls (serfs) does he have?"*

German thought was both a rejection of classical French rationalism and a way of bypassing the realities of the police-state. A whole cluster of German philosophers, beginning with Schelling and going on to Kant, Fichte and Hegel, came in turn to dominate the new intellectual universe. Hegel's influence was perhaps the most durable, doubtless because in its profound ambiguousness the immense apparatus of Hegelian rhetoric has a splendidly mobile pivot; it can be turned in any desired direction. Radicals, conservatives and all intervening shades of sociopolitical affiliation could find justification for anything they wanted in the *camera obscura* of Hegelian doctrine.

But though German metaphysics was absorbed with passionate intensity —lifelong friendships were broken by a quibble over a Hegelian nuance—its intellectual remoteness gradually came to be chafed at.

Social studies began being emphasized in contrast with timeless philosophical lucubrations. France, in a different incarnation, was turned to again. The more extremist or radical thinkers began studying Russia herself, past or present, which in turn led to an avid absorption of French Socialism—Saint-Simon, Fourier, Proudhon, Louis Blanc.

In the 1840s the tournament of opinion threw up two broad attitudes conventionally described as "Slavophilism" and "Westernism". Both words are misleading.

The Westerners were basically humanitarians with a Russian tinge: they wanted to believe in a universal European culture and steep Russia in it so that she could transcend her parochial limitations and achieve world significance. "European culture" was of course a grab-bag of ingredients; since the Westerners had no clear-cut principles they simply took their pick. Entirely heterogeneous in origin, they believed with varying degrees of emphasis in science, constitutional government, liberal values, freedom of expression, etc., and were theoretically, though often tactfully, against serfdom: they also deplored the chasm between the Russian masses and the cultivated elite. They were far from committed to Socialism: one of the leading Westerners, Granovsky, was opposed to it.

The Slavophiles were generally devoted to a glorification of the Russian national past—all quite imaginary. They looked on the West as decadent and enthralled by materialistic rationalism. They also tended to regard the Orthodox Church as the axis of the Russian people and its chief hope for the future.

They came chiefly from the landed aristocracy, and though conservative in the romantic sense indicated above, were by no means in favor of official government policy, though there were

of course points in common. Since they were particularly concerned with Russian Orthodoxy, they were hostile to the Church's political subservience, which had been such a cardinal trait of Russian history. Politically they were opposed to the Catholic Slav nations, which they regarded as traitors. For that matter they were also opposed to Ukrainian nationalism: they thought it disloyal to Great Russia, though this was because they regarded the Great Russian state as the incarnation of true Slavdom, and naturally called Ukrainian nationalism separatism. Up to the Crimean War they were not much interested in the Balkan Slavs.

Slavophilism began by having a world-view independent of official policy; in fact it was often highly critical of the government, but it ultimately dwindled in influence by becoming identified with the official regime. A curious instance of how the same institution can be ideologized in different ways was the Slavophile adoration of the village commune as representing the quintessence of Russian congregationalism—a dominant motif in Greek and Russian Orthodoxy. Their insistence on the commune, indeed, is taken by many to be the essence of their doctrine. Later on the village commune was sponsored by the radical Westerners, who thought of it not as a holy Slav institution, but as the matrix of a future Socialist society.

Perhaps the most attractive and in some ways the most influential of the forerunners of the intelligentsia was Alexander Herzen (1812-1870) a novelist and journalist who was the first of the "conscience-stricken gentry". Herzen was one of the principal channels in Russia for the somewhat vague though extraordinarily imaginative views of Saint-Simon. He had been given a conventional aristocratic education, largely under French influence, and at first was attracted to some extent by Slavophilism. But when the two groups, which though vague about program nevertheless represented differing casts of mind, fell out in 1844—the climax was occasioned, typically enough, by a series of lectures on the history of the Middle Ages—he struck out for himself, fusing together a number of elements in a system of his own, a sort of synthesis of Westernism and Slavophilism, which became known as Populism. It was based essentially on an idolization of the common people—i.e., the peasants—and looked forward to the institution of a form of agrarian Socialism based on the village commune. Thus he retained the Slavophile adoration of the village commune as the source of all good things, while emphasizing its purely economic and organizational aspect and discarding the ethico-religious emphasis of the Slavophiles.

173

Herzen detested the complex modern state. He thought of Russia as a federation of free communes, in which the elements of serfdom, nobility and bureaucracy, introduced by the Romanovs, were essentially alien to the people. Tsar, peasants and clergy were all native—everything else was an exotic and generally pernicious excrescence. If Russia simply flung aside serfdom, aristocracy, bureaucracy and that part of the Church represented by Byzantium and created a new society based on a partnership between the village commune and the workers, she would accomplish an entirely pacific and unfettered revolution. He thought the modern Russian state resembled Chingis Khan's system plus the telegraph. He loathed modern, liberal, civilized Europe, as well as all forms of legalism: he condemned them as engulfing the individual personality, and thrust aside as superfluous the notion of constitutional reforms.

His attitude toward Peter the Great was twofold: on the one hand he admired him for having broken away from the Byzantine conception of the Tsar as a remote unknowable figure to be venerated, turning himself and the Russian people into a nation of democratic workers, destroying the power of the Byzantinized Church, letting in the light and wiping out women's Byzantine seclusion.

But by elevating the nobility and Europeanizing it, Peter also created the cleavage between the serfs and their masters, straddling the divided people by means of a German bureaucracy. Since Peter the Great Russian history was accordingly no more than the history of Tsar and nobility, bridged over only by functionaries and parasites. The people had vanished from history, except for a brief upheaval during the Napoleonic invasion. Only the village commune and the fellowship of the workers had managed to hold out.

Herzen thought it was this cleavage in the nation that explained the profound malaise of Russian life. There were two Russias: European Russia, or the educated classes, wanted one thing, i.e., Western civilization, and old, religious Russia something else. This was how he explained the stock figure in Russian literature, the "superfluous man", as well as a certain ineffectuality in Russian character.

If Herzen was a prime inspirer of the intelligentsia, its technical fathering, so to speak, may be ascribed to Vissarion Belinsky (1810-1848), who exercised great influence not only in publicizing new ideas but as a professional literary critic, the first and perhaps the most important in Russian history.

Belinsky's fame was extraordinary; at the height of his brief career his name was known to every earnest young man in Russia. He was a sort of distillation of the activities of the intelligentsia as a class: just because he was socially unattached—of plebeian origins with no money—not exactly a writer, and not exactly a thinker, but a vehement and dilettantish exponent of others' ideas, he is typical of its dynamic principle. He knew no foreign languages and actually read little even in Russian: his chief function was conversation. He could never write a book, after a tragic and catastrophically received boyish effort; his literary influence was exerted through correspondence and reviews. He worshipped Peter the Great, and also Hegel: he had begun as a believer in aesthetics —naturally understood ethically—and as a Hegelian was also in favor at first of the position taken by Hegel in his celebrated defense of the Prussian monarchy—i.e., whatever is, is right, or at least reasonable (to Hegel's mind, or vocabulary, this was the same thing). He then became a fervent proponent of utility in literature, and so the father of the long line of industrious literary propagandists and moralists Russian literature has become famous for.

Belinsky combines the cardinal traits of the Russian intelligentsia—devotion to "Western" ideals; worship of science;

Early manuscript (1821) by the great Russian poet Alexander Pushkin: *a page from his "Feast in Hell".*

Four Russian writers: *from left to right,* ▶
Krlyov, author of fables, Pushkin, and two other authors, Yukovsky and Gnedich; painting in the Tretyakov Gallery, Moscow.

Pages 176-177.

View of Moscow from the Kremlin, *anonymous early XIXth century engraving. Many engravers of this period copied each other so exactly that the same views appear with very slight modifications. The Swiss father and son, both named Gabriel Lory, and the French artist Guérard de la Barthe made large albums of colored plates for the European trade.*

Socialist doctrine, however vague, as part of the service of mankind, which in its turn is also idolized as a sort of substitute for the mystical emotion of orthodox religion; the powerful expression of the sense of guilt by the longing to atone for the wrongs perpetrated against mankind; philosophizing without knowing anything about philosophy; and above all the infusion of a powerful, though sometimes nebulous moral emotion into the discussion of everything. From this point of view, the arts and sciences are merely material for the moral emotion to work on: only an ethical criterion anchored in mankind makes any judgement possible at all. The point of view also implies personal asceticism and a dedication to duty, in other words the suppression of individual life on behalf of the collective ideal. The sum of these attitudes characterized the intelligentsia throughout its existence.

Belinsky ultimately broke with Hegelianism; he and his friends formed the "Westernizing" tendency described above.

It will be seen that there was a completely matter-of-course interaction between literature and political activity. It is in fact this curious interweaving of the two that may be taken as the hallmark of Russian literature for most of the Nineteenth Century and later; it is certainly this aspect of it that has been accepted abroad as characteristic. Messianism was the significant element held in common by both Westerners and Slavophiles; Belinsky's attitude was in fact largely accepted by the writers themselves, which is doubtless what gives literature its special importance in Russian history.

The very earliest beginnings of modern Russian literature can be traced to the Seventeenth Century; it was an imitation of a Polish imitation of French standards. But with the second quarter of the Eighteenth Century the original source itself was turned to; French classicism became the wellspring of

◄ *C. Brullow:* Monsieur Naryshkin and his wife. *1827. Brullow is the best known and the most gifted of the minor painters who left charming records of life and customs in Russia about the middle of the last century. "Monsieur" Naryshkin, descended from an illustrious line of boyars (his family always considered itself above the rather current title of "Prince" and refused to use it) is, like his wife, dressed in the latest Paris and London style. Looking fashionable was far from inexpensive: at the time the double portrait was painted, there were only two "coiffeurs" in Saint Petersburg, both French. Each one charged five rubles for a cut and fifteen to dress a lady's hair. A horse cost twenty-five rubles then, and a pair of boots, three.*

Russian writing, chiefly through the work of the many-sided scholar and scientist Lomonosov (1711-1765). For decades after him Russian literature was negligible: it is best understood as the digestion of the best of Western writing. Most of the writers were basi-

Nicholas Gogol *(1809-1852). In spite of oppressive censorship literature flowered in Nicholas's reign. The crumbling efficiency of the immense administrative apparatus was satirized in Gogol's novels.*

cally schoolmasters and translators who provided the channels for the new ideas and forms that came not only from France but from Germany and England. Russians were familiarized with various currents of German and English pre-romantic literature and given new models for verse, which finally, in the Nineteenth Century, laid the foundations of Russian modern literature in its truly modern phase. This begins with French classical standards all over again; it was inaugurated by the publication of Pushkin's first book in 1820.

Pushkin (1799-1837), unquestionably the greatest Russian poet, indeed the Goethe and Dante of the Russian language, is both a literary ideal and a symbol of national civilization. For Russians his immense charm is not in his being characteristically "Russian", as foreigners conceive this, but in his universality, his "pan-humanity" as Dostoyevsky put it. He thought of himself as a romantic, but his actual virtues were harmony and restraint: none of his effects is meant to startle. He is essentially a contained, delicate, classical poet.

Yet though he had an enormous influence on literary development, the swift growth of the messianically preoccupied intelligentsia meant his eclipse,

at least in artistic content. After its brilliant classical efflorescence in the beginning of the Nineteenth Century —the epoch of classical poetry lasted scarcely more than a decade—Russian literature slipped into the mainstream of Russian moralizing.

Ivan Turgenev *(1818-1883). The writer was horrified at the contrast between social conditions at home and abroad. His short stories and novels depicting life in his own land drew attention to the evils of serfdom.*

The triumph of Russian messianism, in its two forms of Slavophilism and Westernizing radicalism, meant that after a half-generation of transition following the Golden Age of poetry, the basically dogmatic temperament of the "committed" intelligentsia suffused literature with purposiveness. Romanticism, which had merely been invoked during the brief classical period of Russian poetry, now made up the content of literature. The German influences that flooded the literate class and the struggle of political ideas overwhelmed literature too. Art became the handmaiden of "other" ideas.

This was to have immense significance because it was just at this time that Russia emerged from her ancient spiritual isolation. In the Nineteenth Century the Russian intelligentsia, and above all its writers, left an indelible imprint on the world at large as well as on Russia herself.

The most characteristic effect in literature of the "two heads of Janus"—as Herzen called the Slavophile and radical currents of Russian idealism—was in the creation of the "natural school," a transition in which Gogol (1809-1852) may be considered the pivot.

Gogol's outlook is of course essentially poetic; his first work was a pro-

Count Leo Tolstoy *(1828-1910)*, *photographed as an officer at Sebastopol during the disastrous Crimean war (1853-1856). Tolstoy was to use experiences gathered during this period in "War and Peace".*

duct of a fantastic imagination quite indifferent to the "real" social background that served as its springboard. It was basically a lyrical caricature.

But Belinsky found a social message in it; he explained to everyone just what Gogol had really meant, or what he should have meant. Gogol himself was converted, and though he was not hostile at all to the social order, his choice of material, combined with the interpretation thrust on it by Belinsky and others, persuaded everyone that he was a social satirist. His admirers of 1845 thought him a model of "realism."

With the surrender of poetry to prose as the core of Russian literature the artistic serenity of Pushkin and his disciples was gone forever. The writer now sought some gripping world-truth, and if he found anything solid he could cling to himself he became a preacher. When Gogol failed to find something, for instance, as in the sequel to his *Dead Souls*, where the characters refused to be tailored to fit a moral purpose, he flung the manuscript into the fire.

But it must not be forgotten that aside from actual content, as a literary *genre* Russian realism owes its forms to the French, especially Boileau, Molière, and La Fontaine, who were imitated and developed by a long line of Russian fable-writers culminating in the well-known rhymes of Krylov and Griboyedov, author of *Woe from Wit* (1825). Indeed, while the "realism" associated

with Russian literature stems from the messianic commitment inspired by Belinsky and his followers, its actual language—primarily in the absence of stylistic ornamentation—owes even more to the fine prose of the poets Pushkin and Lermontov. Pushkin's stories of course are pure action, and have none of the character-study the Russian novel and theatre have become famous for, but he at least handed on his own form of realism in the classical spareness of his style.

The "natural school" gave rise to the Russian realistic novel, which, though many distinguished dramas were also written, wholly dominated Russian literature until well into the Twentieth Century. Gogol, in Belinsky's implacably tendentious interpretation, became a sort of model for later Russian novelists.

The realistic novel, though its form changed frequently, at bottom constituted a single school of writing, which was characterized primarily by an overwhelming preponderance of character-drawing over action, an indifference to "fine" style, and the ethical suffusion mentioned above.

The dramatic effect of Russian novelists on world literature is surely due to their intense concentration on the portrayal of character. There is an absence of any distraction from "real" human beings in the interests of superficial story-telling. The converse of this of course is a certain narrative sluggishness, and a general tendency toward the fusion of fiction and biography.

The indifference or hostility to "style" was doubtless a corollary of the real milieu Russian novelists chose to describe with painstaking precision. Between Gogol and the Symbolists there was no attempt at linguistic adornment, which makes up so much of style in other literatures. Russians were preoccupied by a verisimilitude of detail bearing on the important problems of society as a whole; this was bound to forbid any purely stylistic excursions. The literary critics, whose role in Russia was disproportionate, could be relied on to remind an author of waywardness.

But apart from Russian antecedents, the preponderant foreign influence remained French. Dickens was very popular about 1845, but his actual influence was minor. Indeed, until 1917 France was to remain a deep source of Russian inspiration. George Sand was idolized; Balzac's following, though less extensive, was equally devoted. Tolstoy

By 1909 when this photograph was taken on Tolstoy's estate at Yasnaya-Polyana, the writer had lived many years away from the world, surrounded by his family, working the land with his own hands. He continued to write, mainly preoccupied by philosophical and moral questions.

acknowledged the cardinal influence of Stendhal, most of all, of course, in the analytic establishment of personality.

Turgenev (1818-1883) was the first Russian novelist to fix Russian letters in the minds of foreigners. He was far better known than any other novelist of his generation except Tolstoy and Dostoyevsky, and for a time his name outshone any other in Russia. He has since been outdistanced in world fame by these last two, perhaps the best known and indeed greatest Russian novelists—Tolstoy and Dostoyevsky, in whom, together with Stendhal, the

psychological novel of the Nineteenth Century reached its zenith.

Both Tolstoy (1828-1910) and Dostoyevsky (1821-1881) were typical of Russian literature as a whole; they were increasingly preoccupied, indeed obsessed by what they considered the essential problems of life—death and God. The various threads in their writing can be disentangled only by disregarding the profound fusion of both interest and execution in both of them. In Tolstoy especially, we are obliged to probe his lifelong afflictions together with him. It is of course possible to discuss endlessly the ingredients of Tolstoy's art—to analyse his analysis—but even when he was being most purely an artist, before his religious conversion around 1880, the whole of his bulky personality was at grips with the ultimate "reality" he was writing about. After his conversion, of course, his preoccupation became still more explicit, even didactic.

Tolstoy's career, though from a literary point of view it exemplifies the ethical nature of Russian writing, was socially unusual. He received a purely aristocratic education: he had scarcely any contact with intellectuals at all before attending the university, and even there and for the rest of his life he had very little to do with them. Not only are the middle classes and their problems never referred to in his writing, for all practical purposes they did not even exist for him. The only point of view he is aware of as even possible is his own, that of an aristocrat of independent means, and that of mankind at large, which for him boiled down to the peasants. Of all the Russian writers who became internationally celebrated he was the least literary: he was simply

181

race from the depths of his own discontent. With its patriarchal and profoundly aristocratic traits Tolstoy's figure is an arresting contrast to the generally plebeian or middle-class atmosphere of Russian literary life. Indeed, his personal distinction, aside from his remarkable literary talents, is inextricably rooted in his aristocratic outlook: as a writer it made him unique.

Russian literature had a tremendous impact on the international public, but with the death of Chekhov its great period, at least insofar as its world influence is concerned, was practically over. The great age of the novel itself ended about 1880: Dostoyevsky died in 1881 and Turgenev in 1883; Tolstoy's conversion about then also meant the subtraction of his talents from the novel and their application to his hortatory goals.

The growth of the educated classes meant a general flare-up of activity in other arts as well as literature. In music, especially, Russia made the world aware of herself almost as much as in literature, in marked contrast to her status before. The meagreness of Russian music, as far as the outside world was concerned, had been due to the oral transmissions of folk songs and the inadequacy of the few transcriptions available. Religious music had been jealously shielded against secular influence, and since the Russian Church made no use of instrumental music there was no way for it to develop as in Roman Catholic countries. There were actually no music schools in Petersburg or Moscow; music was taught by private instructors, largely foreigners. Consequently Russia

had no operatic or concert music at all worth mentioning until the late 1830s.

Michael Glinka (1804-1857) may be thought the first distinguished Russian composer; his characteristic contribution lay in the application of European technique—he had studied in Italy, Germany and France for several years —to the musical themes he had been familiar with as a child. The result was a combination of technical competence, originality and talent. He wrote two operas, *A Life for the Tsar* (1836), now called *Ivan Susanin* in the Soviet Union, and *Ruslan and Lyudmila* (1842). But his reception was so discouraging that he never wrote any others. The first became part of operatic repertory because of its patriotic subject, in spite of being sneered at by aristocratic audiences as "coachman's music," but the second was withdrawn after a year and never produced again during his lifetime.

Almost every Nineteenth Century Russian composer can be traced back to Glinka's work: Tchaikovsky found the seeds of the whole of the Russian symphonic school in Glinka, even though the latter wrote no symphonies.

After Glinka music in Russia made a sudden leap forward, like so much else that happened there in the Nineteenth Century. A Russian Music Society was founded in 1859; it revolutionized standards in everything, both in teaching and in music appreciation, establishing branches in Moscow and thirty cities in the provinces, and sponsoring the setting up of conservatories in Moscow and Petersburg and music schools in a number of the major

Above : Alexander Borodin *(1834-1887),* one of the Russian composers who made up "The Five" group; the others were Mussorgsky, Rimsky-Korsakov, Balakirev and Cui. Borodin was also a professor of chemistry at St. Petersburg Academy; he could only devote his spare time to music.

Right, Nicholas Rimsky-Korsakov *(1844-1908),* another Russian composer not originally trained as a musician. Before teaching at the Conservatory he was a naval officer. He wrote the first Russian symphony and was a master of orchestration.

a gentleman. His intense nature and idiosyncrasies made him bored or irritated by society, but aside from his writing his life was that of a squire. His external interests were raising his family, farming his estates, and seeing friends of his own class; his artistic interests expressed themselves in stories about peasants and aristocratic families.

It is true that he gave all this up after his religious conversion, but he never became a mere writer. He turned into a prophet, exhorting the human

Russian centers. Symphony orchestras were maintained, while concerts and recitals by Russian and foreign artists were sponsored by the Society. This immense enterprise, which was extraordinarily successful, was launched by Anton Rubinstein (1821-1894), the son of a Jewish convert to Christianity. Rubinstein, who started out as a musical prodigy, was a prolific composer as well as a celebrated pianist.

During the 1860s a group of exceptionally talented composers appeared all at once, known as "The Five." They were Balakirev, Cui, Mussorgsky, Borodin and Rimsky-Korsakov, who provided an effective counter-point to the conservative tradition of Rubinstein and the Conservatory. These five composers, often described as the "Neo-Russian" school, were great admirers of Glinka and of "realism" (they particularly admired Berlioz and Liszt). They thought a composer ought to draw on his national background, including popular songs.

It is revealing to recall that the only trained professional among the Five was Balakirev (1837-1910), who was a pianist and conductor as well as a composer. Cui (1835-1918) was a general in the Army Engineers, while Mussorgsky (1839-1881) was a Guards officer and later a bureaucrat. Borodin (1834-1887) was a well-known chemistry professor; Rimsky-Korsakov (1844-1908) was a naval officer, though he later taught at the St. Petersburg Conservatory.

The Five did not last long as a group: after the 1860s each struck out alone. Borodin and Balakirev are considered

the founders of the Russian symphonic school, while Mussorgsky's *Boris Godunov*, Borodin's *Prince Igor*, and Rimsky-Korsakov's *Le Coq d'Or* have been played all over the world.

Perhaps the most famous Russian composer of the period was Tchaikovsky (1840-1893), whose talents took in every form of composition from romances and chamber music to ballets, operas and symphonies. Though of his eight operas *Eugene Onegin* (1877) and *The Queen of Spades* (1890) are much more popular in Russia than abroad, his symphonies, especially the *Pathétique*, have been international favorites for years.

Painting made a far less flamboyant début than either literature or music. The Academy of Arts was the bulwark of the pseudo-classical tradition; its authority was supreme until the 1860s, when it was successfully challenged by the younger generation. The only portraits thought worth doing were of Biblical, allegorical, mythological and historical subjects. The realism sweeping literature was severely curbed; the only landscapes and interiors tolerated were scenes of upper-class surroundings and of "sunny Italy." Russian themes, unless entirely romanticized, were unacceptable.

Most painters had been trained abroad in any case, especially in Italy, where until the latter part of the century they were simply supposed to copy the work of renaissance masters. The Society for the Encouragement of Artists, founded in 1822, was entirely academic. Consequently, until the latter part of the century, Russian painting was a pale reflection of Western European art.

In keeping with the general ferment that seized the country after the Crimean war, however, painters rebelled against routine: a revolt that had long been brewing against the pseudo-classical tradition of the Academy of Arts came to the boil in 1863, when the entire

Peter Tchaikovsky *(1840 - 1893), first studied law and entered the administration. Later the generosity of his patroness, Madame de Meck, allowed him to pursue an uninterrupted career as a composer.*

graduating class refused to join in the contest on a set traditional theme; they launched the Association of Free Artists, and though soon dissolved this was to lead in 1870 to the establishment of the Society of Circulating Exhibitions, which lasted until the revolution of 1917. The cultural life of the country was at last affected. Perhaps the chief fault painting suffered from was the social commitment that submerged Russian art in the wake of Russian literature. The young rebels against academic convention also attacked all the old masters on principle: having espoused the social-message theory of art in a particularly gross form, they thought art was to be directed at the toiling masses, who of course never came to exhibitions. All questions of talent were subordinated to "social content". In view of the general mediocrity in painting this theory was actually rather well conceived. Even Repin (1844-1930), the most famous painter of this period, is primarily of sociological interest.

Michael Glinka *(1804-1857), spiritual father of indigenous Russian music, painted by Repin. Glinka was of noble birth; like other Russian composers of the period he was trained outside of a conservatory (none existed in Russia until 1862).*

Architecture, because of its collectively symbolic character, suffered most from the narrow-minded constraint of the authorities. Churches, public buildings and sometimes even private houses had to have government approval. Nicholas I took a great interest in

Dmitri Mendeleyev *(1834-1907), chemist. After preparatory work in Russia and Paris, Mendeleyev studied oil in Pennsylvania and the Caucasus. Later he held a chair at the University of St. Petersburg. He wrote celebrated studies on oil and the compression of gas.*

architecture; he considered his taste infallible. The result was that the "Russian Empire" of the Eighteenth and early Nineteenth Centuries, which had a certain charm, succumbed to a vulgar eclecticism rooted in the haphazard mingling of styles borrowed from Western Europe. This eclecticism yielded in its turn to a precise counterpart of the "official patriotism" of the regime: invented by a Professor Ton (1794-1881) it combined what in his opinion were the characteristic elements of Byzantine and ancient Russian architecture. This Russo-Bizantine style was made compulsory for church designs, public buildings, and even cottages in military settlements. The Grand Palais in the Kremlin was one of Ton's best-known works, as was the Church of Christ the Savior in Moscow, which was replaced by the Palace of the Soviets after the revolution.

During the second half of the Nineteenth Century Russian architecture, perhaps in keeping with the dramatic deterioration of taste all over Europe and the United States, produced some of the worst and unfortunately the most

durable buildings, which reflected more than ever its lack of genuine tradition and its low technical standards. This period was particularly disastrous because it was just the time when cities began expanding rapidly, and wood was uniformly replaced by brick and stone.

These signs of artistic efflorescence were both effect and cause of a general intellectual stimulation based on the growth of education, and above all of the considerable absolute, though relatively insignificant growth in the actual numbers of educated people. In spite of all the repressive measures of the Tsarist regime the technology of the Nineteenth Century proved unable to control the longing for information and self-expression through the arts. Nor was there, before the modern totalitarian dictatorships, any conception of the potentialities of social upheaval. No attempt was made actually to extirpate opposition physically, or even to silence effectively every organ of unofficial public opinion.

The reform of the school system was doubtless the beginning. Between 1855 and 1861 progessive circles, with the sympathy of the more enlightened bureaucrats, removed the most oppressive restrictions on the universities. The student body no longer had a limit on size; Russian scholars were allowed to travel and study abroad; inspectors could no longer supervise students' behavior off grounds; undergraduate uniforms were eliminated; philosophy and European constitutional law began being taught again, and the general public was allowed into lectures.

But as though to illustrate the provocativeness of repressive measures half-heartedly applied, the universities, especially after the Crimean War, became the scene of disturbances that remained permanent in Russian academic life until the revolution. Undergraduate agitation, the forerunner of student unrest throughout the world today, became a mass movement. At first the students merely protested against the tiresome vexations of academic controls, living conditions, etc., but the growth of general disaffection throughout the intelligentsia soon gave their protests a political tincture.

The first attempt on Alexander II's life, in 1866, led to a tightening of the screws. A liberal Minister of Education was dismissed out of hand and his place taken by Count D.A. Tolstoy, notorious for his fierce hostility toward Roman Catholics and his virulent opposition to

Right, Ivan Pavlov *(1849-1936), famous physiologist. Pavlov founded the Russian school of physiology. His main research concerned the work of the digestive glands. He was awarded the Nobel prize in 1904.*

the emancipation of the serfs. Tolstoy was in control of both church and schools for some fourteen years; he had an effect on educational institutions that lasted until the revolution. In retrospect, of course, we can see that his attempt to dam the liberal and revolutionary spirit of the universities by police repression—repression, moreover that in the nature of things could only be palliative—was bound to exacerbate matters. A law promulgated by him in 1871, for instance, replacing a more liberal law of 1864, attempted to exploit the ancient issue of classicism versus science in the secondary schools in accordance with Tolstoy's views. This issue was not, of course, entirely academic, since the teaching of the humanities was used as a method of preventing boys with no money or social status from getting into higher schools, an objective openly proclaimed in 1887. The 1871 law launched a secondary school regime described as "Greco-Roman bondage." Both classical languages were made compulsory in all secondary schools. Latin with the first and Greek with the third year; each language was assigned six to eight hours per week for the whole course, which in 1877 was extended to eight years. Mathematics and religion were also given more time at the expense of literature, history, geography, etc.

Of course even in the classics there was no question of the nature of ancient civilization: the time was spent on boring things like vocabulary and syntax.

These classical courses were designed to fill up the young scholars' time in such a way as to deflect their attention from things closer at hand. In discussing the struggle in Rome between patricians

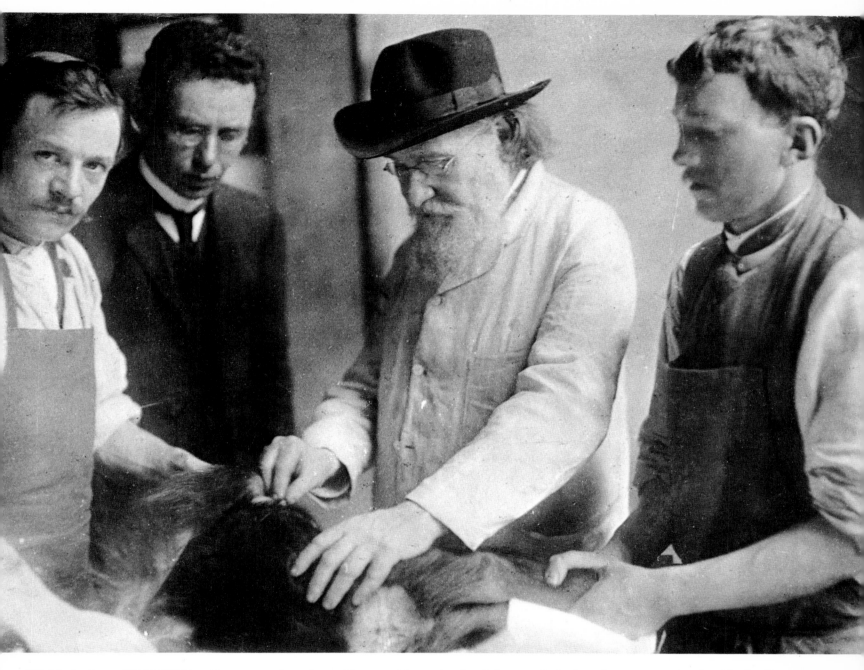

Eli Mechnikov *(1845-1916). After research and teaching in his native land he travelled, then became associated with the Pasteur Institute of Paris. He studied the causes of old age phenomena which he attributed to the formation of intestinal poisons. Mechnikov, shown here injecting virus into a monkey at the Pasteur Institute, won the Nobel prize in 1908.*

and plebeians, for instance, it was to be "strongly emphasized that both parties displayed moderation and self-control at all times." etc.

But the classical secondary schools were a complete failure; very few boys graduated, and it was not even effective as a shield against subversive ideas. The scholastic regime was so deadening and at the same time so futile that revolutionary and liberal ideas spread even among the teachers like wildfire, to say nothing of the students, and even some of the parents.

Despite the restrictions, formalism and grinding foolishness, education was gaining in spite of everything. Women's education made substantial progress, and in the 1860s and 70s a genuine

beginning, however modest, was finally made in elementary education. On the eve of the emancipation of the serfs there had been scarcely any elementary schools to speak of, but even under Tolstoy's regime a start was made that was to have far-reaching effects. The problem in education generally was actually not so much the unreasonable measures of the government as the appalling lack of teachers, the general poverty, and the consequent reluctance of the local communities to take up the burden of a school system, which was largely left in the hands of the harassed and incompetent central government.

By the end of Alexander II's reign in 1881, there were eight universities in Russia with a teaching staff of 600, and

a student body of almost 10,000, most of them (7,700) graduates of secondary schools. Petersburg and Moscow had the largest universities, with 2,400 and 2,000 students respectively, nearly half of them working toward a medical degree. The women's universities that had been established had over 900 students in Petersburg, for instance, and 400 in Kiev.

The elementary school system was still more meagre in terms of the population: in 1881 there were 229 county schools, with 17,300 students; 262 municipal schools with 28,100 students, and 22,800 primary schools with 1,207,000 pupils, including 235,000 girls.

These figures are strikingly low, of course; nevertheless there was a substantial advance over the 1850s in the number of both schools and students. It was typical of Russia to have an Academy of Science long before there were any elementary or secondary schools. The characteristic anomaly of Russian life had not yet been exorcised: the cultivation underlying civilization —science and the arts—sprang from a foreign tradition, and remained exotic.

Nevertheless, in actual achievements, and indeed in talent, the Russian upper class and intelligentsia distinguished themselves; they proved to be an immense reservoir of intellectual ability and moral dedication. The cultural and technological progress launched by the branching out, however meagre, of education after the middle of the Nineteenth Century laid an ineradicable imprint on the younger generation.

During the 1860s and 70s young Russians became impassioned students of all forms of science—chemistry, physics, zoology, geology and everything else, including mathematics. The devotion to science was itself a revolt against the restraints of the official social order, and perhaps even more against the scholasticism and metaphysics that were objects of so much conventional piety. The exact disciplines of science seemed a more effective and rational approach to the comprehension of the universe; in addition, their form was, of course, far more immune to the probings of the police regime. Here again the West played a vitalizing role: though the chief centers for the study of natural science were the Universities of Kazan and Petersburg, most Russian scientists of note were trained, at least partially, in the great universities and academies of Western Europe, particularly Germany; most of them in fact did a good deal of their work under the celebrated German chemist Liebig.

The significance of scientific study is indicated by its extraordinary popularity: not only were learned societies, congresses, and journals produced for the scientists themselves, but as early as 1858 some businessmen built a hall where public lectures were given to packed houses on such subjects as "Galvanism and its Applications". Some of the most notable names in the scientific Russian tradition that was established then, and that was to remain characteristic of Russian life, were the chemist Mendeleyev (1843-1907), the biologist Mechnikov (1845-1916) and the physiologist Pavlov (1849-1936): they are familiar even to laymen.

The success of abstruse science is of course less surprising than the development of a cultivated intelligentsia: just because theoretical science lends a role of such importance to individuals the Russians, even with the small fraction of their population engaged in such studies, were able to demonstrate great versatility and talent.

The realism in the arts, with its tacitly assumed concomitant of political radicalism, that characterized the general unrest and disillusionment of the 60s and 70s, was largely due to the liberalization of the government, however halfhearted and contradictory this was.

The great event, both political and social, of the latter part of the Nineteenth Century was, of course, the emancipation of the serfs, which was widely reflected in literature. The landed aristocracy, which had produced the classical literature of the early part of the century and had begun decomposing a little later, decayed on its estates or floated off to join the evolving intelligentsia. Scarcely anyone but Tolstoy retained a specific class consciousness; nearly all writers and thinkers, even those like Turgenev who individually had patrician origins, became more or less uprooted. By the time of the emancipation the gentry was completely overhauled: the middle layers were finished off by the pressure of the emancipation and its aftermath, and the aristocracy proper was isolated.

Meanwhile the intelligentsia, which had been in the grip of the two broad currents of Slavophilism and Westernizing radicalism, was being polarized still more sharply.

The romantic Slavophilism of the early intelligentsia turned into Russian Pan-Slavism, which simply became a synonym for the ambitions of the Russian state as such. The sentimental theories formerly held about Slav kinship etc., were exploited to provide the autocracy with pretexts for expansion. From the view that the Slavs as a whole were united by deep ties of culture and psychology, the Pan-Slavists, whose influence grew substantially after the national humiliation of the Crimean War, began to formulate a crude theory that it was the mission of Russia to liberate the Slavs from foreign yokes.

Practically speaking the theory, aside from containing differences about all conceivable details, was encumbered by insoluble riddles: for those Pan-Slavists who based their claims of Russia's historic mission on religious grounds the disadvantage was that it excluded all Roman Catholic Slavs, such as the Poles, who were loathed by all Russian Pan-Slavists, as well as the Czechs and Croats, unless they recanted their Catholic "heresy", which was highly unlikely. Since by the end of 1906 all the Slavs in the world were thought to number some 150,000,000, of whom 70% were Greek Orthodox and 23% Roman Catholics, the remainder being divided into Uniats, dissidents, Protestants and Muslims, this was a substantial loss for the religious wing of Pan-Slavism.

The less pious Pan-Slavists disregarded the religious issue, and developed a quasi-ethnic basis for Slav unity: the

cardinal factor in Slavdom's position in the world was the "historic" struggle between the Slavs and Western (i.e. German-Magyar) Europe. Since the only great Slav power was Russia, the conduct of this struggle had to depend on her.

It need hardly be pointed out that all such claims belong to mythology. This is of course very powerful, but in fact the Russians ultimately failed to achieve anything beyond adding one more element of confusion to the imbroglio of the First World War, which Russia was to emerge from so disastrously. On any rational plane, of course, the comparison with Germans and Italians was fatal: unlike them the Slavic peoples had never developed any common culture at all, but had simply evolved under the impact of cultures imported from various points abroad. The Poles, Czechs, Croats and Slovaks, for instance, had been moulded entirely by Western European and Catholic influences. There is, in fact, no such thing as Slavic civilization in the sense in which the term has meaning for French, Italians, or Germans; hence the opposition of "Slavdom" to the "decadent West" was literally senseless.

The interest taken by Russia in her "Slavic brethren" after the Crimean War, was quite novel: beforehand it had been negligible. As for the Russian attempt to involve the Balkan Slavs in the schemes of the Russian state, not many of them were willing to exchange Austrians, Magyars, or for that matter even Turks for Russians. They were not encouraged by what had happened to Poland.

In fact Pan-Slavism was not a genuine emotional focus as its more intellectual predecessor, Slavophilism, had been, but a mere device of statecraft. Its basic significance lies in its political role; it became a rallying-point for the Pan-Russian agitation that preceded the First World War.

At the other end of the spectrum, the former Westernizing movement also began delineating itself far more sharply. The fusion between the educated elements of the middle and smaller gentry and the self-made intellectuals (in Russian the "men-of-all-ranks") who had somehow slipped into an education, formed a milieu that was to take its abstract ideas into the field of action.

A revolutionary movement, armed and organized, took up the ancient heritage of Russian rebelliousness. This sector of the intelligentsia broadened its messianic perspective to encompass the overthrow not merely of the political regime, but the whole of the social order. Simultaneously it created, for the first time in history, an organized movement for the realization of this apocalyptic vision. This movement ultimately swept the field and created a new society over the ruins of Tsarism.

Dissidence Organized

The revolutionary movement carried disaffection to a logical extreme. Almost as soon the intelligentsia became conscious of itself as a special group, with an awareness of the contrast between

1858 launched *The Bell* in London, a little journal that had great influence for several years; it was smuggled into Russia and reached the topmost strata of the regime.

whose abolition at first he hailed enthusiastically.

But when the aftermath of the emancipation shifted the whole peasant question into a far more serious perspective Herzen's influence began declining, though to be sure he gave the nascent revolutionary movement two of its most lasting slogans: in an editorial in *The Bell* of July, 1861, entitled "What Do the People Need?" his simple reply, reflecting his indignant rejection of the results of the emancipation program, was—"the people need land and liberty", a motto that was to become a rallying-cry for generations.

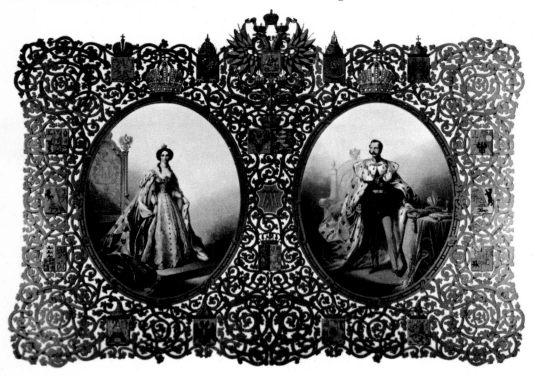

Three illustrations (above, below and opposite) from an album commemorating the coronation in 1856 of Alexander II *(Tsar from 1855-1881). Left, the Empress Maria Alexandrovna (former Princess of Hesse-Darmstadt), right, the Emperor. Brought up to rule, Alexander had a good education and had traveled widely.*

Russia and Europe, a desire to do something about it began growing and ultimately took an organized form.

It was during the second quarter of the Nineteenth Century that Russia for the first time developed an articulate group of people prepared to criticize the authorities—the foreshadowing of "public opinion". Those vitally interested in reform were no longer a handful of people from the social elite, such as the Decembrist noblemen, but represented the plebeian classes. Despite all the efforts of the censorship, journalism, literature, and even the theatre reflected a state of uneasiness, however veiled, about social affairs, though, to be sure, it was confined to the educated few.

It was in this period that "official Russia" diverged from liberal opinion.

Nicholas I began tightening the screws in reaction to the subversive currents agitating Europe toward the turbulent year of 1848; in 1847, Herzen, who had been optimistic about the possibility of working for his ideals in Russia, finally left for good. Having inherited a large fortune, he devoted himself to promoting his ideas, and in

The Empress-mother surrounded by the Grand Duchesses. They wear Russian-style headresses and French crinolines.

Though Herzen had no objection in principle to revolutionary action, he thought everything necessary could stem far more appropriately from the Tsar. His special concern was social and economic reform, especially serfdom

Herzen had left Russia just before the storm of 1848 made Nicholas's police regime even harsher. The radicalized students and intellectuals remaining in Russia were confronted by a repressive apparatus they could no longer elude, though its treatment of dissident opinion was characterized by a mingling of severity and caprice.

This baffling combination was illustrated, for instance, in the case of Peter Chaadayev (1793-1856) an aristocratic dandy and Guards officer, who was an habitué of the aristocratic salons of Petersburg and Moscow and also, curiously enough, a religious philosopher of distinction.

Influenced by Roman Catholicism, he considered the unification of all Christian sects an indispensable step in the establishment of the Kingdom of God. He had a gift for writing, and after his retirement from the army at the age of thirty expressed himself vigorously in "philosophical letters" circulated in aristocratic circles. After abortive attempts at publication, one of the Letters finally appeared in a Moscow newspaper, *The*

The coronation of the Empress. *Cathedral of the Dormition in Moscow. The ladies of the court in the foreground wear the Russian coiffe. From an album printed in France for the Emperor.*

Telescope, in 1836. It was like a gush of cold water on the chauvinistic enthusiasm of official circles; Chaadayev took away from Russia practically everything.

"Hermits in the world, we have given it nothing and received nothing from it; we have contributed not a single thought to the sum total of mankind's ideas; we have not helped perfect human understanding and we have distorted everything we have borrowed from it... Not one useful thought has been born on our soil."

He blamed the Byzantine source of Russia's Christianity for her isolation from Western Europe. But though he infuriated the French and German-speaking proponents of Russian grandeur to the point of suspending *The Telescope*, exiling the editor, and sacking the censor who passed the article,

Chaadayev was simply declared insane. But he was not put into an asylum and his movements were only slightly restricted; he remained a revered figure in Moscow's aristocratic life. It is more than likely that "official" patriotism was confined to a small bureaucratic and imperial circle, and that the regime was already beginning to lose the whole-hearted backing even of the topmost social stratum.

The "Petrashevsky group" was another example, perhaps the most tragic, of the obtuseness of the authorities.

Petrashevsky was a graduate of the aristocratic *lycée* of Tsarskoye Selo and a minor official in the Foreign Ministry. He was an admirer of Fourier, the mildest of visionaries. His literary receptions, very popular with the elite, finally aroused police suspicion. When Petrashevsky and his friends started

talking, among many other things, of forming a secret revolutionary society, and furthermore held a dinner in memory of Fourier in April 1849, the over-excited police spies thought they were preaching sedition. Thirty-nine of the "group" were arrested, though nothing could be proved against them but the offense, non-existent in the criminal code, of a "conspiracy of ideas". Fifteen were sentenced to death and six to forced labor or Siberian exile.

Nicholas I reverted to a sport he had not had a chance to indulge in since the Decembrist revolt of 1825: he examined the "ideational conspirators" himself, with the same skill he had shown twenty-four years before. He decided to commute their sentence, but in order to dramatize things not to inform them until they were already standing on the scaffold. In his own hand he prescribed

189

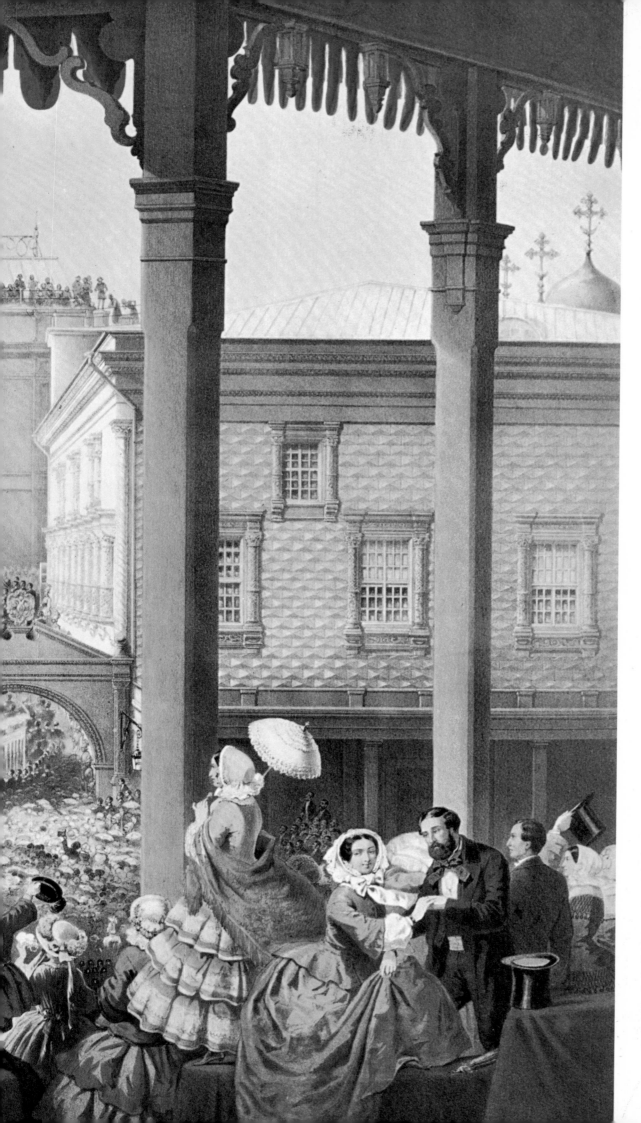

Popular rejoicing after the coronation of Emperor Alexander II *on the Palace Square, from the same album as the previous illustrations. The Emperor stands at the top of the stairs on the left and waves to the crowd. On the right, the cupolas of the Dormition cathedral within the Kremlin. On coming to the throne Alexander announced he would continue the policies of his father in every way. However, the disastrous Crimean war had to be liquidated and reforms undertaken to assuage internal dissatisfaction.*

the distances between gibbets, the number of drum-rolls announcing the bogus executions, and the costume to be worn by the chaplain.

Dostoyevsky, whose first works had come out shortly before, was one of the victims: he was sentenced to four years of hard labor, then six years in a Siberian army garrison. He has left an absorbing record of his travail in his *House of the Dead*.

A comparison between the Petrashevists and the Decembrists is revealing: both were futile, but in different ways. If the Decembrists seemed a hold-over from the Eighteenth Century, with their aristocratic, idealistic, purely personal and socially isolated idealism, the Petrashevists seemed a foreshadowing of the end of the Nineteenth Century, when the action of plebeians, linked to a collective ideal and informed by an abstract idea, would begin to lay an axe to the social order.

A natural reaction to Nicholas I's authoritarianism was its transformation into its opposite. In the 1860s a mood was generated for which the word applied by Turgenev to his famous hero Bazarov—Nihilism—has become standard. The Nihilists denied all authority of whatever origin: not merely the state, family and religion, but science as well, or at any rate absolute Science.

The Nihilists, after replacing the utopians of the 1840s, were succeeded in their turn by the practical revolutionaries. The sentimental philosophizing of the Fourierists yielded to a passionate determination to change society as well as talk about it.

This determination did not bear fruit for a decade. Russia had no revolutionary movement at all during the 1850s: Herzen's *Bell*, published abroad, was the only focus of subversion. But with the optimistic atmosphere surrounding the accession of Alexander II the winds of radicalism began to blow.

There was some justification for thinking Alexander II's reign the beginning of an era of reform. In the late 1850s,

Many of the XIXth century revolutionaries were intellectuals with upper-class backgrounds. Above: Prince Peter Kropotkin *(1842-1921), who contributed vast sums to the revolutionary movement.*

Center: Vissarion Belinsky *(1810-1848), who used literary criticism as a vehicle to diffuse social theories of the intelligentsia. His messianic aspirations and "Western" leanings influenced a whole younger generation.*

Below: Michael Bakunin *(1818-1872), the father of revolutionary anarchy. Wellborn, dynamic, Bakunin founded the First International with Marx. Portrait by the famous French photographer Nadar.*

for instance, the surviving Decembrists and the Petrashevists were allowed to return from Siberia, while the emancipation of the serfs was hailed as the beginning of progress even by radicals.

Under the Tsar-Emancipator the reins of academic repression and censorship relaxed, and the young people, mostly commoners, thronged fairly freely into the universities. Talk was unconfined. Dostoyevsky's novel, *The Possessed*, gives us a glimpse of the excitement of the period: "They talked of the abolition of the censorship, of phonetic spelling, of the substitution of the Latin characters for the Russian alphabet... of splitting Russia into nationalities united in a free federation, of the abolition of the Army and Navy, of the restoration of Poland as far as the Dnieper, of the peasant reforms and of the manifestos, of the abolition of the hereditary principle and of the family, of children, of priests, of women's rights."

But despite the relaxation of controls during the first years of Alexander II's reign, the autocracy could not of course be expected to permit open opposition. The need for secrecy led to the establishment of the "underground" in Russian life—the revival of secret societies that was so typical of the final phase of Tsarism. Indeed, perhaps the most portentous phenomenon of the "Era of Great Reforms" was the rise of the revolutionary movement: it is surely significant that the whole of the generation that accomplished the revolution of 1917 was born between 1870 and 1880.

Broadly speaking, this revolutionary movement was made up of two currents —Populism and Marxism.

The Populist attempt to organize the peasants was rooted in the idea that it was alienated from the official regime and intrinsically hostile to it. But of course the desire to "go to the people" did not mean that the people was available. The Populist movement, in fact, developed a terrorist wing that was far more notorious, and indeed, effective, than any of its other elements, just because the people failed to respond to the ardent enthusiasm of the youths who found a goal for their idealism in the notion of inflaming the sodden, oppressed Russian masses with a broad vision of a new society.

Populism had been launched in a sense by Herzen, though with his essentially humanitarian, social-reformist, perhaps sentimental views, he was quickly outdistanced by the anarchism and political terrorism that became embedded in the new movement. In addition to "Land and Liberty", his other rallying-cry, "Go to the people!" (an exhortation written in November 1861 to the students expelled from the

The terrorists, or Nihilists as they called themselves, were highly articulate and published clandestine newspapers. Here is a scene shown in a French illustrated weekly of 1881: a police raid on a Nihilist press in Kharkov.

universities in a general shut-down) remained magnetic for decades, perhaps because of its inchoate, indeed almost meaningless yet ardent pathos.

Herzen lost much of his Russian support by coming out for Polish independence toward the end of 1861, but his major shortcoming in the new era was that he remained essentially a gentleman. His reasons for hostility to the centralized Russian state failed to strike an echo among the younger radicals flocking out of Russia to London, Paris, Zurich and Geneva in the Seventies and Eighties.

From their point of view Herzen was far too rhetorical and abstractly humanitarian. By 1865, when he transferred the printing-press and editorial offices of *The Bell* to Geneva, now the new centre of the Russian political emigration, it was obvious that the new developments had left him far behind. After 1863 the circulation of *The Bell*, never more than 3,000 copies in any case,

declined considerably. It was suspended in 1867 and Herzen, embittered and characteristically disillusioned, died in 1870.

The men who typified Russian dissidence differed widely in temperament and origins: "going to the people" was the principal idea they had in common.

This notion actually reflected two distinct emotional states: one was the idealistic, misty adoration of The People, as deity, in which the desire was to sacrifice oneself and serve. The other was due to an exasperation caused by the failure of this abstract entity to respond to the love being borne it. The incapacity of the people for mass action doubtless imposed on the frustrated intellectuals a need to express themselves in violence. Thus there were always two emotional currents that bore intellectuals into Populist activity: the folk-worshippers, and the idealistic assassins, doubtless frustrated folk-worshippers themselves, but too impatient

to wait for the people to wake up and storm the fortress themselves.

Perhaps all the successive movements of dissidence rotated around the same axis of differentiation: the desire to serve the historic process one was identifying with oneself, and the headstrong eagerness to force that same process to obey one's will.

It is curious to recall that the "going to the people" associated with the Russian revolutionary movement was also reflected, on an innocuous scale, a little later in England, where university settlements in slums became fashionable, to say nothing of the fad of "slumming" itself: Bernard Shaw's brief career as a vestryman is an echo of the Populist peasant crusades.

From the insurrectionist point of view the success of the Paris Commune of 1871 in actually surviving for several weeks was very encouraging to the "immediate action" groups among the revolutionaries. It influenced their plans

Terrorist activities increased during this period, with repeated attacks against high officials and draconian reprisals on the part of the police. After seven assassination attempts, the second of two bombs killed Alexander II on March 1, 1881. The first hit his sled killing the guard; the Tsar got out to help the wounded and was felled by the final bomb.

Members of the terrorist organization named The People's Will *responsible for the assassination of Alexander II are hung in St. Petersburg. Contemporary news drawings.*

both in the abortive rehearsal of 1905 and the full-dress performance in 1917.

One of the most potent publicists of the period was Chernyshevsky, who in 1861 founded the first new secret society, Young Russia; together with his comrade Dobrolyubov he was a leading figure in the world of "cri-ticism" that moulded so many Russian ideas. In 1862 he was arrested and after being pilloried in a St. Petersburg square deported to Siberia.

Though a "Westerner" like Belinsky, and an agnostic, Chernyshevsky had nothing but contempt for the peasants; nor did he expect much from the workers.

Unlike Marx in many ways, primarily in his belief in the absolute validity of morality, in contrast with Marx's emphasis on the "objective" environment as a precondition to the attainment of any ideal, he resembled him in basing his hopes on the development of society's productive forces through capitalism, as against those who expected miracles to be wrought by the wooden plough and by small groups of benevolent cooperators. He also, like Marx, stressed the role of the state, and above all regarded Socialism as emerging of necessity from the economic situation in and for itself.

He was of course disappointed by the terms of the emancipation; he had fought for the bestowal of land as well as liberty on the serfs. His imprisonment after the 1866 attempt on Alexander II's life was not surprising. The relative mildness of the Tsarist regime—from the viewpoint of later totalitarian states—is indicated by his managing to publish, from prison, a novel called *What Is to Be Done?* Though all the ideas expressed in it are to be found in Owen, Fourier, George Sand, Godwin and John Stuart Mill, the book had a great influence, not least on the thinking of Lenin, for whom Chernyshevsky was a favorite. One of the characters in *What Is to Be Done?* dreams of a Russia transformed into a paradise of beauty and health by the total subjugation of nature to human needs, with the whole community of the "Phalansterie" living in a palace of aluminum and glass (doubtless inspired by the Crystal Palace Exposition of 1851: Chernyshevsky was a great Anglophile). This sort of dream later mesmerized the Bolsheviks; though inspired by utilitarianism Chernyshevsky was clearly one of their forerunners.

Michael Bakunin, born in 1818, was the son of a rich nobleman: of fabulous energy and temperament, he was a sort of one-man hurricane—from the age of twenty-five on the eye of every political tornado in Europe. A founder together with Marx of the International Workingmen's Association of 1864—the "First International"—he soon broke with him, and after many violent disputes was expelled in 1872; he died four years later, as he was about to try launching a social revolution in Italy.

Though something of a Slavophile in his earlier days—he supported the idea of a Slav federation—Bakunin is known primarily as the father of revolutionary anarchism, a logical extension of Proudhon's idea of the negation of the state. Bakunin combined this idea with one taken from Marx, of collective ownership, and pushed it as far as it could go. His personal glamour and exciting presence made him a symbol for all those who craved action justified by some theory, however obscure and even incoherent.

Despite his diffuse, though flamboyant gyrations, Bakunin made a real contribution to insurrectionary tactics, though it was vitiated by a streak of nihilism: he claimed, for instance, that the first thing to do in any outbreak was to set fire to—not seize!—the town hall. Herzen cracked a joke about Bakunin's invariably mistaking the second month of gestation for the ninth, and said he bounded around in the preliminaries of the Polish insurrection as though decorating a Christmas tree. The supporters of the autocracy nicknamed him the "Old Man of the Mountain," after the chief of the Assassin Sect. Nicholas II remarked that he was "a nice boy, but we must keep him locked up."

The tendency represented by Bakunin was counterweighed by the allegiance of many other young revolutionaries to Peter Lavrov, who in a series of historical letters published in 1868-1869 inspired young idealists to help the

At the period the above photograph was taken, Dostoyevsky *the young conspirator has been replaced by this man with ravaged features racked by epileptic fits.*

Vera Zasulich, *young aristocrat terrorist who fired at the Military Governor of St. Petersburg, wounding him seriously. Anti-regime feeling ran so high she was acquitted.*

peasants by going to the villages to teach and awaken them. Lavrov believed in the simultaneous perfection of the individual and of society in a unity that would evade the contrast between individualism and Socialism. He also believed that ideas were the source of power, and hence that a society that repressed the creative minority was doomed to stagnation.

This minority had to be allowed to do its thinking in peace; accordingly the state's coercive power had to be curtailed as much as possible. Lavrov's social ideal consequently boiled down to a form of anarchy, with the sections of society bound to each other by contractual duties, supervised by the benevolence of a natural aristocracy of the intellect.

Though a revolutionary in this sense, Lavrov was hostile to dictatorship, which he thought corrupting; he believed that the people alone ought to wield power. He also believed that these ideas of his should be taught gradually, in accordance with a maturing process. He was editor for a time of the *People's Will,* a magazine that stood for terrorism, which he and his school were not opposed to.

In this pre-Marxist age both Bakunin and Lavrov stood for individual and not mass action; both were revolutionary, and both were terrorist. The contrast was really in their long-range aims: the Lavrov group believed in

Page of the manuscript from Dostoyevsky's The Possessed. *In this work Dostoyevsky used a real life incident he had experienced: Sergius Nechayev, an early terrorist, assassinated a colleague when he suspected the latter of betraying him.*

195

an ultimate transformation of society through gradual ripening processes, while the Bakunin group believed in short-range agitation for immediate insurrection wherever possible. Lavrov thought enlightenment had to come from the intelligentsia, while Bakunin

Left, Frederick Engels *(1820-1895). Philosopher and lifelong collaborator of Marx, was soon translated into Russian and passionately discussed by intellectual revolutionaries. Right,* Karl Marx *(1818-1883). His* Capital, *originally published in 1867, was translated into a foreign language, Russian, for the first time a few years later (see document facing page). The censor apparently did not recognize what trouble it was to foment.*

believed the elemental instincts of the people were in fact the only source of right, i.e., insurrectionary action.

Before Marxist ideas had spread very widely in Russia, this belief in long-range and inevitable historical processes gave the nickname of "Marxists" to the Lavrov group: at this time Marxist doctrine was still considered to be gradualist and merely hortatory.

Typical of the new generation was Sergius Nechayev (1847-1883), a plebeian school teacher and student who was a disciple and even a friend of Bakunin's. Nechayev distinguished himself as the first Russian revolutionary to set up a practical outline for a revolutionary program and organization; at the age of 22 he gave the notion of terrorism a principled formulation. Fanatically devoted to his own cause, he also imposed a puritanical code of personal behavior on his followers, while at the same time resorting to any kind of fraud to magnify his personal prestige. Preceding the myth-making totalitarian regimes of our own day, he personally manufactured his own propaganda, sending out news about his bogus arrests and escapes, even his own death. A premature believer in the cult of the leader, he personally, on conceiving doubts of the loyalty of a blindly devoted associate, decided on and carried out his assassination. The

episode is described in Dostoyevsky's *The Possessed:* it led to Nechayev's trial and life imprisonment. While in prison he kept up regular contacts with his associates and directed their terrorist activities. A thoroughly romantic visionary as well as a matter-of-fact organizer, he devised imaginative plots for popular rebellions to be provoked by fictitious imperial manifestoes. His extravagant ruthlessness led to his repudiation by Marx and Bakunin, but he went on being venerated by the bloodthirstier branch of the movement. Zhelyabov, who organized Alexander II's assassination, vacillated between that and setting Nechayev free: it was the latter who requested that Alexander II be killed instead.

Peter Tkachev was typical of the next two or three generations of revolutionaries; born in 1844, he was first arrested for subversive activities at the age of 17. A radical journalist close to Nechayev, he contributed an element of his own that was characteristic: it places him directly in the line of Lenin's spiritual ancestry. Under the influence of Auguste Blanqui he developed the view that it was not the business of a political party to harangue the people, that is, propagandize the masses, but to seize power. This gave him the reputation of a Russian Jacobin. He thought Russia was perfectly ripe for a Socialist revolution, but that too much talk about it would simply play into the hands of the bourgeoisie, who would have the time to organize and thus jeopardize the chances of an insurrection. Tkachev was far from Marxism: he was primarily interested in the peas-

antry and indifferent to the industrial proletariat: it is his organizational point of view that makes him a forerunner of Lenin's.

The general structure of Populism, originating in Herzen's writings of the late 1840s and early 1850s and elaborated ten or twenty years later by Chernyshevsky, Dobrolyubov, Nechayev, Tkachev, Lavrov, Bakunin and others, rested on the following essential points:

The Russian existing order, which was doomed and had to be overthrown by a Socialist revolution, was different from that of other countries. It was this difference that permitted capitalism to be skipped over altogether and Socialism to be embarked on directly. This was based on the assumption that a couple of specifically Russian institutions — the village commune and the associations of workmen and craftsmen *(artels)* — were in harmony with Socialism; thus capitalism in Russia would be a step backward. The fraternal cooperation taken to underly these institutions was considered to derive from the character of the Russian peasants, who were thought to be collectively minded by instinct and therefore the authentic force behind the revolutionary movement.

It goes without saying that there was no agreement on just how all these objectives were to be achieved. Optimistic fantasy remained inherent in all Populist assumptions about political affairs, and even when it was the general creed of Russian radicals, during the 1870s, its mixture of Socialism, national conceit, visionary idealism and ferocious brutality was not enough to provide the movement with a manual of instructions for bringing about the great upheaval.

Perhaps just because its large-scale program was difficult to formulate the practical echoes of Populism in ordinary life were far from trivial. A long series of revolutionary periodicals began appearing in Russia in the autumn of 1861 and went on until the 1917 revolution. After Chernyshevsky's short-lived Young Russia, secret societies of the modern kind really began in 1862 with the establishment in Petersburg of *Land and Liberty,* the first important one, though it only lasted a couple of years: Chernyshevsky was in close contact with this, too.

The unsuccessful 1866 attempt made against Alexander II's life by Karakozov, a member of an extreme radical group who acted, however, on his personal initiative, led to all sorts of official harassment of students. They kept being penalized, and expelled in addition, to such an extent that in 1882 the Director of the Police, Von Plehve, later Minister of the Interior, thought that it was the excessively harsh police repression that alienated an enormous number of young men from normal society and practically forced them into the revolutionary movement. When women were barred from universities in 1863, Russian girls began flocking abroad, especially to Zurich. They were steeped in systematic propaganda, which by now was becoming dense enough to constitute an entire philosophy of life. It took the government a decade to see the results of this expatriation of able, idealistic young women. By the time it issued an edict promising the opening of higher schools for women in Russia and ordering the students home by the end of 1873 on pain of exclusion from Russian schools and state employment, the result was that though most of the Russian girls came back it was only in order to participate in a mass propaganda campaign among the peasantry that the revolutionary groups meanwhile had decided on. It seemed as though the government's activities, as usual both too extreme and not extreme enough, could only help its enemies.

The movement "To the People!" assumed an organizational character by the "crazy" summer of 1874. Literally thousands of young men and women, frenzied by optimistic reports that the Russian countryside was about to burst into flames, put on peasant clothing and invaded rural Russia. Some of them tried to set up fixed centres for agitation, others roved about preaching. But their ideas were so far removed from the peasants' experience that though they were sometimes listened to with approval the strange crusade, watched in any case with great vigilance by the police, came to little. The revolution-

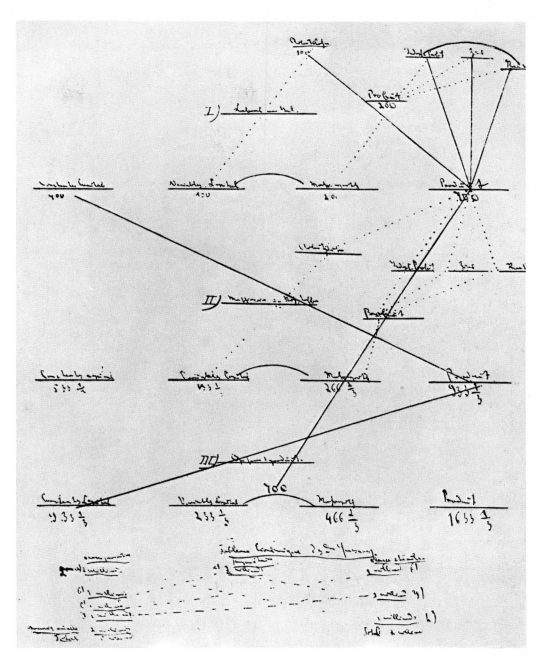

Diagram showing the "Process of reproduction of capital", *contained in a letter from Karl Marx to Frederick Engels of July 6, 1863.*

aries were arrested in droves; the chief Petersburg organization was eliminated in the winter of 1873-74.

The failure of the attempt to appeal to the "people" directly and arouse its conscience stimulated the growth of terrorism. The young intellectuals, despairing of attracting the masses to their idealistic program, decided to fight the autocracy personally, to be sure in the "name" of the people.

In 1878 an organization was formed in Petersburg that revived the name of *Land and Liberty*: it embodied many of the terrorist principles of Tkachev and Nechayev. A new approach "to the people" was made in 1877-78; now the peasants were cajoled not by the mere preaching of individual idealists, but by the revolutionists disguising themselves as important personages, such as storekeepers, trained workmen, teachers,

etc. The peasants remained irremediably apathetic; the only ones to pay attention to the movement in its revised form was the police, and by 1879 the second crusade "to the people" had evaporated. Its failure accentuated the lethal idealism of the youth.

Sometimes, to be sure, there was a peasant response. A peculiar charade was performed in the Province of Kiev in the style of an amusing anachronism. Some flexible revolutionaries talked a few thousand peasants into joining a clandestine organization sworn to the defense of the autocracy: the ringleaders wrote a bogus manifesto in the name of Alexander II giving all the land to the peasants and declaring the emancipation Acts of 1861 a forgery; the revolutionaries called on the peasants to organize in secret and free the shackled Tsar from the aristocratic and bureaucratic

usurpers. This curious modern-dress revival of a Pugachov drama was uncovered in 1877; about a thousand people were arrested for it, including all the leaders. The spirited improvisation, however, had nothing to do with *Land and Liberty*.

Though *Land and Liberty* contained views that were both terrorist and purely educational, the difficulty of establishing effective, indeed, rational contact with the peasantry weighted the balance in favor of terrorism, a trend that was strengthened by the celebrated case of Vera Zasulich.

An unsuccessful demonstration had been staged by *Land and Liberty* in December 1876 in Petersburg; the few dozen participants were roughly handled by the police, and the leaders arrested, tried, and given long terms in goal. One of them, Bogolyubov, was flogged by General Trepov, Military Governor of Petersburg; the revolutionaries decided to protest by killing Trepov. Vera Zasulich, a twenty-nine-year-old aristocrat who knew neither Bogolyubov nor Trepov, but was an active revolutionary who had been imprisoned for two years at the age of twenty, forestalled everyone by firing at Trepov and wounding him seriously in 1878.

Her trial became the symbol of the general indictment of the regime; to the dismay of the authorities she was quickly given a verdict of "not guilty". A huge crowd in the courtroom and outside, including even higher bureaucrats, applauded in rapture. An attempt to arrest her again and set aside the verdict was checkmated; she was slipped secretly out of the country by friends, and returned legally to Russia only after the 1905 amnesty.

Political terror was immensely stimulated by the Zasulich case. A great many Populists were impressed by the popular endorsement of terrorism that was thought to be the significance of the verdict. Outrages on the persons of state officials, including, of course, policemen, became rife, and logically enough led to an attempt on the life of the Tsar.

The issue of regicide divided *Land and Liberty* in October 1879, after Solovyov, one of its members, had fired five shots at the Tsar and missed. Solovyov had used a party gun without authorization, and on this the internal dissension came to a head, splitting the party into the *People's Will* (or *People's Liberty*) and *Total Partition*, led by the later founder of Russian Marxism, George Plekhanov.

Though the *People's Will* used a conventional humane vocabulary revolving around Socialism, faith in the people, the overthrow of autocracy, and democratic representation, in actual fact it was concentrated solely on the

killing of the Tsar, which after seven attempts it finally succeeded in accomplishing by March 1881. Its preparations testified to boundless zeal, painstaking diligence and great personal daring, all in the name of an ideal.

This idealism is perhaps the most impressive thing about the whole Populist movement: though a few of the Populist leaders came of peasant origins, most of them were drawn from the intelligentsia of the upper and middle class: their motives were quite impersonal, and one of the things that baffled the police most in stamping out the movement, which, indeed, they never managed, was just this combination of zeal and selflessness.

The actual membership of all the secret societies was quite small, but except for the peasantry and industrial proletariat revolutionary ideas attracted wide support even in the topmost circles of the bureaucracy and the security police itself. The upper-class origins of many of the revolutionaries meant a copious course of funds; many of them, like Peter Kropotkin, the celebrated revolutionary anarchist, donated their entire fortunes to the movement. The contradictory situation of the Russian upper classes in general was to account for immense sums of money being made available to all sorts of revolutionary organizations, including the later Bolsheviks; capital was substituted for membership. In addition, the police were astonishingly lax.

The Populist movement was apparently exhausted by the assassination of Alexander II: the *People's Will* appealed to his son, Alexander III, offering to cut short all agitation in return for a political amnesty and the convening of a representative assembly. By 1883 most of the leaders were either exiled or jailed, and by the end of the century it seemed moribund.

One of its last spasms of activity was the abortive attempt in 1887 to kill Alexander III. One of the five young men executed for it was Lenin's older brother Alexander; this may have had some influence in shaping Lenin's mind.

The Populist wing of the revolutionary movement underwent a crisis perhaps primarily because of the groundlessness of its two basic assumptions —the political effectiveness of terror and peasant leadership of the revolution. Its basic attitudes were inherited by the Socialist Revolutionary Party, which remained a factor in Russian life until shortly after the 1917 revolution. Toward the end of the Nineteenth Century, however, the Marxist movement, which had already made substantial progress in Europe, began overshadowing it.

Marxism was much later in coming to Russia than Populism, though a Russian translation of *Das Kapital*, published

in 1867, was the first to be made, in 1869. Itself a form of idealism, Marxism was nevertheless rooted in an organic development, the emergence of an industrial proletariat, that ultimately enabled it to realize a comprehensive project of social transformation.

George Plekhanov (1857-1918) was one of the converts to Marxism from Populism; he broke away from *Land and Liberty* at the age of twenty-two and emigrated to Switzerland in 1880. In 1883 he founded the first Russian Marxist organization, the *Emancipation of Labor*.

There is no need here to enter into the details of Marxism. Perhaps its chief appeal for the Russian intelligentsia, even more than for the intellectuals of other countries, was its combination of a powerful messianic emotion with an appearance of scientific methodology that offered enthusiasts the best of both worlds. Their burning desire to change the world was buttressed by sound scientific reasons why this was not only possible, but inevitable.

Marxism in its Russian form may be broadly summed up as the contention that Russian history was a part of universal history, which meant that Russia had to pass through capitalism in order to reach the future Socialist society, that neither the peasantry nor its characteristic institutions, in contrast with the proletariat, were conducive to Socialism, that terrorism must be abandoned, and that the main task of the revolutionary leaders was to create a disciplined working-class party to conduct Russia into the promised land.

This program diverged from Populism on fundamental points, of course, and since for a long time neither group had a mass base the energies of the small number of dedicated intellectuals were expended in arguing with each other. Marx and Engels were translated, adapted, pored over, commented on, and analyzed, so that everything they said could be funneled into the historical conditions of Russia. By 1883-1884 small groups of "scientific" Socialists were formed, chiefly among university students, and by 1887 *Das Kapital* was the most popular book among Russian students. But despite their hope that the motive force for the revolution was to be found in the nascent Russian working-class, these early student Marx-

They did not expect him. *Title of a painting by I.E. Repin of 1884, evoking the return of a political prisoner from Siberia. Tretyakov Gallery, Moscow. Repin (1844-1930), of the late XIXth century Russian realist school, had a successful career as a portrait painter of prominent personalities. He nevertheless criticized the regime, and painted such subjects as political prisoners awaiting execution.*

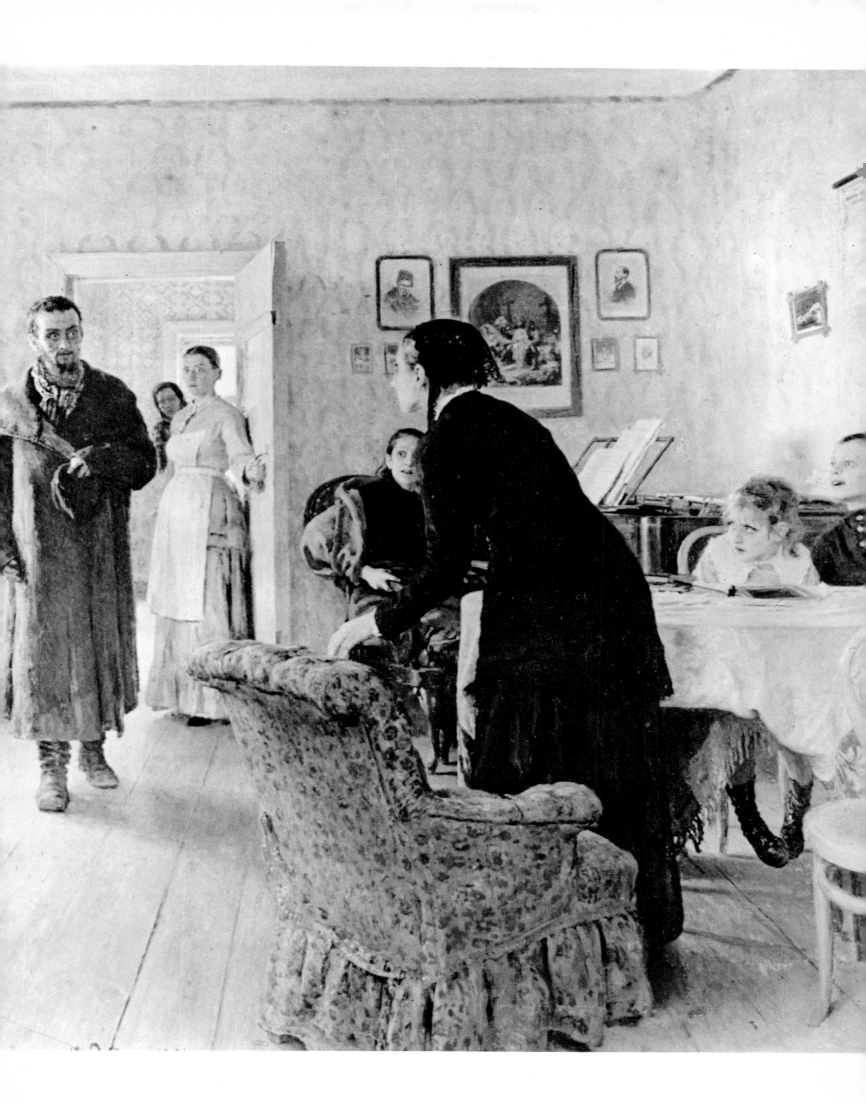

ists had very tenuous connections with the workers or none at all. The great strikes, for instance, that broke out in the 1880s and early 1890s, owe nothing to "ideology"—they were due primarily to the economic grievances that were the growing pains of Russian capitalism. The police and troops found their repression a simple matter. In the beginning Russian Marxism was just as much detached an intellectual effort as the other products of the intelligentsia; it was essentially a literary discussion group.

Marxism's faith in the development of the "objective" forces of society protected it from the Tsarist censors: the notion developed in the early Eighties that the Marxists were actually friendly to capitalism, because of their conviction that Russia had to develop a bourgeois society. To many Marxists the capitalist system was *bound* to succeed feudalism, just as it was *bound* to precede Socialism, and consequently some orthodox Marxists favored capitalism to such an extent that in the calamitous famine of 1891-1892 they were against helping the peasants for fear of hindering the growth of capitalism.

In its early days Russian Marxism was also sometimes identified with the Manchester School of economics: this was doubtless the reason the Tsarist government was to tolerate what was called "legal Marxism" for so long. Aided by its anti-terrorist character, Marxism in this form could be expressed in the legal Russian press, and until the outbreak of the First World War there was, as well as an illegal branch of Marxism, a legal one adhered to by many of the new class of business managers and engineers created by the growing industrialization of Russia.

Until the middle of the 1890s Marxism was a matter of polemicizing against Populists and not much more: factories and workshops were still too remote. About 1893 the word "Social-Democrat", already current in Germany, began to be used for Russian Marxism, to distinguish it by virtue of its theory of social development from terrorist or anarchist opinion. 1895 is perhaps best taken as the starting-point of the movement that in a little more than twenty years was to find itself at the helm of the Russian state. This was when some twenty Marxist discussion and literary coteries in the Petersburg area, under the leadership of Lenin (born Vladimir Ulyanov) and Martov (born Julius Tsederbaum) fused in the *Fighting Union for the Liberation of the Working-Class*. It combined intellectual discussion with practical activity, by unambiguously shifting the Union's emphasis to energetic agitation among the rank-and-file of the proletariat. Moscow and other industrial centres followed suit, and by the end of the century the Marxist movement, though still negligible in size, was a substantial factor in Russian life.

But it was still shapeless. A congress held in Minsk in March 1898 to unify the movement was inhibited by police vigilance. Nine people attended, representing five local organizations and the Russian Jewish "Bund", a Social-Democratic organization of Jewish workers established in 1897. This was to play a stellar role in the revolutionary movement for some years, until Marxism finally rooted itself in the major centres of the Russian working-class proper and the relative importance of the *Bund* subsided.

Russian Marxism, despite the "scientific" methodology it shared with other Marxist movements, was always splintered, perhaps because the message of the scriptures was too elusive to be fathomed with precision. The great arch of deviation was studded with factions expressing every form of opinion from mild reformism to the narrowest views of the dictatorship of the proletariat. Russian Social-Democracy was steeped in the most venomous, implacable, extravagantly expressed factional conflict, to the natural accompaniment of denunciations, splits and excommunications. It would be a hopeless endeavor even to begin to indicate the immense varieties of groupings and regroupings that took place, even after the "unification" that finally articulated the movement.

An early—and decisive—grouping had resulted in a newspaper that appeared first in Stuttgart in December 1900. It was called *Iskra*, ("The Spark", i.e., from the spark, the conflagration); the editorial board was made up of Lenin, Martov, Potresov, Plekhanov, Axelrod and Vera Zasulich, the last three of whom were in exile. This initial attempt at unity was succeeded by the emergence of the Russian Social-Democratic Party from the Second Party Congress, which met in 1903 with a joint program representing twenty-six constituent organizations.

This program, however, though adhered to formally by the major groups until after the 1917 revolution, contained enough ambiguities to allow the factional strife characteristic of the movement to go on even within the framework of a single party. It was really a twofold program—maximum and minimum. The maximum program had

Above: Oil *being transported on camel-back in the Caucasus. 1896. Photograph. The oil industry in Russia was one of the contributing factors to the rapid growth of an industrial proletariat.*

Below: Baku oil wells. *The Russian oil industry was developed, largely due to French and British capital, at the same time as oil wells were being tapped in the United States.*

to do with the ultimate goals of the Social-Democracy—the abolition of the capitalist order and the establishment via a revolution of a new socialist society under the dictatorship of the proletariat. The minimum program dealt with the immediate tactics of the Party and its structure: the overthrow of the Tsarist autocracy, the establishment of a democratic republic, the eight-hour day, etc., including the restitution to the peasants of the land they were thought to have been deprived of by the emancipation of 1861. The charter of the Party laid down the conditions for membership and the framework and reciprocal relations of Party agencies. The basic organs were the Central Committee, the Council (dropped a couple of years later), and the editorial board of *Iskra*, now the Party's official organ.

It was the staffing of the Party agencies and in general the attitude toward membership in the Party that led to a cleavage in the Party that far surpassed all other factional struggles and was never, indeed, bridged over. Lenin's group had managed to elect its candidates to the editorial board of *Iskra*, and the Martov group had refused to take part in any further relations or to accept a representation in the Party's basic agencies. At this particular moment, among this handful of individuals, Lenin happened to have a majority, on the basis of which his group were called Majoritarians—in Russian, "*Bolsheviki*". The converse referred to the Mensheviks headed by Martov; it was with this inconspicuous beginning that these names have since become consecrated by history.

The thing that must seem curious to us is that the profundity of the cleavage, which in the light of past and present history seems such a matter of course, was quite unnoticed by any of the participants in the war of words that went on relentlessly in the tiny world

Workers in a tobacco factory at Rostov-on-the-Don. *Witte's adoption of the gold standard in 1897 encouraged foreign capital; a new class of factory owners and entrepreneurs appeared.*

of the Russian Social-Democratic emigration.

The differences between Bolsheviks and Mensheviks were never formulated with consistency even on the theoretical plane. Broadly speaking, Lenin was distinguished by an organizational preoccupation: he wanted the Party to consist of people whose lives were completely taken up by the revolution. He wanted a group of professional revolutionaries. The Mensheviks were satisfied with a much looser concept of "sympathy" with the revolution: they were willing to accept anyone who supported the movement intellectually. The Bolsheviks were for the caucus as the spearhead of the proletarian dictatorship, the Mensheviks for the mass-meeting.

Still more broadly, this organizational concept was itself the reflection of a more general view of the dynamics of planned upheaval: the Mensheviks considered Socialism impossible without the establishment of an economy of abundance based on a society with the requisite culture and technological competence to undertake the industrialization that alone could make it work. They thought that such a society could only be brought into existence rather slowly as a result of bourgeois democracy, which would also enable the working-class to become mature enough to play its role as the midwife of the new society.

The Bolsheviks, while agreeing with this in principle, thought that the Social-Democracy itself would serve as the accelerator of this historic process, and was indeed the sole channel for the revolutionary education of the proletariat.

This conception of the gradualness of socio-economic evolution gave the Mensheviks a different view of the conditions of "taking power": they assumed that the inevitable evolution of bourgeois society — all factions agreed on the inevitability of everything — would automatically ripen both class relations and technology to the point of making the succession of regimes a mere formality, even though a possibly insurrectionary one. Contrariwise, the Bolsheviks were bound to emphasize the violent nature of an insurrectionary assumption of power precisely because they thought it could be accomplished *before* society *in toto* had ripened to the point of making it a minor matter.

Yet none of these basic differences was clearly seen at the time, which may be why a fabulous amount of hair-splitting and factional wrangling filled the lives of the émigrés. In retrospect we may see that Lenin's distinguishing feature was an immense will-power, doubtless partly derived from the unconscious feeling that in the expression of that will-power he was — in fact and beyond argument — identified with the working out of an ineluctable force of historical development as analyzed and foreseen by Marx and Engels. This injected a special element into the wranglings of the Social-Democratic movement, but since all forms of debate were necessarily expressed in scholastic language Lenin's personal quality was never made manifest, especially since it was precisely this unspoken identification of himself with history that enabled him to be unostentatious, affable, and self-sacrificing. The practical consequences of both Lenin's personality and his interpretation of Marxist doctrine were not to be demonstrated until the autumn of 1917.

In 1900, of course, he was only thirty years old and merely one among other Social-Democratic leaders, far from the ikon he has since become. In addition Populism and the romantic traditions of the *People's Will* revived somewhat; toward the turn of the century, spurred on by the great famine of 1891-92, they began growing again with great vigor. The Social-Democrats still shared the field with the new Populist movement, which in the later 1890s became known as Social-Revolutionaries.

The Social-Revolutionary Party—its name designed to steer a course between the older Populism and the newer Social-Democracy—was formally established in the summer of 1900. In spite of itself its program actually looked something like that of the Social-Democracy, but nevertheless most of the major Social-Revolutionary groups both in Russia and abroad joined up by 1901. The differences between the S. R. Party (as it was usually referred to) and the Marxists were still great; the S. R.s believed that since Russian capitalism was so weak the collapse of the monarchy would lead automatically and at once to Socialism; hence they supported cooperation with the liberal bourgeoisie against the autocracy. They also retained their faith in the peasantry as the motor of the revolution, and were basically hostile to the concentrated bureaucratization they thought inherent in Marxism.

But the most dramatic aspect of their contrast with the Marxists lay in their belief in terror. This, in fact, was the only principle that tied together the otherwise loosely associated segments of the Party, though to be sure the Party also thought that terror had to be linked with the indoctrination of the public.

The Social-Democrats, though they greeted the terrorist exploits of their rivals with a certain amount of glee, thought terror not only pointless but pernicious.

In 1901 the Social-Revolutionaries devoted a specific segment of their own organization to terror; from 1902 to 1907, when there was a slump in the revolutionary movement and the police were successful in catching most of the terrorists, a wave of S.R. atrocities swept the country. The central Terrorist Organization was extremely secret: its members carried their self-sacrificing zeal to a high pitch. Its membership was drawn from every section of society, including professional people and aristocrats. The best known leaders were Gershuni, Azev, and Boris Savinkov, the last of whom, under a pseudonym, was a well-known novelist and the protagonist of melodramatic exploits of an

Erno Azev, *the notorious double agent who worked for the terrorists and the police.*

improbable extravagance. Churchill thought him the most fascinating man he had ever met.

The role of Azev is one of the most extraordinary in political history. It is typical of the complex relations between the security police and the revolutionaries.

The men in charge of the security police were often highly sophisticated; not only did they occasionally sympathize with the idealism of the revolutionary cause or causes, but they were fascinated by the revolutionaries themselves.

Azev was simultaneously an agent of the security police. It would have been impossible to say whom he was *really* working for: he would occasionally organize a terrorist coup while hoodwinking his police superiors, while at

Two Russian writers photographed at the beginning of the century: Anton Chekhov (1860-1904) and Maxim Gorky (1868-1936). Chekhov, author of novels, short stories and such well-known plays as "The Cherry Orchard", depicted the fading bourgeois world and Russia's rural life and peasantry. Gorky was the outstanding literary figure of the revolutionary days. An active socialist, exiled under Tsarism, he returned to his country to take part in the October revolution.

The 18-month Russo-Japanese war (1904-1905) was the result of Nicholas II's reckless ambitions in the Far East. It was carried out with a maximum of inefficiency and involved a series of disasters for the Russians. A Japanese print shows the combat before Port Arthur. The Russian commander abandoned Port Arthur after a siege, although he still had large quantities of food and ammunition.

other times he would ensure his credit with the police by denouncing his terrorist associates. He did all this with immense acumen and plausibility, and in spite of repeated accusations that were dismissed by his political comrades as political calumny, a slander on the Party honor, etc., he survived for years, until he was finally exposed incontrovertibly in 1908 by Burtsev, an émigré journalist and historian. The exposure of Azev was a major blow to political terrorism, which in any case had already begun to wane.

The S.R. organization also followed a policy, entirely logical, of carrying out armed robberies, for which "expropriations" was a handy euphemism. Regardless of the logic involved, however, the Party was not entirely easy in its mind about these robberies; it

claimed it tried to restrict these "exes" to government funds, and not to kill anyone but police officers.

As opponents of terrorism, the Social-Democrats naturally could take a far more lofty line, but Lenin himself was involved in a scandal by authorizing some "exes" of his own, which were carried out very successfully by Stalin among others. The Social-Democrats had no principle to advance in defense of these and Lenin either denied them vehemently or shifted into an attack on his factional rivals.

The interaction between the police and the revolutionaries was so intense that not only were individual agents sometimes psychologically split about their "real" roles, but on occasion even propaganda found its only audience among police spies. Some of Lenin's

activities in exile consisted of delivering lectures; he would spend hours lecturing to tiny classes—perhaps four or five people—most of whom consisted of police spies conscientiously sending reports back to headquarters.

The most famous incident involving Lenin concerned a police agent by the name of Malinovsky, who was not only a faithful disciple of Lenin's for years, but actually served as the major orator of the legal Bolshevik fraction in the semi-constitutional regime that was set up after 1905. Malinovsky was an energetic and talented speaker: he would receive general drafts of speeches from Lenin, go over them carefully with the head of the security police, and then, pursuing a policy decided on by the subtle minds in the security police, exaggerate small points or large in order to widen the already yawning chasm between the Bolsheviks and their fellow-revolutionaries. The theory was that if Lenin was made too much of an extremist he would discredit himself completely and thus weaken the revolutionary movement. Malinovsky was vehemently defended by Lenin, and his critics, including the generally esteemed Burtsev, were assailed with Lenin's usual lush invective. Malinovsky was not exposed to Lenin's satisfaction until the archives of the security police were thrown open after the 1917 revolution. Malinovsky was shot out of hand.

The infiltration of the revolutionary organizations by police agents was given a characteristic defense later by Lenin and his sympathizers, on the theory that after all the facts proved to have been stronger than political espionage, and that the revolutionary organizations grew regardless of the role played in them by individual traitors.

The revolutionary movement was hampered for many years by hopeless factional strife and by its exiguous membership. Despite all their devotion, abundance of funds—the Bolsheviks also benefited by the openhandedness of rich patrons—and tireless energy, the revolutionaries remained alien to the peasantry and for a long time to the growing working-class as well. At the beginning of 1905 a claim of a mere 8,000 members was made by the Bolsheviks; naturally such figures are often exaggerated. Their strength was not, of course, derived from their debating powers in the charmed circle of those with a grasp of Marxist or Populist dialectics, but from the profound disaffection that prevailed in the country

at large, and that gave the propaganda of all revolutionary groups something to sharpen itself on. It was not until 1917 that, in the case of the Bolsheviks at least, the importance was realized of the role in the age of modern technology of simplified propaganda wielded by

During the Russo-Japanese war: *a Russian officer holds up an ikon to the kneeling troops.*

a limber and well-articulated party organization.

It is, in fact, only now that we can see the importance of the seeds of the new world when they first began germinating. In the Russia of the time there was no feeling that anything really serious was actually *happening*: the stability of the regime in a broad sense was quite unquestioned. However ardently the new ideas sweeping the intelligentsia were discussed, "respectable" society went its own way imbued with the sense of stability essential for its peace of mind.

What was far more important on the public horizon of the period was the upswing of liberalism, the somewhat inchoate desire, generally associated with a constitution, for a softening of the monarchy. The famine years of 1891-1892 that were such a stimulant to the Populist and Marxist movements also promoted the spread of liberal ideas.

Of course, in some ways fixing a specific label on this amorphous body of attitudes is a falsification *per se*: the

huge camp between the autocracy and its revolutionary enemies was filled by the bulk of the educated and critical opinion in the country, opposed to the bureaucratic state for its backwardness and arbitrary controls, but not to the point of advocating violent action.

It was the Rural Councils that contained most of the seeds of this pacific, forward-looking movement, which broadly speaking was aimed at the installation of some form of popular representation in the central government and also at the creation of a central Rural Council administration, which would have had the effect of supplementing the cumbersome, highhanded central regime by a flexible, decentralized administration. The liberal sentiment that had suffered in the general movement of repression after the assassination of Alexander II began pushing ahead cautiously during the last decade of the Nineteenth Century and afterwards, invigorated by the relief work done during the famine years of 1891-1892: people were loath to return to the indolence and passivity of normal routine. In addition, by the middle of the 1890s the so-called "Third Element", as the hired employees of the Rural Councils were called—teachers, doctors, nurses, veterinarians, statisticians, agronomists—played an active and growingly effective role. This Third Element became a source of political activity, aimed at the establishment of professional unions and the discussion of the broadest political issues at conventions held with the tacit approval of the Rural Councils. The Third Element —the other two were officials of the crown and the elected members of the Rural Councils—stemmed, of course, from the radical intelligentsia, and many of them were linked to revolutionary

A Japanese general studying his map before the battle of Mudken, *March, 1905. The Russians were forced to retreat after sustaining heavy losses. The war was ended by American mediation when President Theodore Roosevelt arbitrated the Treaty of Portsmouth. Korea was made a Japanese sphere of influence and the Russians were forced to evacuate Manchuria.*

groups. But as a body they reached out beyond the framework of the Rural Councils proper and came in contact with other classes: the interest in professional unions, for instance, infected professional men outside the Rural Councils altogether.

Agriculture, in the wake of the defective emancipatiou of 1861, was still functioning poorly. There was another failure of crops in 1897-1898 and in 1901, and by the end of the century the defects of the emancipation were unmistakable. The general agricultural stagnation and the progressive impoverishment of the peasants had their roots in the staggering taxes and in the paralysis due to the communal tenure of the land. Rural mutinies kept breaking out to illustrate the depressing statistics that accumulated about increasing arrears, meagre crops, and debased living standards.

In addition, the working-class began generating a persistent malaise: the strikes that had begun in the 1890s went on increasing in number and scope. It was not so much their number: the manufacturing, mining and metallurgical industries employed some 2,200,000 workers in the Russian Empire in 1900, while the strikers in the peak years of 1899 and 1903 numbered 97,000 and 87,000 respectively. It was the novelty of mass organized strikes that proved so disturbing, even though the grievances of the working-class had not yet found a politically articulate channel.

Student agitation, which kept growing in importance, added a serious factor to the revolutionary froth. Not only were living conditions still harsh for most students—an indication that the regime's attempts to confine higher education to the upper classes had in fact misfired—but the very juxtaposition of the poverty-stricken students to their elegant, wealthy fellows gave special point to the various levelling theories contending for attention. After a period of relative quiet in the 1880s, student agitation began taking on a more and more truculently political character in the 1890s; in 1899 disor-

ders flared up with exceptional violence for causes in themselves trivial. Assassinations carried out by Social-Revolutionary students became a commonplace.

There was thus a fusion between the various kinds of opposition to the regime. Individuals with a variety of attitudes united in a common detestation of the *status quo*, and though the remedies projected differed in accordance with political outlook the Tsarist fortress found itself besieged from all points in the compass, and incapable of incubating a counter-offensive.

Liberalism was established as an organized political force by the initiative of Miliukov, a history professor, and Struve, author of the Social-Democratic manifesto of 1898, who had shifted over to the extreme right of the Socialist movement. In 1902 they started the first issue of *Liberation*, which was published in Stuttgart and smuggled into Russia; it advocated the overthrow of autocracy and the installation of a constitutional regime. The endorsement of this program by the Union of Liberation, a clandestine organization initiated at a Rural Council Conference in 1903 and formally established in 1904, marked the entry of organized liberalism on the horizon of Russian politics. The Union managed to set up a ramified web of local agencies; it focussed the activities of a great many intellectuals and professional men, as well as those engaged in Rural Council work directly.

The Russo-Japanese War that broke out in January 1904 relaxed the tension for a while, due to the inevitable patriotism manifested even for a war that was generally quite unpopular. But it was no more than a stop-gap; as Russian forces, underequipped and outfought, were struck by one reverse after another, topped by the humiliating surrender of Port Arthur, the whole of the national opposition concerted its campaign against the autocracy.

A spectacular incident — "Bloody Sunday" — gave the mounting tension a focus. Underlying it was a convergence of police action and revolutionary enthusiasm.

A strike that broke out early in January 1905 in Petersburg, and spread to some factories where tens of thousands of workers were employed, had been directed by the so-called Assembly of Russian Workmen, a group organized and financed by the police themselves. Just as mutinies had been led in the name of the Tsar so the police had done a certain amount of dabbling in setting up organizations claiming concern with the interests of the working-class. This one was headed by a priest in the service of the police, Father Gapon, who conceived the notion of a public appeal to the Tsar.

Just as many revolutionaries were stool-pigeons, so many stool-pigeons were identified to some extent with the cause they were being paid to subvert. Whether Gapon was sincere or playing a role, in any case he thought of appealing to the Tsar directly; he organized a parade of columns of workers flaunting a wide variety of grievances. But though the parade was quite peaceful, some of the marchers actually carrying sacred ikons and portraits of the Tsar, and the authorities knew all about it, the demonstrators were stopped by cordons of troops and fired on when they refused to disperse. Official estimates listed one hundred and thirty killed, and several hundred wounded, but the casualties must have been much heavier.

The demonstration and its bloody sequel made a dramatic impression out of all proportion to the number of casualties. The agitation of the Rural Councils and a variety of other bodies was intensified; in February the Grand Duke Sergius, the Tsar's uncle and brother-in-law, was assassinated in a coup planned by the famous S.R. Savinkov, under the protection of Azev, the double agent.

The government reacted sluggishly and irresolutely: from now on nothing it did, including concessions made to liberal opinion, could catch up with the swelling tide of dissidence, which flowed in the two channels of conciliationist liberalism and revolutionary intransigeance. The government felt itself forced to concede the principle of popular representation in an advisory assembly, but this was no longer enough to satisfy the liberals, who were now intent on securing a constituent assembly based on the commonplaces of political democracy in Western Europe — universal suffrage and a secret, direct and equal ballot.

By May 1905, when the Russian fleet was annihilated by the Japanese in the straits of Tsushima, the domestic situation seemed hopeless. Agrarian upheavals, strikes, political agitation of liberal and revolutionary groups countered by the action of the autocracy's supporters, aimed particularly at the Jews, strained the situation to bursting-point.

A tardy concession in August 1905 laying down the procedure to be followed for elections to the State Duma, the name for the consultative assembly announced in February, was greeted by open hostility and mockery. The definition of the franchise satisfied no one, conservative or liberal.

The universities were given a substantial degree of autonomy in an unexpected law of August 1905; the manner in which this was worked out against the background of the relentless pressure of public opinion even outside,

transformed academic lecture audiences into debating assemblies where speakers safe from police interference could erupt to their heart's content.

A by-product of the oratory released by this university autonomy was to be the Petersburg Soviet of Workers' Deputies.

The political tension burst at last, in the form of a general strike that broke out in the second half of September 1905 among the Moscow printers and bakers. A sympathetic strike was organized in Moscow by a union that was functioning in spite of its lack of official recognition; it spread to the whole network in a few days, involving the telegraph and telephone services and halting almost the entire industrial plant.

Though the strikers at first made the conventional demands for a constituent assembly, civil liberties, and an eight-hour day, they soon added purely revolutionary demands: for a democratic republic, political amnesty, disarming of the police and troops, and the arming of labor. This program, inspired by the previous decade of radical toil, was endorsed even by the unions of professional people.

The populace was in a state of delirious excitement: euphoric mobs roved about carrying red banners and revolutionary posters: everything that could shut its doors did so—banks, shops, government offices, even pharmacies and hospitals. Newspapers, electricity, gas, and in some places water were all shut down, and barricades were set up in a number of cities. The country was actually paralyzed.

The Petersburg Soviet of Workers' Deputies met for the first time in October, with only thirty or forty delegates at first, but with almost six hundred by the end of November. In theory one delegate was supposed to represent five hundred workers, but according to Trotsky—who at the age of twenty-five was now to play a stellar role—some deputies were backed by much smaller groups. The elections to the Soviet had been carried out by the

◄ On January 22, 1905, Father Gapon's followers advanced towards the Winter Palace carrying ikons and pictures of the Tsar. Their intentions were presumably peaceable; they hoped to read a petition to Nicholas II. The Tsar was away at the time. The Guards lost their nerves at the size of the crowd; firing directly at the unarmed procession, slashing at the foremost with their sabres, the Guards killed hundreds and wounded thousands. The event, known as "Bloody Sunday", touched off the 1905 revolution. This contemporary news drawing shows the Guards charging in front of the Admiralty, blocking the way to the Winter Palace.

revolutionary parties, chiefly the Mensheviks, who dominated the Soviet and its executive committee. It published an organ, *Izvestiya*, which appeared for the first time on 17 October, the same day the Tsar signed a manifesto transforming Russia into a constitutional monar-

After "Bloody Sunday" a spate of riots and acts of terror culminated in a general strike. Above, metal workers from the Putilov factory at Saint Petersburg demonstrate. Although industrial workers were numerically few in Russia, their concentration around a small group of gigantic enterprises such as this one made them an easy target for Socialist propaganda.

chy. This manifesto, which had been devised by Witte, a former Minister of Finance recalled from semi-retirement to conduct Russian peace negotiations with Japan via the mediation of Theodore Roosevelt, guaranteed basic civil liberties, promised to extend the franchise of the August law establishing the State Duma, and laid it down as an "immutable rule" that all laws had to have the sanction of the State Duma, which was also to exercise a control over crown appointees.

The concessions contained in the October Manifesto, a milestone in Russian political evolution, aroused the consternation of the conservatives and a certain amount of skepticism among the liberals. But the reaction of the public at large was one of unbridled excitement: the big cities were filled with parades, red banners, demonstrations, and counter-demonstrations. The conservative reaction took the familiar form of pogroms against the Jews; during the week after the signing of the October Manifesto hundreds of pogroms

ravaged small towns inside the Jewish Pale and outside, especially Kiev and Odessa. They were generally condoned, or indeed inspired by the police, and created an immense impression outside Russia.

The government was hamstrung by the fact that the October Manifesto proclaimed principles of liberty that the actual law still obstructed or limited; this led to a state of paralysis in the government, especially the police. The official censorship ceased operating, while the Printers' Union began exercising an impromptu censorship of its own, by simply refusing to print whatever displeased it, while allowing scores of radical papers to be printed and to circulate freely.

The Petersburg Soviet disregarded the October Manifesto by carrying on with a general strike. There was, to be sure, a spontaneous and irresistible back-to-work movement following the Man-

Pages 210-211

The intellectuals rallied to the support of the workers in the 1905 revolution. Here women and men university students demonstrate in sympathy with red banners aloft. Although the 1905 upheaval was a failure, Lenin called it a "general rehearsal" for what was to follow.

ifesto, but the Soviet had now become a revolutionary tribune; it proclaimed that the "proletariat would never lay down its arms" until the monarchy had been replaced by a democratic republic. The temporary governmental paralysis, plus the long-range calculations of Witte, who was biding his time, enabled the Soviet to act with a great deal of freedom: it handed out orders and carried on negotiations with the government. A partial amnesty granted a few days after the October Manifesto enabled many political exiles to return and resume their activities.

The revolutionary mood automatically overflowed into the Russian hinterland: over 2,000 manor houses were burnt or plundered, and their owners killed or expelled.

The government finally pulled itself together, proclaiming a state of emergency and sending off expeditions to suppress the riots. In November it arrested the whole Moscow headquarters of the Peasants' Union, a clandestine organization led by radical intellectuals, which had held its first conference in Moscow in August. Witte's calculations were bearing fruit: as the hold of the Petersburg Soviet over the workers began slacking off, the government intervened. Early in December it arrested all the principal leaders, including Trotsky, who had been elected Soviet chairman. Together with fifteen other defendants Trotsky was sentenced to Siberian exile for life; by March of 1907 he was back in Petersburg, but with the ebb-tide in full force he emigrated. He returned ten years later.

A substitute Soviet to replace the one that had been decapitated proved a futile enterprise. By January 1906 the government was in complete control again; order had been restored.

The first "modern" revolution, rooted in industrial relations and powered by abstract ideas, was over. But though the principle of autocracy was shattered, the monarchy had survived and the social order emerged from the upheaval unimpaired. The revolutionary forces seemed to have been submerged once again; Russia was finally embarked on the transformation of the vast illiterate empire, run by an equally vast centralized bureaucratic regime, into a society patterned after the modern states of Western and Central Europe.

But this enterprise was, perhaps, inherently unviable. In the chasm between the summits of society and the illiterate, impoverished masses there were only two bridges: the radical and idealistic intelligentsia, which with the power of its abstractions was trying to turn the whole of society upside down, and the liberal classes, which had evolved rapidly during the latter part of the Nineteenth Century. With no experience of self-government and with no parliamentary skills or established political parties, the liberals were poorly equipped to undertake the perhaps insoluble task of providing a representative government for the gigantic, multiracial, and backward empire. After all, there had been no parties at all in Russia before 1905, while the Social-Democratic Party and the Social-Revolutionary Parties were wholly clandestine revolutionary organizations.

The experiment in trying to introduce even the embryonic forms of a Western-style parliamentary democracy was to last about a decade: in 1914 the battered Tsarist vessel was to embark on the fatefully tempestuous sea of the First World War.

The Extinction of Tsarism

Alexander II's assassination in March 1881 had not affected the regime. The revolutionary mood that had been hoped for as a result of the regicide did not come about: the only result was that one sovereign imbued with traditional ideas was succeeded by another with an even more authoritarian turn of mind. The regime that had stood obdurate in the face of the various currents of thought disturbing the country gave way to another regime still more obdurate. Nor had Alexander II's murder stirred the countryside in any way: the peasants remained indifferent. For all one could tell they were utterly apathetic. For that matter some peasants seemed to think the Tsar had been killed by some landowners working off a grudge.

The new sovereign, Alexander III, was unimaginative, and unusually single-minded. He was indissolubly identified with the old formula, "Orthodoxy, Autocracy and Nationality", in which the element emphasized by himself was autocracy. He was profoundly influenced by Constantine Pobedonostsev (1827-1907), who tutored both him and his son, the future Nicholas II, and who was rightly considered the most powerful man in Russia. Pobedonostsev's strategy combined the defense of the union of the common people and the throne on the one hand, with a systematic attack on the corrupt, self-serving bureaucracy, plus all proponents of constitutional reform, on the other.

Alexander III's regime became more oppressive on all the questions that had been agitating Russia for so long: the press was gagged, the schools were thrown back to the regime of the 1830s, when children were supposed to be educated in terms of their social status, "undesirable" elements, especially Jews, were excluded as far as possible from the educational system, ethnic minorities, local languages and dissenting religious sects were systematically persecuted (Pobedonostsev's letters to the Tsar overflowed with diatribes against Roman Catholics, Protestants, Jews, and Russian dissenters). The treatment of the Jews was singularly harsh: Alexander III himself had a special hatred of them based on a naive acceptance of traditional anti-Semitism —the supposed Jewish responsibility for the Crucifixion. Nor was anti-Semitism confined to conservative and orthodox milieux: in the early 1880s the *People's Will* used anti-Jewish slogans. The Jews were in their classic position of being caught between two fires: their role in dissident organizations (a Jewess had participated in Alexander II's assassination) made them the target for conservative hatred, while their prominence in the newly forming business world attracted the ire of the revolutionaries.

In 1861 southern Russia was swept by a wave of pogroms, connived at, as indicated before, or even instigated by the police. They aroused public opinion everywhere to such an extent that the government had to announce its intention of instituting some sweeping reforms. In the event, however, what the government did, after receiving a report from a highly conservative body recommending that discrimination be discontinued, was to do exactly the opposite: it heightened the oppressiveness of the existing regime. The boundaries of the Jewish Pale were restricted still further, quotas for Jews were introduced in secondary and higher schools (1887), they were excluded from the legal profession (1889), from the Rural

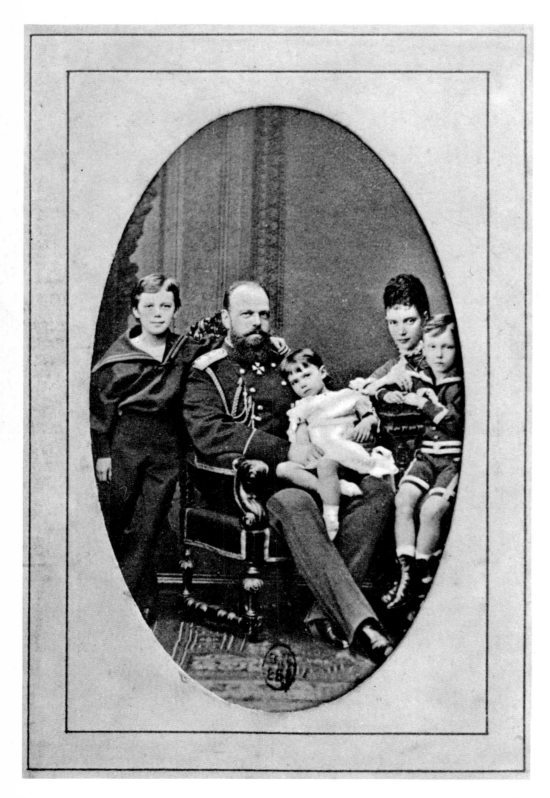

Alexander III and his family. *The Empress was formely princess Maria Dagmar, daughter of Christian IX of Denmark. Alexander III came to the throne (1881-1894), after the assassination of his father by terrorists, dissatisfied with merely liberal reforms. He was a thick-set, red-bearded family man of very simple tastes and narrow ideas.*

A forge in St. Petersburg *at the end of the XIXth century. The industrial revolution arrived late in Russia but made rapid strides after the Crimean War. But while industry expanded, the condition of workers remained worse than in other European countries.*

Councils (1890) and municipal governments (1892). It was even made a criminal offense for a Jew to use a Christian given name.

The severity of this regime naturally increased the vulnerability of the Jewish community to the personal greed of government officials: bribery, renewed exactions and pressure went hand in hand. But perhaps the chief effect of the treatment of Jews during Alexander III's reign was to kindle a spark among Russian Jewry that had far-reaching consequences: the mass migration of Russian Jews to the United States, and the launching of the Zionist movement, which began to form in the 1890s and has since changed the map of the Middle East by establishing the State of Israel. In addition, the brutal-

ity assumed by Russian anti-Semitism during this period evoked a powerful reaction abroad, particularly in the United States and Great Britain: the monarchy was creating enemies for itself both at home and abroad.

In 1894, however, the year of Nicholas II's accession to the throne, the country would have seemed stable and tranquil to any superficial observer. The draconian police regime appeared to have driven all dissident movements out of sight; the revolutionary movement was decapitated, with its leaders exiled to Siberia and abroad. The peasants were motionless; they had not even reacted to the great famine of 1891, in which thousands had perished. As the Russian autocracy entered the Twentieth Century it seemed to have lost

nothing. It looked as tranquil at home as the international outlook seemed secure. Alexander III had been known as the "Tsar Peacemaker", and the international scene was very calm. France had taken Germany's place as Russia's ally, and relations with Great Britain were much more harmonious.

Nicholas II ascended a throne universally considered a rocklike fortress of stability: he was to be the last Tsar. He was sadly outmatched by the events that were to remove his dynasty from the country's helm. Even a monarch with more character and brains might have fallen short of what was required by the gathering turbulence of the epoch, but in the case of Nicholas II we are aware of an utter inability not only to cope with the inherited situation but to understand what was happening. His personality seems invested with a stupefying triviality, unmistakably attested not merely by the opinions of others, but by his personal diary,

Nicholas II, *the last Tsar, reigned from 1894-1917. Weak, charming and limited, convinced of the divine rightness of autocracy, Nicholas was peculiarly unsuited to his role and his times. He married Princess Alix of Hesse-Darmstadt (a granddaughter of Queen Victoria). Converted to Greek Orthodoxy for her marriage, the Empress became fanatically religious.*

which he kept very regularly throughout his life and which gives us an unambiguous view of him.

His diary never fails to mention the weather and his various outdoor activities: playing with dogs, rowing, swimming, walking, picking mushrooms—all are faithfully recorded. Shooting was his favorite pastime, and the day's bag of every hunt was conscientiously listed: when he had no time to hunt he shot the crows flying on the grounds of the imperial residence, with all results recorded. The cardinal events of his reign—the Japanese War, the 1905 revolution, the creation of the State Duma—are hardly mentioned. He had the outlook of an indolent, goodnatured, passive boy. At the age of 26, for instance, he took the trouble to record

Luncheon in the snow *after a bear hunt organized by Prince Yusupov for Grand Duke Cyril in 1896. An account of the hunt mentions that the Grand Duke killed two bears. Among other guests shown here are the French ambassador Count of Montebello, the Austrian ambassador Prince Liechtenstein, and their wives.*

in his diary that he had fought a chestnut battle with Prince George of Greece; two days later he mentions a battle with pine cones.

His passivity, however, was combined with extreme, though mindless stubbornness. 1905 had compelled him to convene a representative institution, the State Duma, and to restrict the sovereign's legislative powers. Nicholas II remained sulkily unreconciled. He was fortified by the unbending nature of his wife, the former Princess Alix of Hesse-Darmstadt, who dominated him completely. Their intimacy was flawless; they remained utterly devoted to each other until the end.

The Tsarina, whose mother was Princess Alice of England, had been brought up by her grandmother, Queen Victoria; she and Nicholas wrote to each other in English. After somewhat reluctantly embracing Russian Orthodoxy to marry him, she became an ardent devotee of her new religion: her mystical nature felt itself wholly fused with her conception of the union of the "people" with the crown, with a concomitantly virulent loathing of any curb on the autocratic power. The Tsarina was both shy and sickly, and though her health was impaired by the birth of four daughters, the desire of the imperial couple for an heir to the throne was strong enough to make them turn for advice to shady adventurers, faith-healers, and various quacks. A longed-for heir was finally born in 1904; when the infant was only ten weeks old the parents learned with grief that he had hemophilia, an incurable disease hereditary in the males of the House of Hesse but transmitted as usual through the mother.

Lilies of the valley egg *by Carl Fabergé, presented by Nicholas II to his mother Maria Fyodorovna, dated April 5, 1898. Fabergé's name has become synonymous with the type of luxury peculiar to the last years of imperial Russia. The Russian goldsmith became celebrated for making yearly eggs for the Tsar to give the Tsarina and the Dowager Empress at Easter. These were made of precious stones and colored enamels and always contained an intricate "surprise". The "surprise" of the Lilies of the valley egg is the fan of three miniatures, of the Tsar and his two eldest daughters, Grand Duchesses Olga and Tatiana, that is released mechanically when a pearl on the side is turned, and folds back when the pearl is turned in the opposite direction. Messrs Wartski collection, London.*

The savior sent by providence, which the anguished mother appealed to for salvation, was Rasputin, a semi-literate peasant from the Siberian wilderness, whom an enormously powerful body, magnetic personality, and unintelligible talk had established in a coterie of Petersburg society neurotics. One of the characteristically Russian fraternity of self-constituted religious teachers living by their wits on hand-outs from naive believers, Rasputin had an attractive combination of erotism and mysticism. His creed was based on the logical assumption that forgiveness could only be given if there was something to forgive, i.e., the act of sinning; he promised eternal salvation to the believers who achieved true humility by way of sexual license.

Rasputin seems to have been trained by a professional medium. He was

actually successful, according to a number of trustworthy witnesses, in stopping young Alexis's bleedings. His performance of this miracle was enough to embed him solidly in the Empress's confidence: not only was he the incarnation of her beloved "people"—rough-hewn and filthy—but he was a divine prop of the throne. She dismissed all rumors of his debaucheries as evil gossip, and sought his advice on matters of state policy as well as the welfare of the Imperial family. Rasputin gradually realized the great power given him by his strategic position with the Imperial family, and his growing influence was exploited by all sorts of bureaucrats, businessmen and adventurers. In the minds of the public at large, as well as of the summit of society, by the time the First World War broke out he was one of the cardinal elements in the pall that overhung the monarchy.

The beginnings of the parliamentary system laid in 1905 had had reservations that made its actual functioning difficult. Not only did the government dig in its heels after the setbacks of 1905, but the parties that emerged from the storm proved equally rigid with respect to each other. Before 1905, after all, no political parties at all had any official status: the Social-Democratic and Social Revolutionary Parties that were to play such a decisive role in the upheaval of 1917 were basically underground organizations.

The constitutional regime set up after 1905 established a spectrum of political parties that resembled their Western models—at a casual glance. Opinion organized itself into groups that spread from Left to Right, beginning, of course, from what we should now consider the Centre. Extremist liberalism was represented by the Constitutional Democrats—known as "Cadets", from their initials—a party, led by Miliukov, that had emerged from a campaign by the Rural Council groups. Its program was approved by the first and the second (January 1906) party congress; it naturally represented a compromise

of contending views. The "extremist" demands for a democratic republic and a constituent assembly based on a direct and universal ballot were eliminated; the party as a whole came out for a constitutional monarchy, with the State Duma being given a full-fledged role in the establishment of the new constitution. The Cadets sponsored broad social and economic reforms, including the expropriation of great estates against a fair indemnification.

The more conservative elements set up their own parties, the most important of which was the "Octobrists", headed by Guchkov: it was founded in December 1905. Basing itself, as indicated by its name, on the October Manifesto, it vigorously opposed the more far-reaching socio-economic demands of the Cadets, especially the expropriation of the big landowners. Conservative extremists joined in the Union of the Russian People.

With the shaping up of the parliamentary regime the Rural Councils subsided as the expression of liberal opinion; until the abolition of the monarchy the new Russian parliament remained the arena of conventional politics.

With a slight ineptitude due, perhaps, to inexperience, the first two Dumas were far more radical than the regime had been counting on. In the First Duma, for instance, inaugurated April 27, 1906 (O.S.), though the peasantry was well represented and was counted on as a traditional bulwark of conservatism, the 200 peasant deputies (of a total of 500) turned out to be unexpectedly liberal; they took the most inconvenient line on all questions to do with the land.

Count Sergius Witte *(1849-1915) was born into the minor nobility. He first occupied a modest post as a railroad clerk. Later, in 1891, he activated the building of the Trans-Siberian railroad and became Minister of Communications the following year. As Minister of Finance he negotiated immense foreign loans and battled against the archaic structure of Russian economy. Opposed to the war with Japan, he negotiated the peace treaty after the Russian defeat. Nicholas II disliked him, but nevertheless made him Premier. As his last act, Witte obtained a manifesto from Nicholas creating a constitution.*

Center, Peter Stolypin *(1862-1911) able, lucid, was Minister of the Interior (1904), then Premier. A large landowner himself, he was responsible for agrarian reforms that so ameliorated the peasant situation that Lenin considered him a menace to the revolution. He antagonized the Empress by banishing Rasputin from St. Petersburg in 1911. The same year he was assassinated while attending the opera at Kiev with the Emperor.*

Below, Constantine Pobedonostsev *(1827-1907) rigid reactionary, close adviser to Alexander III and then to Nicholas II. He was a jurist, procurator of the Holy Synod, and against any form of parliamentary system or liberal thought. Pobedonostsev drafted Nicholas's accession speech, making it clear that the autocratic principle was to be upheld.*

This Duma was dominated by the Cadets, who were very disturbing to the conservative elements; though the Duma represented twenty-six parties and sixteen national groups, the Cadets had between 170-180 members, and were generally supported by the Labor

Democrats and S.R.s had taken part in the elections—Lenin had been impressed by the First Duma's propaganda potential—and the Second Duma had some 65 Social-Democrats and 34 S.R.s, while the Cadets fell to 92 and the Labor Group to 101.

Of the four Dumas Tsarism was destined to see, the Third Duma was the only one to complete its full term: it lasted from November 1907 to June 1912, and was ruled by the conservatives. The Rightwing, moderate Rightwing and nationalist parties had about 150 members, as did the Octobrists. The Cadets sank to 53 and the Social Democrats and the Labor Group had 14 each.

The last Duma—November 1912 to February 1917—was even more conservative: the Rightwing had 185 deputies, the Octobrists 97 and the Cadets 58. The Social-Democrats kept their 14 while the Labor Group sank to 10.

Both the Third and Fourth Dumas were boycotted by the Social-Revolutionaries.

Witte's return to public life in 1905 had been cut short through his becoming the target of attacks from all quarters equally—conservatives, liberals and revolutionaries—and especially by Nicholas II's detestation of him. Witte's reverence for Tsarism, coupled with his contempt for the Tsar, perhaps made it impossible for him to apply his considerable talents to the efficient performance of his duties as President of the Council of Ministers (the equivalent of Prime Minister) under a pseudo-representative regime. His resignation was accepted a few days before the convocation of the First Duma, and his place taken by an elderly routine functionary, Goremykin (1839-1917), whose career was firmly grounded on obsequiousness to the Tsar, which made him an ideal choice, from the latter's

In June 1905 some sailors of the Black Sea fleet mutinied on the battleship Potomkin *off Odessa. This major naval mutiny was to strike Russian imagination with peculiar force. It remained a heroic legend to the sailors who played such an important role in the revolutionary activities of 1918. The Potomkin sailors finally entered the ship into the Rumanian port of Constanza, where they were interned. Above, the battleship off Constanza.*

Group, which had over 100 members. The latter was made up of a merger of ten groups that were even more liberal than the Cadets, especially about the land, but were not Socialists or revolutionaries. The ethnic groups, such as the Poles, Ukrainians, Letts, etc., had about 60-70 members: they backed national autonomy and had a generally radical tinge. The Social-Democrats, now legally recognized, had a small separate fraction. There were no conservative deputies at all.

But the First Duma lasted only a few months. The very fact of its radical composition, as expressed in the demands made in its program, adopted practically unanimously, which insisted on universal suffrage, a one-chamber parliament, and a land reform based on expropriation, implied a rapid demise. By July it was dissolved.

The second Duma, scheduled for February 20, 1907 (O.S.), was even more radical in composition than the first and just as short-lived: it lasted a little more than three months. Both Social-

The surprising radicalism of the First Two Dumas indicated a defect in the arithmetic underlying the theory of representation. It was rectified quite simply: merely by reducing the number of deputies to be elected by industrial workers and increasing the landowners' ratio a fairly conservative Third Duma was ensured.

The mutinous sailors on the deck of the Potomkin. *The pretext for the mutiny came when, after conditions in general had become impossible, some sailors refused to eat rotten meat served for their meal. The commander ordered the malcontents shot; the firing squad refused to execute the orders. In the ensuing violence the commander and six other officers were killed. The mutineers only spared those officers necessary to run the ship.*

The Potomkin mutiny became part of Soviet mythology. In 1925 Serge Eisenstein made a remarkable film, The Battleship Potomkin, *in which much of the action takes place on the Odessa steps (above). The population of Odessa flocked down these steps to the docks, carrying food for the mutineers. The Guard appeared and shot down the sympathisers, including women and children. In a celebrated sequence, a pram bumped down the steps and turned over, after the mother pushing it was shot.*

point of view, for supervisor of the new constitutional regime.

Perhaps the most distinguished newcomer to the government was Peter Stolypin (1862-1911), Minister of the Interior in the apocopated First Duma and later a powerful, resourceful, and able President of the Council of Ministers.

By temperament Stolypin was more of a landowner than a professional functionary. Marshal of the Nobility for Kovno Province, where he owned a great deal of land, and afterwards Governor there as well as in Saratov on the Volga, he combined a high degree of Pan-Russian militancy with a far-reaching originality of outlook and a grasp of the peasant problem that led him to embark on a series of agrarian innovations. Stolypin's attempt to revise the communal system of peasant administration was the only serious effort of the government to cope with the imbalance in land relations inherited from the defective reforms of the 1860s.

It was his aim to enable the peasants to own land independently of any other institution, thus stilling the congenital restlessness of the peasant countryside. He wanted to eradicate once and for all the village commune, zealously preserved in the settlement of 1861, and thus launch for the first time in Russia a class of peasant proprietors, whose political influence he of course hoped to benefit by. The basic part of a somewhat ramified scheme to accomplish this was embodied in a law of November 1906 giving an individual peasant the right, once he secured the consent of two-thirds of the village assembly, to consolidate his scattered strips in the common fields into a single plot, which from then on was to be personal property in perpetuity.

Stolypin's legislation did not actually destroy the peasant commune all at once: in 1917 the great bulk of the peasantry were still being governed by it, but his agrarian reform was in fact spreading in wider and wider circles and laying the groundwork of a new peasant economy. By the outbreak of the 1914 war about a quarter of the peasant households in European Russia had transformed all their holdings into personal property, with about ten per cent already consolidated. It would have seemed to be a mere question of time before the process spread throughout rural Russia and radically transformed its entire face and outlook: Lenin, indeed, considered Stolypin's reform the most substantial single obstacle in the way of the Bolsheviks' making any progress in the countryside.

Stolypin accompanied this far-sighted and radical transformation of rural

Born in Siberia, Rasputin *arrived in St. Petersburg in 1903 where he was rapidly adopted by an aristocratic coterie imbued with mysticism and the occult. In November 1905 Nicholas II wrote in his diary: "We met a holy man, Gregory from the province of Tobolsk". This illiterate and lustful monk, with an intensely magnetic personality, dominated the Empress. Worry over her son's health had undermined her mental stability.*

Russia with a ruthless repression of radical activity. There had been an upsurge of terrorism after the turbulent events of 1905; the Social-Revolutionaries had managed to arrange the assassination of almost 1,600 people in 1906, mostly officials of all grades, and more than 2,500 in 1907. This wave of murders reflected a general belief, shared by Lenin, that another armed revolt was in the offing. In August 1906 the "Maximalists", a newly formed S.R. group, blew up Stolypin's summer villa, killing thirty-two people, including the bomb-throwers, and injuring twenty-two, including Stolypin's son and daughter; he personally was unscathed. Though the S.R. Central Committee declined to take any credit for this particular outrage, the terrorist movement had frightened the regime, which

under Stolypin's energetic direction reacted with brio. The security police were given immense latitude; the activities of the terrorists were countered by the lawbreaking of the security organs themselves.

The extensive use of agents-provocateurs directly involved the police in the most extravagant enterprises. Stolypin himself, in fact, found himself indirectly one of the victims of this regime of reciprocal lawlessness: a prison-break was arranged on behalf of one of the Maximalists, Solomon Ryss, who took advantage of the liberty given him by the police to organize the attack on Stolypin's villa. Ryss also organized a lucrative hold-up in the heart of St. Petersburg; it increased the Maximalist treasury by 400,000 rubles.

But the wave of terrorism did not last long. The strength of the revolutionary movement at this time was altogether illusory. In 1907 the central S.R. organ was arrested and liquidated; by the end of the year almost all local groups had vanished. The activities of Ryss himself were finally noticed by his police sponsors, somewhat belatedly, and he was hanged in 1908. The terrorists who escaped arrest fled abroad. By the end of 1907 the Central Committee of the S.R. Party, which after the amnesty of October 1905 had returned to Russia, was obliged to emigrate again. On top of this the exposure in 1908 of Azev's double-dealing, while highly embarrassing to the government, was even more so to the S.R. movement; it nearly wrecked it.

The Social-Democracy was also in a parlous state: still rent by factional strife, its members arrested in droves, it almost broke up entirely. Even its fitful spurts of propaganda fell on stony ground. After Trotsky, Lenin emigrated in 1907, while Stalin, arrested in 1908, was deported to Siberia. By the spring of 1908 Russia was practically cleared of the whole of the revolutionary leadership.

The liberal movement, its premature hopes withering, was hard pressed. The conservatives were winning at all points, including the Rural Councils that had once seemed such promising arenas of agitation. The government had abandoned its intention of keeping its hands off the parliamentary process and was lavishly providing the Rightwing organizations with secret funds; it also openly patronized even the arch-conservative organizations that began springing up with increasing boldness. The most prominent of these was the Council of the United Nobility, though a stellar role was still played by the Union of the Russian People, which split in 1908 and brought forth the Union of the Archangel Michael.

The notoriety of the Union of the Russian People's activities is a striking index of the political corruption of the period between the 1905 upheaval and the First World War. It was public knowledge that the Union of the Russian People was engaged in actual criminal activities, including the organization of pogroms; its president, Dubrovin, had successfully conspired to murder two Cadet deputies to the First Duma, and had also made two abortive attempts to assassinate Witte. Nothing was done about these notorious enterprises; Nicholas acknowledged a flood of telegrams organized by the Union demanding the dissolution of the intractable Second Duma by calling the Union the "mainstay of the throne".

Stolypin's Pan-Russian zeal led to an intensification of the nationalist element in his program. In practice nationalism

—perhaps inevitably, considering the inherent blurriness of the concept—took the form of persecuting the various minorities of the Empire and of artificially ensuring the predominance of Russians in the quasi-representative institutions that had been imposed on the regime.

Russian was rammed down the throats of the minorities; it was made the language of instruction in the Ukraine, a special target of government ire. The regime made no secret of its hostility to the Ukrainian nationalist movement, which was suspected, doubtless rightly, of separatist tendencies, fortified by the autonomy accorded Ukrainians in the adjacent Austro-Hungarian provinces.

The qualified liberties the Finns had once managed to wrest from the Tsarist regime were nibbled away at; in 1910 the Russian government resumed its authority in questions affecting Finland if they went beyond purely Finnish interests, as conceived, of course, by the Russians. This involved a variety of issues, such as the assessment of Finland's contribution to the Russian budget, the taxes needed for it, army service, education, etc., all extremely irritating to the Finns; the upshot was naturally their alienation and embitterment.

The position of the Jews also deteriorated. The discriminatory regime they had been accustomed to for so long was intensified. In 1906 the Council of Ministers, without going so far as emancipation, recommended a slight liberalization of the anti-Jewish restrictions by the elimination of some mea-

The Tsar's daughters: *Maria, Tatiana, Anastasia and Olga. Brought up in genteel seclusion, they had no reason to believe their quiet lives were to be shattered by future events.*

This pretty child shown proudly wearing his first pair of trousers is the Tsarevitch Alexis Nicolaievitch, *photographed a few months before his third birthday in May, 1907. In spite of his round cheeks, the Tsarevitch suffered from hereditary hemophelia. The disease attacks males but is transmitted through women. It was common to inbred royal families and was brought to the last generation of Romanovs by the Empress, born in the House of Hesse.*

sures that simply led to abuses and in any case were unenforceable. The Council of Ministers argued that it would be good public relations, in the jargon of today, to ease up on the Jews, who might then be counted on to increase Russian chances of securing foreign loans. Nicholas took a personal interest in the Jews and reacted to these proposals with unusual vivacity; referring to the "inner voice" he had always been guided by he turned them down in spite of what he admitted was their persuasiveness. The outcome was that Jewish disabilities were actually reinforced, most flagrantly in a law passed in 1912 restoring the institution of Justices of the Peace, which had been abolished in 1889. Until 1912 Jews, though never appointed to any judicial office under Alexander III or Nicholas II, had never been excluded as a matter of principle; now they were specifically made ineligible.

Perhaps the most illuminating indication of Russia's anachronistic attitude toward the Jews was the revival of the notorious ritual murder accusation, made against a Jew named Beilis in March 1911. For more than two and a half years, until Beilis was finally acquitted, and for some time afterwards, the validity of these long-since exploded remnants of medieval superstition was vehemently discussed in the press.

Vaslav Nijinsky, *the legendary star of Diaghilev's Ballets Russes, in his costume for* Les Orientales, *first performed in 1910. The virtuosity of the dancers, the opulence of the décors, and the barbaric vitality of the music, swept western Europe off its feet when the company appeared in Paris in 1909. It provided the first national artistic triumph for the Russians beyond their own frontier. After creating leading roles in such ballets as "L'Après-midi d'un Faune", "Spectre de la Rose" and "Petrushka", Nijinsky went completely mad; from 1917 until his death in 1950 he remained in a lunatic asylum.*

and that were forestalled, ironically enough, only by his assassination in September 1911.

His death was actually a ricochet of his condoning of the ramified police network of double agents, spies, and agents-provocateurs. His assassin, Dmitri Bogrov, was one of the revolutionaries on the police payroll.

The next President of the Council of Ministers was V.N. Kokovtsov, who had been Minister of Finance since 1904, except for Witte's brief return; he retained this office while President of the Council. Kokovtsov was cultivated, complacent, and bureaucratic; he prided himself on the fine speeches he made in the Duma, though his real feelings about representative government were summed up in a famous *bon mot:* "Thank God, we still have no parliament!"

It was under Kokovtsov that the security police made their brilliant coup in secretly getting Lenin's trusted friend and spokesman Malinovsky elected to the Fourth Duma. The more visible activities of Kokovtsov's ascendancy in 1911-1914 included the rise of Rasputin and its public repercussions. In spite of Nicholas's efforts to hush things up there was a series of scandals following the appointment of V.K. Sabler, one of Rasputin's selections, as Chief Procurator of the Holy Synod; they involved all sorts of church figures, including dissolute monks. Rasputin was actually denounced on the floor of the Duma by so reactionary a personage as Purishkevich, leader of the Union of the Archangel Michael, as well as by Guchkov, head of the Octobrists.

On Kokovtsov's retirement in January 1914 Goremykin, by now seventy-

Considered according to the criterion of Stolypin's aims his career might have seemed successful. During his regime the revolutionary forces reached their nadir, while his land-program, despite the failure of many conservatives to appreciate its significance—it was June 1910 before it was passed by the Duma—had effected a comprehensive metamorphosis of rural Russia.

Stolypin was actually considered an enemy by the conservative elements in the government and at court; his boldness and energy, expressed with an arrogance perhaps due to his awareness of his superiority, kindled hostile intrigues whose success seemed ensured

Right, Costume for Les Contes Russes, *a ballet based on Russian popular legends, by Michel Larionov, 1915. Serge Diaghilev, the animateur of the Ballets Russes, gathered artists and musicians around him who introduced colorful elements of local folklore into the classical ballet. Center, Dancer from* Le Sacre du Printemps; *the controversial ballet with music by Igor Stravinsky created a public scandal when the Diaghilev company first danced it in Paris in 1913. Far right, Bronislava Nijinska dancing in* Petrushka, *another Ballets Russes production using folk material in a new way, to a score of the young Igor Stravinsky (1911).*

five and somewhat senile, again became President of the Council of Ministers. His professional credentials of unquestioning loyalty to the Tsar were fortified by his association with Rasputin: the two relationships were doubtless interlocked. It was in Goremykin's palsied grip that Russia was to slide into the First World War.

Apart from the radical transformation of the peasant village launched by Stolypin, other structural changes were being manifested: after 1905 the cooperative movement grew with great rapidity. The first Russian cooperatives had appeared some forty years before, though they had made very little progress. But between 1905 and 1914 the membership of the cooperatives was ten times larger; it had increased from less than 1,000,000 to more than 10,000,000. While not impressive in absolute terms, the potentialities of this movement are obvious.

The most portentous development in Russia before the First World War was the great industrial boom, which achieved its unusual dimensions precisely because it took place within the framework of general Russian backwardness. At the peak of Tsarist prosperity before the war the national income per capita was 8-10 times less than in the United States; this is quite understandable when it is recalled that in 1913 the totality of people engaged in all nonagricultural pursuits—industry, commerce, transport, etc.—did not amount to more than one-seventeenth of the whole population, whereas in the United States about 2 ½ were engaged in industry for every one engaged in agriculture.

The industrial expansion, which had

been particularly rapid in 1893-1899, slowed down in the first decade of the Twentieth Century, and speeded up again in 1910-1913. During the 1890s

some 15,000 miles of railway, including the Trans-Siberian, had been built; this had been the chief single cause of the business boom, which then slowed down

Serge Diaghilev, creator of the Ballets Russes, *revolutionized the dance world with his synthesis of music, decoration and ballet. He had the gift of discovering young talent and using it to advantage. Above, some of his collaborators photographed in 1915: seated, Natalie Gontcharova, painter and scenic designer; standing, Leonid Massine, dancer and choreographer; seated, Igor Stravinsky; Michel Larionov, painter; Léon Bakst, designer.*

because of the turmoil of the opening years of the Twentieth Century. All in all industrial production in Russia increased by roughly 100 % between 1905 and the First World War.

But what was far more important was the character of the industry that sprang up: Russia's very lateness enabled her to dispense with the obsolescent features that constituted a substantial element in the capitalism of older industrial countries.

Thus, while agriculture and peasant life had not risen much beyond the level of the Seventeenth Century,

Pages 226-227

A gouache by Natalie Gontcharova for Coq d'Or, *1914, private collection, Paris. The artist did the costumes and décor for this ballet to Rimsky-Korsakov's music for Serge Diaghilev and his Ballets Russes. Its brilliant color and use of folklore material is characteristic of the new note introduced into the classical dance field by the Diaghilev company and its artists.*

The usual aridity of statistics is relieved in this case by the realization that the concentration of vast numbers of workers on the same premises was a *political* factor of capital importance: it was vital in heightening their *esprit de corps*, discipline, political vulnerability—in a word, their "solidarity". It was to prove decisive in 1917.

The industrial boom, to be sure, was not reflected in the actual living conditions or wages of labor; though there seems to have been a rise in real wages in the decade before the First World War, the workers' entire income was almost exhausted on the basic necessities of the meagrest possible life.

A substantial element in the great industrial boom of this quarter-century was the flow of money from abroad: by 1914 foreign companies owned about one-third of the total capital investment of Russian industry, or about 1,342 million roubles; it was foreign money that accelerated the industrialization of the south. About a third of the investments came from France; England contributed 23 %, Germany 20 % and Belgium 14 %. France is supposed to have controlled almost three-quarters of Russia's output of coal and pig iron.

But of course these aspects of the growth of Russian capitalism, confined as it was to a small sector of the population, and even more to the external world of socio-political affairs, are only one indication of the evolution of Russian society. The cultural isolation of Russia from the West, which had lasted so long, was now a thing of the past. The Russian educated classes were at last on a level with their counterparts in other countries.

Although the international situation in July 1914 was already very tense following the assassination at Sarayevo, the state visit of President Poincaré of France to Russia was not cancelled. But the increasingly alarming news made him cut short his stay and abruptly return to Paris. Above, Poincaré's arrival before the imperial tent at the Krasnoye-Selo camp where military fêtes took place to celebrate the Franco-Russian alliance.

Russian industry—in *technique* and *structure*—was well up in the forefront of international capitalism. More important than absolute industrial growth was the density of the production process, which while already noticeable in the very first stages of Russian industrial development became still more marked in the twenty-five years before the First World War.

A comparison with the United States is illuminating. In 1914, 35 % of all American industrial workers were employed in small enterprises with fewer than a hundred workers apiece, while in Russia there were less than 18 %. The two countries had about the same ratio of businesses employing 100 to 1,000 workers, but in the giant enterprises, about 1,000 each, less than 18 % of the workers were employed in the United States, while in Russia there were 32 % of all workers in 1901 and over 40 % in 1914! The figure is still more striking in the main industrial areas: in Petersburg, for instance, there were over 44 % and in Moscow more than 57 %. Russian textile and metal industries were dominated by gigantic plants.

Russian infantry units parade before the two Chiefs of State. Immense in number, poorly equipped and poorly commanded, these units were soon to be decimated at the beginning of the First World War.

In spite of all obstacles the number of students at higher schools had substantially increased. In the beginning of 1914 there were sixty-seven higher schools numbering 90,000 students; this included some thirteen women's institutions with 21,000. There were 36,000 students attending universities, 22,000 in the engineering and other technical schools, and 10,000 in specialized institutions such as agricultural colleges, etc.

The secondary schools also showed some progress, and the primary school system became an object of immense concern even to the conservative Third Duma, which with considerable success undertook a general reform. The general background of the problem, to be sure, remained depressing: in 1914 49 % of the children between 8-11 did not go to school at all, and in its broad outlines the problem of general illiteracy remained unsolved.

Nevertheless, despite the flimsy underpinnings of the educated classes, there was a very lively development of the press and arts. After 1905 the press was largely free, in spite of the censorship regime. The broad spectrum of opinion expressed in the 2,167 periodicals that in 1912 appeared in 246 cities and towns (excluding Finland) took in even Marxist writers, who found it entirely possible to express the substance of their views in public. In 1924 the Communist Academy made a survey, which it admitted to be incomplete, of the Social-Democratic literature—Menshevik as well as Bolshevik—that was legally published in St. Petersburg and Moscow in 1906-1914: it came to almost 3,300 items. In spite of the government's heightened program of russification minority languages were

extensively used: the large number of periodicals mentioned above appeared in 33 languages, including Polish (234), German (69), Lithuanian (47), Estonian (45), Hebrew and Yiddish (31), etc.

Escorted by Cossacks, driven by the traditional Russian coachman in top hat, President Poincaré is taken through Saint Petersburg in a court victoria.

Indeed, in 1906-1914 the Russian press was freer than at any other time.

The industrial and political fevers of the turn of the century as well as the increased freedom of the press after 1905, had a stimulating effect on literature and the arts. The realism Russian literature had become famous for during the 1860s and '70s was sustained by a

group whose leaders were Tolstoy, Gorky, Anton Chekhov (1860-1904) and Ivan Bunin (1870-1953). Tolstoy, in fact, loomed bulkier than ever, perhaps just because of his religious "conversion" around 1880 and his ascetic repudiation of his purely "literary" writings before then. Becoming a world sage, after evolving a highly simplified form of Christianity that he himself considered "primitive" and that involved the repudiation of authority, violence, and all institutions, in short of the whole fabric of accepted society, he went on living on his estate in Yasnaya Polyana. His contradictory life filled him with growing revulsion, to be sure, but he ultimately achieved a certain degree of spiritual consistency by attacking the Orthodox Church and all its works until the Holy Synod, which had shown great forbearance because of his name, finally recognized a *de facto* situation and excommunicated him in 1901.

The success of the writers in winning Russia a name in world literature was echoed more faintly in other arts: from 1900 on Russian painters began appearing at international exhibitions. All the movements of contemporary art found their exponents in Russia—impressionism, post-impressionism, expressionism, cubism, futurism, etc. During the decade preceding the First World War Russian art had in fact altogether caught up with Europe. It did not, to be sure, make a particularly original contribution of its own; because of its rapid growth it was contaminated by many signs of precocity—meaningless, rootless extremism, slavish imitation of foreign models and so on, but at the same time it had freshness and boldness.

Russian music was by now entirely acclimated all over the civilized world: Stravinsky and later Prokofiev were the most famous of the newer composers. The pre-World War generation produced a vast array of celebrated interpretive artists—Rachmaninov, Vladimir Horowitz, Scriabin, Leopold Auer, Ephrem Zimbalist, Jascha Heifetz. Russia, indeed, was one of the most brilliant spots on the horizon of international music-lovers: St. Petersburg had four opera-houses with a full season each; Chaliapine was famous all over the world. Stanislavsky's theatre started an international reputation that has survived to this day. The ballet, which had been introduced into Russia in 1672 and struck root under Catherine the Great, who founded a ballet school modelled on Paris, was finally defrenchified to some extent by the turn of the

century; a host of Russian ballerinas became internationally celebrated. Fokine, the youthful choreographer of the Petersburg ballet, completely recast its traditions; choosing the works of the most famous Russian composers, Tchaikovsky, Rimsky-Korsakov, Glinka, Borodin, Stravinsky, as well as Schumann, Wagner and Weber, he established a fusion between dancing and music. He also laid special emphasis on the role of mass dancing, which increased the importance of the *corps de ballet* in relation to the prima ballerina. All these innovations, framed in splendid new costumes and décor, created by Diaghilev, were introduced in the summer of 1909 at Le Châtelet in Paris.

Before the First World War upper-class Russians were characteristically immersed in an intense intellectual activity, demonstrated by the extraor-

dinarily wide range of the press and an immense variety of different currents in literature, music, painting and theatre. The court itself was considered rather stuffy, though many Grand Duchesses and aristocratic matrons had intellectual salons that established a national tone. Outside the circle of the Tsar's immediate entourage educated Russians tended to be urbanely critical of the existing order; in cultivated circles, the State Duma, for all its parliamentary imperfections, was the object of absorbed attention.

Ties with Western Europe were very close: upper-class children were habitually taught to speak French, German and, somewhat less frequently, English: foreign literature was widely read, Russians flocked to all the capitals and resorts of Europe. Educated Russians were thoroughly Europeanized

by the end of the Nineteenth Century.

But this complete assimilation to European culture was simply another index of the profound chasm that has been referred to so often. Precisely because of these European influences the upper classes were completely alien to the bulk of the country. The cosmopolitan tendencies streaming in from abroad were concentrated socially in the upper middle-classes, and territorially in the capital: Petersburg, with its baroque Eighteenth and Nineteenth Century palaces, constructed by Frenchmen and Italians, and its splendid embankment was entirely westernized, physically and temperamentally. Even the court and the bureaucracy were highly accessible to foreign influences. But the farther one got away from the capital, the farther one sank into a

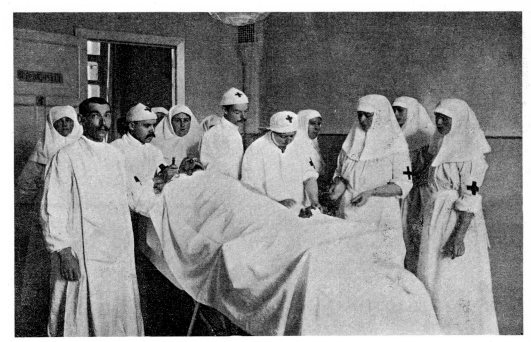

Even the Empress was galvanized by the war. The January 1915 photograph above shows her with her daughters, the Grand Duchesses Olga and Tatiana, nursing the wounded.

quagmire of life altogether alien to Western Europe. Even Moscow had a certain provincialism, and in the small provincial towns the imprint of the West faded fast, being altogether absent in the remoter cities. These were cities only in name, and actually no more than peasant villages with no modern amenities to speak of. Indeed, 87 % of the population, according to the 1897 census, lived in the countryside, and from the point of view of any Western European capital might just as well have lived on Mars. Both in custom, way of life and thought, and even language, there was still nothing in common between the peasants and the tiny educated class. Except for aristocrats who took a personal interest in their land the peasants and the upper-class had no interests whatever in common.

The egalitarian effects of the vigorous and lively popular press were inhibited by illiteracy, which remained widespread, though by the beginning of the First World War it was doubtless a little less than the 79 % recorded in the 1897 census. On the other hand, it must also be recalled that in official reports "literate" might mean nothing more than school attendance in childhood and not the slightest contact with a book or newspaper since, perhaps not even the ability to sign one's name.

When Russia entered the war in 1914 a surge of patriotism obliterated the social bitterness that had torn the country. Rallying faithfully around the Tsar, men flocked to the colors. Here, the entire male population of a village near Moscow responds to the mobilization order.

There were no organized sports, nor did the Russian Church have the cultural or unifying influence of the Protestant or Roman Catholic Churches; this kind of disunity and backwardness was further exacerbated by the persecution of all the national and religious minorities.

Russia plummeted into the First World War, accordingly, with her ancient lopsidedness still embedded in her social and economic structure. The backwardness of the immense majority and the cosmopolitanism of the upper-class elite were radically out of balance: Russia's profound structural flaws were merely plastered over by her façade of monolithic placidity.

Tsarism had been dented, not shattered by the 1905 revolution. But the First World War had undreamed—of consequences for Russia.

If the First World War is broadly thought of as a struggle for the organization of the world, Russia's role was curiously pathetic. Any struggle for world dominion in a race with the industrial states of Western and Central Europe was plainly beyond her capacities and her conceptions. Her own war aims—the control of the Dardanelles, Galicia, Armenia—were parochial; they could be achieved only insofar as the victors in the great conflict permitted them to be.

There is no need to discuss the causes of the First World War or for that matter the course of its development. Russia was involved in it with the same curious mixture of blindness and irresponsibility that characterized the actions of all the Great Powers, from Austro-Hungary to Great Britain. Europe had not had a war for so long, and the technological and organizational background of society had meanwhile changed so profoundly, that it proved impossible for even the most astute statesmen to speculate intelligently on the conduct of an armed conflict involving the mobilization of millions of men. So deeply rooted was the consciousness of security in the minds of all the educated classes that not merely were forecasts in detail utterly falsified by events, but the very fabric of society, thought to be fissure-proof, was to be shredded by the war and its aftermath.

The economic as well as political structure of the Russian state was hopelessly outdistanced by the demands of a modern war. Russian leadership proved to be completely inadequate from both the military and the economic points of view. Having slipped into the maelstrom of a comprehensive conflict even more unprepared than the other Great Powers, Russia found herself short of armaments as well as of war aims. Two contrary tendencies were embodied in the Tsarist state —the essentially medieval and still exclusive prerogatives of the throne, and the defective but existent popular representation in the State Duma and in the scattered institutions of local government. The characteristic wartime concentration of the executive power on the one hand, and the involvement of masses, reflected in the representative institutions, on the other, accentuated both these tendencies.

The authority of the crown was reasserted: the incompetent Tsar's per-

sonal rule was buttressed by the Empress's personal ascendancy and Rasputin's backstage role; the cumbersome Tsarist bureaucracy was circumvented. As for the Duma itself, as well as the

Alexander Rodzianko, *a large landowner, was President of the Tsarist Duma. On February 27, 1917, after several days of strikes and meetings, the Petrograd garrison announced it had withdrawn its loyalty from the Tsar. Rodzianko telegraphed Nicholas begging him to abdicate. The Tsar answered by an order to dissolve the Duma. Rodzianko and party leaders decided not to obey.*

Rural Councils and the municipalities, they were called upon to enlarge their functions in order to cope with the magnified tasks of recruitment, supply, and all the aspects of economic functioning. These two tendencies collided and helped shatter the whole system.

Politically speaking the war was supported, though with varying degrees of enthusiasm, by all parties in the government with the exception of the Bolshevik fraction of the Social-Democratic Party, which took the intransigent position that the proletariat ought to fight against the domestic "bourgeois and imperialist" regime instead of the enemy's armies. This attitude was eventually to help them, but at the time it simply meant the arrest of the five Bolshevik deputies who made up the legal, parliamentary section of the Bolshevik group and their exile to Eastern Siberia in 1915.

One of the major atmospheric elements, so to speak, leading up to the 1917 revolution was the towering role Rasputin had been playing in state affairs. In the topmost circles it had become so disturbing that a plot was finally set afoot to get rid of him. He was assassinated in the palace of Prince Yusupov in December 1916; no action was taken against the assassins, who included a nephew of the Tsar as well as Yusupov himself.

Rasputin's influence had damaged the prestige of the monarchy, and helped alienate the most conservative elements in the country from the support of the throne. But it would be a gross extra-

The parliamentary system *in Russia was largely a fiction. In spite of the regime promised by Witte's Manifesto of October 17, 1905, autocracy soon took over as completely as before. The First Duma was dissolved after 73 days of existence, the Second after 103 days. The Third, called "the nobility's Duma", was made particularly inoffensive by a restrictive electoral law. The Fourth Duma, elected in 1912, only met once until war-time; public opinion forced Nicholas to convoke parliament on several occasions. Above, the Tsar at the reopening ceremonies of the February 14, 1916 session. That day, 300,000 workers went on strike to manifest their solidarity with the parliament.*

vagance to think of it as a genuine factor in the making of the 1917 revolution, whose roots must be looked for in the lopsided structure inherited from the past and now subjected to an unendurable strain by the exigencies of a great war.

The crumbling of national morale that led to the events of 1917 took place only gradually. A patriotic fervor swept the capital in the summer of 1914, as indeed it swept every capital that went to war, and it was shared at the time by every visible social group. Huge

◀ Nicholas *sincerely loved his people although he had no conception of their problems. On Easter Sunday, 1916, the Tsar himself gave a traditional Easter egg to each member of a front line unit. The "little father" is seen here, kissing one of the soldiers in the Russian manner.*

crowds collected to express their dislike of Germans and Austrians, the mobilization went off smoothly, and the strike movement, which in the summer of 1914 had set a record since 1905-1906, simply evaporated.

But the façade of orderly devotion to a common cause began splintering at once. The immediate factors in the disintegration of the patriotic mood were the successive defeats of the army, the chaos of the administration, and a growing irritation among the masses with a war that remained entirely incomprehensible to them.

The Duma spoke only for the bulk of the upper and middle class, but the peasants and workers had no interest at all in general politics; their restlessness began increasing because of the perfectly simple economic grievances they blamed on the incomprehensible war.

Prices were going up and the necessities of life were going down; these facts, plus the overcrowding, naturally squeezed the population, especially the poorer part of it. Except for the better-paid workers in the war industries, wages receded from the already low level of 1915-1916. As for the families whose male members were drafted, they were in a desperate situation; the government only gave them enough to buy food with and nothing else.

As labor felt the pinch it began striking again: in 1915 more than a thousand strikes took place, involving more than half a million workers. In 1916 there were 1,400 strikes involving more than a million, and the strike movement kept mounting in January-February 1917. These wartime strikes, though actually somewhat below the figures for the first half-year of 1914, which had been, moreover, partly "poli-

and the mercy of St. Nicholas, patron of Holy Russia".

It was primarily the defeatist mood of the peasantry and industrial proletariat that the Tsarist regime, immersed in a war it was technologically baffled by, was to founder on; it also undid the Provisional Government that succeeded the monarchy in 1917.

None of the discontent arising from the wartime conditions was guided by any revolutionary centres: the police repressions that had taken place after the strikes of 1914 had exterminated all the clandestine revolutionary organizations, and it was not until the end of 1915 that the Central Committee of the Bolshevik faction began working very quietly in Petersburg again.

None of the future revolutionary leaders was in Russia. Lenin was in Switzerland. Trotsky had made his way to New York after being expelled from one European country after another. It is true that though the revolutionary movement had been decapitated thousands of its members and sympathizers were scattered everywhere, throughout the army and the wartime agencies and factories, but their propaganda was limited to the propagation of ultimate revolutionary aims: there was no question of planning for a revolution.

Though all the revolutionaries kept dreaming about a revolution, and kept reassuring each other of its imminence, when it actually came, in February of 1917, everyone without exception, including all the leaders of all factions both inside Russia and out, was completely taken by surprise. Both the timing, the magnitude and the form it took were completely beyond expectations.

The capital was completely calm the week before February 23 (Old Style).

Grandson of Nicholas I, Grand Duke Nicholas Nikolayevich was named Commander-in-Chief of the Western front upon declaration of war. Profoundly devoted to his task, energetic, loved by his men, this giant lacked the intellectual qualities necessary to a modern military leader. It was not the Russian defeats that brought about his replacement in 1915 but his opposition to Rasputin, which had won him the animosity of the Empress.

tical", were quite spontaneous; they had nothing to do with either political perspectives or trade union leadership, except for the "class conscious" and relatively highly paid metal-workers. As for the peasants, though economically they were better off than the industrial working-class, it was they who had to bear the brunt of the staggering war casualties, which for the First World War amounted on the Russian side to more than 7,000,000 men, the bulk of whom, in consonance with the representative quality of a conscript army, were peasants.

The people at large could not grasp the remote and profoundly meaningless war aims of the "nation": not only did the peasants desert *en masse*, but entire regiments would panic and flee for the most trivial reasons. In 1915 the Minister of War, Polivanov, was reduced to proclaiming his faith in "the immeasurable distances and impassable roads,

Prince Yusupov, *shown here as a young boy painted by the society portraitist Serov, was married to the Tsar's niece. He belonged to the highest spheres of court circles where the plot to kill Rasputin was woven. The execution took place on December 29, 1916 in the Yusupov palace. This nocturnal scene of poisoning followed by revolver shots and drowning remains one of the most theatrical murders of history.*

The Duma had been convoked on February 14, and on the 22nd the Tsar left for army headquarters. The excitement caused by Rasputin's assassination

to the broad and initially unguided movement in the streets of the capital during the first few days after the food disturbances.

Duma, there convened, with no guidance, no mandate, and no plan, the Petrograd Soviet of Workers' Deputies, which on March 2 changed its name

Rasputin *a few weeks before his assassination, surrounded by his court.*

had died down completely during the first few weeks of the year.

All at once disturbances that seem to have begun among the irritated housewives queuing up in front of food-shops spread with incomprehensible rapidity to the working-class suburbs, then flowed back through the main streets and squares of the whole capital. There was no violence, and no hostility was shown by the police and troops; the city authorities were not at all alarmed.

At some point it became apparent that orders given to troops to stop unarmed demonstrators from proceeding along streets or over bridges could not in fact be carried out. When a commanding officer gives an order that is not carried out, and he cannot punish anyone for it, military discipline is at an end. This was what happened

The absence of authority was noticed all of a sudden: it was embodied most dramatically in the simple fact that all gendarmes had vanished. Once that happened, the subjective feeling of anarchy had found a spectacular symbol.

The Duma session was cut short, but after some vacillation the Duma leaders decided to remain informally in session; on February 27 a "Provisional Committee" was elected consisting of the leaders of the "Progressive Bloc" of the Duma plus some Leftwing representatives, Kerensky, a temperamental young lawyer of Populist sympathies, and Chkheidze, a Menshevik leader. This committee had nothing subversive in mind: in the terms of its mandate it was simply supposed to "restore order and deal with institutions and individuals".

On the very same day, February 27, in the Tauride Palace, the seat of the

to the Soviet of Workers' and Soldiers' Deputies.

During the afternoon, while the Petrograd garrison was *de facto* sapping the foundations of the old regime, some Leftwing Duma members, political prisoners just released, and a variety of journalists, doctors, lawyers, Rural Council employees, and so on, had set up the Provisional Executive Committee of the Petrograd Soviet, which was not yet in existence, and in the evening hundreds of people of unknown antecedents held a plenary session of the Soviet confirming the Executive Committee.

The idea of reviving the 1905 revolutionary assembly seems to have sprung up by itself. No one has ever claimed credit for it, and the idea must have occurred more or less simultaneously to a number of labor leaders and intel-

lectuals. At the time it seemed to be a haphazard assembly, but the birth of the Petrograd Soviet is surely a turning point in world history.

It should of course be emphasized that the Soviet—simply the Russian word for "council"—which was later

presentative" is, to be sure, a conveniently capacious term.

By March 3 the Soviet had 1,300 members, and a week later 3,000, of which 800 represented factory workers, and the remainder various army units, in itself significant since there were far

the following day was sent off by train with his family to captivity and ultimately death. That same day he wrote in his diary: "I had a long and sound sleep. Woke up beyond Dvinsk. Sunshine and frost... I read much of Julius Caesar."

When the photograph on the opposite page was taken, Nicholas still ruled. The crowd (above) had lived through a cataclysmic series of events that started during the last days of February. The old order was gone. The Duma saw its role weaken in favor of the Petrograd Soviet. This body, which was to give its name to the Bolshevik regime, was at first a council (Soviet) elected by workers and soldiers of the city. Bolsheviks were far from having a majority in it. The Soviet had promulgated its famous "Order Number One" instructing the soldiers to keep their arms, to form committees and to obey only the orders of the Soviet.

retained to characterize the present-day regime of the Russian Communist Party, initially had no such political connotation. In origin it was a genuinely representative institution, though "re-

◄ *At 10 in the morning of February 27, 1917 the subaltern Astakhov induced some soldiers of the Volhynia guard to leave their barracks. Without difficulty these persuaded their friends in other regiments to follow them, and soon all the soldiers of the Petrograd garrison were in the streets, mingling with the workers and singing the "Marseillaise". Left, a typical scene from the first days of revolution.*

more workers in Petrograd than soldiers. Thus, even before the collapse of the Tsarist regime, the Tauride Palace became the seat of two sources of power that instantly proved themselves to be more authoritative than the whole of the former governmental apparatus.

Thousands of soldiers and civilians suddenly began streaming into the vast and stately halls of the Palace; the whole building was turned into an arena for a seething mass of shabby and headstrong mobs, with the more sedate quarters reserved for the Duma and its hangers-on.

By March 2 the Tsar had signed a document of personal abdication, and

The Tsarist administration collapsed: in the space of three days the apparently unshakable edifice of Tsarist authority had simply been pulverized. Nothing whatever was left of it, and this was felt by everyone in the capital.

But the throngs of people teeming in and around the Tauride Palace had no clear objective. It was the conservative Fourth Duma that was first turned to by many of the upper and middle-class Russians, who naturally gravitated toward it as the new source of state authority.

The Soviet, however, though a diffuse throng in many ways, was aware of its *general* attitude, which was against the retention of monarchy with or without Nicholas II. On March 2, by the time a Provisional Government had been formed by the Provisional Committee of the Duma, after a laboriously arrived of course conditioned activity of the ordinary inhabitants of the city, plus the disaffected garrisoned soldiers. The rest of the country and the army as such played no role in the revolution.

to prefigure the entire framework of political life for the next period. The axis of the celebrated "dual power" was an inherent contradiction that in the event was settled by a further shift of state power when the Bolsheviks in their turn leaped into the seat of authority.

at agreement with the Executive Committee of the Soviet, it was evident that a constitutional monarchy, which had been hoped for by the conservative Duma leaders headed by Miliukov, was no longer a possibility. Soviet insistence had excluded it, and the liberals, who had been hoping for the accession to the throne of the Tsar's brother, to serve as regent for the Tsar's young son and heir Alexis, were confronted by the *de facto* elimination of monarchism as a principle of government. The ancient Russian historical tradition was simply extinguished. The Provisional Government, despite its having been engendered by a conservative Duma, found itself forced by circumstances to be just as revolutionary an institution as the Soviet itself. Against its will it was obliged to assume the direction of the state, and thus consecrate the rupture with the past.

The monarchy had evaporated with a sort of fabulous ease, though casualties amounted to some 1,500. It was a *coup d'état* carried out without organized leadership, by the spontaneous, though

Above, soldiers riding on the mud-guards of an automobile, red flags fixed to their bayonets. Right, officials guarding corpses after a skirmish. While these scenes went on, life continued apparently normal. As late as March 9, Buchanan, the British ambassador, cabled: "A few disturbances took place today, but nothing serious".

This was simply accepted throughout the country, with or without enthusiasm, as an accomplished fact.

For eight months now the political destinies of Russia were to be enacted against a background of democratic liberties in the midst of the continuing war. Politically Russia was freer than at any other time in her history.

The establishment of a twofold source of authority in the Tauride Palace was

The Soviet leaders, almost uniformly Social-Revolutionaries and Mensheviks, did not contest the authority vested in the Provisional Government that had sprung out of the Fourth Duma. Their own authority had been forced on them long before the authority itself was juridically "recognized", which did not actually take place until the eve of the Bolshevik insurrection in October. The trade-unions, the industrial working-class generally, and the peasants kept their eyes glued on the Soviet: the trains would not move, the municipal institutions and the police were paralyzed, and the most basic functions of administration were inhibited unless authorized, sanctioned or specifically ordered by the Soviet, which according to the official "theory" of the Provisional Government remained a "private" body. And despite the theoretical sovereignty of the Provisional Government it was actually living only by the grace of the "private" Soviet, which in turn declined to acknowledge its own authority theoretically while nevertheless in *de facto* control of all administration.

This contradiction in the behavior of the Soviet leaders can only be explained by the character of Socialist theory I have hinted at before. The Soviet was directed largely by the Mensheviks, who some months later also joined the Provisional Government, and in fact were the head of it until the Bolsheviks became powerful enough to suppress it.

Soldiers and sailors, and a few men and women civilians, listen to a speech by Rodzianko in the great Catherine Hall of the Tauride Palace, where the Duma met: March 1917.

Now, the Mensheviks were actually precluded from the assumption of power by their view of politics, which briefly put consisted of the conviction that a Socialist society could only come about after society had matured; thus a bourgeois society had to be established first, and consequently run by the bourgeois parties. Even if they were given a position of authority, as they were in spite of themselves during the eight months the Provisional Government lasted, they felt themselves compelled to act as the custodians, so to speak, of bourgeois power. Their theory tied their hands; they could do nothing to upset the bourgeois regime. As a matter of fact events proved that though Bolsheviks and Mensheviks were equally "doctrinaire", the Mensheviks were far more "fanatical"—they actually destroyed

their personal careers as well as the effectiveness of their party by failing to adjust pragmatically to a situation in flux.

The Bolsheviks, on the other hand, had a more plastic view of theory: they simply moulded it to suit their purposes, and did this plausibly enough both to establish their dynamic leadership and to conserve their virtuous allegiance to tradition.

But of course it was not the Bolsheviks as a group that leaped from theory into action-plus-theory: it was Lenin, who came back to Russia in April 1917 in the famous "sealed train" put at his disposal by the German authorities. Both Lenin and the Imperial German government were naturally making their own calculations, with different degrees of success.

When the revolution broke out, Lenin had been in Switzerland together with a great many other revolutionaries, including Martov, who had actually conceived this plan of returning to Russia via Germany. The "sealed train" —as well as the legend of "German gold"—was to become a persistent motif in the propaganda of Lenin's opponents.

I have referred to Lenin before, in the context of the revolutionary movement as a whole. On his return to Russia he was simply the leader of a small fraction in the restricted universe of the Russian revolutionaries; no one would have had the slightest premonition that in a few months he was to become one of the most famous personalities in history, and the architect of a new social order.

A discussion of Lenin, often considered the "Bolshevik Peter the Great", would lead far afield. I shall merely situate him socially.

Vladimir Ilyich Ulyanov (1870-1924) was born into a prosperous family. His father was a professor of mathematics and an academic supervisor who had been given a noble title in accordance with the Table of Ranks. His mother was the daughter of a well-to-do physician; she spoke four languages, sang and played the piano—i.e., she was the product of an extensive education implying family tutors and governesses.

In spite of the legend carefully propagated by the Soviet government, Lenin was, in short, the son of a land-owner. As he once said: "I too lived on an estate belonging to my grandfather; I too am the son of a landowner. Is that a reason why I am unworthy of being called a revolutionary?"

Until he was 27 the question never arose of his having to earn a living. Afterwards the combination of family and Party allowances, as well as what he made by his pen, enabled him to live in circumstances that from a vulgarly material point of view were perfectly "bourgeois", though the personal frugality of Lenin and his wife made them indifferent to such questions.

Alexander Kerensky, *a lawyer and socialist deputy of the Duma, the most moderate member of the Soviet Executive Committee, was 36 years old when he joined the government of Prince Lvov. The Soviet had exacted its participation in this government. On July 7, after Lvov's resignation, Kerensky became its President.*

The propagandistic attempt to pretend that they lived in poverty deliberately misses the point that they enjoyed the luxury of being able to do just what they wanted—work for their own ideas and their own cause.

In the brief general discussion of the Socialist theory of taking power I have mentioned Lenin's matter-of-fact, unverbalized conviction that he was himself an "objective" force of history. This penetrating conviction, allied to a highly rationalistic, utilitarian approach to specific circumstances, was now to enable him to achieve a fusion between theory and practice other intellectual groups found denied them by too rigid a conception of theory.

Throughout his experience as an émigré Lenin had shared the general Socialist assumptions mentioned above. He ascribed greater importance in the process of political maturation to the leavening effect of the revolutionary Party—i.e., his own caucus—but he was in general agreement with other Social-Democrats on the preconditions for Socialism in general.

Now, however, he came to Russia armed with a theory that gave him the

necessary justification for taking power.

This theory was provided by Leon Trotsky, whose name was now to be closely linked to Lenin's in the preparation and execution of the Bolshevik insurrection.

Leon Trotsky (1879-1940), born Bronstein into a fairly well-to-do Jewish farmer's family in the Ukraine, is generally known as a brilliant speaker and writer. A prolific writer on many subjects beside politics, he had remained without stable Party affiliations throughout the years of exile he shared with so many others. During the revolutionary depression that followed the 1905 turmoil, Trotsky had spent most of his time trying to reconcile the Bolsheviks and Mensheviks, without being a member of either group. His attempts at intra-party unification were all the more futile since he could never hold the personal allegiance of more than a few people at a time. This defect in character has of course been interpreted variously by friends and foes.

In any case, when he arrived in Russia about a month after Lenin, his theoretical ability fused with Lenin's organizational preoccupation to launch the first successful revolt of armed intellectuals in history.

The theory Trotsky had developed was not, to be sure, his alone: it had been suggested by Parvus, a Russo-German cosmopolitan Marxist, and in the unflagging clatter of argument among Russian émigrés was naturally no novelty.

This theory was to the effect that the Russian bourgeoisie was actually too weak to overcome Tsarism alone and to reform capitalism adequately *before* the Russian workers grew strong enough to push it out altogether; hence it was necessary for the working-class itself to take power in order to accomplish the bourgeois revolution *on behalf* of the bourgeoisie, and thus create a situation in which it could construct Socialism later on.

Lenin seized on this theory when he came back to Russia in April; he insisted that the Bolsheviks must take power and waste no more time waiting for the Russian bourgeoisie to reform capitalism. Lenin arrived at the Finland Station of Petrograd on the evening of April 3rd. He was forty-seven years old. Though at this time his name was unknown outside political circles, he was given a gigantic reception by a great throng that filled the square. His speech ended with a slogan that at the time was utterly alien to all Socialist, including Bolshevik thought— "Long live the Socialist revolution!".

Revolutionary street scene *in Petrograd. Shots fired from a window in the Nevsky Prospect make the crowd run for cover.*

Sukhanov, a semi-Menshevik journalist and economist who has left us the only full-length memoir of the eight

One of the first acts of the Provisional Government was to proclaim the liberty of the press. Seen here are the new revolutionary newspapers being distributed to the crowd. The main Marxist papers were Izvestia *(The News), organ of the Executive Committee of the Soviet,* Novaya Zhizn *(New Life) of Gorky and* Pravda *(Truth), publication of the Bolsheviks, which was Lenin's platform (he took the title from Trotsky).*

revolutionary months of 1917, happened to slip into the celebration of Lenin's arrival at the Bolshevik headquarters, the palace of the famous ballerina Kshesinskaya, where he had been driven from the Finland station on top of an armored car, "holding a service", as Sukhanov says, at every street-crossing to throngs of gaping people.

Sukhanov gives us a vivid description not only of Lenin's oratorical style, but of the emotional impact of his impromptu departure from Socialist tradition, for even though Lenin, while not yet ikonized, had immense authority within his faction, his new theory absolutely flabbergasted his disciples—he had to conquer them before acquiring a mass following. Here is Sukhanov's eye-witness account:

"...The celebrated master of the order got to his feet. I shall never forget that thunder-like speech, which startled and amazed not only me, a heretic who had accidentally dropped in, but all the true believers. I am certain that no one had expected anything of the sort. It seemed as though all the elements had risen from their abodes, and the spirit of universal destruction, knowing neither barriers nor doubts, neither human difficulties nor human calculations, were

hovering around Kshesinskaya's reception room above the heads of the bewitched disciples.

"Lenin was a very good orator—not an orator of the consummate, rounded phrase, or of the luminous image, or of absorbing pathos, or of pointed witticism, but an orator of enormous impact and power, breaking down complicated systems into the simplest and most generally accessible elements, and hammering, hammering, hammering them into the heads of his audience until he took them captive.

"Afterwards, about a year and a half later, hearing him as head of the government, one was bound to regret the former orator, the 'irresponsible' agitator and demagogue. After Lenin had changed from a demagogue and insurrectionary into a statesman, Lenin the orator became flat and faded, losing both his power and his originality. His speeches came to resemble each other like two drops of water..."

Sukhanov goes on to give us some typical reflections of Lenin's opponents:

"...the conversation turned upon Lenin. Skobelev told Miliukov about his 'lunatic ideas', appraising him as a completely lost man, standing outside the movement. I agreed in general with this estimate of Lenin's ideas and said that in his present guise he was so unacceptable to everyone that now he was not at all dangerous for our interlocutor,

Prince Lvov's Provisional Government *pursued a precarious life for a few months with no real force or authority behind it, the power divided between the government and the Soviet. It was first dominated by the Constitutional Democratic Party (Cadets) and the Prince's own party, the Progressives. Then on May 5 it had to give a larger place to the Socialists, and it disappeared altogether at the beginning of July to be replaced by the Kerensky government. Here is the Lvov government as it was initially constituted, with Kerensky as Minister of Justice. Later Kerensky replaced Prince Lvov as Prime Minister and also filled the post of Minister of War.*

Miliukov. However, the future of Lenin seemed different to me: I was convinced that after he had escaped from his foreign academic milieu and entered an atmosphere of real struggle and wide practical activity, he would acclimatise himself quickly, settle down, stand on firm ground and throw overboard the bulk of his anarchist 'ravings'. What life failed to accomplish with him, the solid pressure of his party comrades would help with. I was convinced that in the near future Lenin would again be converted into a herald of the ideas of revolutionary Marxism and occupy a place in the revolution worthy of him as the most authoritative leader of the Soviet proletarian Left. Then, I said, he would be dangerous to Miliukov. And Miliukov agreed with me.

"We refused to admit that Lenin might stick to his 'abstractions'. Still less did we admit that through these abstractions Lenin would be able to conquer not only the revolution, not only all its active masses, not only the whole Soviet—but even his own Bolsheviks.

"We were cruelly mistaken..."

During the eight months the Provisional Government lasted all parties except the Bolsheviks supported the war; it was this burden, inherited from Tsarism, that was to prove their undoing. The war situation could not be remedied: the material difficulties kept accumulating, and though there was a brief

Like so many other revolutionaries, Georgi Valentinovitch Plekhanov *belonged to a prosperous land-owning family. He founded the first Russian Marxist group in 1883; for a long time he was revered by Trotsky and Lenin as the intellectual leader of Social-Democracy. But these two admirers were far more radical than their old master in their theoretical views and principles of action. Plekhanov is photographed here at Petrograd next to a French Socialist. He was to die soon after the Bolsheviks came into power. These gave him a grandiose funeral before letting his name sink into oblivion.*

surge of enthusiasm in favor of the Provisional Government, and Kerensky himself would have seemed to any outsider to be a durably popular political leader, the hardships of the war and its incomprehensibility to the bulk of the population made the task both of the bourgeois parties and the former revolutionaries in the Social-Revolutionary and Menshevik groups unbearable.

For in actual fact, however much the Bolsheviks theorized about what they were doing, and in their well-worn polemics against old and new political opponents used the old logico-rhetorical apparatus of Marxism, in their appeals to the masses they presented no complex theories at all. On the contrary, they made the most simple and basic of all promises: they were the only party, in fact, that cut through all the verbiage political questions in general are enveloped in and the pathos attendant on carrying on a war, and simply promised the masses what they wanted, in the celebrated tripartite slogan of "peace, bread, and land".

The Bolsheviks proved to be highly flexible, indeed opportunistic. Once Lenin made up his mind that he was willing to take power, the corollary of this implied the needlessness of educating the masses in general theory. Since it was not the masses, ripened by lengthy experience of a bourgeois environment, who were to take the

power, but a small, limber and highly disciplined team of professional revolutionaries, there was clearly no need to waste time on lengthy indoctrination in the theory that in effect was reserved for the Party elite.

In his veneration of sacred texts Lenin thus combined extreme scholastic rigidity with a perfectly practical view of how things could get accomplished, and since his immediate goals were all on the order of power politics, he could reserve his theoretical preoccupation for what he would do *after* taking power.

It must be further recalled that the decision to take power was made against a background, common at least during the early period of the revolution to all shades of Socialist opinion from Lenin to Plekhanov and Kerensky, that the revolution in Russia would be imitated in Western countries. On October 7 Lenin wrote that "the worldwide workers' revolution had begun... doubts are impossible. We stand on the threshold of the world proletarian revolution."

It was against the background of this general expectation that the decision was taken at a secret meeting of the Central Committee, on October 10, with twelve of the 21 members present. The discussion (which took place, curiously enough, in Sukhanov's flat, without his knowledge) lasted for about ten hours; Lenin's resolution that the "armed insurrection is inevitable and the time for it fully ripe" was passed by ten to two. Trotsky, who had been chairman of the Petrograd Soviet since September 23, was also chairman of the Military Revolutionary Committee that had been established by the Petrograd Soviet to secure the revolutionary defense of the city.

The actual *coup d'état*, freely discussed everywhere beforehand, was child's play: against the general background of civic disintegration, mass apathy, and more particularly the utter incapacity of the Provisional Government to conceive of either a program that might rally support, or a firm tactic that might at any rate give it

Below, the presidents of the Peasant Congress groups which met in May 1917 at Petrograd. The Social-Revolutionary Party (S.R.S.) had always considered that the peasantry and not the proletariat would be the real ferment of the revolution in Russia. This party dominated the Congress. It was also to dominate the Pan-Russian Congress of the Soviets held at the beginning of June. The popularity of the S.R. Party was immense at that time. The Bolsheviks underestimated it when they launched the movement to upset the Provisional Government too soon, which only resulted in the bloody "July days".

244

On July 3, 1917 *the Bolsheviks organized a huge demonstration against the Provisional Government. A counter-demonstration took place and the exchange of shots was murderous. Next day the Kronstadt sailors—always an extreme radical element—joined the Bolshevik ranks. After firing on the Cossacks who were faithful to the government, they went to the Tauride Palace to demand that the Soviet take over. The executive committee of the Soviet hesitated and the Provisional Government seemed about to use real energy for a few days. An order of arrest was sent out for the Bolshevik leaders but these, warned in time, had escaped. Soon the process of decomposition continued.*

the benefit of its own armed forces, the Bolsheviks found it simple to apply a plan of their own. In spite of what Trotsky admits to have been its crude, hasty, and improvized character, it was

General Lavr Georgievitch Kornilov, *former Military Governor of Tsarist Petrograd, was made Commander-in-Chief of the Provisional Government forces by Kerensky. Kornilov prepared a military coup d'état for September; the plot failed after various heroic-comic adventures. The General had hoped to replace Kerensky.*

enough for the purpose. The insurrection was, in fact, a very flabby affair; its success can only be explained by the bewildering indolence of the Bolsheviks' opponents.

On the night of October 24 the Military Revolutionary Committee sent armed detachments to occupy the key-points of the capital—railway-terminals, bridges, the state bank, the telephone exchange, the central post-office, and various public buildings. Though the troops were apathetic, they were at any rate "for" the Bolsheviks, except for a few "neutral" regiments, including the Cossacks; there was no bloodshed or opposition. A day later nearly all the Ministers of the Provisional Government were arrested, except for Kerensky. They were taken to the Peter-Paul Fortress to join their Tsarist predecessors.

The insurrection was so easy that no one was aware of what was happening: most of the shops, theatres and cinemas were open: on the afternoon of October 25, when the insurrection was supposedly at its height, city life looked practically normal.

That same afternoon Trotsky took time off from the insurrection to preside over a session of the Petrograd Soviet: here Lenin, who had been in hiding from the Provisional Government since July, finally emerged to take over publicly the reins of the power seized by his Party. After the preceding months of tension, wrangling and apathy, the mood was now very enthusiastic: Sukhanov reports the scene:

"Long-drawn-out ovations alternated with the singing of the Internationale. Lenin was hailed again, hurrahs were shouted, caps flung into the air. A funeral march was sung in memory of the martyrs of the war. Then they applauded again, shouted, flung up their caps. The whole Praesidium, headed by Lenin, was standing up and singing, with exalted faces and blazing eyes... Applause, hurrahs, caps flung up into the air..."

The Bolsheviks, in the teeth of Socialist tradition and theory, had decided to govern entirely alone, independently of all other Socialist forces as well as bourgeois society.

The Bolshevik subordination of theory to power politics was illustrated dramatically by the total absence of any program. The Bolsheviks simply snatched the power left dangling in the air by the exhausted Provisional Government, and *then* proceeded to work out a program.

A striking instance of improvization was the Bolshevik promise of land to the peasants, which was implemented in a Land Decree. This abolished all private ownership in land, making it impossible to buy, sell, lease, mortgage or alienate it in any way. The whole of the land reserve was subject to periodic reapportionments, with provisions for the mass resettlement of the rural population.

Now, this scheme, which revived the most unworkable features of the obsolescent village commune, was lifted bodily from the arsenal of Social-Revolutionary theory, which the Bolsheviks had been laughing at for years. Lenin admitted this, but defended this incorporation of his opponents' theories as expedient!

The fact is that the Bolsheviks had not bothered working out any plans at all for the remaking of society. Their decision to take power did not arise out of any theoretical view of the tasks of a Socialist party at the helm of an agricultural state—theoretically inconceivable—but was a reflection of a concrete power situation.

The theoretical justification for doing this was the hope and indeed, as indicated above, the expectation that the more advanced industrialized countries of Western Europe were already ripe for revolution, and were certain to have one of their own from one day

to the next. It was this expectation that provided Lenin's party with its theoretical justification, since regardless of the differences indicated above between Mensheviks and Bolsheviks on the feasibility of *taking power* in a backward agricultural country, all Socialist theory was in accord on the utter impossibility of *realizing* a Socialist society in a country where the overwhelming majority of the population had not yet evolved into capitalist techniques. At bottom Lenin's view was that the Bolshevik Party would simply have to hold on to power for a little while, until the trail-blazing Russian revolution was caught up with and then pulled along in the train of the revolution that was bound to take place in a country with a massive industrial base like Germany. Then an equilibrated industrial-agricultural society would be established in which the

The garrison had deserted in large numbers, leaving only a small force that included 130 women. Kerensky was away at the front, the remaining Provisional Government ministers held out in one room, hoping for reinforcements which never came. Bolshevik shelling terrified the Women's Battalion into prompt surrender. Red Guards stormed the Palace and arrested the ministers, taking them off to the St. Peter and St. Paul dungeons.

principles of Socialism could be realized.

He was really applying one of his favorite quotations, a remark of Napoleon's: "You commit yourself, and then —you see". The fact that the revolution failed to materialize in other countries, despite a number of abortive attempts in the aftermath of the war in Germany and Hungary, meant that the Bolshevik faction, with no theoretical foundation for running an agricultural country, with an inadequate control of the population—since the Bolshevik regime was not accepted so quickly by the country at large—and with no administrative cadres, was setting out to run a large backward, and ruined country with its own resources alone. The Bolshevik Party made this leap into the unknown in response to nothing but Lenin's high spirits. It was now to collide with "objective" reality, and in doing so remake society not by planning, but by improvizing one institution after another.

Page 248

The Russian delegates at the Peace Conference are greeted at the Brest-Litovsk station by German officers. The Bolsheviks wanted to sign an immediate peace but they found it difficult to accept the stringent conditions imposed by the Germans. Begun at Brest-Litovsk in December, the negotiations were broken off several times. The play of contradictory elements made the situation extraordinarily complex: the changeable attitude of the Allies, the efforts made by counter-revolutionary elements, and the fraternization between Russian and German soldiers, which worried the Kaiser's command. The Bolsheviks estimated that the Germans needed fresh troops for the west too badly to launch a new offensive. Besides, they hoped to temporize until the proletarian revolution in Germany, which they believed to be near. The result of these delays was that the peace treaty finally accepted on February 23 was even more severe than the one originally proposed by the Germans.

The New Order

The material situation inherited from the war was calamitous. The Bolsheviks would have been incapable of embarking on any scheme of social reconstruction even if they had had one when they took power. Their energies were completely consumed by the termination of the war, and then, after the war, by the combination of civil war and foreign intervention that went on for more than four years.

Since the exhausted Russian forces had to get out of the war at all costs, the Germans were able to impose a particularly savage peace settlement on them that included the surrender of vast chunks of the national territory. It was only the defeat of the Germans that enabled the Bolsheviks to surge back into the control of Russian lands, progressively defeating both the organized domestic forces of the "White" opposition, as well as the improvised and defectively supported expeditionary forces of their former allies.

By the time the First World War ended in the peace settlement of 1919, the Soviet heir of the Tsarist Empire was substantially mutilated. A *"cordon sanitaire"* had been set up by the disgruntled Allies to contain the Bolshevik infection: the Baltic States, Poland, Finland, and part of Rumania were all lopped off and made independent. The Tsarist boundaries had been pushed back. It was thus within a reduced sphere that the Bolshevik Party was now to embark on its innovations.

The Bolsheviks had begun with a regime of "War Communism". This simply meant the massive expropriation of all the major institutions of the country: the banks, the merchant marine, the grain-dealers, the mines and the oil industry, as well as all enterprises with a capital of between a half-million and a million roubles. Only businesses with less than ten workers were left untouched. But this first

attempt at centralized direction was done so amateurishly, against such a background of devastation, that when the civil war was over the country was utterly reduced.

Vast areas had been lying fallow for years. The battlefields had been constantly shifting around, especially in the Ukraine, where the destruction was general. Harvests had been destroyed over and over again; industry was completely shattered, with production down to a *seventh* of the pre-war figure. Most of the factories were simply standing idle, while many mines had been physically annihilated. Pig-iron amounted to only 3 % of what it had been before the war. The stocks of metal and industrial products were exhausted: the most basic commodities, food and fuel, were unavailable.

The workers were profoundly discontented: wages had been lost because of this shutting-down of factories for lack of raw materials and fuel.

Lenin and Trotsky *in Moscow, on Red Square, during a demonstration organized at the end of 1918. On the right, a photograph of the same demonstration published in a recent Soviet book on Lenin. It can be seen clearly that retouching has made Trotsky disappear from the picture.*

Commerce had also been halted; small as well as large businesses were shut down; private trading was altogether prohibited in 1920. All cash had to be deposited in the state bank, and all precious metals surrendered.

A black market naturally arose to take the place of the normal market. This squeezed the workers and the city-dwellers in general very severely, though of course it favored the peasants. Prices soared: between 1920 and 1921 the price of bread went up 11 ½ times. The early enthusiasm that despite the immense opposition had attended the Bolshevik seizure of power, and all the

excitement of civil war and intervention had quite evaporated. The Bolsheviks found themselves at the helm of an utterly ruined country that in addition had lost practically all its educated classes. In the aftermath of the Bolshevik insurrection some 2,000,000 Russians, nearly all of them belonging to the aristocracy and cultivated classes, emigrated, leaving the Bolsheviks the immensely difficult problem of finding and training technicians and administrators for an unprecedently comprehensive government program.

The new position of the state made all economic activities political *ipso facto*. Since it had taken the place of the private employer it now collected all revenue from production, and thus played the same supervisory role as the private employer before it, with of course the added advantage of an immense apparatus of coercion. In this way what the Bolshevik slogan of "socialization of the means of production" meant in practice was a highly centralized network of production subordinate to the governing apparatus and backed by a concentrated police power, duplicated on the consumers' side by the cumbersome bureaucracy required for large-scale distribution.

In the early part of 1921 the rations of the Petrograd factory workers had to be cut because of the widespread shortages; this brought about a wave of massive strikes, which were political in their very essence and which culminated, in fact, in a first-class insurrection headed by the naval base in Kronstadt, across the gulf from Petrograd. This insurrection was highly political from the very beginning. The sailors had always been militant Bolshevik suppor-

ters; the insurrection marked their disappointment. It was not aimed at the restoration of democracy, but called for a revolutionary regime *without* the Bolsheviks —a "third revolution".

During two and a half years of civil war, Trotsky *travelled along the fronts held by the sixteen armies which he galvanized and directed. He led the military operations against the Whites, and organized propaganda for the civilian population.*

The Bolsheviks found themselves outflanked on the Left; to defend themselves they instituted a ruthless campaign

In April, 1918, the former Emperor with his wife, son and his four daughters was transferred from Tobolsk to Ekaterinburg in the Urals (today Sverdlovsk). After a few miserable months, on July 16, they were ordered into this room; an armed guard entered and shot them dead. Grand Duke Michael and Grand Duke Sergius were among other members of the family murdered during the same period in this district. Fear of approaching White armies, which captured Ekaterinburg a few days later, probably precipitated the slaughter.

against the Kronstadt uprising, which by the middle of March was completely shattered. The Kronstadt garrison of 14,000 men, of whom 10,000 were sailors, was completely liquidated: the

◄ *Since the abdication, Nicholas II and his family had lived quietly at Tsarskoye Selo where the deposed Emperor, completely forgotten, went in for gardening. A suspicious correspondence had been seized in July 1917, and the Petrograd Soviet insisted that the imperial family be exiled to Tobolsk in Siberia. In this photograph taken at Tobolsk, the Tsar and his family sit on the roof of a hot-house belonging to the provincial governor's house, which had been given to them as residence. The Empress, ill, was not photographed.*

survivors of the Bolshevik attack, which encountered indescribably ferocious resistance, were shot or sent to prison camps.

The Kronstadt insurrection was the first of the feuds within the Bolshevik fold; it has remained a source of Communist soul-searching ever since. With its dense intermixture of political and economic factors it was an obvious danger-symptom; it was clear that a way out of the economic quagmire had to be found. The conclusions Lenin first drew from the Kronstadt mutiny involved a tightening of the security police system to forestall the danger of any further insurrectionary movements, but ultimately it made him turn aside from the program of planning—a national planning commission had been establish-

ed in the early part of February 1921 —and look for a radically different way out of the material devastation exacerbated by the chaos of "War Communism".

His solution was simply a return to capitalism: the political regime, still too enfeebled for planning on a national scale, had to stimulate the peasants' interest in producing for a market, ensure the food supply, start up commerce again, and fortify the industrial plant.

The Bolsheviks, while tightening the political controls essential for their monopoly of power, made a bold about-face. In the so-called New Economic Policy, approved at the Tenth Party Congress in March 1921, they established a mixed economy in which the concerns that still remained nationalized were to compete with a reborn private enterprise. The theory was that the socialized sector of the economy would gradually grow at the expense of the private sector, but that this would come about through

national aid committee directed by Herbert Hoover, later president of the United States, was established after an appeal was sent out written by Maxim Gorky, and the Soviet government accepted its help.

economy with state controls—had not yet been touched.

Politically, though the Bolsheviks retained their power monopoly, their former revolutionary associates, the Mensheviks and the Social-Revolutionaries, had been allowed a good deal of latitude. As late as August 1920 a Menshevik Party congress could be held in Moscow, perhaps because the Mensheviks still had strong points of support in the trades unions.

But the Bolsheviks were beginning to concentrate their power. By the beginning of 1921 the chief Menshevik leaders, Martov, the friend and comrade of Lenin's youth, and Theodore Dan, as well as the Social-Revolutionary Chernov, went abroad. It was the beginning of the new radical emigration.

A general campaign soon followed, first against the Mensheviks, then against the Social-Revolutionaries; by February 1922 arrests—the first of a long, long series—began to be made against the Bolsheviks' former fellow-revolutionaries. In the summer of 1922 the first political trial mounted by the Bolshevik Party took place, directed against the Social-Revolutionaries, with the celebrated terrorist Savinkov a defendant. The court handed down fourteen death sentences, and only two acquittals. As the Bolshevik utopia receded into the misty future politics was acquiring a serious look. The Social-Revolutionary movement, heir of so much agrarian, communizing, and anarchist tradition, was practically liquidated.

The Bolshevik Party itself began to take on an entirely different form: it was no longer subject to the purely polemical and theoretical considerations that had dominated it in exile. The problems confronting the Party, which all boiled down to the administration of

The Georgian, Joseph Vissarionovitch Dzhugashvili, called Stalin *(1879-1953), was a militant Bolshevik for a long time, but nothing indicated that he was destined to become one of the most extraordinary dictators of all time. This photograph shows him just before the Bolsheviks took over. Shortly afterwards, he was made People's Commissar but with the relatively modest post of Minority Nationalities.*

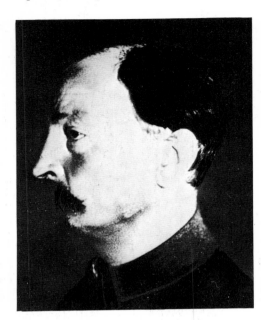

Right, Dzerzhinsky *had been deported three times to Siberia in Tsarist days. After the Soviets came to power he organized the "Extraordinary Commission created to fight the counter-revolution", known by its initials, the Cheka. This police group, formed by December 7, 1917, has changed its name over the years. It has brought its method of spying, denunciation and execution to a terrifying degree of perfection.*

the natural operation of economic forces and not be hastened by political action. The large industrial plants, transport, the banking system, and foreign trade were to remain the monopoly of the state apparatus, but the rest of the industrial sector and domestic trade were to be open to private initiative. The right to private ownership was restored within limits; the peasants could once again sell some of their produce on the open market. Foreign capital was solicited, and foreign firms invited back to Russia, even into heavy industry. This conciliatory move on the part of the Bolsheviks went hand in hand with generally successful attempts to restore international relations with the non-Bolshevik world, via treaties and trade pacts.

The new policy bore fruit, though not at once. The 1921-22 winter was very severe and the harvests quite inadequate during both years; reserves were of course non-existent. Even if the New Economic Policy could have been rapidly effective it came too late to prevent the first great famine of the Soviet era, in which some five million people are supposed to have died. An inter-

But in spite of everything the country gradually recovered: production started up again, in both agriculture and industry, and commerce became much livelier in the money economy restored by the N.E.P. By the beginning of 1923 the country as a whole seemed to have weathered the storm, and for the first time in seven years the economy began to take on a viable look.

Of course, from the point of view of the Bolshevik leaders it was primarily the merchants and peasants who benefited by the restored opportunities for accumulating capital: the basic problem of the regime—how to industrialize the

The poet Vladimir Mayakovsky *in the opening years of the revolution. Many avant-garde writers and artists greeted the new regime with high fervor, thinking it would encourage the most audacious intellectual efforts. This honeymoon was short and the innovators were soon ostracized. Mayakovsky, one of the most gifted poets of our times, had lent his talent enthusiastically to the Bolshevik cause. In 1930, smothered by the ultra-conformist atmosphere, he committed suicide.*

Lenin *haranguing the crowd in 1919, while Trotsky listens at the foot of the platform. The two Bolshevik chiefs had complementary gifts : Trotsky's imagination and dynamism were constructively counterbalanced by Lenin's more considered personality.*

rural, backward Russia within the framework of a concept that called for an antithetical type of country, split up the ruling group, and by Lenin's death in 1924 factions were definitely formed. The criterion of differentiation may broadly be said to be the various attitudes possible toward the solution of this basic problem—the institution of a collective, socialist economy in a rural and illiterate country.

It was still thought a revolution would take place in industrial central Europe, and at bottom the question was whether the Bolshevik regime would be forced to let the country lapse back permanently into some form of capitalist enterprise, or else whether with the help of the powerful industrial working-class

of some other country—by now only Germany could play this role—it would be able to institute some form of Socialism.

Trotsky's prestige in the country had been enormous after his stage-management of the October insurrection and even more his restoration and command of the Red Army during the tense days of the civil war. With his oratorical, literary and organizational abilities, he was the chief man after Lenin. He occupied an "international" position, logically inherent in Socialism as understood by all Socialists up to that time: that Socialism was inconceivable without an industrial plant capacious enough to ensure the potentialities of an economy of abundance.

In these novel circumstances, however, no "logical" alternative survived the grueling test of power. Despite his personal prestige and abilities, Trotsky proved incapable after Lenin's death of withstanding the emergence of a factor no one had foreseen—the potency of the administrative apparatus.

Strangely enough, despite the intellectual acumen of the Bolsheviks individually, this factor, though manifestly inevitable, had never been taken into consideration in any forecasts of what would happen after the Bolshevik seizure of power.

Before taking power the Bolsheviks had been much the same kind of intellectuals as their fellow-revolutionaries: their principal preoccupation was

ПРОЛЕТАРИИ

УНОВИС 1920

◄ A 1920 poster *showing Lenin delivering a speech from a lofty construction under a sign in Russian bearing the word "proletariat". The artist, El Lissitsky, had been in the vanguard of the modern movement in the early Soviet period. He remained in favor by switching to far more conventional forms of applied art.*

a coterie of intellectuals into a corps of administrators.

It is a platitude of Marxism that the material base of a community determines its spiritual superstructure: indeed, if this is put with such ambiguous diffuseness it is common sense as well. Consequently it should have seemed self-evident that even if the Bolsheviks had been a band of angels they were bound to be radically changed upon undertaking the gargantuan tasks of reconstructing a peasant society, especially since by taking power they had committed themselves to a project that from the point of view of their tradition and theories was unfeasible.

Yet no one foresaw this: the assumption by the numerically insignificant Bolshevik Party of the monopolistic administration of this vast country accelerated the growth of a bureaucracy, and since the authority of the Bolshevik Party found its locus within this huge apparatus it was obvious that the power over the country in reality boiled down to power over the apparatus—the bureaucracy in general and the administrative centres of the Party in particular.

The transformation of the Party into an administrative structure was signalized by the emergence of Stalin, known beforehand essentially as an able "practical" on the non-theoretical levels of political life.

As the prospects of foreign revolution faded, leaving the Bolshevik Party in sole charge of the country with no outside help, the specific weight of the administrative apparatus increased, and the authority of Stalin, the General Secretary of the Party—i.e., the head of structure, personnel, and the allocation of functions—increased with it.

The purely theoretical discussion that had been raging in Party circles about the nature of the reconstruction to be attempted once the tempest of civil war, famine, strikes and war destruction had died down, rapidly yielded to the pressure of Stalin's apparatus.

In coping with this Trotsky was inhibited in the first place apparently by profound problems of character, which prevented his appearing as a candidate for power, and which he naturally veiled from himself in a web of rationalization. Intellectually he failed to perceive in time the immense power bound to fall to anyone in control of the apparatus the country was administered by.

theory. It is true that their theory bore on the reality they were determined to change, but until they came in contact with that reality they were bound to spend most of their intellectually creative time in fixing their ideas within the framework of pure abstraction.

But when these intellectuals found themselves guiding the practical affairs of a large community they were willy-nilly drawn into the necessity of coping with concrete practical matters from an administrative point of view. Thus, whatever the theoretical discussions taking place at the apex of the Party, an actual apparatus of administration was in the nature of things bound to emerge overnight, and as the Bolshevik Party began growing after its seizure of power it was only natural for it to be transformed with corresponding speed from

The Grey House *by Marc Chagall, 1917. Paul Pechère coll. Brussels. All his life Chagall has continued to paint poetic evocations of his native Russian town, Vitebsk, as it was in the first decades of the century. He had left the family isba and the farm animals that appear in so many of his canvases for Paris, in 1910. At the outbreak of the war he returned to Russia, and after the revolution he was put in charge of Fine Arts in his region. Like other artists such as Kandinsky, Pevsner and Gabo who also became émigrés, Chagall had expected to continue his work unhampered. But soon the rigidity of Stalinist rule stamped out all individual expression and Chagall left his country for good. He has lived in France since then.*

What emerged from the conflict of views concerning the implementation of a collective economy was neither the restoration of capitalism nor the establishment of Socialism.

An intermediate course was embarked on, summed up in the formula of "Socialism in one country" and linked to the name of Stalin, who elaborated this idea in 1924 as part of his struggle against Trotsky. It is an illuminating example of the interaction between sacred exegesis and indispensable administration. The idea that Socialism could be confined to one country, however large,

Makhno and his staff. *For two years, the Ukraine was the scene of a tangled skein of revolutionary and counter-revolutionary agitation. Armies and groups were formed and dissolved, became allied, then fought between themselves. Makhno was the chief of one of these bands; for a long time he terrorized the countryside.*

the Georgians who were touched by Marxism, however, became Mensheviks, Stalin was one of the few Georgian recruits in Lenin's faction before the revolution; in his practical way he helped in Lenin's "expropriations". Because of Stalin's Georgian background Lenin regarded him as useful on the "nationalities question".

Negligible as a speaker, writer, or theoretician, Stalin was confined to this view of his reputation until the aftermath of the revolution, when his administrative abilities marked him out in the civil war and in the organization of the government.

During the intense game of intrigues that followed Lenin's death Stalin played a progressively bolder role; he outplayed all other factions, and in a few years was *de facto* master of the

would hitherto have been merely non-sensical to any Marxist for the reasons given above. Socialism, as the next higher stage of social organization after capitalism, naturally had to cover at least a substantial section of a world-wide economy, and in any case have an advanced industrial base of its own to operate on.

This had been a commonplace with all Bolshevik leaders, including Stalin himself up to 1924. In the early part of 1924, for instance, in his *Foundations of Leninism*, Stalin agreed that the proletariat might seize power in a single country—the Bolsheviks maintained that in their seizure of power they "represented" the proletariat—but it could never create a Socialist economy. The efforts of a single country, however large, were not enough to ensure the final victory of Socialism.

However, the world revolution was not—in fact—making its scheduled appearance, and in the event Trotsky's persistence in clinging to the breadth of outlook inherent in Marxist discussion deprived him of an intellectual weapon in his struggle with the secretariat controlled by Stalin. In the bureaucracy, expanding in the new state-controlled economy together with the growth of its administrative assignment, the theory of Socialism in one country, despite its break with all Marxist tradition and perhaps with common sense, was an effective ideological umbrella for the new and portentous role of the General Secretary.

Stalin (1879-1953) was born Joseph Vissarionovich Dzhugashvili into an impoverished family in Georgia. His

native language was Georgian; he was never entirely at home in Russian. He had been given some theological training in the Greek Orthodox Seminary in Tiflis, but at an early age had been affected by the currents of political agitation sweeping from Russia far into her outlying territories. Georgians, in fact, played a disproportionately large role in the Russian revolutionary movement, perhaps because the national oppression of the Great Russian state sharpened their rebelliousness. Most of

General Wrangel *at Sebastopol in 1920.* ▶
Many elements refused to accept the Bolshevik regime, including officers of the imperial army incensed at the humiliation of Brest Litovsk. Generals from this group formed a counter-revolutionary force led by General Denikin which amounted to 150,000 men, well armed by the Allies. Starting from the Cossack country of the Don and the Kuban, Denikin advanced as far as seventy miles from Moscow. Red resistance, Cossack defections and disagreements within his own general staff stopped the offensive. In March, 1920, discouraged, Denikin handed over his command to his rival, Wrangel, seen here taking possession of the southern government on April 7. Wrangel led some successful raids on the Dnieper and the Kuban, but soon his army was forced to withdraw in disorder to the southern Crimean coast. There, in November 1920, 135,000 fleeing elements hastily boarded 126 boats and headed for Turkey, from where they scattered all over Europe. This débacle marked the end of the civil war.

Party. Trotsky was first demoted, then exiled to Siberia, then deported altogether by 1929; Zinoviev and Kamenev, Lenin's closest associates, were reduced to a completely subordinate status.

Stalin's triumph was not, of course, merely personal: it was the triumph of the administrative apparatus that had grown up beneath the Party's intellectual shell, cracked it, and finally sloughed it off. Stalin can only be understood as the prime executor of the compromise between the theoretical background of the Bolshevik Party, its seizure of power and the practical consequences of its application.

On his death-bed Lenin had a belated premonition of what this meant. Shortly before dying he had added a codicil to his "testament", recommending that Stalin be removed from his post

as General Secretary for his "rudeness" —a big word in Lenin's mouth—and had followed this up by breaking off all personal as well as political ties with him. By this time, of course, it was far too late: the "forces of history" were digesting the human material at their disposal.

Stalin overcame all his opponents within the Party by a characteristically conciliationist method that gave him the air of a middle-of-the-road, practical administrator. He made selective borrowings from all programmatic proposals, and on this eclectic basis outlined a new program, which he presented on the occasion of the Tenth Anniversary of the revolution.

In 1917, at the time of the Bolshevik seizure of power, Lenin had coined a phrase: "Either die, or overtake and

pass the advanced capitalist countries." After a decade of political and economic tempests this slogan was now to be implemented by a government united behind the Stalin faction, in a program that established the matrix of the modern Soviet state.

The new governmental structure evolved organically out of the two cardinal goals Stalin set for the state-planned economy: the massive collectivization of agriculture, and the establishment of a powerful industrial plant.

The "Draft Program" proclaimed by Stalin was ratified by the Fifteenth Party Congress that convened in December 1927, and the State Planning Commission was entrusted with the elaboration of the first Five-Year Plan. This was the first attempt in history to encompass the entire national economy,

including the boundless ramifications of retail distribution, in one unified plan.

The collectivization program was started in 1928. Since it involved a vast agricultural revolution, it had a purely political side: the rich peasants—"kulaks"—had to be eliminated in the countryside before the program could be carried out. In fact the collectivization of agriculture was launched under the slogan of an "offensive against the kulaks".

In early 1928 the Political Bureau decreed numerous emergency measures, consisting of sudden raids on kulak farms, requisitions, and mass arrests. But they were not yet expropriated; it was not realized what drastic measures would be necessary. The first Five-Year Plan, which was presented and accepted late in 1928, did not provide for the collectivization of more than 20 % of all the farmers by 1933, and as late as the spring of 1929 Stalin said in public that private agriculture would play a fundamental role in the national economy.

But the collectivization movement established its own momentum. Private agriculture was soon doomed explicitly; by the end of 1929 Stalin called for the "liquidation of the kulaks as a class". The material base of the so-called "rich peasants"—"rich" in a style that would have seemed laughable anywhere else—was to be destroyed by unqualified expropriation, and in 1929 the kulaks were wiped out.

An attempt had been made by the Soviet theoreticians to break down the peasantry into 5-8 million poor peasants, 15-18 million middle-income peasants, and 1 ½-2 million kulaks, amounting to a grand total of 25 million peasants, exclusive of families.

For some reason the planners thought that the middle-income peasants were potentially friendly to collectivization, and could be won over. It was naturally assumed that the poor peasants would be mad with joy.

But if the poor peasants welcomed the collectivization program, their determination was not strong enough to carry it through. The program in fact turned out to depend for its implementation on the police. Not only the kulaks, but the so-called middle-income peasants fought it tooth and nail. The measures taken by the government to overcome their resistance illustrate the new factor introduced by modern technology into the treatment of this outburst of peasant despair, the latest in a long line of peasant revolts against state power that had recurrently churned up Russia since the earliest days.

The peasants were determined not to turn over to the government what they regarded as theirs: vast quantities of food were stored away, the cattle scheduled for the new farms were slaughtered, the crops were set fire to, and the tools were smashed.

The peasants must have calculated that such tactics would in fact simply halt the government's impetuous drive toward collectivization and force it back into a reasonable attitude.

They were sadly mistaken. Since mere administrative measures were futile, the government turned the army loose as well as the secret police. Mutinous villages were simply surrounded by units with machine-guns and forced to surrender. The kulaks, both real kulaks and those who were suddenly called kulaks because of their opposition to the collectivization program, were rounded up in droves and deported to Arctic regions by the hundreds of thousands. By the end of 1929, as Stalin said, even expropriation was no longer sufficient: the kulaks had to be excluded from the collective farms entirely. Millions of peasants of all kinds were simply exiled, jailed or killed.

This violence had been so unexpected that by March 1930 Stalin was forced to slow down the collectivist program himself. He did this, characteristically, by saying that the functionaries who had been supposed to carry it out had become "dizzy with success"—the headline *Pravda* gave the proclamation of the slow-down. In this way Stalin was giving a modern counter-point to the old theme that between the Tsar and the peasants the bureaucrats were responsible for thwarting the benevolent Tsar.

In any case, by the end of the first Five-Year Plan 60 % of all holdings had been turned into independent economic units consisting of large and small holdings, with the land jointly cultivated. Seventy-five peasant families were the average number of members of a collective farm (abbreviated in Russian as Kolkhoz) for which they had to work between 100-150 days a year. All produce was supposed to be turned over by the Kolkhoz to the state, which would thus be in a position to handle the distribution of food to city-dwellers, workers, etc.

Stalin had embarked on this dual program of collectivization and industrialization on the basis of purely abstract considerations, in the teeth of both Left and Right Oppositions. As the great compromiser he had simply borrowed from all relevant sources, taken a middle course—not in terms of actual programmatic content, but as a method of fortifying his position personally—and then gone ahead with the implementation of this program, which in the event was extremist in both scope and method. The "agrarian revolution from above" that was effected in 1928-30 proved as calamitous for the country as the devastation of the civil war. Some years later — in January 1934 — Stalin felt free enough to disclose some figures:

During the great Russian famine, Herbert Hoover, future President of the United States, again took over the direction of his committee which had done such fine work in Belgium during the First World War. Through it, America provided food for a million Russian children.

In the autumn of 1921, representatives of villages struck by famine *come to the main square of Kuybishev, on the Volga, to get seed for planting crops the following season. They have travelled in large carts drawn by dromedaries, camels and horses.*

of the 34 million horses Russia had had in 1929 less than half were left; some 30 million head of cattle and almost 100 million sheep and goats had been slaughtered. As in the civil war of the preceding decade vast areas of land lay fallow. Untold damage had been done to farm implements, etc.

This calamity on the land naturally created a famine of unparalleled scope. The regime was of course reluctant to reveal any figures, but in spite of itself the news crept out. It finally was forced to admit, in a piecemeal way, that literally millions of people—a conservative estimate is six million, though some specialists think ten is nearer the mark—died of hunger due to the bureaucratically induced famine of the

early Thirties. In modern conditions, with no other political parties in existence, and no peasant organization even

This banknote issued in 1921 shows the inflation that was rife in Soviet Russia. It is worth 100,000 roubles, which was about one American dollar at the time.

remotely conceivable, there was no way of expressing discontent, nor could the ferocious rebelliousness of the tormented

Lenin's funeral in Moscow. *Towards the end of 1921 Lenin, troubled by dizzy spells and insomnia, was only partially directing affairs of state. He had a first stroke the following spring but was able to return to the Kremlin to work at a slower rhythm than usual. In March 1923 a second stroke left him dumb and he was never completely himself again. He died January 21, 1924. A crowd of over 300,000 gathered in Red Square for his funeral in bitter cold weather.*

peasantry find any outlet. The regime was still, perhaps, too novel for political discontent to organize itself, once the full-dress opposition of the early anti-Bolshevik forces had been wiped out.

The crisis in agriculture was further compounded by its direct effect on the industrialization program. The slaughter of the horses meant that the land could scarcely be cultivated at all: even if it had been customary to use cattle as draft animals, which it was not, the cattle had, after all, been killed off too. The consequence was that the tractors envisaged as part of the industrialization program had to be provided at once, to cut short the devastation of the famine. The need for tractors was all the more vital since Russian agriculture is extensive; the Kolkhozes were spread

out over vast areas, and could not even begin to be cultivated without tractors. This of course had been realized even before the horses had been slaughtered in such vast numbers, but now the speedy implementation of the industrialization program was literally a matter of life and death.

Consequently Russia found herself thrust brutally into the thick of a problem that even without the attendant crises would have been difficult to solve —the creation of a highly trained industrial working-class that could provide agriculture with the new implements it needed for its mechanization, cope with the increasing needs of the country as a whole, and above all re-establish the country's armed forces. Since the cadres of the industrial working class already

in existence in Russia were exiguous to begin with, the training problem became particularly acute: people to train people were both indispensable and unavailable.

To accomplish these tasks the strait-jacket of the secret police became tighter and tighter. Beginning with the Thirties the Russian people was put through an ordeal doubtless unique in history.

It has become fashionable among the many students of Soviet affairs, even those unsympathetic to Communism as such, to praise Stalin for his "ruthlessness" in carrying through these twin breakneck programs of collectivization and industrialization that imposed so many sacrifices on the Russian people. But the amusing thing, if amusement is to be derived from such events, is that he was quite simply unaware of the probable consequences of such a program. He seems to have had the feeling that the words "mechanization", "collectivization", etc., were talismans: despite his reputation for "practicality" he had a romantic, not to say magical attitude toward the power of these ideas, and scarcely imagined the practical difficulties likely to arise. He was actually astonished by the degree of violence the peasants opposed to the government's projects, and by the practical consequences of their violence. He had not, that is, foreseen the difficulties and then staunchly hacked his way through: he had launched the enterprise with a baffling lightmindedness, all the more curious since both Left and Right Oppositions had given him enough material for a more rational perspective. Afterwards, of course, he kept his nerve during the devastations and massacres that followed the application of "Socialism in one country"—his character withstood the strain.

The Five-Year Plans successively became the foundations of the formidable industrial plant and technical elite the Soviet Union has at its disposal today. The vast Russian sacrifices in consumption made possible an immense concentration on heavy industry. Stalin's name is thus indelibly associated with the present foundations of Soviet power: all questions of tactics have been irrecoverably engulfed by the slipstream of history.

With the onset of industrialization Stalin's political power within the country also became consolidated. At the death of Lenin the vital importance of the pivotal position of General Secretary

Photograph taken in 1922 when Stalin managed to have himself named Secretary General of the Communist Party. This post seemed to be of only secondary importance, but it was essential to the realization of his projects. The picture was widely distributed during the Stalin era. The dictator always wanted to appear as the close companion and most trusted follower of Lenin. Actually, although Lenin appreciated the Georgian's possibilities, he had no illusions about Stalin. In Lenin's "political testament", which was only revealed officially to the Russian people by Khrushchov in 1956, he warned the party's higher echelon against certain aspects of Stalin's character.

Even before Lenin's death, countless plots were woven around his succession. The NEP (New Economic Policy) displeased advanced factions which were in Trotsky's orbit because of the concessions to capitalism involved. To ward off this menace, in the summer of 1923 Stalin allied himself with Lev B. Kamenev, opposite, and Grigori Zinoviev, veteran revolutionaries who had worked closely with Lenin, whose popularity at the time could counterbalance Trotsky's. Kamenev had married Trotsky's sister. As of 1928 Stalin remained sole ruler: Trotsky was in exile, Kamenev and Zinoviev were nonentities.

was not yet obvious: the fact had not yet been digested. But by the beginning of the Thirties there was no longer even a question of effective opposition.

Stalin had made a tactical alliance with the Right Opposition in order to destroy Trotsky and the Left Opposition: after the Fifteenth Party Congress in December 1927 that definitely eliminated Trotsky, Zinoviev, and Kamenev, the leaders of the Right Opposition, indeed, thought their own policy had prevailed. But with the onslaught on the kulaks early in 1928 and the intensification of the collectivization drive, the gap between Stalin's bureaucratic machine and the Right Opposition widened. The Right Opposition found itself in exactly the same position as the Left Opposition before, but this time without even the existence of the Left Opposition to act as a counterweight to Stalin's now overwhelming bureaucratic power. By pulverizing both Oppositions in turn Stalin was now in complete and unquestioned control of the entire Soviet government.

Another wave, or rather trickle of émigrés made its way abroad. Actually the methods of the new regime were far more efficient than those of Tsarism before it; hardly any Oppositionists were able to escape.

This struggle for power within the Soviet regime was to have international repercussions: splinter movements developed in Leftwing political organizations all over the world. The Communist Parties, wholly under the thumb of the Kremlin dictatorship, found themselves defending the vested interests of the bureaucratic oligarchy now running the Soviet Union.

Stalin's progressive victories at home were to produce a phenomenon scarcely paralleled in history. All social activities, both material and spiritual, fused into what has since come to be known as totalitarianism. A decade before this would have been unthinkable. It was the specific contribution of the Stalin regime and perhaps a characteristic institution of our century.

At its inception the Bolshevik regime, despite the rigors of War Communism and the civil war, had demonstrated a marked though relative degree of tolerance. New forms of expression were not only allowed to flourish, but were zealously sought after. Even the Bolshevik

excesses within the purely social sphere during the first decade after the revolution exemplified a utopian enthusiasm. The initial Bolshevik euphoria manifested itself, for instance, in a social radicalism involving the denigration of the family as a "bourgeois" institution, the laughableness of marriage, the absurdity of sexual morality, the laudability of sexual license, the reactionary outrageousness of scholastic discipline, etc. It also went without saying that religion as the "opiate of the people", in Marx's celebrated remark, was to be generally despised in official circles, though none of the Churches had actually been proscribed.

Academic and university education, which had been severely curtailed during the civil war, began to revive afterwards. It met with the greatest difficulties, since Russia's intellectual life had almost completely collapsed during the years of crisis. Vast numbers of intellectuals, who belonged chiefly to the upper classes, had died in prisons or been killed by hunger and cold. The chief scholars of Russia had joined the huge White emigration. But during the N.E.P. education revived substantially, initially with the collaboration of the bourgeois experts who had managed to survive.

Moreover, there was a great efflorescence of artistic creativity during the first decade of Bolshevik rule. Some strikingly original poets became prominent, such as Yesenin, Mayakovsky, Blok, and Pasternak; Prokofiev and Stravinsky also had marked influence, while Shostakovich was perhaps the best known of the younger composers. An immense international impression was also made by the cinema; Eisenstein's films were considered a revolu-

tionary innovation. The theatre and ballet revived once again, to be sure without launching anything novel. In the arts in general the tendencies that had been considered "decadent" were now hailed as expressions of the vanguard.

This relatively liberal situation lasted until 1928, the year that marked the consolidation of Stalin's power. Things now began to change rapidly: censorship, discipline, and enforced conformity blanketed the country.

A foreshadowing of this sweep toward totalitarianism is doubtless to be found in Stalin's inauguration of the Lenin cult in 1924, in a ceremonial "oath" he read aloud at the Second Soviet Congress.

A street scene 10 years after the Soviets came to power gives an idea of the atmosphere of the times. Women selling hats at the market were mostly from formerly wealthy families ruined by the revolution.

The first of numerous Five-Year Plans was launched in October 1928. Seen here is one of the countless construction projects undertaken in all parts of the country with whatever material was at hand. A huge propaganda campaign created a real collective psychosis of enthusiasm among party members and large portions of the population. During this first period, the magic word "piatiletka" (five-year plan) symbolized the hopes for the future, the tasks of the present and the hatred of the past.

Lenin's funeral was at this time being exploited by Stalin as part of his campaign against Trotsky: by misinforming Trotsky of the date of the funeral—when Lenin died Trotsky was in the Caucasus, a singular piece of obtuseness on his part—Stalin became the dominant figure at the ceremonies. The "great pledge" Stalin read out at the Second Soviet Congress in January 1924 is an intriguing mixture of the two types of catechism Stalin had been familiar with in the course of his career: the Greek Orthodox litany he had learned as a boy at the seminary in Tiflis, and the basic documents of Marxism.

This pledge, or oath, was the start of the cult: Lenin was placed on the same pedestal as Marx—a position he would have regarded as grotesque and inconceivable, actually almost meaningless, since he thought of himself merely as a faithful expositor of the master's teachings. But the establishment of a Lenin cult enabled Stalin to make himself its beneficiary; it was, so to speak, *his* Lenin cult, and it enabled him to represent himself as the heir of Lenin's spiritual and intellectual heritage as well as, of course, its executor.

With the rise of Stalin as the visible and uncontested power in the new Soviet state, the Bohemianism of the early regime was not only sloughed off, but the authoritarian atmosphere of the Stalin regime permeated all aspects of life.

Discipline and the iron hand of the teacher were restored in 1935; report cards and marks, hitherto regarded as a piece of bourgeois reaction, were reintroduced. The death sentence was restored, and extended to children from the age of 12 on.

The family was not only re-established as the basis of the state, but was buttressed by curiously old-fashioned safe-

Pages 266-267

Like all dictatorial governments, the Communist party has always gone in for mass propaganda and displays of physical force. This giant red star made up of 2000 athletes was the highpoint of a gymnastic display at Kiev in 1929. It was neither the first nor the last of such events destined to arouse popular enthusiasm.

265

guards: divorce was made much more difficult, and families with children were given exemptions and subsidies; abortion was declared a criminal offense unless medically justified. This question of abortion was actually submitted to the population at large in factories,

Having perhaps realized that the intelligentsia is the most dangerous single social element when disaffected, the Stalin regime simultaneously straitjacketed and coddled it. Combining the classic drives of bribery and punishment, it managed to establish a mould for the

early Bolshevik hostility to "bourgeois" culture; apparently rather discouraged in exile, and aging, he was cajoled by the Soviet government into returning in 1928. Gorky had the unusual charm of being a genuine proletarian. He had been internationally celebrated as a

Stalin *photographed with high Soviet officials on the occasion of Kalinin's "jubilee" as President of the All-Russian Central Executive Committee in March 1929. Few of the group survived politically. From left to right:* Molotov, *who held important Foreign Affairs posts off and on; after Stalin's death he was brought back to head Foreign Affairs until relegated to a minor ambassadorial post by Khrushchov.* Mikoyan, *skilful survivor, still functioning in his Commerce post.* Stalin, *died in 1953.* Petrovsky, *an old Stalinist, executed in 1937.* Kalinin, *retired in 1946.* Smirnov, *tried and assassinated in 1936.* Tolokonzev, *who has faded from the picture.*

offices, collective farms etc., for discussion, but though the reaction was universally hostile the government disregarded the popular verdict, which it had evidently not reckoned on, and applied the new restrictions with great harshness.

The armed forces were also put under an old-fashioned regime of tradition and discipline, and in keeping with the Soviet practice now becoming general of building up Soviet patriotism by assimilating the specifically Russian tradition of the past, the military glories of even the Tsarist empire were absorbed.

The new Soviet patriotism, quite distinct from the ideology of Marxism, was expressed in the unparalleled subsidizing of the intelligentsia as a class.

expression of all artistic and intellectual impulses that was securely embedded in the general structure of the Soviet government.

The effects on literature were of course the most direct, though painting, music, architecture, and for that matter science too were subordinated to the centrally guided corps of censors. Stalin's tastes in these fields as in all others were decisive.

Perhaps the strongest single influence in literature, after the experimentalism of the "soft" period of Soviet intellectual life in the Twenties had waned, was Maxim Gorky (1868-1936), one of the few talented writers inherited by the Communist Party. Gorky had actually left Russia in 1921, disgusted by the

writer, and in addition was the only non-Bolshevik personal friend of Lenin. On his return to Russia the regime made him an official monument. The "Socialist realism" he was considered a splendid example of became a dominant trend in Soviet culture, and has remained so. Fundamentally ambiguous, it is, like its predecessor the old Tsarist slogan of "nationality", a mere synonym for "official patriotism". It has been lived

From the very beginning, the Soviets made ▶ *a great effort to indoctrinate the young. Anti-religious campaigns were a fundamental aspect of their program. Here are young recruits emptying the Simonov convent before this was destroyed in 1930.*

up to as well as possible by most of the well-known Soviet writers—Fadeyev, Sholokhov, Simonov, etc.

There is no need to describe the totalitarian consolidation of culture the Soviet regime may claim credit for: its effects are universally familiar. The theory of the Soviet state, based on a crass simplification and ikonization of some elements to be found in the Marxist scriptures, is by definition

universe, the Communist Party is the custodian and the Soviet state is the executor.

The outcome of this canonization of the Trinity of Party, State, and Theory was that Stalin himself, in the full view of his own generation, became the emblem of the God-head. In the course of a few years he was made the object of a cult that glorified him beyond all imagining.

where. All speeches, the entire press, every expression of literary, political, and scientific opinion referred to him insistently with the most extravagant floweriness. Not merely was he placed in the direct succession of leaders beginning with Marx and going through Engels and Lenin, but he was conventionaly and unreservedly referred to as the greatest genius in world history, the peer of every thinker the human race has

To industrialize Russia and modernize agriculture *the Soviets needed foreign machinery and personnel. America sold her machinery and furnished technicians. The summer harvest of 1930 is shown here in a kolkhoze of the Salsk district. US engineers show Russian peasants how to work the newly imported American equipment.*

comprehensive: the "dialectical materialism" that is its axis encompasses the natural and social sciences, philosophy and law, the study of man, and the very process of thought itself.

This concentrated intellectual apparatus is itself a reflection of Soviet patriotism. It is explicitly declared to be in the service of the Soviet state, i.e., the caucus in power. In the dialectical process of history, understood to comprise both the activity of mankind and the objective functioning of the

◄ *Women operating a textile mill in what formerly was a church. 1927 photograph.*

The profound change in Stalin's status was symbolized by the contrast between the celebration of his fiftieth birthday in December 1929 and that of Lenin's in 1920, which had been markedly quiet. In the nine intervening years the government apparatus had expanded by leaps and bounds, and the Party's grip over it had tightened enormously. Stalin was whirled aloft in the process; at the very pinnacle of this towering structure he became a quasi-deity.

This birthday celebration marked the beginning of the Stalin era. Huge portraits of him were pasted on buildings and walls all over the Soviet Union; his bust was displayed every-

known, in short the greatest man in the world past or present. He became an arbiter on all questions, from party organization to science, from linguistics to zoology. The whole history of the Party was rewritten to give him a prominent place in it from his adolescence on. Until his death twenty-five

Pages 272-273

One of the main projects of the first Five-Year Plan was the construction of the Dniepropetrovsk dam. This huge enterprise holding back the Dniepr river in the Ukraine was to furnish 800,000 horse power of energy to factories of the region.

tion. Thus what had been a foible in the discussions of the pre-revolutionary Russian Social-Democrats now became an iron rule enforced by the police department. The plastic, living intelligence of Marx was mummified and uncomprehendingly revered. As for Stalin's own writings the less said about them the better. With the rise of Stalinism all Communist debate became a matter of rhetorical anathematizing or hosanna-shouting, in which slogans, catchwords, and sacred references replaced discussion or for that matter thought. This is doubtless why Marxism in any rational form has become a dead letter in the Soviet Union: in forty years, despite the backing of a powerful government, no contribution to Marxist literature worth mentioning has come out of Russia.

Stalin's glorification was of course a way of glorifying the growth of the state he symbolized. The early Marxist views of the ultimate "withering away" of the state as soon as it had completed its task of ushering in a Socialist society were shelved altogether, and the new concept of the all-powerful Soviet state substituted. By the time the "Stalin Constitution" of 1936 was published the profound changes that had been taking place both in the government structure and in the Party's thinking were made manifest. Though the "withering away of the state" envisaged by Marx was still paid homage to as the ultimate goal of Communism, it had to wait until capitalist "encirclement" was put an end to. Until then the fight against capitalism had to be conducted by the Soviet state, which the civil service, art, literature, philosophy, morality, law, etc., were all subject to without qualification. This idea of the omnipotence and omnipresence of the

Kirov's funeral ceremonies in 1934. Kirov, who had replaced Zinoviev at the head of the Leningrad Soviet, was assassinated by a young member of the "left-wing opposition". This unleashed a nightmarish series of reprisals. After the mass trial of 1936, Zinoviev, Kamenev and fourteen other important Bolsheviks were sentenced to death after making confessions which astounded the outside world. The trial of the "seventeen Trotskyites" took place in 1937, and, the same year, seven important military leaders were executed.

years later Stalin was to enjoy adulation unprecedented in history.

The most striking single trait in this trinitarian cult of Party, State and Theory is the ritualization of Marxism it involved. It is true that Marxist parties had been doctrinaire in the sense of being able to find a cosmology in the pages of a few books, but Marxism had depended, after all, on an attempt to analyze data empirically and to seek concordances based on induction. Except for its apocalyptic purposiveness —the notion that the utopian classless society must "inevitably" emerge from

the womb of history—Marxist debate could be conducted rationally.

Its ikonization changed all this. With the sanctification of the Marxist texts debate became impossible: everything could be "settled" by the right quota-

Zinoviev, who had done so much to aid Stalin's accession to power, had been excluded from the Communist Party as of 1927. After Kirov's murder he was sentenced to ten years of prison, then judged again and condemned to death during the trial of the Old Bolsheviks in 1936.

new Soviet state embraced the lives of individuals as well as of institutions; it became the basis of the new Soviet patriotism.

The somewhat theoretical constitution that had been devised to unite the family of Soviet republics in 1924 was manifestly outdistanced by the development of the monolithic one-party state, The Stalin Constitution was simply the administrative expression and recognition of this fact.

The formation of the new elite also grew tremendously with the growth of the economy; indeed, the Communist Party itself ceased being the small elite it had originally been. In 1923, only a few years after the revolution, the membership of the Party was still only half a million, but by ten years after Lenin's death it had become a mass party of 3 ½ million. In his domestic struggles Stalin at first resorted to the method of flooding the Party in order to swamp his opponents: in 1925 and 1926 alone some 200,000 new members were admitted. By the beginning of the Second World War it was more than 2,300,000 and ever since it has been relatively on the increase, except for the casualties of the war itself.

Though the Communist Party does not exercise any governing functions formally, it is of course the decisive power within the state, or rather its topmost executive organs contain the personalities who exercise all power. The actual leadership of the whole complex is in the hands of the Political Bureau, though groups within the Political Bureau itself are the *de facto* rulers in a manner too elusive for outsiders to grasp.

Even this importance of the Political Bureau is actually a formal fiction. During Stalin's regime it was the Party Secretariat, and particularly his own private secretariat that had developed within the structure of the Secretariat proper, that exercised real control.

Trotsky in exile. *By January 1925, Trotsky lost his position as Commissar of War to be given an insignificant place as member of the Higher Council for National Economy. Zinoviev and Kamenev, already estranged from Stalin, joined forces with him in the struggle against the Georgian. At the tenth anniversary celebrations of the October Revolution, important anti-Stalin demonstrations took place in Moscow and Leningrad. Trotsky was then excluded from the Communist Party. In January 1928 he was deported to central Asia, then exiled to Turkey. For twelve years he led an itinerant existence trying in vain to rally the international communist masses to his anti-Stalin platform. The Georgian dictator had him assassinated in Mexico at the beginning of the Second World War.*

The cardinal development in the Party structure during the Thirties, of greater significance socially, was the loss of its working-class nature. The number of actual proletarians within the Party dropped to less than a third, while the new Soviet intelligentsia, the Party officials, the upper strata of academic life, the executives and managers, etc., were about half. This has been signalized by the secrecy, prevailing since the Thirties, concerning the social origin of the Party members. Like all forms of suppression this fact is eloquent. The Eighteenth Party Congress in March 1929 erased even the fictitious preeminence of the proletariat and by promoting the intelligentsia in the broadest sense to equality with the workers and peasants established the social primacy of the upper government functionaries.

Two Old Guard Bolsheviks and revolutionary intellectuals accused as "Trotskyites" and liquidated after the mass trial of 1936: left, Radek, far left, Bukharin.

Stalin and Voroshilov at the Kremlin *by A. Gerassimov (1938). The official Soviet art doctrine is "Socialist realism". This formula covers a rigidly controlled system of propaganda art. Here is what a Soviet art critic wrote of this chromo during Stalin's lifetime: "The reason for the extraordinary popularity of this picture stems no doubt from the fact that it represents two men very dear to each Soviet citizen... Stalin and Voroshilov are shown here as inspirers and organizers of the Soviet state, constructors of the new world".*

By the end of the Twenties, with the suppression of all forms of opposition to the Stalin faction, any onlooker would have thought political life fairly consolidated. Not only was there no overt sign of resentment on the part of the political people and functionaries Stalin had neutralized, but as far as could be told from sources both inside the country and outside, there was actually no opposition left to speak of. This does not, of course, mean that Stalin's regime was popular: the extraordinary growth of the secret police, forced labor camps, and the intensification of terror in general would have been the living proof of the opposite.

But no organization of the opposition was possible: without means of communication or expression, without a structure of relationships, and above all, without a program, where could an opposition exist?

Within the framework of the Communist Party itself, and indeed even among its revolutionary rivals, no program of opposition could be formulated. All factions in some sense accepted the Soviet state run by the Communist Party: they may not have liked what it was doing, but since there could be no appeal to the public, and since they were actually excluded from the governing caucus, there was no

way to oppose the regime except by denouncing it *as such*. No group in Russia was prepared to do this. Thus Stalin's regime would have seemed to be shielded against any attacks from within the Leftwing camp.

Yet in 1935 a process began that through a progressive reaction of arrests, interrogations, and executions, culminated in the great trials of 1936-1938, an extraordinary phenomenon known as the "Great Purge".

The Trials completely wiped out the entire corpus of Old Bolsheviks, and the tidal wave of arrests that followed them throughout the country engulfed all former oppositionists of all kinds, former Mensheviks and S.R.s, anarchists, members of the Jewish Bund, sympathizers of pre-revolutionary Left-wing parties, returned immigrants, Party people whose duties had sent them abroad, everyone who had corresponded with anyone abroad, foreign Communists taking refuge in the Soviet Union, members of all religious sects, anyone who had ever been excluded from the Party, any Party member who had resisted the purging process itself, and, above all, the armed forces. All strata of the population were represented, from top to bottom, and all occupations.

This sounds like a long list, and so it is. It is taken from Soviet sources, since possibly the most grotesque element of the purges and especially of the "show" trials was their publicity. The Soviet press gave substantial accounts of them, which while glossing over statistical implications nevertheless enable an estimate to be made.

The most conservative estimates indicate that between seven and eight million people were killed during this two-year period. Some students of Soviet affairs have made estimates ranging considerably over twenty million.

The "theory" of these trials and interrogations was that the Soviet regime was menaced by a conspiracy that was responsible for all the hardships of the Five-Year Plans, the collectivization drive, poor harvests, and famines, to say nothing of earthquakes and bad weather. The trials swiftly concentrated on the person of Trotsky, exiled from the Soviet Union since 1929: they were a systematic attempt to tie together all the disparate elements under fire by leading them back to a central "nucleus" in his study.

The public trials were conducted on the basis of evidence provided over-whelmingly by confessions: the value of objective data was marred by their non-existence. Hundreds of journalists visited the trials; lengthy accounts were published everywhere, and much was written about the complexities of the Russian soul and the tortuousness of the Marxist mind to explain the spate of confessions from some of the veteran Bolsheviks, who after spending their lives fighting capitalism were now beating their breasts and admitting to having conspired with Hitler, the Mikado, *et al.*, in their determination to restore capitalism.

These upheavals were set off by something apparently insignificant: the murder of the Party Secretary for the Leningrad region, Kirov, who was killed in December 1934 allegedly by a student linked to Trotsky.

On the basis of the Soviet disclosures made some years after Stalin's death the whole Grand Guignol is now seen to have been a trumped-up manœuvre on the part of Stalin, but for years all political events in the Soviet Union were interpreted by reference to the "Trotskyite wreckers" who were holding up the realization of the Soviet dream.

By the end of the Thirties a vast network of forced labor camps extended over northern Russia and Siberia: for the years 1935-1937 the number of the inmates is conservatively estimated at 5-6 million; it is thought to have risen to about 10 million between 1940-1942. These figures are of course arrived at by inference, buttressed by accounts of those who have escaped, of whom there have been hundreds. Some economists give a purely economic explanation of the camps: since on an average the camps contained about 10 % of the labor force of the Soviet Union they can be explained as a reflection of a primitive stage in the development of the great state-controlled industrial plant.

The most spectacular aspect of the Great Trials was the catastrophic effect they had on the strength of the Red Army. In a world situation dominated by Hitler Germany, the Stalin regime, on the basis of charges now exploded by Soviet sources themselves, instituted a purge of the army apparatus that during 1937-1938 cut down the membership of the Supreme War Council by 75 %, liquidated three out of five marshals, 13 out of 15 army generals, 62 out of 85 corps commanders, 110 out of 195 divisional commanders, and 220 out of 406 brigade commanders. Probably 65 % of the officers from colonel up were arrested, numbering, together with those in the lower echelons arrested, some 20,000 officers. Fifteen hundred of the 6,000 high ranking officers were killed, while the others vanished, at least for a time, into various forms of detention.

Had Hitler actually been plotting against the Soviet regime from within he would seem to have had an outstanding success.

Since Stalin's death the victims of his purges have all been rehabilitated, either explicitly or implicitly.

The slaughter during the Great Purge of 1936-1938 was so extravagant, so debilitating to the country, and so unrelated to its ostensible goals that its origins are surely to be sought in the realm of mythology, that most potent of political factors. In order to vindicate the sacrifices of the Five-Year Plans, of which the first two had been particularly clumsy, wasteful, and brutal, the regime had to create a fictional structure to give its conduct a rationale. This "rationale", of course, was far

Molotov and Ribbentrop had signed a Nazi-Soviet agreement in August, 1939. Right, Molotov, with Ribbentrop at his side, reviews a German unit during an official visit to Berlin, 1939. France and Russia signed a non-aggression pact in 1933. When the Germans menaced Czechoslovakia in 1938, the Soviets declared themselves in favor of supporting the Czechs. France also was committed to Czechoslovakia by a military alliance. France decided not to intervene, and the result was Munich. Faced with a steady deterioration of the international situation due to Hitler's aggressive policy, a French military mission was sent to Moscow. It was met with bland words but little else. Shortly afterwards, the Soviet Union and Hitler Germany signed a non-aggression pact. Assured that he would not have to fight on two fronts at once, Hitler unleashed the Second World War on September 2, 1939. After defeating the French, he turned on the USSR, attacking in 1941.

The German General Staff used the blitz technique in the USSR that had been so successful in Poland and France. Mechanized units advanced rapidly in the summer dust and autumn mud. Then the defense stiffened, and the invader had to face the terrible Russian winter. Hitler's forces had never expected their enemy to hold out long and were unequipped for the killing temperature. Above, German infantry marching through frozen country. Opposite, above: German motorcyclists slosh through muddy roads.

more destructive than what it was supposed to explain, but precisely by soaring beyond the tedious logic of facts it summoned up the faith made necessary by the absurdity of the claims advanced, and thus reinforced the faithful in their faith while subjecting disbelievers to the dangers of anathema.

At bottom what the regime had to justify was its existence. And it did this by intensifying the concept of siege in a dual form: encirclement from without and betrayal from within. This gave the increasingly monolithic structure, under the umbrella of the grotesque inflation of Stalin's personality, enough tension to legitimize its authority.

But surely the element of personal dementia, while of course repugnant to up-to-date historians, must also be considered. Stalin seems to have become obsessed by the vision of Trotsky even when the latter had nothing much left but his ideas, whose power was, after all, confined to a rather restricted milieu. While the Trials and the vast propaganda apparatus devoted to their popularization concentrated on Trotsky's defamation, the Soviet secret police worked on his assassination. Both activities, in acute disproportion to Trotsky's political influence, were successful.

Trotsky's assassination was finally accomplished by an agent of Stalin's in August 1940 in Mexico, where Trotsky had been given refuge after a series of expulsions from one country after another, largely inspired by Soviet pressure and concurred in by the legion of those indifferent or hostile to his movement.

But what is curious is that the Trials, though preposterous even at the time to any uncommitted observer and long since exploded officially, nevertheless seem to have laid a stigma on Trotsky's reputation. The mere repetition of the word "traitor" is enough in politics to justify a collective opinion that there is no smoke without fire. If Stalin was subtle enough to realize this perhaps he thought the killing of several million people well worth it.

The symmetry between Stalin's magnification and the systematic blaming of the hallucinatory "opposition" for all the shortcomings of state planning was given its literary expression in a short textbook on the history of the Communist Party of the Soviet Union that appeared in 1938, the last year of the purges. Since all the leaders of the early years, the Old Bolsheviks, except Lenin and Stalin, had been charged with treachery and desertion, the whole

The German-Russian alliance had lasted less than two years when Hitler turned his troops against Russia on June 22, 1941. The attack was spread over 2000 miles: from the White Sea to the Black Sea. At the beginning of the campaign, the Germans won impressive victories. By mid-December 1941, they were within thirty miles of Moscow, the furthest point of their thrust towards the Soviet capital. ▶

history of the Party had to be rewritten from beginning to end—to say nothing of countless reference books, encyclopedias, etc.—in order to point out that Stalin had been Lenin's chief friend and disciple, and shared the full credit with him for the whole of the October insurrection and the laying of the foundations of the Soviet State.

To sustain the growing network of propaganda-control underlying the fusion of ideology and administration a new bureaucratic intelligentsia had to be added to the administrative apparatus as a sort of spiritual lining: cultural affairs, the sciences, mass media, as well as public health education, etc., required both experts and executives.

The bureaucratic managers of the state economy—the "apparatchiki"—increased by leaps and bounds. Official statistics number them as about 2,000,000 in 1926, 9,500,000 in 1937, 11,500,000 in 1940, and by 1949 between 15 and 16 millions. By now they must be far more numerous, and if one considers that the general tendency of the government has been to soft-pedal the ramifications of the "apparatus-people" the specific weight of the bureaucracy in Soviet society is obviously substantial.

Concomitantly, the Soviet differentiation in wages has become even more acute than in capitalist countries, including the United States. Though the apparatus accounted for only 14 % of

the working population, its share has been estimated at 35 % of the national income, while the corresponding figures are 33 % for the workers, who are 22 % of the population, and 29 % of the

peasants, who are 53 % of the population.

These figures are heavily underplayed in official statistics, which also cast a veil over the countless perquisites of government service. Motor-cars, houses, railway travel, vacations, medical treatment, etc., substantially elevate the real income of the privileged groups,

a curious parallel to capitalist regimes in which the expense-accounts of business executives have become such an important factor in living standards. The special privileges of the upper

strata of Soviet society have been consolidated in many ways. Until 1932, for instance, 65 % of all students had to be workers; by 1938, when this requirement became obsolete, working-class students had dropped to 33.9 % while bureaucrats' children went up to 42.4 %. Since then the whole question has been veiled by the silence of official government

The Znamensky cathedral at Novgorod was one of many casualties during the years of heavy fighting on Russian soil. Countless industrial installations, houses and monuments were totally or partially destroyed. At the end of the war, 25,000,000 Russians were homeless.

sources, in itself, of course, highly significant.

It is plain, in short, that in the space of a couple of decades the Bolshevik decision to wield a monopoly of power in the framework of state planning, with the resultant administrative apparatus, has produced an entirely new society, with its own stability, stratification, momentum and mythology.

As we have seen, the original Bolshevik expectation of a world revolution, or at least a revolution in the industrial heart of Europe, was soon disappointed. The political turmoil in Europe in the aftermath of the First World War created insurrectionary situations in a number of countries—Hungary, Bulgaria, Germany—but despite the attempts made by the distracted and enfeebled Soviet government, with varying degrees of consistency and with a curious combination of overoptimism and timidity, no break-through was

achieved. The regime was compelled to suspend its apocalyptic perspective.

Chinese prospects were much brighter: from the October revolution on the Bolsheviks had been friendly with the Chinese Nationalist movement, and after the civil war in Russia a working alliance was arrived at. On Stalin's initiative the Kuomintang was given full support, doubtless partly in an effort to compensate for the disastrous setbacks of the Communist movement in Europe. The Political Bureau agreed not to build up the Chinese Communist Party, founded in 1921, independently of the Kuomintang, but to support the Kuomintang directly.

However, after the death of Sun Yat-Sen in 1925 and the rise of Chiang Kai-Shek the situation changed abruptly. Chiang Kai-Shek, now head of the Kuomintang, broke the pact Stalin had been shielding so carefully against opposition elements, and by a ruthless

massacre of Communists and industrial workers in April 1927 brought the collaboration between the two movements to an end.

Thus, by the end of the Twenties the subsidence of the revolutionary elan, signalized in 1924 by the formulation of Stalin's theory of Socialism in one country, was a basic fact of the world situation, and with the loss of this elan the velocity of Soviet policy gradually shifted.

Churchill, Roosevelt and Stalin at Yalta, ▶
February, 1945. When the Big Three met in devasted Crimea, the Russians were approaching Berlin, Eisenhower's armies were getting ready to cross the Rhine and Japan was a few months away from capitulation. During this meeting which was to give its shape to the post-war world, Stalin obtained important concessions in eastern Europe and the Far East.

From the very beginning Bolshevik affiliates in other countries had been altogether subordinate to the Russian Party. The founding of the Third International in 1919 had established a new allegiance for all the forces that the successful Bolshevik faction, renamed the Communist Party after the revolution, could split away from the Second (Socialist) International, discredited in Lenin's eyes by its sponsorship of the "imperialist" First World War.

As the imminence of an auxiliary revolution in Europe receded, the various local Communist Parties lost any claims to autonomy they might have had, and were automatically transformed into instruments of the Soviet state in its struggle for self-preservation. Hence the tactics of any given national party were no longer seen in the increasingly chimerical perspective of an international revolution, but through the prism of Soviet self-interest.

The most dramatic example of this is of course the celebrated "People's Front" of before the Second World War, and its numerous parallels since.

The Soviet regime and the Comintern had clung to their intransigent tactics throughout the Twenties, but after the disappointment of one revolutionary hope after another in Germany, and with the success of the Nazi movement, the Soviet regime saw itself confronted by a specific and unmistakable foreshadowing of catastrophe when Hitler came to power in 1933. The Nazi movement had been successful, after all, not only because it was supported by German industrialists, but because Hitler's foreign policy of "expansion east-

ward"—i.e., the annihilation of the Soviet Union—secured the tacit though effective support of influential elements in Great Britain and France. Stalin was obviously right in considering it the

gravest danger yet faced by the Soviet Union. The Soviet regime now turned its previous intransigence inside out *vis-*

à-vis all capitalist regimes and more particularly its Social-Democratic rivals —Communist rejection of a united front with the Social-Democrats had helped put Hitler in power—and launched the

At the end of August, 1942, the Germans decided to seize Stalingrad *at all costs. They wanted to cut off navigation on the Volga, the only route still open for Caucasus oil to reach central Russia. The furious combat lasted for months, first on the outskirts then in the streets of the city itself. Resistance was fanatical. Relieving Russian forces eventually encircled the enemy, who were hopelessly cut off from outside help. The Germans capitulated on February 2, 1943, leaving 91,000 prisoners to the defenders of the city including twenty-four generals and a marshal: Von Paulus, who had just been promoted to this rank.*

celebrated "People's Front" of "liberals and Socialists" for protection against the rising tide of Fascism.

But the momentum of the forces involved was uncontrollable. Though the rise of Nazi Germany frightened Western Europe, it did not frighten it quickly enough, or seriously enough, to make it give the Stalin regime the insurance it demanded against an attack by Hitler, and so, six years later, Stalin abruptly reversed positions again: in August 1939 the news of his pact with Hitler stupefied the world, especially since the preliminary discussions had been successfully kept secret.

Stalin's reasoning is of course obvious

actual conduct of the war as well as official disclosures after his death show this pretence of guile to have been a clumsy apologia.

At first all went well: the net effect of the Hitler-Stalin pact was the partition of Poland, extinguished as a sovereign state for the fourth time. The Soviet Union adopted a new role as "gatherer of Russian soil" and the executor of ancient Russian claims. The eastern territories of Poland, part of the ancient Kievan realm, regained by Catherine the Great by the First Polish

a torrent of supplies flooding in from the United States.

In the beginning the German army did brilliantly well; by the end of 1941 it controlled about 40 % of the total population of the Soviet Union, in an area containing 65 % of its pre-war coal production, 68 % of its pig-iron, 58 % of its steel, 38 % of its grain and 84 % of its sugar, as well as about 40 % of the railway network. Between June and November Soviet industrial production had fallen by more than half and steel production by more than two-thirds.

Stalin died on March 5, 1953. Here he lies in state, surrounded by leading party mourners. Group on the left, l. to r.: Molotov, his ardent supporter, now exiled as ambassador to Outer Mongolia; Voroshilov, a mere figurehead for many years, now retired; Beria, dreaded head of Stalin's police, hastily executed after his master's death; Malenkov, demoted to an obscure technical position after a brief period heading the Soviet hierarchy. Group on the right, l. to r.: Bulganin, eclipsed after a stretch of public celebrity; Khrushchov, now the master; Kaganovitch, pensioned off and retired; Mikoyan, wizard of Soviet commerce, still important today.

enough: he profoundly mistrusted Great Britain and France, partly because he doubted their determination in the face of Hitler, and particularly because he was afraid that Hitler's basic anti-Soviet policy might be successful in persuading them to leave the Soviet Union to confront the German army alone.

Stalin's mistrust of the Western allies in the context of the period was quite understandable; what was astonishing was his apparent faith in the inviolability of his agreement with Hitler. His gullibility *vis-à-vis* Hitler—whose acumen and dash he greatly admired—was demonstrated when Hitler, on finally breaking the agreement and attacking the Soviet Union, found it in a state of total unreadiness. Stalin naturally later explained his pact with Hitler by saying it had given the Soviet Union a year and a half to prepare, but the

◀ Anniversary celebrations *in Moscow, 1950, of the October Revolution. Five years after the Allied victory, in spite of the devastations she had suffered and the loss of 20,000,000 men, Russia was more powerful than she had ever been before.*

Partition of 1772, a bone of contention during the reign of Alexander I, and forcibly detached from the Tsarist Empire by the First World War, were now integrated with Soviet Russia, as were the Baltic States and Bessarabia in 1940. The Soviet Union was creeping back to the old borders of Tsarism; the Versailles settlement of 1919 was nullified.

Nazi Germany had of course entered the pact in order to secure her eastern flank and thus avoid the terrifying prospect of a war on two fronts, the undoing of Hohenzollern Germany twenty-five years before. In the event, however, Hitler was bound to perceive that even a successful assault on Great Britain, even after the occupation of France in 1940, would leave Germany so weakened that she would be defence-less against the Soviet Union. Thus, in the summer of 1941 the German Army, with no warning, flung the bulk of its strength against the Soviet Union.

The Stalin regime now found itself forced by military necessity to accept Great Britain as an ally, and for that matter France and a little later the United States as well. Its ideological frustration was compensated for by

But the German military successes were not sweeping enough to compensate for Nazi provincialism. The many sources of Soviet disunity, from religious hostility to the Communist regime to the peasants' hatred of the collective farms, were disregarded by the Nazis, enthralled by their obsession about the Slavic "submen". Hitler's touch of dementia in this respect, and perhaps even more decisively the utter inflexibility of agencies like the Waffen-SS in the treatment of Russians, Ukrainians, and Poles, made it impossible for the Germans to benefit by any factor outside their military campaigns. The fabulous mass surrenders of the Russian armies during the first six months of the German onslaught, which should have indicated the internal weaknesses of the Soviet regime, were misunderstood: like Napoleon before it the German High Command depended on the army alone.

The Moscow campaign proved a failure, partly because of an unprecedentedly cold winter; the disastrous campaign against Stalingrad in 1942, undertaken as an alternative, undid the German forces completely.

By December 1941 the Japanese attack on Pearl Harbor put the United

States directly into the war, and as the vast amounts of all kinds of supplies were increased still further the Russians gradually began moving westward again.

Even the staggering losses they were now suffering did not give the Nazis any more political flexibility in dealing with the Russians. They were even principal shortcoming was that he was a Russian patriot, and hence opposed to the atomization of the Soviet Union that the Nazi geopoliticians took for granted even while their realm was melting away. Vlasov was finally half-heartedly accepted and after a meeting in Prague in November, 1944, he was sustained the German onslaught, even with the massive aid afforded by the United States and Great Britain, and made a westward advance with its own armies put it in a favorable position. This position was bolstered by the political incapacity of the American leaders and their insistence on fighting

The Soviet rulers have never spared any effort to form a scientific élite. Above, the buildings erected since the war to house the Scientific *Department of the University of Moscow. The architecture is academic, but the equipment is the very latest.*

reluctant to make use of a first-class political figure, Vlasov, a captured Soviet general who was a sincere political opponent of the Stalin regime and was eager to lead an army made up of Russians and other ethnic units against the Soviet Union as long as he retained some degree of autonomy. Though the Nazis had had almost a million Russians serving in the German army itself, Vlasov's ambition made them hesitate until 1944, when it was far too late. From the Nazi point of view Vlasov's

◀ *A permanent* Exhibition Park *in Moscow, open since 1954, draws a steady crowd. It contains examples of Russian developments in agriculture and industry. Pavilions in the regional styles of the Soviet republics show their particular accomplishments. The Sputnik has a building to itself. On the photograph, left, USSR tourists walk past the large central fountain with its gilded bronze statues.*

elected president of a committee formed of representatives of the Orthodox Church, of the "Eastern workers" dragooned by the Nazis into German factories, and numerous Tsarist émigrés, as well as official German delegates. The highlight of his manifesto was a demand "to overthrow Stalinist tyranny, to liberate the people of our homeland from the Bolshevik system, and to give them back the rights they had successfully fought for in the popular revolution of 1917".

But the Vlasov army was not allowed more than a few divisions, a hopelessly small number and an indication of persistent German mistrust. It was smothered in the converging Soviet and American advances, and after being interned by the Americans in Prague Vlasov was handed over to the Russians and executed in 1946.

The Soviet Union emerged from the ruins of the war in a commanding international position. The fact that it had the war from a parochially military point of view. This astigmatism not only made them go out of their way to allow the Soviet armies to take Berlin, Prague and Vienna, but enshrined these quite artificial military positions in a series of diplomatic accords.

The Yalta Conference in February 1945 granted the Soviet Union a dominant position in the Far East, which an American occupation of Japan could balance only partly, and the whole of Eastern Europe except Greece. While some compromises were effected at Potsdam in the summer of 1945, the net result was favorable to the Soviet Union's interpretation of the accords that had been reached both at Yalta and in Teheran in the winter of 1943. Soviet territory was extended by about 193,000 square miles; not merely were the Baltic countries absorbed totally, but the Soviet Union also engulfed Eastern Poland and Bessarabia, North Bukovina, the northern part of East

Prussia, parts of Finland, etc. Moreover, an impressive array of buffer states was established by Soviet authority; these were bound to become satellites, and did so immediately or very quickly: Poland, East Germany, Czechoslovakia, Hungary, Bulgaria, Rumania, and for a

Soviet control of East Germany secured 36 % of Germany's 1936 industrial capacity, for instance, and the system of reparations between the Soviet Union and the satellites was heavily weighted in favor of the former. Incalculable assets streamed into the Soviet Union;

our present era of the "Cold War" —the political axis of our generation. A history of the Cold War would be a mere commentary on current events: I shall disregard it.

As the Soviet Union emerged from the Second World War in an immensely

By declarations of friendship, assurances of pacific aims, promises of aid, by intimidation, the Soviets pursue an immense effort to draw formerly colonial countries into their orbit, making the most of hypersensitive nationalist susceptibilities. Here, Marshal Bulganin, before he fell from grace, visits India and joins in the ancient ritual greeting.

time Yugoslavia. Soviet gains totalled roughly 110,000,000 people.

By 1945, the Soviet Union had been propped up by the "bastion of world capitalism", the United States, and was at a pinnacle of political authority far removed from its nadir in 1938. Its influence reached from Finland to the Aegean Sea and the Adriatic, and beyond Manchuria. Soviet troops were in Berlin and Vienna, had come as far as the Elbe, controlled the Danube area and the Balkans as a whole, and had occupied Manchuria.

These spectacular political successes were a dramatic counterpoint to the material devastation of the war, which was on a scale comparable with the havoc of the First World War and the Russian civil war. The total loss of life in the Soviet Union was estimated at about 20,000,000, with the homeless numbering some 25,000,000. Countless towns had been levelled; the housing shortage was catastrophic.

The material losses were made up for, on the other hand, by the harnessing of the industrial power of the satellites.

German talents of all kinds, including nuclear physicists, were imported wholesale.

Despite the easy-going political nonchalance of the American leaders, the military coalition with the Soviet Union collapsed completely the moment the war was over.

More mistrustful of the West than ever, perhaps through the contemplation of the industrial might revealed in the American war effort, culminating in the construction of the atom bomb, the Soviet regime withdrew to a characteristic position of defensive aggressiveness. Rejecting the Marshall Plan aid offered by America and mobilizing its Communist Parties all over the world, it began systematizing the ideology of the "Socialist society" as constituting an acute and ineradicable contrast with the capitalist West. The Third (Communist) International, buried in 1943 as a peace gesture, was revived in 1947 in the shape of the Communist Information Bureau, and the West, countering through the American policy of "containment", found itself projected into

strengthened international position, its new profile was more clearly defined.

The pre-war tendency of the Stalin regime to amplify Soviet patriotism through the incorporation of traditional Russian patriotism was greatly reinforced by what was officially known as the "War for the Fatherland". In November 1941, in a speech Stalin made to the troops and people's defense units in Moscow, under the threat of the German guns, he had struck a note characteristic of the whole Soviet war. Disregarding the Communist pantheon, he had held aloft the "virile images of our great ancestors—Nevsky, Donskoy, Minin, Pozharsky, Suvorov and Kutuzov".

In waving before his listeners' eyes the national saints of Imperial Russia Stalin brought Soviet patriotism, kindled during the Thirties, to its logical

Daily life in Moscow: *the personality* ▶ *cult no longer applies to Stalin, but every day delegations and tourists from all over the USSR queue patiently through Red Square to visit Lenin's mausoleum.*

conclusion. He drove the point home at a reception for the Red Army commanders in the Kremlin in 1945, when, with Germany shattered, he gave a toast, not to the multiracial citizens of the Soviet Union, but to the health of the Russian people—"the outstanding nation among the peoples of the Soviet Union".

come on which Japan would be defeated and this blemish be erased. For forty years we, the men of the older generation, have waited for this day. Now it has finally come."

A magnificent piece of irony! Lenin had hailed the victory of Japan as a prologue to the rising of the European proletariat, and even "bourgeois" libe-

fusing all available social elements. The upsurge of Soviet chauvinism, potentially irresistible once the formerly ideological movement was nationalized, became more intense in 1943, with a campaign initiated by an attack of the Party organ, *Bolshevik*, on an apparently harmless volume in a series on the history of philosophy.

Two aspects of the health and physical strength cult *as expressed today in the Soviet Union. Above, in the Moscow central telegraph office, operators go through physical culture movements. Right, women athletes march in Moscow during a sports demonstration, 1959.*

This singling out of the specifically Russian strand in the skein of Soviet patriotism was heightened to the absurd in Stalin's explanation of the precipitate Soviet entry into the war against Japan, on the same day the second American atom bomb was dropped on Nagasaki. Aside from taking the credit for the defeat of Japan—America's role in the end of the Japanese war is still not mentioned in Soviet historiography—Stalin described Soviet participation as an act of revenge for the Japanese victory over Tsarism in the 1905 war! "The defeat of the Russian troops in 1904 left bitter memories in the hearts of the Russian people... Our people hoped and believed that the day would

rals in Russia had been overjoyed by the defeat of Tsarism. Stalin was once again overturning the early doctrinal foundations of the Soviet state, while pretending characteristically that everything was still the same as ever, or even more so.

This assimilation of the Russian "national tradition" was the natural outcome of the ethnocentrism inherent in the theory of "Socialism in one country". As the concept of Socialism itself was denatured to adapt it to the specific conditions of Russia, so the Russian national concept was amplified and incorporated in the conservatism of the bureaucracy that was busily plastering a new tradition together by

This violent attack inaugurated the contemporary epoch, characterized by the blanket eulogy of everything Russian or Soviet. Russians began to be given credit for everything under the sun, from the invention of the steam-engine to radio and penicillin. The present cultural posture constitutes an indignant rejection of the old charge of "backwardness", commonplace among all students of Russian affairs. The new campaign demanded—under severe penalties—the demonstration of Soviet superiority in all areas of science, art, and literature. The intellectual censorship of the regime was intensified, and achieved special notoriety in the Lysenko case that came to a climax in 1948.

◄ *A corner of the Maniezev studio, one of the principal sources of propaganda statuary.*

The imposition of the Party line on the biologists who opposed Lysenko's theories of genetics marked the entry of the new-style Soviet metaphysics into the realm of abstract science.

Soviet self-insulation, at least in this acute form, lasted about a decade, until the summer after Stalin's death in 1953, when a "thaw" set in. Stalin's death, indeed, was the end of an era, though its consequences were not manifested immediately: it was not, after all, a mere individual who had died, but an institution so mighty that Khrushchov's major achievement may turn out to have been its demolition.

This cult, built up over a quarter of a century by all the resources of a great state and doubtless a major factor of alienation in Soviet relations with the world, was smashed all at once without warning; the fact that Khrushchov was a veteran Stalinist and heir to the power, though not the glory of the General Secretary, makes it all the more ironical.

The explosion took place at a secret session of the Twentieth Party Congress in February 1956. With obvious authority and in copious detail Khrushchov, apparently overcome by emotion, bitterly attacked Stalin's megalomania, sadism, cowardice, and incompetence. For seven hours he aired in public charges that among opponents of the Stalin regime had been commonplace for decades. Lay opinion was startled. For a time faithful Communists everywhere were paralyzed by doubt; the pious who had actually believed the illusions manufactured by the Soviet propaganda machine were naturally upset by the abrupt annihilation of the orderly mythical world a whole generation had grown up in.

Apart from its effects on Communists the new movement of "de-stalinization" was naturally taken advantage of by disaffected elements in the satellite countries. The workers' riots in Poznan, Poland, in June 1956, which were suppressed with great bloodshed, and the first-class revolt that broke out in Hungary in the autumn of the same year, may be ascribed to the awakening —and swift disappointment— of hopes generated by the change of regime.

Speculation about personal byplay in the Kremlin is somewhat futile. Professional experts — "Kremlinologists" and "Sovietologists"—have pandered to the inquisitiveness of the public by contriving complex analyses of the Kremlin backstage, but of course it is a milieu that is quite impenetrable for outsiders. As expertise, in fact, it is not worth much more than a gossip column. In discussing Khrushchov's

motivation, or the machinations that established his primacy, or shifting positions in the top official stratum, we have little to fall back on but commonsense: it does not lead far.

Visitors to Moscow are always struck by the variety of racial types seen in public places. The vastly different nationalities of the Soviet Union itself, plus the quantities of foreign delegations from China, the satellite states or sympathetic "underdeveloped" countries add to this impression. Here Chinese and other Far Eastern students in the Lenin Library.

It may well be that the Stalin cult was too stifling for the new, more cultivated and far more numerous educated classes to submit to any longer, and that the Khrushchov faction was simply trying to exculpate itself from the opprobrium of the preceding generation; or perhaps the attack on the cult was entailed by a shift in the play of factions offstage. It is difficult to pierce the fog.

In a general account it would be equally pointless to indulge in speculation about the future. There have been three important developments since Stalin's death, in addition to his debunking: the slight, though unmistakable raising of the Iron Curtain, the relaxation of police controls (i.e., terror) signalized by the release of throngs of prisoners from the forced labor camps,

and perhaps most significantly the proposal made by Khrushchov in 1958 for the decentralization of the top-heavy Soviet administration. If these developments are indices it may mean

that the Soviet regime, immersed though it is in the enduring Cold War, is slowly changing.

It is changing on a much higher level of technique. Lenin's premature slogan of 1917—"Die, or overtake and pass" capitalism—repeated by Stalin in 1931 as the leitmotif of the planned economy, may be on the verge of realization.

This prospect was dramatically expressed in the summer of 1953, when the Soviet government, after dumfounding the United States by duplicating the atom bomb, announced that it had succeeded in making a hydrogen bomb.

The West suddenly found itself deprived of the nuclear weapons that had been thought to guarantee its world hegemony. Within the space of a few years the Soviet government, obviously advancing

291

rapidly in all technical areas, announced that by launching a "sputnik" in 1958 it had outclassed the best engineering talent in the United States. The Soviet Union seemed not only to have drawn level with America in rocketry—the accuracy required to aim a large sputnik obviously puts the whole question of the vulnerability of remote spots in a new light—but to have definitely outdistanced her in at least some branches of science, both abstract and applied.

Soviet success in rocketry at last managed to draw the attention of authoritative Americans to what was actually a matter of common knowledge years before, that the Soviet Union was producing vast numbers of well-trained engineers in addition to the handful of abstract scientists it had already become known for.

In short, despite all sacrifices and wastage, the state-planning of the Soviet Union has finally evolved a first-class technical elite. In a typically Russian way it has jumped over intervening stages: just as it had been easier in the Nineteenth Century for Russia to develop a cultivated elite than to educate the masses, so in the Twentieth Century the new regime, still unable to compete with the United States in the provision of commodities for mass consumption—houses, motorcars, refrigerators, etc.—, has found it easier to match American achievements on the most rarefied levels of technique.

In our own epoch, moreover, this development of an elite has become relatively more important because of the unprecedentedly high degree of concentration required for the production of complex instruments like nuclear weapons, rockets, etc. Mere manpower, though the Soviet Union still disposes of great quantities of it, has become to that extent less indispensable to a modern state.

But even though the Soviet Union is now panoplied by the combination of numbers, wealth, and technique that is a basic requirement for any would-be powerful state, its political effectiveness is peculiar to itself.

For the first time in history a nation has arisen identified with an idea powerful enough to bypass the national interests of other states, and gain devotees everywhere regardless of origin.

The messianic impulse, in short, that generations ago inspired the Russian intelligentsia has been inherited by the Communist Party despite its bureaucratic metamorphosis. And just as the revolutionary idea congealed into the administrative apparatus of the Soviet Union, so the messianic elan has been

The pre-war drive towards the mechanization of industry, already intensive, has been resumed at an accelerated pace.

transformed from an idea into an intitutional complex.

It is this institutional complex that has now been cast abroad.

Since the Twenties the Soviet Union has been a unique example of this clusive trait—the factor of allegiance.

It is allegiance to the Soviet regime as such that is the hallmark of Communist world organization. This allegiance is not the mere zeal of purchased agents; it is this identification with the of political life, and can benefit by the attraction the Soviet Union now exercises in many underdeveloped areas of the world by virtue of its own institutional complex: the combination of state-planning plus a mass movement

The Soviet technological drive applies to agriculture on a large scale.

fusion between idea and institution. As a powerful state, with all the accoutrements of a state, it stands among the nations of the world. But unlike them it has pretensions to a universal ideal, the old utopia of the revolution it claims to be embodying. To the minds of its believers this ideal denationalizes the Soviet Union, and millions of followers abroad see in it not a state like another, but the prefiguration of a universal goal.

The membership of Communist Parties outside Russia do not consider themselves traitors to their "own" countries—on the contrary, the idealistically minded consider the Communist ideal to encompass the whole of the human race, hence any particular country as well. Simultaneously, however, this ideal is no longer served by the mere exhortation of a nondescript public, but by submission to a central headquarters.

This is illustrated by the singular pallor of Communist program considered from the point of view of mere content. Communist program generally is no more "radical" or "Left-wing" than the programs of other Socialistically-minded parties: it is often less so.

What characterizes it is no longer its purely intellectual values, but an ex-

ideals professed by the Soviet regime that kindles the ardor of mass parties.

It is, of course, this factor of allegiance that is now dividing the world. The revolutionary offshoots engendered abroad by the institutionalization in Russia of the early Marxist idea have themselves been bureaucratized and planted all over the world as vested interests. Inspired and organized by a foreign center, they are nevertheless sustained by the malaise of local societies, a malaise that makes them authentic exponents of authentic mass movements.

Thus, as genuinely indigenous factors they participate organically in all forms directed by a party in control of propaganda and the police.

In the new Arab republics, in the embryonic nations of Black Africa, in Cuba, in Indonesia, this institutional complex is particularly attractive. It harmonizes potently with a characteristic syndrome of our epoch: the assumption of power in poor countries by youthful reformers based on a mass movement.

A revolutionary caucus is bound to make its following imaginative promises for the comprehensive overhauling of society. Since it lacks capital, at any rate in relation to its ambitious projects, state-planning, plus the control of the

With the explosion of the first Soviet atom bomb in 1949, and the launching of a "Sputnik" in 1958, it became obvious that the Soviets had succeeded in training scientists and engineers of the highest caliber. Above, a photograph taken at an interplanetary experimental station.

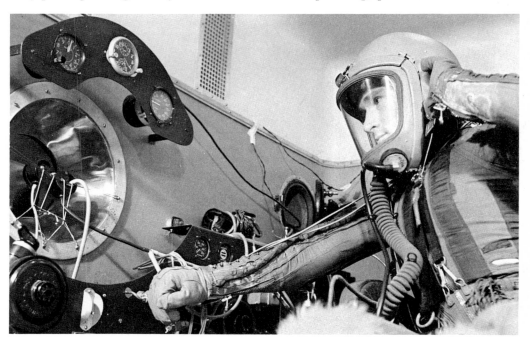

police and the propaganda media, becomes a magnet for it independently of theory.

This is obviously a situation in which Communist Parties can be effective with or without taking power: there is no obstacle to collaboration either between

The acquisition of China for the Soviet idea is of course altogether incalculable. The industrialization of such a gifted and numerous people within the framework of Soviet-style institutions is obviously a primary factor in world history.

into the thick of Middle Eastern affairs; it has inserted itself with ease into the Algerian imbroglio, as well as into the Iraqi insurrection of 1958 and the recent emergence of a cluster of new African nations; with the Castro rebellion in Cuba it seems to have gained a

A rocket is pulled past the reviewing stand on Red Square during a military display.

a local regime and a local Communist Party, or between a local regime and the Soviet government itself, which indeed may even bypass a local Communist Party altogether if tactics call for it.

During the early years of the Soviet regime the colonial areas of the world were not seriously agitated by the harangues of the Russian Communist Party. Its enterprise in China was a failure; the rest of Asia, the Middle East, Africa, and the Western hemisphere were scarcely ruffled. In industrial Europe the only mass movement it produced—the German Communist Party—proved a fiasco.

But as the Soviet regime blossomed out in the postwar period it began having one success after another. It is true that in France and Italy, despite the springing up of mass parties, the question of taking power was never serious, but in the colonial and underdeveloped areas of the world the Soviet Union has made gigantic strides.

The prospects are almost equally full of portent even in those countries of Asia, Africa, and Latin America where the question of outright conversion or conquest has scarcely presented itself. "Sovietism"—as independent of or at least distinct from Communism—has been reaping an exceptional harvest.

The Soviet alliance of technical achievement at home and political success abroad has made Soviet foreign policy more and more supple. With its enormous periphery the Kremlin has been able to swing back and forth at will, applying pressure at any desired point and so retaining the initiative.

In 1946 in Persia it drew in the horns of a satellite mass movement when it collided with Western resistance; in 1950 a stalemate followed in Korea, far away on the Soviet periphery; crises around Berlin have been improvized whenever desired; the simple device of having one of its satellites provide the new Egyptian regime with arms in 1955 thrust the Soviet government

stable foothold in the Western Hemisphere for the first time.

With a third of the human race contained by the Soviet bloc, and with its worldwide influence now assuming an endless variety of forms, the Russian people has come a long way. It has consummated the historic mission so often ascribed to it at a moment when the technology it has been longing for since Peter the Great has evolved to a point where mankind can extinguish itself. If the Soviet regime has a dialectical view of its present slogan of "coexistence" with the capitalist world it will have to find a subtle synthesis to implement it.

These men marching with rifles are train- ▶
ed to use devastating atomic weapons.

Page 296

All through her history, Russia has only been ruled by dictators. Ending this book, the latest of the series : Nikita Khrushchov.

Index

Numbers in italics refer to captions

This book was made with the collaboration
of Monique Schneider-Maunoury
Dominique Raoul-Duval
and Marie-Geneviève de La Coste-Messelière

Lay-out by Robert Delpire

Color photographs

Brian Brake /Magnum: *page 78* — Cornell Capa /Magnum: *pages 25, 113*
Courtesy Faber and Faber, "The Art of Carl Fabergé": *page 217* — Giraudon: *page 119*
William Klein: *page 289* — Erich Lessing /Magnum: *page 63*
Chris Marker: *page 60* — Meyer-Henn: *pages 142-143, 170-171*
Claude Michaelides: *pages 71, 91, 127, 136-137, 157, 190-191, 226-227*
Pic/Cercle d'Art: *pages 32, 50* — De Schutter: *page 261* — Vatican Library: *page 17*

Black-and-white photographs

Agence de Diffusion et de Presse, Paris — Archives France U.R.S.S. — Bildarchiv-Foto Marburg
André Bonin — Brian Brake /Magnum — Jacques Brosse — Cornell Capa /Magnum
Henri Cartier-Bresson /Magnum — Cossira — Mme Djordjadzé — Eliott Erwitt /Magnum
Fleming, London — Giraudon — International News — Simonne Jacquemard — Keystone
William Klein — Mansell Agency, London — Archives Chris Marker — Meyer-Henn
Claude Michaelides — Pic/Cercle d'Art — Rapho — Roger-Viollet — Sirot

The editors wish to extend their thanks to the following: Mmes E. Cournand, E. Lange;
MM. V. Elisseeff, P. Pechère; Armory Museum of the Kremlin, Moscow; Bibliothèque Nationale, Paris;
Department of Prints and Drawings, British Museum, London; Hermitage Museum, Leningrad;
Historical Museum, Kiev; Historical Museum, Moscow; Bibliothèque d'Art et d'Archéologie, Paris;
Kensington Palace, London; Kunstmuseum, Berne; Matenadaran, Erivan; Museum of Architecture,
Moscow; Musée des Beaux-Arts, Nancy; Musée du Louvre, Paris; Russian Museum, Leningrad;
Tiflis Museum; Tretyakov Gallery, Moscow; Vatican Library.

Printed July 31st, 1960
on the presses of the Imprimeries Réunies S. A.,
at Lausanne, Switzerland